# REFUGE

## CALIFORNIA 1985

By Joan Strojny

EVENING STAR Text copyright 1994 Joan Strojny

This as a work of fiction.  Names, characters, places and incidents either are the product of the author's imagination or are used fictitiously, and any resemblance to any actual person, living or dead, or locales is entirely coincidental.

To my daughter, Pam Ferraro and to all immigrants

*I will love you while the stars have motion*

*When the storm clouds race a willful tide*

*I will hold you so much closer that a drop*

*Of water would be too dense to intercede*

*In daybreak of your erupting fire I will*

*Match your ardor with white flames and not expire*

*I love you now and when my old*

*Bones turn to dust I'll love you then.*

*Mario's Song*

CHAPTER ONE

"Mary, Mother of God, cross the desert with us to freedom," murmured Mario, squinting up at the dying sun. "We're ready," he said to his wife, Marcella, and daughter, Rita, sitting beside him in the shade of a tree. He fished his topographical map out of his backpack for one last look before starting, and Rita peered over his shoulder.

"Here's where we are," he said, pointing to a spot on the map. "And here's where we're going tonight." He touched the x he'd made at the mesa with his index finger. "Marcella, look here at the map."

"I see better looking at the land," she replied, with a laugh, glancing at the mesa poking up in the distance out of the vast flat desert.

"It wouldn't hurt to know how to read this map." Mario fixed his gaze on the low mesa forty kilometers to the northwest where they'd camp at daybreak. A thrill of apprehension touched his heart, but his spirit was too proud to nourish it. He had to be a good example to Rita. He must be strong if they were to dare the desert, and the unknown beyond, and make it.

When Mario was a small boy, he'd learned English from a doctor, who came from America to help the war refugees in El Salvador. He and Marcella had started planning their escape the day they met in Guatemala twenty years ago. They'd worked their way north, Mario in mechanic shops, kitchens, and fields, Marcella in kitchens and fields.

As soon as Rita could walk, they'd begun taking her on night hikes to condition her legs and develop her stamina. When she was old enough, they often hiked on the desert from dusk to dawn with as little rest as possible. Mario had crossed alone first to scout their course and map it.

"I'll be back before another new moon. We'll start on the rise of the next moon," he'd told Marcella and Rita.

On his first journey, confused and exhausted after five nights on the desert, Mario detected movement too far away to see what it was. Probably it was a mirage. His vision often betrayed him after days on the desert assaulted by the sun, solitude and the profoundly still monotonous terrain where motion lurks, teasing, just below the ability to perceive it.

He proceeded toward the movement until he made out an automobile with the hood up. A middle-aged couple, so distraught they didn't see Mario approach, stood leaning against the car. The woman, in a sleeveless royal blue Christian Dior dress, a floppy white hat, and white high heels wore tiny diamonds in her pierced ears. Her blonde hair, short and wavy, curled around her face. The man wore dark blue trousers with a white shirt with the sleeves rolled up, the top two buttons open. A red tie lay flung on the back seat, and his suit coat was on a hanger in the rear.

"You've got to start walking, Alv," she pleaded. "There's not going to be another car down this road." She fanned herself with a paper envelope.

"Listen here, Diane. I'm not walking anywhere," said Alv. "I'm having a hard enough time standing in this goddamned heat. Walk! You walk!"

"I've heard of people dying on the desert when their cars broke down. Don't you remember, Alv? It was in the newspaper. They drank their own piss until they died. I told you we should bring water. They always say that; never go on the desert without water."

"I know, I know. It's all my fault. Why didn't you bring the goddamn water? You never make a mistake. You can't get water by yelling about it now. So shut up about it." Alv moved to the front of the car and peered under the hood again, leaning on the car, but the engine at rest retained its secrets.

"I'm scared, Alv." Diane appeared at his elbow. "This place gives me the creeps. I told you not to cut through the Indian reservation. We haven't seen a single soul. It's too quiet and desolate." The tops of her arms were sunburned, and the air stirred slightly around her face as she fanned herself with a paper envelope.

"Excuse me, please," said Mario, coming up behind them, his sneakers silent on the sand. Diane shrieked and jumped. Startled, Alv whirled around.

Mario smiled the practiced, reserved mask he used on strangers when the outcome of the encounter was as important as uncertain.

"Oh, my God," exclaimed Diane, her hand on her heart, catching her breath. "You scared me to death. I didn't hear you sneaking up behind us." Moving closer to Alv, she then clutched his arm, which he promptly liberated with a jerk. Little sputters of nervous laughter escaped Diane, and she covered her mouth with her hand.

"How did you get here?" she asked, looking everywhere but Mario's eyes. "Where's your car? We need help. We need a ride to town. Are you broke down on the road?" She shaded her eyes with her hand, searching in one direction, then the other.

"I know a little about engines," said Mario. "May I see if I can fix it?"

"Please," said Alv, his face flushed with anxious aggravation.

Mario quickly scanned under the hood for the obvious but saw nothing amiss. He sat in the driver's seat and turned the key. The engine sputtered but didn't catch.

"I'm afraid to wear out the battery," said Alv, leaning on the car. The skinny, sun-shrunk desert rat looked like he never saw a car in his life. Suppose he damaged it irreparably?

Mario got out and unscrewed the nut holding the air filter in place.

"Do you think you can fix it?" whimpered Diane, watching what he was doing. "We can give you a lift to town if you help us. We've been stranded here for hours. It's so hot," she said, fanning herself.

"Yes, I see what's wrong," Mario answered. He picked up a little stick of sagebrush. Removing the air filter, he then held the butterfly valve of the carburetor open with the stick.

"Try to start," he said. Alv slid behind the wheel, turned the key and stepped on the gas. The engine sputtered and then revved.

"Thanks friend," said Alv, with a deep sigh of relief. He mopped his brow with a handkerchief and smiled, the sweat glistening on his forehead and under his nose.

"Thank you so much," said Diane, sliding into the passenger seat.

"How did you do that?" asked Alv, leaving the engine running and getting out of the car.

"See here," said Mario, showing Alv how the valve worked before replacing the air filter.

"Thanks pal," said Alv. "Thanks a lot."

"How far to town?" asked Mario, pointing west.

"Seven miles," said Alv.

"That way?" Mario pointed to the east.

"About seventy-five miles." Taking his billfold out of his back pocket, Alv quickly thumbed through the bills to find a twenty, but three hundreds, a few ones, and one five were all he had. He handed Mario a hundred dollar bill and got back in the driver's seat.

"Thanks," said Mario, shoving the bill into his pocket.

"Get in," said Diane. "Hurry up. We'll give you a ride. Where's your car?" She was already buckled in. "Come on, let's get out of here. Get in, get in."

Mario stepped back and waved, the leather of his sun-cured face crinkling into creases around his eyes and mouth.

"You don't want a ride?" asked Alv. Mario shook his head no, and Alv pulled away. Watching the car disappear, Mario silently thanked the Virgin of Guadeloupe, pulled out the bill, folded it neatly, and tucked it into the pocket Marcella had sewn into the inside of his jeans.

Mario searched for a landmark by which to locate the road from a distance and spotted a few boulders about a foot higher than himself with a flat rock balanced on top. The rock formation looked like a door, but from a distance it wouldn't stand out against the brown desert. Locating a large quartz rock that gleamed in the sun, he then placed it on top of the flat rock. He'd be able to see it from a great distance, and he marked the location on his topographical map.

He followed the road back about a mile, and a gravel trail led off of it behind a wall of boulders. At the end of the trail was a small oasis that would be a good place to sleep before hiking the last seven miles into a town. The rock formations concealed it from the road, and a natural artesian well had sprung up into a little pool. Mario refreshed himself there with a drink and a bath. He washed his clothes in the pool before going back.

When he returned from his scouting expedition with his hundred dollar bill, he was ready to make the trip with Marcella and Rita. Looking down at Rita, he saw Marcella in her face, with her determined chin, penetrating gaze and high cheekbones.

Marcella studied Mario's face intently, bringing him a twinge of pride, as the trio faced the passage between two worlds.

"Let's go," said Mario. "A journey to the free world or to anywhere you want to be starts with the ground beneath your feet."

"Si, Papa," said Rita. Catching her error, she amended it. "Yes Dad." Mario hugged her.

"You'll make it fine," said Mario.

"We'll make it," corrected Rita, laughter bursting out of her large brown eyes, proud of knowledge acquired in school when she had the opportunity to attend. She was always looking for the chance to use it.

"We'll make it," repeated Mario. He tousled Rita's long, black hair, pleased with his daughter's self-confidence.

Flaming streaks softened to orange and would soon turn gray in the evening sky as the nearly-full moon rose over the mesa. "See that brightest star, how it points to the center of the mesa?" he asked. Rita nodded.

"That's Polaris. Watch how it stays over the mesa as we walk. That's how we know where we're going. It's called the North Star because it shows you which way is north." As the hike took all their effort, they stopped talking conserving everything for the task

A few hours into the night the stars fully revealed their splendor. The black beguiling void had a hypnotic effect on Mario because of his steady motion. It pulled him into its mysterious embrace against his will, and he lost the fight to concentrate on the Virgin of Guadeloupe, so he wouldn't have to think about his past.

Death had dominated that world like the mesa ruled this one. Orphaned at five, Mario had lived in refugee camps since then. The hundreds of others like himself showed him that he wasn't alone in his plight. He'd wanted to get away from the fighting and killing, but the guns, the tanks, the midnight rousts, the burning villages, the sudden screams in the night followed him when he was relocated to another country.

He'd watched the blood of his people water the earth and tried to figure out why, but he couldn't fathom it. He didn't want to hurt or kill, but that's all the other boys talked about.

"Por que?" he asked his friend.
"To be valiant."
"Why is it valiant to kill a person?"
"To stay alive: when somebody tries to kill you, you have to kill him first."
When he was ten, Mario went to the chapel to pray and ask the Virgin of Guadeloupe why this must be because there was no one else to ask. The answer came to him. *Go to North America. There is no war there.*

There was no war in the United States. He'd go there. He'd already begun his odyssey when he met Marcella. Hiking the desert with Marcella and Rita, his heart pounded with the excitement of making the dream real.

Memories of Mario's mother and father ambushed his thought in the silence of the desert. His father's death in the night as Mario slept by his side haunted him like an angry demon. He used to wonder who would be next. It might be him. The rapacious cannibal war, that devoured his family, was shattered bones and bloody heads, chopped off arms and blown up legs, his father's warm blood blinding his eyes, the horrible taste engraved in his memory. He'd clamped his lips like a vice pinned under his father's body as his life ran out.

Mario had wished he could sleep through the night without terror of the bomb, the guns, the rustle of combat boots tromping down the dried leaves and twigs around the tent. He'd heard that in the United States people slept peacefully. He wanted to escape war and didn't want Rita to know it.

He led the hike for hours without stopping or speaking. When Mario prayed, instead of the faded, chipped plaster statue of the Virgin of Guadeloupe, he was surprised to envision his mother laughing. It was funny how much Marcella reminded him of his mother.

About midnight the vision of his mother quit laughing and covered her face with her hands. She disappeared suddenly as Marcella grabbed his arm. Mario stopped dead, resting his hand on Rita's shoulder to stop her.

Still as a rock, Mario heard the rattle of a rattlesnake but couldn't see it. Listening, he scanned the concealing night. Rita on his right and Marcella on his left were motionless. Soundlessly, he unsheathed his knife, straining his eyes in the dark. The hiss, like air from a flat tire, drew his attention to the snake coiled to the right of Rita's boot. Holding the knife in his teeth, he lifted Rita with lightning speed to the other side as the snake struck.

Missing Rita, its fangs sank into Mario's right heel. Mario screamed in pain. Quick as the striking snake, he slashed the serpent's head off, sat in the sand and pried the fangs out with his knife. He yanked his boot and sock off. Darts of pain were already shooting up his calf.

Bending over him, Marcella began sucking the poison out, spitting it on the ground. When she was finished, she took a swig of water from her canteen and swilled it around in her mouth before spitting it out. She repeated the rinse several times.

"You'll be okay, Dad?" asked Rita, anxiously, looking down at Mario's foot.

"I'll be okay. We'll rest here and eat him. He's a big one. Walk quiet to get wood and listen good; maybe there're more." Mario spoke softly, and Rita began scavenging the area for wood, listening for another rattle and hiss.

Marcella removed her backpack, got her flashlight out and examined the wound. The fangs had pierced deeply. Already the wound was flaming red and swollen.

Pain fired up Mario's shin and radiated through his foot to his toes. "The poison's not all out," he said. For his family's sake, he wanted to be too strong to get sick. He swung his backpack off his shoulder onto the ground, unzipped the front pocket and took two aspirins out. He downed them with a swig of water.

"I'll do what I can, Mario," said Marcella, softly. Gritting his teeth, Mario watched her wash the wound with a little water from her canteen. Opening her backpack, she removed a vial of peroxide, medicinal leaves and a rolled up gauze bandage. She unwrapped the medicinal leaves. After pouring peroxide into the wound, she applied the leaves and held them in place with the bandage. Cutting the bandage from the roll and tying it, she then replaced the items in her pack.

"I better find you a walking stick," said Marcella, getting up. She went to scout the area.

Rita started the fire with wood she'd gathered as Marcella returned with a suitable straight stick.

Working by the light of the moon and stars and fire, Mario skinned the snake and roasted it.

"Your snakebite's bad, I can tell," said Rita, squatting by the fire, sensing Mario's easy going good nature turn into an inner struggle.

"Yeah, it's real bad," said Mario.

When the snake was done, Mario let it cool a little on a rock before cutting it in sections and handing Marcella and Rita each a piece. He ate wolfishly. Marcella ate slowly, and Rita couldn't finish hers. She cut what she had left in half and gave half to Mario and half to Marcella. Mario took a little sip from his canteen.

"The aspirin and the leaves you put on the bite help," said Mario. "It's not as bad now."

"Good," said Marcella.

The sudden wail of animals pierced the stillness followed by a series of rapid yelps; and the beat of paws vibrated the sand as a pack passed nearby.

"Sounds like jackals," said Marcella, uneasily.
"There're none around here," said Mario, softly.
"It's not coyotes."
"I know."
"If it's not jackals, it must be hyenas."
"It sounds like that, but there're no hyenas around here either."
"What is it then; that runs in a pack and makes that noise?" asked Rita.
"I don't know," said Mario.
"Must be wild dogs," speculated Marcella, with a shudder. "Domestic strays gone wild and bred with coyotes. We don't have to get to the mesa tonight, Mario. If we rest here, we'll get there sometime anyway."

"We'll get there before dawn," insisted Mario. "There's a place to sleep out of the sun and two canteens of water I left there."

"It's not too far away, Dad."

"It's much farther than it looks. We'll walk, and walk, and walk all night until it feels like we're standing still, and everything else is moving."

"We can go back," said Marcella. "We can wait to make sure you don't get sick and start again."

"No," said Mario. "It could happen anytime again or something worse could happen. It's very bad to start and then turn back. How far back could we go...to before we were born? We waited for this moon; we worked hard for everything to be just right, and now we have to go on. We're lucky it wasn't Rita who got bit. We can thank the Virgin of Guadeloupe; we still got each other."

The unyielding tenacity in Mario's voice indicated that he couldn't change his mind if he wanted to. "Now everything's changed," he said. "We have to walk very fast and get to the mesa much sooner in case I get sick."

Mario found their direction by the North Star over the black mesa, its outline visible in the moonlight and stood up using the walking stick Marcella had found. Marcella and Rita got up, and Marcella kicked sand over the dying embers. Rita helped her until the coals were dead. Marcella shouldered her backpack.

Mario set the pace, going much faster. His head was afire with pain. He wrestled down the urge to vomit, and he was hot with fever and the extraordinary state of perception that goes with it. He determined to remain in motion if he had to be sick. He might not be able to start again if he stopped.

"Watch out for snakes," he joked. Marcella and Rita giggled.
"Maybe something was wrong with it," said Marcella.
"There's something wrong with it now," commented Rita. Mario and Marcella laughed.
Mario limped on the ball of his foot using the stick to hold his weight. Every time his foot touched earth a sharp stab of pain went from the bite to his knee. The worse he felt, the faster Mario walked. Marcella and Rita speeded to a slow jog to keep up.

Mario tried not to look at the stars because they turned into explosions of bombs from his childhood with flashes of light and the rat-a-tat-tat of machine guns. A comet sparkled out of the night sky, but the sign of good fortune turned into a blast from a gun so powerful that it moved all the stars in the firmament; and a red glowing curtain descended between the stars and Mario's eyes. He shook his head to make it go away, but it wouldn't go. Wiping the sweat from his face with a rag he kept in his pocket, he wished to tie it around his head to stop the sweat from running into his eyes, but he couldn't afford to stop.

Every step brought him closer to the mesa. How would Marcella and Rita get to it if he stopped and couldn't start again? The constant throbbing in his heel forced him to unwittingly increase his speed until he was running. He heard Marcella and Rita breathing harder beside him. The sound of his own hard breathing mingled with theirs before they fell behind. Then all he could hear was his own breath and the pounding of his feet and walking stick and heart against the eternal machine gun fire.

The Virgin of Guadeloupe appeared in the sky on the other side of the translucent red curtain. That meant they were safe. He silently thanked the Virgin. She turned into his mother. He watched his mother in the sky washing their clothes in the river as he ran.

The black void sucked up the stars and disappeared pulling the red curtain with it into a blazing sphere. Suddenly, the sun was shining out of a bright blue, cloudless sky.

Mario, a small boy, sat naked on the bank of the river watching his mother wash clothes. Laughing, she sang; and pulling him into the water, she washed him with a clean shirt.

The cold water splashed all over him as she soaped his hair first and then his whole body. Throwing the shirt over her shoulder, she pulled him through the water by his hands to rinse him off. Laughing, she splashed him and let him duck her.

The cold water numbed the pain in his foot, and the sky burst into gunfire as the first hint of dawn crept out of the east. His mother was caught in the crossfire. The desert sand was transformed into the river roiled with his mother's blood. Her eyes gaping lifeless, the current dragged her corpse rapidly downstream out of reach.

"Mama; Mama!" he shouted. Tears stinging his eyes, he tried to get to her; but the river swirled her rapidly out of reach until he could no longer find her. He started scrambling to get away; swimming, crawling stumbling on the rocks. Mario fell down and got up. The current dragged him down again and again. He clamped his mouth shut. Rat-a-tat tat, rat-a-tat tat, the bullets flew all around. Coming to the rocky place in the stream where it was shallow enough to stand, he climbed over the river rocks to shore.

Scrambling up the bank, he ran back to where his mother had tossed the clothes after washing them and pulled on his shorts, jeans and tee shirt quickly.

He ran as fast as he could toward the mesa through the weeds that grew along the river. The relentless rat-a-tat-tat, assaulting his ears pierced his skull and rang in his brain. He ran faster, faster to get away from the sting of his mother's death and the breath of it on his neck and back and legs and arms, the sound of it ringing in his ears.

Running through grass that was higher than his head, he had to get to the cornfield. He knew his way through the cornfield and to the village on the other side where his people were. Tears blurred his vision.

He was shot in the heel. It was nothing but pain, and he knew pain. He stumbled on, falling and crawling, dragging himself, staggering forward. The desert floor hit him in the face again and again, but each time the sand in his nose or a spine from a cactus pricked him awake. Puking, overcome with pain and exhaustion, he yearned to sleep there endlessly. He felt the shadow creeping over him, whispering, a wind in his ear and on the back of his neck. He felt it rippling his shirt against his back and the tap of it on his shoulder.

"Go away," he thought. "They won't make it without me." An unknown force gripped him by the nape of his neck and dragged him forward, his rubber legs churning, to the mesa looming ahead in the morning twilight. Where was the cave? The enemy closed in. He had to get to the cave or he would die. His foot was killing him.

Marcella and Rita ran after Mario as he widened the space between them. Outdistancing Rita, Marcella turned to see her wave, indicating she could manage. Marcella made out Mario's black silhouette stagger and fall and get up repeated over and over until she didn't see him rise.

She dared not look back again, keeping her eyes on the spot where he fell as she ran. Stopping where she thought she saw him go down, she gasped for breath, her hands on her knees, scanning the ground ahead in the faint moonlight. A large scurrying lizard called her attention to drag tracks and disturbance in the sand. Mario hadn't stayed where he fell. Waiting for Rita to catch up, Marcella vaguely indulged in the luxury of wondering what she was going to do.

Rita caught up, and she, too, rested her hands on her knees gasping for breath. Marcella pointed out Mario's track, still breathing too hard to talk. Rita nodded, panting.

When Rita was ready, Marcella tracked Mario to the mesa. She and Rita found him face down at the entrance to the cave unconscious.

"We'll have to drag him inside," said Marcella, taking one arm. Rita got the other, and they pulled him into the cool cave. Marcella unbuckled Mario's backpack. She removed it and rolled him over

with the backpack under his head for a pillow. His body radiated heat. He muttered something unintelligible through cracked and bleeding lips.

Marcella trickled a little water into his mouth, and she drank a few swallows, as much as she dared.

"He looks awful," said Rita. "Is he going to be all right?" Her voice cracked, and talking made her throat itch. She drank a little water.

"I don't know," said Marcella.

Rita threw herself into her mother's arms. Hugging each other, they rocked back and forth. Rita then took off her backpack and threw it on the ground next to her father and fell on top of it exhausted.

"Goodnight, Mom," she said.
"Goodnight," said Marcella.

## CHAPTER TWO

Curling up next to Mario, a human heater in the cold morning, using her backpack as a pillow, Rita fell asleep. Marcella slept stretched across the mouth of the cave.

Mario's meaningless babbling woke Marcella later in the day. She sat up, stretched and knelt beside him. He was still hot with fever. She removed his shirt, boots and socks.

Rita awoke and sat beside Mario, watching her mother peel away the bandage and absorbent leaves from the snakebite. It was infected.

"He's not all right," said Rita, observing the angry red lines from the wound.

"No. We'll make a fire, very little," said Marcella, and Rita went to find some sticks.

"How small will the fire be?" Rita asked, returning to the cave with wood and kindling.

"That's plenty," said Marcella. After making the fire near the mouth of the cave, Marcella held the blade of her knife in it until it was red hot. She cut away the infected skin and pus as Rita watched. Holding it on the knife, she took it away from the cave, scraped it off in the sand, wiped the blade clean with sand and leaves, heated the blade again, and repeated the procedure.

"What should I do?" asked Rita.

"Bury that mess, but be careful not to touch it," said Marcella, pouring the remaining peroxide into the wound. Getting her package of leaves out, she then applied new leaves and cleaned and sterilized her knife with sand and fire.

Rita dug a hole about a foot deep and shoved the infected matter into it with her knife. She covered it over and sterilized the knife.

Searching out a young sage, Marcella then cut two slim, pliable branches the same size. Carefully, she wove them together fashioning a six-sided star while Rita watched. She placed it on Mario's chest over his heart.

"This will draw away the fever, Mario," she said.

Marcella made Rita kneel on one side of Mario, and she knelt on the other. They clasped hands, each one taking one of Mario's hot hands in theirs.

"Our Father, in the name of Jesus, make Mario well," said Marcella. She and Rita repeated the words together. Mario sat up screaming, his eyes popped open, staring without sight. Three bats flew out of the cave, and Marcella and Rita looked up to see the ceiling of the cave covered with bats.

"He's just as bad," said Rita, watching the bats. She hoped they'd stay where they were. "Do bats get in your hair and drive you mad?" she asked.

"No," said Marcella. "They don't go out in daylight either, but we frightened them."

"I'm hungry and thirsty. Dad left some water here." A quick search turned up two full canteens. Rita drank three gulps from her canteen, and they left the spare water deep inside the cave.

"Let's find some food," said Marcella. She was ravenous.

"Good," said Rita. "I could eat a whole snake now."

Marcella handed Rita a stick of beef jerky from her backpack and took one for herself. Leaving everything from her backpack that she wouldn't need in the cave, she then shouldered the nearly empty backpack.

The sun was past its zenith when Marcella and Rita started climbing to the top of the mesa. Noting its position anxiously as they hiked, Marcella judged that it took about two hours to reach the top. Standing on a flat rock, she surveyed the vast expanse of brown hills and towering peaks to the south, wiping the sweat off her dripping face and arms with a bandana.

"It looks like you can see to South America," said Rita, taking off her hat, wiping the sweat off her face and pushing her hair back before replacing it.

Marcella laughed, surveying the terrain. "I didn't know we'd be this high," she replied.

About a mile to the east was a ravine about a hundred yards long marked out of the surrounding brown cliffs and boulders, ledges and endless sand by lush green stands of pine and fir trees. The ravine was surrounded by tall, sandstone cliffs and weird rock formations. A brown boulder the size of a small building rested precariously atop a curved pole-like rock like an office building perched on a pointed sword.

"That's where we'll find food," said Marcella, pointing to the ravine. "There's water, too. See how green it is?"

"How do you catch a snake?" asked Rita, as they started hiking. "Not like Dad did."

Marcella laughed. "I don't know, Querido," she said. "But we'll have to catch something."

They hiked rapidly as the sun cast shadows over the rocks creating optical illusions. Boulders, scrub trees and an occasional pine concealed tunnels, narrow passes through the rocks and eerie, dark caves.

"Don't ever go in those caves," warned Marcella. "Mountain lions live in them."

"Can you eat them?" asked Rita, hungry enough to try anything.

Marcella looked at Rita, laughing. "Catch one and we'll see!" she said. Rita laughed with her. They explored the ravine into mid-afternoon without finding food.

"There are hundreds of lizards," noted Rita, hopefully. "We could eat them."

"Let's keep on looking for something better than that," said Marcella. "I don't know if we could eat them, but I think we could catch them easier than anything else."

"How?"

"Like this," said Marcella. She watched one motionless in the sand, and when she stooped down beside it, it remained still. She grabbed it and let it go just as quickly.

Coming upon a flock of a half dozen brown desert turkeys, Marcella took a dried apple from her backpack, cut it into tiny pieces and threw one piece at a time. The flock followed the apple pieces eating them, so she and Rita lured the fowl to their feet with bits of apple. Marcella tried to grab a large tom by the neck, but he pulled in his neck and stepped back. She kept trying, and though he drew back sharply every time, her empty stomach spurred her to move quickly.

"Who's hungrier, you or me?" she asked. As she spoke, she grabbed the large male by the neck as the others scattered. He put up a fierce struggle, flapping his wings and kicking. Marcella fought with the bird that had a four-foot wingspan. She twisted his neck until his life ran out as Rita watched.

"I can't believe a wild animal let you catch it," said Rita.

"Some domestic turkeys must have escaped from a ranch somewhere and bred with wild," said Marcella. Dizzy and nauseous under the relentlessly burning sun, she carried the catch by its feet. She and Rita started hiking rapidly back to camp.

"When we get back, make the fire right away while I clean and dress him," Marcella said. "We have to hurry to get back before the sun sets. I don't know if we can find the cave at night." The return trip, almost all downhill with Marcella and Rita practically running to get back before dark, was half as long as their hike to the ravine. The sun turned the sky to a blazing flame, and then painted it with purple, scarlet, gold and brilliant orange hues over the mesa.

Returning to camp, Rita began looking for wood as Marcella worked on the turkey. A little distance from camp, because she didn't want to bring wild animals close, she hacked off the head with her knife.

Hanging the bird from a tree by the feet, she then plucked the feathers, eviscerated it, cut off the legs and buried the offal. Carrying their catch back to camp, she was ready to cook it.

Rita had started the fire near the mouth of the cave. She had a little wood stacked nearby and had gone back to the brush where she'd found a dead tree. She broke off an armload of large pieces and carried them back to slowly feed the fire.

"Where are the feathers?" asked Rita. "I'm going to keep some of them."

"What for?" asked Marcella.

"I don't know; I like them. Don't you think they're pretty?"

"Yeah, but I don't want to keep them. I'll show you where they are as soon as I get this bird on the fire." She carefully placed rocks on each side of the fire, building them to a height of a foot. Then finding a flat rock, she called Rita over. "Help me lift this over the fire. We're going to put it on those rock posts."

"Okay," said Rita, lifting one end of the flat rock as Marcella took the other end. They hauled it to the fire and placed it on the rock posts. Marcella cut the turkey in pieces and put them on the makeshift stove.

"Let's get the feathers," said Rita.

"This way," said Marcella, returning to the butchery. As Rita picked up some of the feathers and selected the best ones to keep, Marcella went to Mario in the cave. She daubed as much water from the canteen on his hot face as she dared.

Rita returned humming, and Marcella turned the turkey which smelled heavenly.

"I think it's almost ready," said Rita, hopefully. She fanned out a handful of feathers in front of the fire, and the light behind them made them glitter and change colors. "They're so pretty," she said.

"Yes, but so is the sunset," said Marcella.

"You keep some of that," said Rita. "I'll take the feathers."

"All right," Marcella replied, seriously. "I will keep some of it. I'll need it."

Rita imagined the sunset and understood how Marcella could keep some of it.

"We got food, Mario," said Marcella. "For you, too, as soon as you can eat," she said.

"Why do you talk to him, Mom? He can't hear you."

"There're many levels of hearing," said Marcella. "He can hear me, only he doesn't know it."

"I hate when you say things I don't believe and I can't prove I'm right, even when I know I am."

"You think you're right, because you have no experience with the truth in my words. Someday, something will happen to make you understand, but you're very young. You haven't had time to experience as much as me."

"You never tell me wrong, so maybe I am. But I hate it because it doesn't make sense. How can he hear?"

"There are things in life you must take on faith," said Marcella. "But I'm glad you don't believe anything you don't understand, because the world is full of people who try to make you believe all kinds of nonsense."

"What was your experience that made you believe?"

"When I was just about your age, I caught the measles. I got them from my friend, and she went blind. I was afraid that I would go blind, too. My grandmother hung blankets over the doors and windows, so no light could come in the room, and she put a bandage over my eyes. She held my hands, and we prayed. She told me that when the measles were gone, I would see as well as before if I believed that God would make it true. I asked her how she knew, and she told me the same thing I just told you. I've tried it many times in my life, Rita. Will you hold your flashlight while I wash Mario's snakebite?"

Rita nodded and followed Marcella into the cave. She turned her light on Mario's wound as Marcella removed the bandage and changed the medicinal leaves. Mario's leg was a massive blue, purple and black bruise from his toes to his knee, but the angry red lines coming out from the wound had faded away.

"The bite's not as bad," noticed Rita.

"That's right," said Marcella. "The infection is going away." Marcella left the wound open for the air to heal.

Rita took her turkey feathers out of her pocket and put them in her backpack as Marcella returned to the roasting bird. With the feathers safely stashed, Rita joined her mother.

Marcella speared a piece of meat with her knife, put it on a rock she'd selected for a table and sliced into it. It was done.

"This is for you, Rita," she said. "There's more than we can eat, so take as much as you want." Marcella removed the rest of the turkey from the makeshift stove and put it on the table rock. When it was cool enough, they ate wolfishly.

"This is the best meal I ever ate," said Rita.

"We might as well be in a fancy American restaurant to be eating like this," said Marcella.

"It's good luck," said Rita.

When they were finished, Marcella sliced the remainder as thinly as possible, wrapped it in cheesecloth and hung it from a dead tree limb near the mouth of the cave.

With a full stomach, tired from the day's events, Rita went into the cave, curled up next to Mario and fell asleep on her poncho.

Marcella sat at the mouth of the cave watching the stars until she, too, got sleepy and fell asleep. When Marcella woke in the morning, Rita was chewing on a turkey bone.

"We have to find more water. What Mario left in the cave with what we brought won't be enough. We'll go back to the ravine," said Marcella.

After eating more turkey, they hiked to the ravine and walked it from one end to the other crisscrossing back and forth without finding water.

"There's water in barrel cactus," said Rita. "I read it in a book at school."

"We'll see," said Marcella, selecting a small one about a foot tall.   "Should we try this one?"

"Looks as good as any," said Rita.  The plant was tough and fibrous and extremely difficult to cut down, but with Marcella and Rita taking turns hacking at it, they managed to eventually separate it from the desert floor.  Marcella cut it in half long ways, and the inside fiber looked dryer than the turkey's juicy bones.

"My book was wrong," said Rita, disappointed.  She cut a little piece out to chew on just in case there was water in it that she couldn't see, but it tasted bad, and no liquid came from it; so she spat it out.  "You can eat prickly pears," she said.  "I saw them in a grocery store."

"I cut a piece off of just a small one," said Marcella.  "I couldn't eat it, though.  Why don't you try?"

"No," said Rita.  "I cut a piece off, too.  I thought maybe you knew how to get the spines out."

"Maybe the ones we see in the store are specially grown for food," said Marcella.  "They don't have spines."

"Look!" said Rita, pointing.  Marcella looked up from a dry wash at three young, wild donkeys staring at her and Rita.  They had almost no manes and skimpy tails and were shorter and stockier than domestic donkeys.  Their large bright eyes contained enormous black pupils.  Rita took a few steps forward, and the donkeys ran about twenty feet, stopped and turned to watch them.

"I wonder where they get water.  They sure look fat and healthy," said Rita.

"There's a lot more of them, too," noted Marcella, pointing to the dried evidence in the sand.  "If we could catch one and break it, we could carry Mario back on it."  The donkeys stood motionless watching them, but as soon as Rita approached, the animals ran a safe distance before stopping to look back.

Removing a coiled rope hanging from her backpack, Marcella made a lasso. Handing it to Rita, she then pointed out a tree. "Try to get to that tree without spooking them, and climb up in it. Tie the rope tight to a strong limb. I'll drive one under the tree, and see if you can drop the lasso over its head," said Marcella.

"Okay," replied Rita. Hanging the coil of rope over her shoulder, she then jumped to catch the lowest branch of the tree and swiftly climbed it. Tying the end of the rope around a branch, she called softly, "I'm ready, Mom."

Marcella tried to drive the donkeys, but she couldn't get close enough. Every time she approached, they ran away.

"No luck," she said. "I'm going back to the cave to see how Mario's doing."

"They'll be back," said Rita, climbing down from the tree. "I'm going to stay here and practice with this rope." She threw the lasso at a tree branch; and when she could rope it without missing, she practiced on rocks. Developing concentration and skill, she loosened up and became comfortable with her task. She then tried roping branches or shrubs while on the run.

Marcella found Mario raving fitfully in his fevered sleep. She looked at how far the sun had moved across the blue cloudless sky since they'd gone to search for water and noticed the position of the shadow of a particular shrub. She watched an eagle fly overhead and admired the grace and beauty of the animal in flight until it turned to head into the sun and became a silhouette.

"It doesn't like to be watched, and it's been watched before," she thought. At noon the sun penetrated the cave, and she dragged Mario deeper into it, bending her knees to shift most of his weight to her thighs and relieve her back.

Kneeling beside him, she tipped his head up and poured a little water into his mouth and on his swollen lips. She washed his face and sprinkled a few drops on his chest over his heart; the chest that had been so strong, so determined that she could always lean on it if she needed to. She'd never seen Mario helpless before, and she felt his pain. Her heart ached to see the familiar smile on his lips, the crinkles around his eyes when he laughed, the muscles ripple under the skin of his arms and shoulders and back. She longed to hear the sound of his voice and his laugh when Rita made a joke, to see him clown around to make her laugh when she felt like the world was coming to an end.

On an impulse, she removed her shirt and lay down on top of him. Taking his jaw in her hand, she breathed hard into his mouth forcing the air from her lungs into his. Inhaling the bad air out of his lungs, she exhaled into the air, took a deep breath and breathed into his lungs again. She continued to breathe in that manner, compelled to exchange something from her body with his.

After praying silently that he'd live and that his brain wouldn't be damaged by the long fever, she replaced the star and put on her shirt. The idea of his death tried to stick in her mind, and with a struggle fiercer than it took to kill the turkey, she banished the shadow of it. Her grandmother had taught her the importance of retaining images one wants to occur and throwing off the bad ones.

Rita returned with the rope coiled over her shoulder at twilight after practicing roping until it was too dark to see her targets.

"The desert's a mystery at night," said Rita, "and especially at twilight. There's a moving shadow; I can't see what it goes to." She pointed, but by the time Marcella looked, it was gone. The boulders and mesquite around the cave loomed gray out of the darkness before it swallowed them up in the flutter of time between sunset and moonrise when no stars were yet visible.

"Yes," said Marcella. "The desert's more alive at night when everything else seems to sleep, and something of it dies at sunrise."

Marcella sat in the entrance to the cave, and the fierce howling followed by staccato yelps she'd heard after Mario got bitten broke the stillness of the night.

"What could it be?" asked Rita, crowding close to Marcella.

"I don't know; not jackals, not hyenas, maybe wild dogs." The loud yelps continued as the shadows deepened, and darkness settled over the mesa. The piercing barks sent chills up Marcella's spine.

"It sounds like they're getting closer," said Rita, her eyes wide.

"Yes, it does. We've got trouble, Mario," said Marcella. "The wild beasts we heard when you got bit - they're back." Rita gave her mother a curious look.

Marcella started gathering rocks and piling them at the entrance of the cave. Rita worked on a pile opposite Marcella's. "If they come in a pack, we'll drive them off with the rocks, you on that side, and me on this," said Marcella. Marcella's life had been hard and sharp as Mario's, and she had to act on the threat of immanent disaster with which she was surrounded.

Early schooling had dulled the edges of Rita's experience, and her pliable thought searched out possibility. She wanted to try the dead ends to see if they led to deeper rivers below the surface.

"Fire would be easier," said Rita.

Marcella stopped collecting rocks to give Rita her full attention. "Next time we cook a bird we'll look farther for enough wood. We can spare the rocks easier."

"I see," said Rita.

"You're going to get well, Mario," said Marcella, softly. "We'll go on with our journey. Deep inside you can hear me. I know you believe me."

"Goodnight, Mama," said Rita, tired from carrying the rocks, practicing with the rope, exploring the desert and looking for food and water. Curling up back in the cave by Mario because he was hot and the desert got cold at night, she fell asleep immediately, listening to the dogs. The yapping faded into a dream of a loudly ticking clock.

Marcella sat, her eyes as half-closed as her consciousness, watching bats fly out of the cave. She wasn't sleepy.

Mario's heat branded his hollow cheeks scarlet, and their water was almost gone. Much of the water to last the journey she'd used on Mario's face and wound. Her throat was parched and dry, but she took only a stingy sip, not daring to drink too much.

The night was lit by the moon and stars. Standing and stretching wearily, Marcella heard the wild dogs getting closer. Trying to pinpoint the sound, she stood outside the cave and turned in all directions. She seemed to be in the center of a circle surrounded by animals closing in.

Testing her theory that the cave was the focus the sounds sought, she moved away from the cave. She still felt herself to be in the center of the hysterical, staccato yapping. Yet, the farther she went, the more subdued it became. About fifty feet away, the noise was replaced by a steady hum like the whir of a hummingbird's wings. That turned into buzzing in her ears.

Then, in a weird juxtaposition of perception, the sound was emanating outward from her brain. She saw, breaking the irregular black line of the horizon lit by a star directly below the moon, a single column of smoke. Smelling smoke, she walked toward it repeating the Lord's Prayer, afraid but drawn to it. Before she reached the smoke, it dissipated; but she stood on the spot it had risen from, the odor still strong.

She heard the wild dogs again, but this time they raised terror in her heart. Had she been lured to this God-forsaken spot away from the safety of the cave, away from her husband and daughter? By what...or whom...for what purpose...some crazy sacrifice to a pack of wild hounds while her daughter lay sleeping, her husband ill in a cave full of bats?

The yelps of the animals wailed over the sand and cactus louder and louder until she felt the vibration of their paws shake the earth. Marcella tried to run, but she was stuck to the spot by an invisible force.

The first waves of beasts came from all directions, leaping at her throat, fangs bared, drooling and frothing, giant wild mongrels, part wolf, part coyote, yapping and growling, amber darts firing out of their glowing amber eyes. She covered her head and face with her arms as they lunged again and again and fell away again and again.

She was protected by an invisible barrier the beasts couldn't penetrate. Her arms fell to her side, and a sharp flicker of pain beginning in the center of the pupil of each eye radiated outward turning into light as it went until the pain diminished and then vanished. Marcella could use those radiations to see as far as she dared. Shielding her eyes with her hand to protect them from the extraordinary brilliance of a strange white light seen with an inner eye, she was free of the shield that held her in place and protected her from the creatures.

They crumbled into heaps of flesh, panting and heaving with exhaustion from the frenzy of their attack. Decomposing, they were drawn down beneath the earth, their brown and tan bodies turning into sand spreading under her feet as the ground moved and squirmed. All that died beneath her feet met the life in Marcella's body at the surface and struggled in the invisible crack between.

With an intense exertion of will, she kept that which belonged below the surface beneath the soles of her feet, as the living force surrounding her and from above came through the center of her right palm and the top of her head, leaving through her left palm. Death pitted against life, she stood on the intersection of opposing forces with her feet together and her hands stretched up to heaven.

The ages rolled away under her expanded vision to reveal the place on which she stood before humanity inhabited the earth, desolate. The awesome loneliness of God prior to the creation of her earliest ancestors descended, and grief of infinite solitude forced her to one knee and bowed her head to earth. Covering her face with her hands, Marcella wept passionately.

Sensing a light from above, she raised her head and saw earth from a distance. Looking directly into the face of evil without turning aside; she saw a maelstrom of stinking, smutty city air and poisoned sea, poverty and despair and the petty, ignorant prejudice of centuries that breeds crime and decay.

She watched in fascination as the planet turned in upon itself swallowing the darkness in the minds of human individuals from which light began to emanate that would've blinded Marcella had her eyes not been prepared.

The experience dissipated, and she returned to the cave utterly exhausted. Mario appeared to be sleeping peacefully; though his breathing was too slow, and his fever persisted.

Rita stirred and sat up. "I dreamed you fought wild dogs and defeated them," she said. "I don't hear them anymore."

"They're gone," said Marcella.

"I'm tired," said Rita.

"Go back to sleep, Querido. I'm tired, too." Marcella sat near the mouth of the cave quietly, listening to Rita's even breathing. "Rita, are you sleeping yet?"

"No, Mom."

"Mario's going to be all right before another full day has passed."

"How do you know? He doesn't look any better. The fever has stayed so long." Rita's voice was sleepy.

"I know because of the wild dogs, and I wanted you to know, so you could sleep better."

"I believe. Good night, Mom." As she spoke, Rita believed, surprising herself with the subtle yet unmistakable *experience* of belief.

CHAPTER THREE

At daybreak, Rita finished half of the remaining bird, leaving the rest for Marcella. Taking the lasso, she then returned to the glade where she'd seen the donkeys. Spotting a herd of seven, including a large gray female nursing a foal in front of a low, jagged cliff behind her, she wanted the mother.

Soundlessly, Rita snuck to the other side of the boulders. Climbing steadily, the rope coiled over her shoulder, she approached the top of the cliff dislodging a rock that served as her foothold. Dangling precariously, clutching a small tree growing out of a crevice, she scrambled for another footrest. Loose rocks clattered down the steep rock, and her shin hit the canyon wall. It ached fiercely. Her foot found solid rock, and she made her way down the other side until she was on the ledge above the asses.

Creeping to the edge, Rita peered over and caught her breath. The donkey nursing the foal was below. Crawling along the ledge until she was directly above the beasts, she then looped the end of the rope over a jagged rock and tied it tightly, testing it with her full weight. Confident that it would hold, she threw the lasso, and the skill behind every practice rope she'd thrown went into that rope, as it sailed for a moment and dropped neatly over the donkey's ears and around her neck.

The mare went into a frenzy kicking and bucking, and the colt bolted. Rita scampered like a mountain goat, half sliding, down the front face of the rocks near the frightened donkey thrashing and bucking wildly. Standing still, Rita spoke to her softly out of range of the flying hooves.

"It's all right. Don't be afraid," she repeated. "I'm not moving until you quiet down. I'm going to stand right here talking to you."

Catching sight of Marcella approaching, Rita continued to speak softly to the frightened creature.

Marcella walked up silently and stood beside Rita. "Rita, that's nice work. Great work," she whispered, patting Rita on the shoulder. "She's thoroughly wild."

"Can you tame her good enough to carry Mario on her?"
"Yes, I can; and she's got milk."
"What are you going to name her?"
"Liberty."
"That's a good name. Can you make her live up to it?"
"Yes. I picked her out special."
"I'm going back to the ravine to catch another turkey. If you can milk that animal, we'll eat better than all the times we lived on tortillas and beans."

Rita laughed. "Maybe we should take up residence here."

Marcella chuckled softly. "I've got to go. That sun's getting hotter by the minute." Sweat rolled down Marcella's face and arms as she rested for a few moments before plodding through the sand, picking her way around barrel cactus, prickly pears, mesquite and sagebrush to the ravine. The shade of the pine trees and the canyon walls renewed her vigor, but as the sun crossed the sky she combed the canyon from one end to the other without finding the flock that had volunteered previously.

"I'll catch a rabbit," she said to herself, almost tripping over one that brazenly crossed her path. She watched another, still as a stone, for a long time. Spotting a loose rock within reach out of the corner of her eye, it occurred to her to pitch it at the animal, but before she could reach for the rock, the rabbit vanished into the sage. She made a trap which brought no better results.

"How do they know?" she asked herself. "Why don't the turkeys?" The only answer she could think of was that the turkeys were not completely wild.

Marcella sat down to rest and think of what to do when the flock of turkeys came strutting straight to her. She threw them pieces of dried apple, and they fell for the same trick. She caught a fat male with ease.

Returning to camp triumphantly at twilight, the temperature began to drop drastically, and Marcella went to check on Mario. "I love you, Mario," she said, the dead turkey dangling from her hand. "It's hard to wait here like this. Hurry up and get well. You've been out long enough. I want us to move on. I see things on the desert - shadows and riders in the starlight that aren't there - the afternoon sun glinting off the quartz, like fields of diamonds - a lone eagle winging into the sun, something squirming in its claw - the shadow following us, flickering over the hill - a hundred rabbits I can't catch - how do you catch them, Mario? Your map doesn't tell me too many things."

Sighing, she took the bird to the butchery to clean and dress it. She then built the fire, cut up the bird and put it in on the hot rock to cook.

Rita had been working with Liberty all day. She understood animals, and talking to her until she could touch her, she felt the donkey's fear and calmed it. She then fashioned a halter for Liberty so she could lead her to new foraging areas. When Rita smelled the roasting bird, she tied Liberty to a tree and returned to camp.

"Hi, Mom; the smell of that turkey roasting makes me hungry. That must be why the wild dogs came," she said.

"I don't think they'll be back tonight," said Marcella. "How's your Liberty? Is it hopeless to ride her?"

"We're making progress," said Rita. "Can I have your plastic glass?"

"Sure, it's in my backpack. You're going to milk the donkey?"

"Yeah; the colt is what slowed her down enough for me to get her, and the milk is why I chose her."

Marcella gathered the empty canteens and plastic glasses from her and Mario's backpacks and handed the glasses to Rita. She walked back to the donkey with Rita, carrying the empty canteens.

Sitting on a rock, Rita held the glass between her knees and started to milk the donkey. Liberty shied at first, but was greatly relieved as Rita filled the glass, and she stood quietly. When the glass was full, Rita eagerly tasted the milk. It was warm and raw and felt like the nectar of God in her empty stomach. She drank it down, and refilling the glass, she then handed it to Marcella.

Marcella drank it all and set the empty glass and canteens beside Rita. "Good work, Rita," she said. "You saved our lives. I couldn't have caught that animal."

Marcella returned to the fire to turn the bird. As it roasted, Rita finished milking the donkey and brought a full glass of milk to camp, and two full canteens. Marcella sipped the warm, raw milk slowly. Sitting side by side by the roasting bird, mother and daughter drank their fill.

"We'll drag Mario outside tonight. The night wind will blow the fever away," said Marcella.

"How do you know that, Mom? Why don't I?"

"I don't know how. I see farther and deeper after last night. Something happened to my eyes."

When the bird finished roasting, Marcella put the pieces on the table rock, and they ate, watching the fire dim.

"Are you going to have anymore, Rita?" asked Marcella.

"No, when I'm finished with this leg that's all for me."

Marcella got up and sliced the remaining meat thinly before wrapping it in cheesecloth and hanging it high from the tree. She sat on a rock with a pleasantly full stomach, gazing at the last of the dying embers. Rita sat so they were back to back. In that way, they could lean against each other. Marcella dozed, and starting to fall over, she woke up.

"We have to move Mario outside," she told Rita.

"Okay," said Rita, getting up. They went into the cave, and Marcella put the star in her pocket and put Mario's shirt and socks on him. "We have to drag him head first," she said, taking one arm near the shoulder. Rita took the other arm.

"Watch out for cactus," said Marcella, as they turned Mario so his head was at the mouth of the cave.

"We have to move you, Mario. Let this motion sink into your heart and brain and start to move your thought from deep inside, let the motion work, Mario," said Marcella, as they dragged him out of the cave. He was hot as a rock in the noonday sun.

"Help me get him onto that flat rock," said Marcella, pointing it out.

"Okay," said Rita. As they laboriously dragged him through the sand around cactus and through sage and mesquite and then rolled and pulled him onto the rock, thunder crashed; and low black clouds rolled out of the east over the mesa. Jagged pink, fuchsia and orange lightning crackled in a fantastic web of iridescent hieroglyphs, moving with terrific speed, casting an eerie colorful glow over the terrain, illuminating flashes of desert scenery like still surrealistic camera shots. A few drops of rain came down, and soon torrents drenched them.

Marcella ran into the cave and dug a bar of soap out of her backpack. She took it outside near the rock Mario was stretched out on. Quickly undressing, she then soaped herself thoroughly. Tossing Rita, who had already discarded her clothing, the soap, she caught it, giggling, as Marcella let the rain rinse her off.

"No point drying," she said, going into the cave for clean clothes.

"A shower never felt so good," said Rita. After lathering herself and luxuriating in the cleanliness, she dropped the bar of soap on Mario's chest. "Should I help with Dad?" she asked, getting dressed. Shivering in the cold rain, it was too refreshing to complain about the temperature.

"No," said Marcella. "I'll do it."

"I feel like a prune turning into a plum," said Rita, making Marcella laugh.

"I know exactly what it feels like," said Marcella.

"I'll get Liberty to water she can drink," said Rita, and scrambled over the rocks to the donkey. She untied Liberty and led her to a puddle of water made by a depression in a rock, and Liberty drank thirstily.

"This is the time to wake up, Mario. It must be now in the rain. Life is in this wind and this water. Let your body and mind and spirit drink it deep, Mario. Drink up this life, your gift from God and your Virgin of Guadeloupe, drink." As she talked, Marcella undressed Mario as though he was a rag doll.

She scrubbed his hair first, massaging the soap into his scalp to get all the sand out and worked up a lather for the rain to rinse off. Laboring over his head and shoulders, she remembered them moving of his volition. She wished to see him move again, to feel the rush of his emotion and to share her feeling with him. Her prayer today was to imagine him getting up, moving, opening one eye and then the other. She willed him to wake, wanting it more than she'd ever wanted anything.

She worked over his sore leg, still swollen with bruises, gently and washed his feet last, scrubbing them clean. When he was rinsed by the rain, she turned him over and did the other side.

"Talk to me, Mario. The fever's going. I can feel it going. Talk to me." Throughout the ordeal, she'd imagined his brain turning to ice in rebellion against the devouring fever, refusing it, and she spoke often to him. Somewhere in the soul of him, he'd hear and in that secret space, he wouldn't leave her stranded in the desert with Rita; he couldn't leave her.

"I won't let you go, Mario. Your brain is your most important part, and we need it to get out of here."

Marcella scrubbed all their dirty clothes with soap, laid them out on the rocks for the rain to rinse, and washed and filled the canteens with rain water where it ran off the rocks in rivulets.

Turning Mario over once more she felt the last of the fever drain out of him. When the rain stopped, Marcella undid the sage star and buried the pieces in the wet sand.

A soft, low, guttural groan came from Mario. His eyelids fluttered open. He looked into Marcella's eyes, and saw something that hadn't been there before.

Bracing Mario's head, Marcella held a canteen to his lips, and he drank slowly feeling the water trickle down his parched throat. Marcella helped him sit up and lean against a rock abutting the one he was sitting on, and he took the canteen in his hands and drank thirstily.

"I love you, Marcella," whispered Mario. "I never knew how much before." His voice was like sandpaper, and he rested his arm on her shoulder, drinking more water.

"I love you, too, Mario. Maybe our love is what kept you alive."

"Where's Rita?"

"She caught a donkey. She's with her. She's fine."

"I feel like I'm awake from the dead."

"We were scared, but we knew you'd be all right."

"How long was I gone?"

"This is the fourth night. It rained and gave us water. I killed two turkeys with my hands. The first one was hard."

"I could've died. I feel how close I was."

"No, Mario. I couldn't let you die. I would've died, too, and Rita. I won't speak of it. I wouldn't think of it while you were sick, and I won't think of it now."

"Some day one of us will die before the other, Marcella."

"I'm not going to worry about something that might not happen for fifty years." Marcella tossed her head. "I might not wake up in the morning, but what will these words mean then?"

"I'm happy to be alive! God, I'm so happy to be alive!" said Mario, laughing. Hugging Marcella, he then tipped the canteen up and gulped lustily, and the world he woke into was different from the one he touched death in. The air itself was alive, and the white cloud in the distance teemed with life. He'd taken the clouds for granted before, but in this new world, he wondered why the clouds on the desert were flat and straight on the bottom. Watching a lizard, motionless, he thought that unlike him, the lizard never knew a moment of taking the world for granted.

Marcella helped Mario dress in his clean clothes. The swelling was very slight in his foot and leg, but his leg was still badly bruised.

When he was finished drinking as much water as he wanted, Marcella kissed him on the mouth. His lips were softer than the brittle, cracked leather she'd pressed when she breathed into his mouth. An unfamiliar power worked under his weakness from being sick. Joy and gratitude for life stirred Mario's heart as he embraced Marcella, aware of a deeper life force awakened by the brush of death.

"I'm starved," he said.

Marcella ran to the cave and returned with a plastic glass full of milk for him. "Rita caught a mother donkey," she explained.

Mario took a long slow sip of the milk. "That's amazing," said Mario. "How did she do that?"

"If I knew that! She loves animals. She has a way with them I don't understand. They probably speak to each other in a language I don't know." She laughed.

The milk gave Mario strength, and he drank it slowly, pausing after each swallow.

Rita returned from working with Liberty, bringing more milk in the early morning twilight.

"Papa! Dad!" yelled Rita, handing Marcella the glass. She ran to Mario and flung herself into his arms. "Dad, you're okay!" Mom knew it. She told me, but I was scared."

"Marcella was right. Maybe she kept me alive by the power of her knowing it; and you kept us all alive with your donkey milk when the water was running out. I'm proud of you, Rita."

Marcella took down the meat hanging from the dead tree, opened the cheesecloth and took it to Mario and Rita so they could eat. She took a slice, too. Mario ate and drank sparingly.

He tried to stand. Dizzy and faint with red spots before his eyes, he quickly sat down and leaned against the rock. He sat still until he felt better, drank a little more milk and ate another piece of dry meat. His heel throbbed where the snake's fangs had gone in, but the pain was gone. With Marcella and Rita flanking him, he got up again. They helped him stand, and he leaned against the rock until his legs felt firm beneath him and he wasn't dizzy.

"I want to do it myself," he said to Marcella and Rita, and they let go of him. He walked a few steps until his legs refused him, and he had to sit down. He edged himself back to where he'd been leaning against the rock, took a few sips of water and tried again. This time he got up by himself; and mustering all his determination forced himself to walk a few yards before returning to where he could sit, leaning against the rock.

He watched Marcella hanging the turkey that was still left on the dead tree by the mouth of the cave and realized her separateness from him at the same time she was part of him. His eye caught the walking stick leaning against the wall of the cave, and he made up his mind to walk to it. Resting until he was ready to move again, he stood and again he felt dizzy and faint, but he remained on his feet, leaning against the stone wall until the faintness went away. Then he walked the distance and took his stick. He sat just inside the cave in the shade, his eyes flickering around the encampment, taking everything in, proud of Marcella and Rita.

"I'm going to get some sleep," said Marcella, going into the cave and stretching out.

"I'm going to break Liberty so we can get out of here," said Rita, bounding out of sight.

"I'm going to walk a little more," said Mario. He took his walking stick and pulled himself up with it. Out of the sun, he didn't get dizzy when he stood up. He made it twice the distance of his first few trials and returned to the cave with such ease that he was obliged to do it again, pushing himself to his farthest limit this time. When he returned to the cave and eased himself down next to Marcella, he felt as if he'd been working hard for a long time and fell asleep immediately. Before dozing off, Marcella listened to Mario's normal breathing beside her.

"How different a man getting well is from when he was wrestling death," she said to herself.

Rita coiled her rope, hung it over her shoulder and went to see Liberty. She'd tied her to a tree near a natural basin of rainwater where she'd have shade, water and forage. Though the sun was hot and bright, Rita could still smell the rain in the air. A brilliantly marked butterfly caught her attention, and she sat in the sand watching it light on a red barrel cactus flower that had bloomed in the rain. Rita let her thoughts rest in the bright colors of its motionless wings.

Suddenly, she stretched and jumped to her feet with the careless exuberance of youth. The desert was abloom with flowers and a little of the drab olive of the sparse green had turned to jade. The air smelled of water and life, but the sand was already dry.

Standing on her toes, Rita reached as high as she could with open hands catching the sun's early rays. She leaped to grab a low branch of a gnarled, twisted Douglas pine tree, a scrawny post with a few faded olive needles stuck to its topmost limbs. Letting her body swing back and forth, the lethargic remains of inactivity from sitting watching the butterfly shook out. It felt delicious. Her muscles and blood and bones sang with pleasure, and she dropped to the ground and went to Liberty.

To prepare her for riding, she patted and petted the donkey's back repeatedly. "You're going to learn something today, Liberty," said Rita, leaning on the donkey's back. Liberty squirmed restlessly, but Rita kept up the pressure, increasing it little by little until she could tolerate it.

"See, Liberty? It's okay," she said. Pressing on Liberty's back, she then jumped beside her without mounting, and led her by the halter. Rita tied one end of her long rope to a tree and the other to the halter before holding her around the neck, and throwing one leg over, as she tried to jump onto the donkey's back.

Liberty bucked, and Rita landed painfully on the ground on the other side of her. Trying again, this time she quickly leaned forward and grabbed Liberty around her neck with both hands and hung on until she quieted.

When Liberty got used to Rita sitting on her back, Rita made reins from her long rope and began her riding lessons. After practicing riding over the desert the rest of the morning and into early afternoon, she triumphantly rode Liberty back to the cave.

Hearing the animal approach, Marcella awoke and went out to meet the donkey and rider. Mario woke when Marcella got up and used his walking stick to stand up. He followed Marcella out.

"Rita!" said Mario, standing in the entrance to the cave. "You broke a wild animal! You're going to get us out of here yet!" Rita beamed.

"If I could handle animals like that, it would be a miracle," said Marcella. "It's a gift you have, Rita."

"I'll order one large glass of milk," said Mario.

"Will do," said Rita. Alighting, Rita then tied Liberty to the dead tree in front of the cave, got the glass, milked her in front of Mario and handed him the glass of milk.

"Every man should have such a daughter," said Mario. He drained the glass and gave it back to Rita who filled it again and handed Marcella the glass. Rita drank next, and they passed the glass around until everyone had enough, but Liberty still had milk. Rita then rode Liberty back to a grazing place and milked her out, letting the milk run into the desert sand.

"I better go and catch another bird," said Marcella. "This one's almost gone." She left for the ravine, and Mario got up to walk strength back into his legs. The wound from the snakebite throbbed when he walked, but he felt no pain. He passed the time resting and walking, resting and walking until Marcella returned carrying a turkey by the legs.

"I married a woman and got a hunter," said Mario.

"It's good to know how to do this," said Marcella. "But next time, I'm going to be the one to get bitten by the snake."

Rita returned from working with Liberty and started the fire beneath the rock oven, and Mario took the bird from Marcella to clean and dress it.

"C'mon, I'll show you the butcher shop," said Marcella. She took him to where she'd cleaned and dressed the turkeys, and in the almost pristine wilderness, Mario could detect the foreign feeling of an alien act repeated. Marcella was happy to let him cook it.

After they gathered at the fire and ate, Mario took out his topographical map to study. "Are you ready to go tonight, Marcella?" asked Mario. .

"I can't wait to get out of here," Marcella said.

"How about you, Rita?"

"I think I'll hang around for a couple of years enjoying the scenery."

Mario and Marcella laughed.

"I'll go get Liberty," said Rita.

"Good," said Mario. He went into the cave to help Marcella pack their things and shoved his canteen loops through his belt that was now so loose it felt like it might not hold his pants up. Rita returned with Liberty, and Mario hung their packs from her back with rope before mounting the donkey, sticking to the original plan to travel at sunset.

"Suppose they won't let us stay?" asked Rita, walking beside Liberty, as they continued their journey.

"Who?" asked Marcella.

"I don't know. Anyone."

"We have to be careful not to get caught," said Marcella. "Many people find a way to stay, and we will, too. Don't think about what you don't want to happen."

"It's hard not to. If we think about it, we can think up things to do ahead of time," replied Rita.

"No, you could make it happen," argued Marcella.

"If anyone asks where we live, we can say Nogales. That's a town in Arizona on the border. I saw it on a map at school."

"Good. Arizona," said Mario. "We're from Nogales. That's where we live, Nogales, Arizona."

"Nogales, Arizona," said Marcella. It sounded foreign, and she repeated it. "It sounds nice, Nogales, Arizona."

"After we get to America, I want to go to New York," said Rita.

"Why New York?" asked Mario.

"We learned about it in school. There's no desert in New York, but there are many, many lakes and forests and mountains; great, high mountains covered with big trees. It snows in winter. They cut holes in the ice on the lakes and go fishing. In summer it's warm, but not as hot as this. All kinds of people live in New York, and they speak every language.

"The biggest city in the world is in New York. They have everything in it. I want to see that city. A statue of a lady holding a torch, the Statue of Liberty, means freedom. We can all work there. We can go to school, too, and learn how to do the jobs they have in New York. Then we can buy a house and live like everyone in the free world with no war and plenty of money."

"How about it, Mario?" asked Marcella. "Want to go to New York?"

"Okay," said Mario. "After we see how to get there, we'll go to New York."

Traveling was welcome after the long stop, and they moved briskly for three hours. When they rested, Mario got off the donkey and was sore from riding. He had to walk a little, but now the problem was not in his legs. Marcella distributed wild turkey, and Rita milked Liberty. They sat down to eat and drink and rest.

As soon as they were all finished eating, Mario said, "Let's go. I need to practice walking."

Marcella and Rita, anxious to put the desert behind were happy to accommodate him. Mario walked as long as possible with the walking stick, enjoying the return of strength to his muscles and independence to his spirit. Only when he slowed down the party would he ride and then only long enough for a fifteen or twenty minute rest.

"This way," Mario said, veering off course and heading for a large boulder and rocky area several hundred yards away. The rock formations loomed up in the darkness, like an ancient castle and surrounding grounds against the midnight sky.

"We have to stop here and wait until dawn. The last part of the journey must be made in daylight. It's too dangerous to go in the dark," said Mario. "We have to cross the Valley of the Wind."

They made camp, Rita milked Liberty and Marcella rationed out the turkey. Rita finished eating quickly. "I can sleep here," she said, stretching full length on a dolmen. Moving around, she found a place where the contour of the rock fit so comfortably with her body that the hardness didn't bother her. Within minutes she was snoring.

When Mario and Marcella finished eating, Marcella lay on her back on her poncho on the sand in a dry wash alongside the mountain of rocks, looking at the stars.

"The stars are bigger and brighter and more on the desert," she said.

Mario spread his poncho beside her and lay down facing her, his elbow bent, his head propped on his hand. "Something's different since I got sick. We're all different, but I don't know how," he said.

"I can't explain what happened when you were sick, but it changed how I see. It made me stronger, and I knew you'd be all right if we believed strong enough," replied Marcella.

"I can't stand being this helpless, Marcella."

"We'd die here without you. You read the map and figure out the way. Even when you were unconscious, Mario, I talked to you, and you helped me."

"It takes time to get all my strength back. Waiting is the hardest thing in the world for me."

"Yes, you always like to do things. That's why I love you so much. Waiting is just as hard for me as it is for you. When you were sick, it was harder than breathing almost."

Mario kissed her slow until they were seized with passion, and they made love in the moonlight. Their pleasure was intensified because Mario had recovered, and now they allowed their emotion to reach a crescendo in the sliver of the crescent moon. Slow and fast and slow and steady and fast, and it lasted a long time until they both had given up and taken everything the other offered.

"Your body's different," he said hoarsely, running his hands over it. "Stronger, harder, leaner, more, but you're my same Marcella." Mario held her in his arms, and she embraced him.

"Ah Mario, I knew you had to come back to me. I knew it like I knew I'd take another breath, but knowing something good is going to happen is nothing like when it really happens."

"What you say with your acts and with your feeling is more than you can ever say with words," said Mario.

Marcella giggled, playing with his hair. "I guess that's why we don't talk so much," she said.

Listening to Marcella's soft even breathing and Rita snoring on the rock, Mario fell asleep satisfied that his strength had returned.

CHAPTER FOUR

Rita woke first in mid-morning, the rock hot from the sun, while Mario and Marcella slept in the shadow of the high rocks entwined in each other's arms. She explored the rocks, hopping from one to another.

Marcella woke next, got up and stretched anxiously glancing up to see how high the sun was. The longer they remained in the desert wilderness, the more she couldn't stand to be there. Her one purpose was now to get free of it and into civilization. If it wasn't for Mario and Rita, she thought the sun overhead and the sand beneath her feet would drive her insane. The rocks that had sheltered them stretched out in a low ridge rising into low mountains in places. The ridge ran as far as her eye could see. Not seeing Rita, Marcella called, "Rita! Rita!"

Mario woke and got up, and Rita came leaping over the rocks back to camp.

"Time to eat and get moving," announced Marcella. Mario and Rita settled themselves on a flat rock, and Marcella went over to the donkey and took the last of the turkey from the cheesecloth tied to her backpack. She patted Liberty on the neck and returned to Rita and Mario. Dividing the meat into three parts, she handed it out, and they ate it all.

"I'll milk Liberty this time," said Mario.

"Good," said Rita, happy to relinquish the chore.

Rita and Marcella stood by while Mario filled the glasses. He handed the first one to Marcella, and she emptied it. They drank until they were full. After breaking camp, hiking was fairly comfortable for Marcella and Rita because the sun hadn't reached its zenith, and they stayed in the shadow of the rocky ridge. Mario rode Liberty to conserve his legs for crossing the Valley of the Wind which had demanded all his strength when he was in the peak of health.

When the line of rocks curved to the right, Mario kept them on a straight course. "We're close to the Valley of the Wind on the border of North America," he said. They picked up speed, the excitement of being close to their destination and desire to get out of the desert inspiring Marcella and Rita to a quicker pace.

"Here," said Mario, stopping at the edge of a cliff. From their height they looked across a steep, circular depression in the earth on the border of Mexico and the United States. The descent from rim to floor was a jagged two hundred yards all around. The wind raged noisily in the valley and ripped at the vegetation which was permanently twisted and bent to its force. The tree trunks and branches skewered like corkscrews bent so far over that their tops swept the sandy earth. Sand blew wildly, filling the air to the rim, and mesquite and sagebrush hurled every which way caught in the crossfire of the wind which seemed to be blowing in all directions at once.

Mario pointed across the bowl of wind. "That's it," he said. "That's where we're going. That's the free land of the north." Marcella's heart sank. Across the windswept desolation the terrain looked exactly like the desert behind them.

"It's not far across," said Rita.

"The wind howls down there. You won't be able to hear me talk. It tries to pin you down. It's twelve or thirteen kilometers, but it takes as long to travel one step as it takes to go fifty up here. You're going to ride Liberty, Rita."

"Why don't you ride, Dad? My legs are good and strong."

Mario shook his head. "No, you have to ride. You're not heavy enough. The wind might carry you away."

Rita mounted, and Mario tied a rope around her waist and looped it around Liberty's belly to the other side, fastening it securely.

"If me or Marcella lets go of the halter, stop and wait until we're both holding on again," he said.

Mario got three pairs of goggles and three red bandanas out of his backpack and distributed them to Marcella and Rita. "We'll need these," he said. He put on the third pair of goggles and tied a bandana over his nose and mouth. He then pulled up his poncho and held it over his face with one hand.

"You look like Pancho Villa," said Rita. She and Marcella laughed, but Mario didn't laugh. He stood staring solemnly at them, waiting for them to put on their goggles and bandanas and cover their faces with their ponchos.

Rita put on her plastic goggles, and Marcella laughed at her. "You look like a barn owl," said Marcella.

"Put yours on. Let's see what you look like," said Rita. Marcella put on the goggles, adjusting the strap to fit comfortably. "You look like a sea frog," said Rita. It was her turn to laugh.

Mario got an undershirt out of his bag and started to tie it over Liberty's nose and mouth. She tossed her head and tried to rear, but before she could get on her hind legs, Marcella grabbed her halter from the other side, and she and Mario held her down with Rita shortening the reins. Mario tied the shirt around her muzzle to help keep the sand out of her nose and mouth.

Bowing their heads against the fury of the raging wind, Mario and Marcella pulled with all their strength on the halter of the reluctant Liberty, but she wouldn't budge.

"Go, Liberty!" yelled Rita, kicking hard with both heels, urging the donkey forward with her body

As Liberty took the first few steps into the long march, Mario kept his head and face covered with his poncho and goggles, holding the poncho in place with his free hand. The piercing, frenzied wind blasted sand showers from the ground and all sides. Cutting through the furious chaotic gusts, slower than a desert tortoise, they fought for every forward step.

The outreaching branches of the scrub pinion trees tore at their hats and clothing. Some of the wind-warped trees appeared to be kneeling in prayer.

Mario lost his footing on the steep ascent, and holding onto Liberty's harness, he managed to right himself; but he couldn't keep his advantage and slipped again and again.

Proceeding down the steep slope, Rita was positioned at an untenable angle, and clung to the donkey's sides with her legs and knees, keeping balance with her arms; but it took far more strength to stay on Liberty than it would take to run a mile. Though she preferred to keep her eyes closed, she had to open them from time to time to get her bearings, but all she could see was sand hitting the goggles, as the wind lashed at her head and back and shoulders and whistled through her ears, blowing all her thought out of her head until there was nothing left in her brain but the sound of screaming wind.

Tumbleweed caught in Liberty's mane and pounded on their hats in its crazed journey, and glass-like slivers of sand slashed Rita's face, invading her nose and mouth through the bandana and poncho. The environment was alive with missiles of pebbles, stones and uprooted vegetation propelled by the wind.

The screaming gusts caught Marcella, knocking her into Liberty and throwing Marcella off her footing. When she stumbled, it tore the poncho from her face. Holding to her lifeline, she found her footing, but when she was on her feet, Mario was knocked down. Only Liberty didn't stumble.

Rita discovered the way to alleviate the battering from the wind and the debris it hurled everywhere was to lean forward into Liberty's neck with her body flush with the donkey's and her head buried in Liberty's neck. She felt that if she hadn't been tied, the wind would have lifted her off Liberty's back and whirled her away.

Pinned against Liberty, Mario found that he could walk more easily and lose his footing less frequently when he leaned on her. Keeping his shoulder against the donkey's shoulder, Mario closed his eyes, but the whistle of the wind in his ear disoriented him, making him lose his balance, and he had to open his eyes. Liberty had swerved slightly from his direction, but the wind was less violent, so they could make better progress. He corrected the course later, working with the donkey. She instinctively moved with the strongest wind to their backs, making use of it, instead of approaching it head on, as they'd been doing.

Marcella, feeling a change in procedure, as they moved faster and more easily, also, discovered the advantage of leaning against Liberty with her eyes on the ground.

Clutching the poncho with one hand, holding onto the halter with the other, Mario's legs screamed for rest, but there was no choice. He forced them to churn on. Feeling a tap on his shoulder, he looked up, and brushing the sand off his goggles, he saw Rita motioning that she wanted to walk. He shook his head no. He wanted to tell her they couldn't afford to stop in the Valley of the Wind, but he couldn't open his mouth. She nodded to let him know she understood.

Marcella was thrown into a barrel cactus that spiked her in the knee in three places. She leaped aside, still holding onto the halter, with a cry, and her mouth filled with sand. Turning her head, she tried to spit it out, but the force of the wind was too great, and she thought she could hold it in her mouth, but little by little it went down. Breathing became a battle, and she tried to hurry Liberty. She couldn't wait to get out of the valley. "This must be the place on earth where the wind is born," she said to herself, because it blew from all directions.

On the homeward side of the valley, the battle against the fury of the tumultuous blasts reached its apex. The wind in its rage seemed to have volition, to desire their death in the valley, and all of them, even Liberty, sensed the war with death, knowing that they had to make it together and felt the common purpose of survival as one being.

Proceeding slowly and steadily they stepped over a skull of a lost steer, the entire skeleton of a donkey, and many coyote bones. At one point, Mario tripped over a human skull, and as he made his way further along, the rest of the bones of a human body stuck through the sand in places followed by more skulls. He counted only the human skulls and stopped counting when he reached twelve.

Struggling uphill out of the bowl, with every forward step, the wind pushed them back two. Liberty balked, and Rita sat up straight, risking being yanked from her mooring and blown away, kicking with all her strength, but the donkey wouldn't budge.

"Hie!" shouted Rita, relaxing her position to try to sit up and show Liberty who was boss, but the wind blew the shout back down her throat with a mouthful of debris, and she didn't think Liberty heard it. The branch of a pinion tree, driven by a gust shoved Rita, and bowing into Liberty again, she flattened herself against the donkey, but it brushed her to the side, so that she was clinging by her arms and the leg remaining over the donkey's back, pressuring Marcella, who tried to push her back onto Liberty's back.

Clutching Liberty with her arms and legs, every muscle seemingly under pressure, Rita hung onto the side of the donkey, trying to squirm her way squarely onto Liberty's back. A tree limb snagged the tee shirt protecting Liberty's mouth and nose, and she was at the mercy of the violent wind. Inching her way up, Rita was still in the path of the branch and couldn't get back. The seconds stretched to eternity, and she couldn't hang on much longer.

"It doesn't have to be much longer. It only has to be until Liberty gets past that branch," she said to herself, and holding the one idea of her salvation, that it may be just for one more second or fraction thereof, she held on, and then she felt Mario grab her leg.

Rita took a deep breath of relief, pulling her way back to a riding position, with the leverage of Mario holding onto her leg. Marcella kept her from falling on her side, and Liberty finally passed the barricading branch of the pinion tree.

The wind shifted suddenly, and Marcella got the rare opportunity to open her mouth. "Come on, Liberty," she said, putting her mouth in the donkey's ear. "We're almost there." Liberty stopped still, her ears forward nearly parallel to the ground. She stood like a stone for a second and then galloped straight up the hill at full speed, Marcella and Mario racing on each side to keep up.

"Stop!" yelled Rita, as Liberty jerked the reins out of her hand with a forward thrust of her head. Rita grabbed the donkey around her neck, and Mario and Marcella were forced to hold onto the halter with both hands, but their weight couldn't slow the desperate animal.

Mario lost his footing as Liberty bolted out of the Valley of the Wind and dragged him the last twenty feet before Rita could get her to stop. He let go of the rope, blood dripping from his hands and rolled away from Liberty's wild hooves. The wind on this side was dead, and the family had the feeling of going through the turmoil of hell to death itself as utter silence took the place of chaos. Liberty stopped suddenly. Marcella tried to let go of the halter, but her fingers were frozen to it. She had to wait a few minutes, and even motion seemed frozen in death. Rita broke the spell.

"You can let go now, Mom," she said.

"Thanks for telling me," said Marcella. It took a few moments for her right hand to relax enough to loosen its grip.

Mario struggled to his feet, and limped back to Liberty as Rita untied herself.

"Good girl, Liberty," said Mario. He patted her on the neck with the back of his hand, and then fell on his rear, watching Marcella, too exhausted to speak.

Marcella painfully pulled the three cactus spines out of her knee. She took off her jeans and poured a little water from her canteen over the wounds in her hands and knee. After drinking a little, she limped to her backpack and found her medicinal leaves in the zipper pocket. Unwrapping them, she then applied two to her knee which she held in place with a strip from the roll of gauze bandage.

Before putting her jeans back on, she shook as much sand out of them as possible, turned them inside out and brushed all the sand off the inside. She whisked sand off her body letting her actions substitute for thought because her head was utterly vacant. Her whole being was still infused with the action of getting through.

Mario poured water from his canteen into one bloody hand and then the other, welcoming the extraordinary stillness of the calm desert magnified by the absence of wind in his ears, though he could hear it in the distance ravaging the valley.

After throwing the loop end of Liberty's rope over a tall jagged rock, Rita returned to the edge of the valley of wind and looked back over it, watching the sandstorm in the violent chaotic gusts, the swirling mesquite and smaller rocks blowing like paper down a city street in a summer breeze, and a chill went up her spine. She'd looked death in the face and had been spared. Mentally returning to the point where she'd thought of death, she wondered if one of them had slipped up, if they'd all have died. She knew Liberty would have gotten through without them, but she relived the meeting ground of life and death with an unexplainable and unspeakable thrill of the knowledge that human beings rarely survive. Returning to Liberty, she then put her goggles and bandana in her backpack.

"There's a campground not too far ahead," rasped Mario. Breathing came hard. He spat out a wad of phlegm full of sand; and then they all started hawking up sand, spitting it out, blowing sand out of their noses, and picking it out of their ears.

Marcella got out her pocket knife and scraped sand from under her fingernails. "This side looks the same, but it's different," she said.

"Yes," agreed Rita. "It feels different, like people have been here."

Marcella dropped down beside Mario, tilting her wide-brimmed straw hat to shade her face. The sand had penetrated her shirt and stuck to her skin. Perspiration ran down her face and body, increasing her discomfort and she felt she'd go mad from the itching it produced. Sitting up, she tried to comb the sand out of her long thick hair, but the comb, too, was full of sand.

Rita scratched her arm and her leg and her belly. Fanning with her shirt, she then swiped at the sand stuck to her skin, and screamed. "I want to go back! I hate this goddamn desert! I'm sick of it! I don't want to go another step!"

"Sure, Querido," said Marcella, pleasantly. "Get back on Liberty. We'll dance on back through the windy valley, and next week we'll be at the mesa if one of us doesn't fall off a cliff or step on a snake or die of heat exhaustion."

Rita felt like crying, but she was no baby.

"It's all right," said Mario. "It feels good to complain sometimes, even when you know it can't help." He laughed, and Rita looked at him like he was crazy.

Marcella laughed, too, and then Rita had to laugh. Mario scratched his armpits, like a monkey, making faces. Rita and Marcella laughed harder, and forgetting his agony momentarily, Mario leaped to his feet, raised one leg and then the other, scratching himself all over in a hilarious monkey mime. Facing him, Rita mimicked him. They aped each other, each one outdoing the other, and Marcella laughed until tears rolled down her cheeks.

She took a long swig from her canteen in a moment of careless abandon, and the water slid down like something sacred. Mario dropped down beside her and also drank. Falling backwards, he covered his face with his hat, but the sun was too hot, and he was too uncomfortable to remain there for long. He tried to get up, but his legs wouldn't work.

"Rita," he said. "Would you get me my topographical map?" She brought it to him. Rolling over on his side, propping himself on his arm, he looked at his map studying it for a long while.

Marcella looked at the map, too. "Where are we?" she asked. He pointed out their location.

"We have to push on," she said. "I can't stand this sun."

"Agreed," said Mario. "Too bad my legs won't get me up." He coughed up another wad of sandy phlegm and spat it out.

"Rita, let's be Mario's legs," said Marcella. Marcella stood and took one of Mario's arms. Rita grabbed the other, and they helped him stand. On his feet, his legs took over their natural function. He walked a half mile to strengthen them before getting on Liberty's back, and Rita and Marcella walked side by side for several hours.

Mario looked at his topographical map for the fourth time after emerging from the Valley of the Wind. Permitting Liberty to help steer them through the valley, he wasn't sure he hadn't left some of their direction to her. If so, she'd surely try to circle around the wind bowl, returning to her place of origin.

When the sun began to set, he saw that he'd been veering slightly off course and turned Liberty to the northwest adjusting his direction. At twilight he saw one of his landmarks about a mile due north and headed straight for it.

"See the way the sun glints off that quartz rock on that tall rectangular boulder standing alone that looks like a door?" he asked, pointing in the distance. Marcella and Rita scanned the terrain.

"Yes, I see it," said Marcella.

"Where?" asked Rita. Marcella leveled her face with Rita's and pointed to it.

"Oh yeah," said Rita.

Look directly to the right of it, about a mile, I guess," said Mario, pointing. They both looked. There are a few boulders with a flat rock on top. That's where the man in the broke down car gave me a hundred dollars. There's a road near it, and it's seven miles to a town."

"I see it," said Rita.

"There's a clearing there where we'll camp. There's a natural spring, too, and a dirt road on the other side of those rocks. The road ends there. I put that quartz on top of that rock to mark it. See, here it is on my map." He showed Marcella and Rita the map, and they both looked with interest.

They arrived at the abandoned camp site after dark, and Mario slid off Liberty's back. The afternoon ride had rested his legs, and he didn't collapse; but his back ached, and he had a hard time standing up straight until he walked the kink out of his back.

A natural artesian well provided a spring of running water; and spotting it immediately, Rita and Marcella ran to it. Mario led Liberty to the spring for a long cool drink before finding a place to secure her and returned to Rita and Marcella.

"Water!" yelled Rita. She knelt in the shallow water beside the spring where it bubbled out of the ground in a little pool and drank from it before moving to the edge of the pool and splashing it all over her face and head. Pine trees and shrubs grew all around the spring, and the wild grasses sprouting along it were soft not brittle like the rest of the desert flora.

"We're on the other side!" cried Marcella. "We made it over the edge! Here's the second sign of civilization." She put her face in the water, drank some and threw water over her head and arms.

"Look at Liberty," said Rita. "She knows it, too, and she's afraid. We're closer to our turf, but she's farther from hers." Liberty's ears twitched, her eyes rolled and her ears flayed back. Her feet moved nervously in a kind of frenzied dance.

Rita splashed water over her face, and Marcella drank again from cupped hands.

Mario knelt and drank. He threw a handful of water at Marcella, and she retaliated. Then he scooped some over the top of Rita's head. Soon they were all laughing and throwing water at each other, cavorting in the pool.

"You go first, Rita," said Marcella, refreshed. Rita ran to Liberty and got her bar of soap and the clothes Marcella had washed in the rain out of her backpack. The clothes were soft from being so tightly rolled, and she returned to the pool with them. She stripped off her clothes and plopped into the water, as deep as her navel. Leaning back, she then soaked her hair through before soaping herself and her hair and rinsing off. When she was clean, she got out and dressed in clean clothes.

She found Marcella resting on a rock hidden from the spring by boulders. "I'm finished, Mom," she said. "Where's Dad?"

"Finding a rabbit for us to eat," said Marcella. "I'll take my turn, and you can make the fire."

"Sure," said Rita. "Look at all the wood around here." She gathered enough tinder and kindling for a decent start, as Marcella headed for her backpack. Larger sticks were plentiful, and when Mario returned holding a dead jack rabbit by the ears, the fire was ready.

He left the camp site to skin the rabbit. Bringing it back, he then began roasting it over the fire.

Returning clean and refreshed from the spring, Marcella said, "Smells like food." She laid out her clothes which she'd washed on a nearby rock to dry.

Mario left the rabbit cooking to take his turn at the spring. Taking clean clothes and his soap, he went to the water, stripped and toppled in. He worked up a lather, singing loudly off key.

> *"From this valley they say you are leaving,*
>
> *We will miss your bright eyes and sweet smile,*
> *For they say you are taking the sunshine,*
> *That brightened our pathway awhile,*
> *Come and sit by my side if you love me,*
> *Do not hasten to bid me adieu,*
> *But remember that awful windy valley,*
> *And the man who has loved you so true,"* he bellowed

His noise caused Liberty to bray, and Rita started laughing. "Where did he learn that?" she asked Marcella.

"I don't know. I never heard him do that," she said. "Maybe from the American doctor who taught him English."

Mario returned to the fire and shaved, ebullient that they were on the other side, not that he'd ever doubted.

"Where did you learn that song, Dad?" asked Rita.

"From an American doctor who taught me English," he replied. "Do you like it?"

Rita giggled. "No. Too bad he couldn't teach you how to sing."

Mario went to turn the rabbit, but saw that Marcella had already done it, so he got the hard, brown soap out of Marcella's backpack and went back to the spring to wash his clothes while the rabbit finished roasting.

"Aaagh! The sand and grime won't come out!" he shouted. He laid the shirt on a boulder and started beating it with a rock, grunting like a cave man. Hearing him clowning, Marcella went to the spring, laughing. She snatched the shirt, knelt by the spring and soaped it. Then she rubbed it between her knuckles, held it up, dunked it and repeated it several times.

"Like this," she said.

"Oh," said Mario, as though he hadn't seen her do it a hundred times. She threw the shirt over his head, and he finished washing his clothes.

Rita milked Liberty. "Soon we're going to be free," she said. "You too, Liberty. Thanks for helping us." Liberty turned her head to look at Rita as though she understood.

"It's true," said Rita. When the glass had been filled, the milk drunk, the canteens refilled until Liberty ran dry, Rita untied her and took all their packs off. She walked Liberty to the spring and tied her in the shade. When she returned to the fire, the rabbit was ready.

The delectable aroma of the roasting rabbit betrayed the taste. Tough, dry, almost tasteless and chewy, it would've been inedible if there was anything else to eat.

"When we get to New York, you can make a fortune cooking in a fancy restaurant, Dad," Rita joked.

Mario sat straight, tall and poker faced. Then he stood solemnly in front of the fire and bowed, like one accepting a compliment. He turned his back and bowed in the direction of the Valley of the Wind. "Thank you for letting us through," he said.

"This rabbit was getting ready to die of old age when you caught it," said Marcella.

Sitting down, Mario's expression changed to one of incredulity and then his lower lip puckered.

"That's how Dad could catch it," quipped Rita, giggling.

"It'll toughen you up. Your teeth need exercise, just like your brain," said Mario, in the tone of a teacher.

"Good thing we got this workout," said Rita, before ripping a piece of meat off the bone with her teeth. She chewed it for a long time in order to swallow it. "Now we can walk out of here on the strength of our teeth and iron digestions."

After she ate, Rita washed her clothes which she'd left beside the pool. When she returned to the glowing coals, Mario was sleeping, Marcella stretched out beside him. Rita spread her clothes on a nearby rock to dry, unrolled her poncho on the other side of Marcella and curled up to go to sleep.

CHAPTER FIVE

The belch of a truck's motor on a dusty trail on the other side of the rocks woke Marcella early the next afternoon.

"Wake up, Mario! Wake up, Rita!" She shook Mario awake, and Rita got up, too. "Here comes someone."

"I'm going to let Liberty go," said Rita, and ran back to the spring. She held the halter briefly and whispered, "Thank you for saving our lives." She unsheathed her knife, cut the halter and yanked it off. Liberty took off across the desert her scraggly tail straight out behind her. Rita untied the rope from the pinion tree, coiled it and hung it over her shoulder. She returned to Mario and Marcella as three men approached.

Mario studied the men. Though they were more like him than Alv had been with deeply tanned, wrinkled working outdoor faces, hands and manner, he keenly felt his vulnerability.

The lead man spoke to them quietly. "What are you doing here? Can I help you?"

"Our car broke down," said Mario, pointing across the desert toward the east along the road. "We've been walking all night. We had to rest."

"Where do you live?" he asked, studying Mario's face.

"We're from Nogales, but we're traveling. We're going northwest," said Mario.

The man spoke to his two companions in his native language, and Mario realized that they were on the Pima reservation. One of the others answered him, and there was a long hesitation before the leader spoke again, and the third man joined the conversation. The leader turned to Mario. "Want a ride to your car?" he asked.

"No," said Mario. "We're lucky to be rid of it, nothing but trouble. I'm tired of pushing it. Can you give us a ride to town?"

"Where in the northwest are you going?"
"California," popped out of Rita's mouth.

The man looked down at her and smiled. "Crop pickers?" he asked.

"Yes," said Mario. "Crop pickers."

"Come on," said the man. "We can give you a ride to Bakersfield."

Rita shouldered her backpack, and Mario ran to get his and Marcella's backpacks as Marcella grabbed all their clothes off the rocks. She deftly rolled them into a neat bundle and followed the party to the end of the road where an old pick up truck was parked.

Mario threw the backpacks into the bed, and he, Marcella and Rita climbed in. The Pima men climbed into the cab, the leader in the driver's seat. Soon they were off the gravel trail clipping along on an asphalt road.

"I knew we'd have good fortune," said Mario. "I never knew we'd be this lucky." The truck rumbled through the well-conserved reservation. The wind drying the scorched leather of his face, etching in the wrinkles, Mario watched the desert give way to grazing land and irrigated fields.

Marcella felt the danger of the desert crossing lift as they left it, and she looked ahead at the land rushing by, the mountains in the distance, poised on the edge of a world she didn't know.

Rita imagined going to a life where they could stop running. She'd learn new and extraordinary things and dream up fantastic solutions to her problems where people didn't live to kill and maim, and nothing but her personal limitations would slow her down. A teacher in Mexico told her once that in America the air was full of freedom and girls and boys could grow up to be whatever they wanted even if they started out poor. Anybody could get a job. In the breath of that rarefied air that every persecuted soul looked toward, she would discover her talents and shortcomings, and there would be nothing to keep her from acting on them. On the brink of change, she felt incredibly lucky to have this chance, the more so because she'd left so many children behind that never would.

"Whatever the new world brings, I'm going to make the best of it, not get by in it, but take it and use it and blaze a trail," she said, her voice determined, her chin set squarely, her brown eyes gleaming.

Suspended between two worlds, one impossible to live in and the other unknown; the precariousness of their situation attacked Mario's sense of logic and reason threatening to unbalance him. He spoke to reassure himself. "My life, from the day I was born, has been a flight from death," he said. "I want a little time before it catches me to see what I can do besides run."

"You can do anything you want in America," said Marcella. "I know just what I want - a little bungalow with a white picket fence all around it and a white gate. It'll have big trees all around, and I'll plant vegetables in the back and flowers in the front. We'll work hard and see how they do things, and then we'll live good and happy like everybody else in America."

Mario laughed. "That's okay with me, Marcella, because I won't be running."

The driver proceeded for several hours before stopping to buy gas, and Mario, Marcella and Rita took advantage of the pit stop on the outskirts of a small town to get out and stretch.

They went into the store at the gas station and used the restrooms. Mario bought a loaf of bread, a package of lunchmeat, a quart of milk, a large bag of corn chips, cheese, salsa and three gallons of water. He handed a gallon to Marcella and one to Rita.

"I'll take two of those hot dogs," said Rita. The clerk took them off a spit and put them on rolls. Rita, also, got a cold can of soda, a bag of potato chips and a package of two little cakes.

"I'll try one of those hot dogs, too," said Marcella. She, also, put a quart of grapefruit juice on the counter. Mario handed the clerk his hundred dollar bill.

They all gathered around the man counting out the change, watching eagerly. Taking the change, Mario then handed Marcella two twenty dollar bills and Rita a ten. They hurried back to the truck and got in before the Pima men were finished gassing up, checking the oil and paying inside. They were soon on the road again fortifying themselves with the food and beverages they'd bought.

Rattling through town, small brick ramblers lined up neatly along each side of the road. Some of them had large shady trees in the front yards, and Rita pictured herself living in such a house. She saw two boys about her age throwing a baseball back and forth as a small terrier yapped after it leaping in the air trying to catch it.

The houses soon thinned out giving way to ranches, some with little houses and a barn off in the distance. Some were surrounded by large trees. Watching the orchards and fields roll by, they each retreated into their own thoughts. The sound of traffic and wind made it too difficult to talk.

The driver stopped for gas again just before the sun reached the horizon. Mario, Marcella and Rita climbed out of the truck to stretch and use the restroom.

The Pima men went into the store at the gas station, and Mario, Marcella and Rita remained outside by the bed of the truck. When the men came out of the store, they climbed back in, and the truck rolled down the highway.

After dark Marcella stretched out flat in the bed of the truck wrapped in her poncho. Mario lay beside her on his back, looking up at the stars, and Rita snuggled against Marcella. Dozing off and on, Mario knew by the soft breathing of his wife and daughter that they were sleeping. One of the small towns, like those they stopped for gas in, would probably be home for him and his family. As he thought this Rita asked a question, and he thought she was talking in her sleep because she didn't move and her breathing didn't change.

"How long does it take to get home?" she asked sleepily.

"It depends on how far you have to go," he replied, before drifting into sleep himself.

When the truck stopped late at night, Mario woke up and got out of the truck to use the bathroom and get another drink. Marcella and Rita slept through. The truck hit the road again, and Mario dozed off and on without sleeping deeply.

The sun rose as they neared the end of the Mojave Desert, and Mario was surprised that they were back on the desert. Though it was hot and dry and there was no traffic it wasn't remote as the desert they'd crossed on foot. Mario took a long swig from his water jug and made a sandwich. He ate it and some chips dipped in salsa and cheese.

Marcella sat up and stretched her stiff back and arms and legs. Looking at Rita jouncing in the bed of the truck, she asked, "How did I sleep through that?"

"The same way she is," said Mario. "I slept, too."

"We're back on the desert? We're going the wrong way." Marcella reached for the chips and cheese and salsa.

"There's desert in California, too. I saw a sign when we crossed the border into California a long time ago. This is the great Mojave."

Marcella drank a long drink from her water jug. "This is the way I like to cross a desert," she said, munching corn chips.

"I'm not so sure," said Mario. "I don't know what kind of snakes they've got here. I don't like to get bit, but when you know what bit you, you know what to do about it."

Looking around the bed of the truck, Marcella lifted Rita's poncho and looked under it at her sleeping daughter, searching for a snake. "You're wrong, Mario. There aren't any snakes. This is way, way, easier."

"Much," said Mario.

"Much, much easier."

Rita woke up rubbing her eyes. She sat up and looked around. "Where are we?" she asked.

"California," said Mario, smiling at her.

"All right!" said Rita. "So, California's a desert, too, but not as solitary as our desert." She took a long drink of water, and helped Mario and Marcella finish the groceries. The desert faded into mountains and the mountains soon opened into a valley green with orchards and crops climbing the slopes.

The Pima men stopped at a general store with an island of two gas pumps in front on the outskirts of Bakersfield. Noticing the location of the sun, Mario figured that it was about two o'clock. The Pima man who spoke to them first got out of the driver's seat and walked over to them.

"From here we're going over the mountain to Los

Angeles, and then we're going south down to Mexico. After that we're going back to where we picked you up," he said.

"Thanks for the ride," said Mario, jumping down from the truck with his backpack. He shook the man's hand. Marcella and Rita gathered their backpacks and water and climbed out of the truck. Rita stretched and started walking the kinks out of her back.

With the temperature pushing a hundred and five, the men put gas in the truck, went into the little store and returned. They all got in the truck and rattled off. Mario looked around with misgivings. The land sweltered, flat and dusty covered with tinder dry grass, sparse and brown. An old wood picnic table with benches attached on each side stood under a large cottonwood tree.

They went into the small store which offered a fair selection of groceries and settled on bologna, a loaf of bread, sodas from the cold drink case and a large bag of tortilla chips, cheese and salsa. Mario put three gallons of water on the counter and a newspaper which he folded to read later. "This'll tell us more about America than anything," he said.

The clerk noticing their attention when she gave change counted slowly and deliberately. She looked Hispanic and spoke perfect English. She had long dark brown wavy hair that fell around her plump shoulders and wore a bright yellow blouse with flowers and parrots on it. Her khaki trousers hung baggy as a skirt, and she wore a mask of heavy cosmetics with cherry red lipstick.

"Are you from around here?" she asked.

"Nogales," said Mario.

"I see," she nodded slowly, deep in thought.

"They're hiring orange pickers around Delano and Porterville," she said.

"Which way?" asked Mario.

"North."

"How far?"

"Delano's maybe fifty miles, Porterville sixty-five. People always stop here on their way north. It won't be hard to get a ride."

"Good," said Mario. "Thanks."

"Do you get a lot of customers out here?" asked

Marcella. "It looks like not much here but the highway."

"That's all I need. Most of my business is gas and refreshments for the road," she said. Marcella stayed in the shop where it was cooler, talking to the woman.

Taking the groceries outside, Rita then started making sandwiches at the outdoor picnic table. Mario sat down swatting at bees and flies with the rolled up paper. He ate one of Rita's sandwiches as soon as it was ready.

"Not too bad," said Mario, munching on his sandwich.

"Better than your rabbit."

"What do you mean? You're talking to the famous chef in the fancy restaurant, don't forget." Mario opened the newspaper and started reading it, and Rita sat next to him with a sandwich, also, reading.

Marcella walked around the store noticing everything. She watched as a late model Ford with a blue-eyed blonde woman and four North American teenagers in it pulled up. They were all well-dressed and moved with the self assurance of those who are comfortable with their place in the system.

One of the teenagers put gas in the car, and the others came inside talking and laughing. Marcella watched out the store window as another woman stopped and put gas in her car. Two children emerged from the car and came into the store, and when the woman was finished gassing up, she came in, too. The boy was just a little younger than Rita; and looking at him Marcella saw how different his life had been than Rita's; and though Rita's had been harsh and sharp, she felt Rita knew more about life than he did. Life had given Rita a far different base. Watching the Americans and their transactions carefully until they left, Marcella then went outside to the picnic table with Mario and Rita.

An ancient pickup truck rattled to a stop, and a man got out. As he filled his gas tank, Mario strolled over to him. He looked Hispanic, and Mario thought by his face and clothes and hands that he worked hard outdoors.

"We need a ride north, my wife and daughter and me," Mario said to the man. "Can you give us a lift?" The man's dark eyes swept over Mario and his family. "Where are you going?" he asked.

"Delano," said Mario.

"Sure." The man smiled and nodded. Hearing his reply, Rita then went over to the truck and threw her backpack into the bed. She went back for the food and started to climb into the back with some bushels of beans and bags of fertilizer.

"There's enough room in the front," said the man. Mario threw his backpack in the bed and Marcella tossed hers back. Mario climbed in first; Marcella sat in the middle and Rita squeezed in between Marcella and the door.

Driving north, large moving machinery dotted field after field of orchards. Marcella made a bologna sandwich. "Want a sandwich?" she asked the driver. He shook his head no.

"What are those machines?" she asked.

"Oil drills. Oil conglomerates own a lot of California, and they hire business managers from back east to manage the farms on top of the oil."

"We're going to Delano to pick oranges," said Mario. "We heard there's work."

"You can find work," he said.

"Is there a school?" asked Rita. "Yes, and there's a law you have to go. Since it doesn't open until September, you get to start right out picking oranges."

"No, no, no, no," said Mario, laughing. "We'll work, Marcella and me."

Farther up the highway they passed orange groves for miles on both sides of the road growing out of a bright orange sea of fallen oranges.

"Why do they leave the oranges so deep on the ground instead of selling them?" asked Rita. Thinking of the rabbit she ate on the desert, it was inconceivable to her that anyone could be rich enough to throw that much food away.

"They can't sell 'em. Government regulations," said the man, turning off the highway and down a dirt road.

"We're going to get jobs picking oranges," said Mario. "How can we pick them if they can't sell them?"

"They can't sell all of them," replied the driver. "There's plenty to pick to sell, but don't you worry about that. All you'll have to do is pick."

He made several more turns to a large field where rows of homemade tarpaper shacks lined dirt trails barely wide enough for the truck to pass. Children playing in the road scattered when the truck approached and as soon as it rattled by were back at their game. An old man leaning on a stick he used for a cane came out of one of the shacks.

"Get away from there!" he yelled at the children. "Go play in the field!" He waved them away with his stick, and the children moved to a parallel lane, laughing and chatting.

The driver stopped at a shack covered with shingles painted bright yellow. "You got to get out here," he said. Rita opened the door and jumped to the ground. Marcella climbed down with the bag of food, and Mario followed with the water. He handed the plastic jug to Rita and climbed into the bed of the truck to throw their backpacks out and jumped off the truck. The driver waved, grinning and drove back to the highway.

A large sloppy Latino man with an enormous belly came out the door, bending over so his head wouldn't hit the door frame.

"He looks like he's pregnant," whispered Marcella, under her breath. Rita giggled and Mario chuckled.

"Lookin' fer work an' a place ta rent?" he asked. Lighting a cigarette, he wheezed and was racked with coughing.

"How much to rent?" asked Mario.

"Three hunnert a month. I only got one. A fambly just moved on this mornin'."

"Can we see it?" asked Marcella.

"This way," said Manuel, glaring at Marcella.

Mario, Marcella, and Rita followed Manuel threading his way through the jumble of small children playing in the roadways. The shanties the migrant workers called home lined the narrow lanes. Each dwelling was different as a result of the occupant's improvements using scraps of wood, shingles and tarpaper salvaged from the wrecks Manuel no longer rented.

Almost all the habitats included vegetable patches with corn as high as the makeshift structures, tomatoes, peppers and squash. The gardens were fenced with chicken wire.

The shack Manuel showed them was partitioned into two sections. A filthy mattress stank on the floor in a corner of the first section. A rat scurried from a pile of debris where the ceiling had caved in.

"What do you do when it rains?" asked Rita, gaping at the sky through the hole.

Manuel laughed so hard he had to stop walking. He huffed and wheezed for breath, flicking his cigarette ash on the pile of debri, ignoring Rita's question.

"How did they cook?" asked Marcella.
"Outside. They had a grill, but they sold it when they left."
"Why did they leave?" Marcella asked.
"They had a fight. One of 'em got lazy and figgered they wasn't gunna work no more. Happens ever' day." Manuel shrugged, nonchalantly.

Behind the partition was a toilet and shower stall. A hose, hooked to the water spigot outside, came through the open window and hung over a curtain rail into the shower stall. Under the drain a six-inch space between the floor of the shack and the drainpipe in the center was muddy sludge.

"Someone goes out an' turns the water on ta take a shower an' fill the toilet tank," said Manuel.

"How much do they pay to pick the oranges?" Marcella asked.

"Depends on how much ya pick. The truck comes at six a.m. and ya pick til four p.m. Ya get a half hour off fer lunch. I gotta contract ya kin sign.

"If yas fergot yer identification, yas got no choice." Manuel's mean grin showed his two front teeth missing. "No questions ast," he added.

Mario glanced dubiously at Marcella.

"We need a little time to think about it," he said.

"Well, while yer cogitatin' figger this. Mr. Painter got a li'l store behind my place, and I run it fer'm. Ya kin rent tow'ls fer a buck apiece a week. Soap runs two buck a bar, and a loaf a bread'll run ya three bucks. We got everding ya need ta keep body and soul tagedder. Ya kin git a pound bag a beans fer two bucks and corn meal and lard. We even gotta launder with a cupple washers and dryers."

"Where are the other stores?" asked Marcella.

"Nine miles down the road." Manuel had another coughing fit between sputters of laughter.

"I want to talk to some of the people who live here," said Mario.

"I'm rentin' this place ta da first person who signs da contract," said Manuel. "I gotta bizniz ta run fer Mr. Painter. He likes ta keep his properties fully operational."

An old rattletrap full of Latinos, a squalling baby in front and fighting children in back, pulled up at the yellow house, and the driver got out. Manuel turned and started waddling up the dirt lane to go meet them.

"I'll sign the contract," said Mario. Turning back, Manuel eyed him suspiciously. "Don't try nudden' stupid," he said. "Or ya'll wish ya was dead."

Mario, Marcella and Rita followed Manuel back to the shack with bright yellow shingles.

"Don't got noddin'," he yelled at the Latino man who'd emerged from his car and was leaning against the door. "Jus' rented da last place. Go on now. Go on," he waved his arms at the man as if he were shooing a calf.

"Donde?" asked the man.

Manuel looked at him and shrugged. "Don't know," he yelled. "Outta here 'fore I call da police. Policia! Policia!" Frowning, the man got in the car. It sputtered to a start, and he drove away with a backfire of the engine like the report of a pistol and a puff of black smoke from the exhaust.

   Lumbering up the three front stairs and ducking to go into his shack, Manuel returned in a few minutes with a printed sheet of paper. He pulled a pen out of his shirt pocket and handed it to Mario. "Sign here on da dotted line," he said.

   "I'll read it first," said Mario, starting to read the document, but Manuel yanked it out of his hand.

   "Hey! Yas want da place er not? I ain't got time fer foolin' aroun'." Another old jalopy turned onto the dirt lane, and Mario looked at Manuel in disgust. He signed the contract, and he Marcella and Rita returned to the shack.

   None of them wanted to go inside, so they sat outside in back leaning against the shack.

   "We have to hurry and get to work on this wreck," said Mario. "Let's go look at some of those falling down heaps of junk Manuel doesn't rent anymore. We'll have to find stuff to patch the roof."

   They began walking down the dirt road, and children stopped playing to stare at them until they passed. Mario stopped in front of a shack that had once been a home with the roof caved in. "I can find boards, tarpaper and shingles here," he said. He began pulling and prying out materials.

   "There are only small kids, no parents or kids my age here," noted Rita.

   "They're not back from the orange groves," said Mario. "Marcella, the first thing we need to buy when we have money is a hammer."

   "I'll go find one," said Rita.

   "Where?" asked Mario, but she was already running down the lane, and he watched as she talked to a small boy a half block away. He pointed to a slightly older child Mario estimated to be about five, and Rita and the child disappeared around the corner and were lost to view. Mario looked at Marcella and laughed.

   "She's going to borrow us a hammer," said Marcella.

Mario rescued a large solid piece of tarpaper that would fit over the hole in the roof. He pulled it loose and tossed it to the ground. Marcella rolled it up, carried it back to their house and returned for more.

When she got back to the collapsed structure, Rita was gathering an armful of boards that Mario had pried off with a hammer. "So, you got us a donkey first and now a hammer," said Marcella. "What would do without a daughter, Mario?"

"Sleep in the rain?" asked Mario. He pounded rusty nails out of the wreck, and tossed them to Rita one by one. Prying enough shingles from the only outer wall still standing to cover the hole in the roof, he then threw them down in a pile, and Marcella gathered them up.

When Mario had removed everything usable from the wreck, they returned to their shanty. "Rita, go find the store, and buy us a broom, would you?" asked Marcella.

"Okay," she said, handing Mario the nails and went to locate the store.

Mario put the nails in his pockets and climbed to the roof using the bathroom window as a step ladder, and lay on his stomach facing the ground. "Hand up the stuff, Marcella," he said.

She handed up the tarpaper and followed up with the hammer

At the store Rita found that a cheaply made plastic broom like she could buy in Mexico for two dollars cost ten, so she returned to the house of the boy who'd lent her the hammer. She returned with a broom, a shovel and a bucket. "I didn't buy the broom," she announced. "It cost ten bucks."

"Good for you," said Marcella, disdainfully. "I'm glad you didn't waste our money."

"That Manuel must be a highway robber," said Mario. "Or is the handle made of gold?"

"Maybe he flies on it," said Rita, to the amusement of Marcella and Mario.

Marcella shoveled the debris from the fallen-in roof into the bucket; and when it was full, Rita hauled it to a mountain of similar trash in a field behind the shacks and dumped it. Though the ground was dusty and hard at the shanty, her feet squished around the trash mountain on lower ground.

Small children played on the heap, and Rita paused to watch them. They climbed to the top, slipping and sliding part way down and trying again until they reached the top. Some kids would roll down or slide all the way down on their rear ends in an avalanche of rubble, whooping and hollering.

When Rita returned with the bucket, Marcella started filling it again. Something fell on Rita's head; and looking up, there was nothing but the hole in the ceiling and the sky above. She felt it again, and Marcella, also, looked up at the hole. Marcella brushed some woodchips out of her hair.

"Hey!" yelled Rita. "The sky's falling on my head."

"Mario," whispered Marcella. She went to the bathroom, got the hose and pulled it into the main room. "Go outside, and when I yell, turn the water on," she whispered in Rita's ear.

Giggling, Rita ran outside and waited by the spigot.

"Now!" yelled Marcella, as Mario looked through the hole, grinning with a handful of woodchips.

The water came on instantly, and Marcella held her thumb over the nozzle to create pressure and squirt Mario. He disappeared from view, and Rita turned off the water and ran in laughing.

"How am I going to get this roof fixed when it's raining from below?" Mario's face appeared in the space, dripping wet.

"If you don't get it fixed today, you can sleep under the hole, and maybe it'll rain from above," said Marcella. Giggling, they heard the hammer on the roof. Before the final board closed the opening completely, a last handful of woodchips came down on their heads.

Mario covered the tarpaper with boards, nailed them down and nailed shingles on top. When he was finished with the roof, he dragged the stinking mattress into the field, adding it to the mountain of debris.

Marcella hosed one of the walls. She and Rita scrubbed it with the brown soap they'd brought and rags they'd found at the wreck. When Mario returned, he helped them, and they finished scrubbing all the walls and floors of the inside of the shack.

After their shanty was repaired and cleaned, Marcella sat behind it, leaning against the outside wall. Mario sat beside her as Rita went to return the hammer, bucket, shovel and broom.

"This is not good," Mario said. "We'll be paying too much to live in this rat hole."

"Yes, but what else can we do until we find out how things work?"

"Nothing but pay too much to live in a rat hole."

"It's a good thing you signed anyway, Mario. Someone else would have got it, and we might all be in jail right now. We don't know anything about how they do things, and if we got caught camping where we could not, who knows?"

Their food was almost gone, and they waited for Rita to return to eat. "What could be keeping Rita?" asked Mario. "Why did someone lend her those things?"

"Rita can take care of herself. They lent us the stuff because they were in the same spot once. She must be scouting the neighborhood."

"We don't know who we can talk to beside other people in these shacks. We don't know what happens if someone finds out we're illegal," said Mario.

"We're from Nogales, no matter who we talk to."

"I mean, Marcella, we need to communicate without giving ourselves away. We have to learn how to get papers or whatever we need to enter the main way where everybody legal is."

"I don't think we're so lucky anymore," said Marcella. "That big belly is like the snake that bit you, Mario."

"We'll make some money and save all we can. We'll get out of here," Mario promised.

Rita came running back and sat cross-legged opposite Mario and Marcella. "We have to go stand in front of Manuel's house at six o'clock to get a ride to the worksite. Julio told me. He's my age, and he goes every day. We get more money if I go, too."

"No, you don't have to go," said Mario, opening the bag of leftovers which quickly disappeared. They were still hungry.

"Should I stay here and play with the babies on the mountain of rubble?"

"Oh, okay, but for now we have to eat something." Mario took out a five dollar bill and held it out to Rita. "Go buy some food. Even if it costs too much, buy something we don't have to cook."

She shook her head no. "Julio's mom told me to come and get some corn and tortillas and beans when we're ready to eat. She was cooking supper. She says not to buy from Manuel's store."

"Why not?"

"He charges your hand and your foot, and Caretta comes in a truck on Saturday to take someone to Delano to shop at a real store. We take turns so different ones get to go."

## CHAPTER SIX

Mario and Marcella went with Rita to Julio's. His mother was handing out cookies to children at the front door. Marcella was tempted to take one, and Sedar held out the box to her. She took a cookie, and Mario and Rita each snatched one before the children emptied the box.

"Thanks," said Marcella. One of the boys, with large, sad eyes caught Marcella's eye, and she smiled at him. "What's your name?" she asked.

"Enrico," he replied, shyly.

"You kids go play," said Sedar. They ran away, Enrico last. The smallest, he was nearly left behind.

"Enrico's family's new here," said Sedar. "That's why he's so shy. They don't know nobody. They stay to themselves. I think probably they're illegal. But they got food. We make sure."

"How will they get legal?" asked Marcella.

"I don't know. They'll find a way. Just a minute, you got food, too," she said, going inside. She returned with a brown grocery bag containing a gallon ice cream carton full of cooked pinto beans with jalapeno peppers, a stack of tortillas, a chunk of cheese, a half dozen ears of corn, three cucumbers and three tomatoes.

"Here's stuff to eat with, too," she said. She handed Rita a bag containing three plastic plates, forks, spoons and cups.

"Thanks. When we work and get paid, we'll pay you back," said Mario.

"This is how you pay back," said Sedar. "Not to us, when somebody else comes like you. That's the way when you get here. Someone helps. When we came, we had the shirts on our backs, nothing more. Now we got the garden, but it's not good here."

"We just got here today. We got the place someone just moved out of yesterday," said Marcella.

"No one lived there for weeks," said Sedar, her voice dripping with contempt for Manuel. "If you don't come, the place falls down, like the wrecks you use to fix it with. Now you fix it, pigstuff can rent it."

"Thanks for the food," said Marcella. She held out a five dollar bill to Sedar. Pushing Marcella's hand away, Sedar shook her head no.

"We got plenty. How'll you get up in time to go to work tomorrow? You be too tired to wake up. I know that place you rent. It needs work all day to live in it. Coons live in it before you."

"Maybe we won't get up," joked Rita. Everybody laughed.

"I'll send Julio to knock on the door at five thirty. Come in and meet Salvadore. He's out in back, but he'll be right in. If you need to borrow something; tools, dishes, maybe we got it."

They trooped in, and the house was hot from the stove. Salvadore came in from the garden, perspiration running down his face and neck, wiping his hands on his jeans. "Hi," he said. "How about a beer? I'm Salvadore." He shook Mario's hand.

"Thanks. I'd love a beer," said Mario. "I'm Mario, and this is Marcella."

"I'm happy to meet you. We already know Rita. Want a beer, Rita?" Salvadore laughed and Rita giggled.

"I'll take a big, cold foamy," she said. Salvadore laughed heartily.

"Marcella?" he asked.

"Yes, thanks," she said.

Salvadore got Rita a root beer and Mario and Marcella each a can of cold Mexican beer out of the three foot high refrigerator. He had built cabinets all along the narrowest wall of his shack. Sedar had a four burner propane stove that Salvadore had rescued from a disabled shanty. He and Sedar had spent a whole day scraping and scrubbing it clean. Their abode was much larger than Mario,

Marcella and Rita's and had doorways leading to three other rooms Salvadore had added on. He handed out the drinks.

"We can't stay," said Mario, popping the tab. He took a long drink, and it was like water on the desert. "We've been fixing the dump we got to live in all day, and now we're tired and hungry."

"I know tired and hungry. I was you last year, but I had relatives here," said Salvadore. "We'll be your relatives."

"Thanks, Salvadore," said Mario. "I got something to laugh about. I got a friend...." Mario was interrupted by Julio and two other boys racing to the house from the field.

"Socorro! Socorro! Pronto!" yelled Julio. He was out of breath, breathing hard. "A wreck shack fell on Enrico! We can't get him out!"

Salvadore ran behind his house and got a shovel. He raced after Sedar, Mario, Marcella, Rita and other farm workers already streaming to the collapsed shanty. Digging with spades, shovels, and their hands, they tossed out boards, shingles, broken bricks, rubbish, dirt and mud. The ruin had collapsed into a sinkhole from the soggy wet ground without adequate septic system.

"Enrico!" shouted his father, Diego. "Can you hear me, Enrico?" There was no answer. Enrico's mother was beside herself, crying and digging frantically, hysterically with her hands like a dog after a buried bone. Diego pulled her back.

"Stop, Lavina. Please, stop that."
"He must be still alive!" she sobbed.
"We'll see when we get him out," said Diego, holding her in his arms.

Julio flung a board out of the wreckage. Rita noticed that when Julio wiped the dirt and sweat from his face it was mixed with tears.

Two men emerged from the site covered with grime, and Mario and Salvadore took their places, digging furiously. When Mario got too winded, he came out; and someone from the surrounding crowd, anxious to help, took his place. After ten minutes of steady work, Julio spotted a hand in the slime.

"Here he is!" shouted Julio. He helped Salvadore and Diego carefully dig the boy from the muck as everyone gave them breathing room. Enrico was dead.

Clamoring out of the pit with his son's body, Diego then handed the dead child to his mother. She sat, holding him, sobbing and rocking back and forth.

"Leave us a little while alone," said Diego. The campesinos faded away to their homes to find materials for the coffin and to gather flowers from their gardens for the funeral.

Rita saw Julio run across the field into the woods. Sedar cried, returning to her home with Salvadore. Mario, Rita and Marcella walked with them. "I wish I didn't tell them to go play, Maybe they'd have stayed in the front...maybe...."

"No," said Marcella. "It was there waiting to happen."

"That stinking Manuel! He don't even come out of the house! We don't count with those pigs. Where's Julio? Julio!" she shouted, cupping her mouth with her hands. "Julio!" There was no answer.

When they reached their house, Salvadore kicked the wooden step viciously before going in. "That's for Enrico," he said. "I have to go help make the coffin and dig the grave."

"I'll come and help," said Mario.

"Dad," said Rita, tugging on his sleeve. Since she didn't speak up, Mario bent over so she could whisper in his ear.

"Julio was crying. I saw where he went. Maybe you better talk to him first."

"You go, Salvadore. I'll be along pretty soon," said Mario. He went with Rita to the woods along one side of the encampment. Rita spotted Julio, sitting leaning against a tree, drinking from a bottle of cheap whiskey.

"There," she whispered, pointing. Mario motioned her to go back. She left, and Mario went over to Julio.

"I came here to be alone," muttered Julio, looking away, wiping his dirty tear-streaked face on his sleeve.

"I'm Mario, Rita's father. We just got here today."

"I hate this shit! They don't think we're people!" He took a long swig from his bottle, and Mario squatted beside Julio who handed him the bottle. Mario drank a little and handed the bottle back.

"I know death, too," Mario said. "And I know how it feels to be treated like dirt."

"There's got to be a way to get away," said Julio. "People weren't made to live like animals in pigsties. Other guys live like human beings. The older guys at school drive cars. They go out with girls, they buy clothes. They live in a different fucking world five miles down the road, and if they read about us in the paper or see something about it on television, they laugh. You know what, Mister? Some day I'm going to get out of this world and into that one. I'm going to get out of it, or I'm going to blow the fucker up!" Julio stood and flung the empty bottle as hard as he could.

"It'll be better tomorrow because you talked about it today. Don't ever stop talking to your friends, Julio. As long as you can do that, you'll never have to blow up or blow anything up."

"I'm going to get out of this garbage dump if it kills me," vowed Julio, his voice quiet and low. He punched the tree he'd been leaning against, and his knuckles came back bloody.

"I'm an illegal alien, Julio. Look at my hands." Mario held them out palms up. The wounds from holding onto Liberty's harness hadn't yet healed. His hands were scarred, weathered working hands with calloused palms and fingers. Two of his fingers were crooked where they'd been broken at one time. "I came through hell to get here, me and Marcella and Rita. When I was five, my father was killed in the war in El Salvador. I was pinned under him. I tasted his blood, Julio; and then my mother was shot, and I watched her die."

"I see," said Julio, nodding.

"I swore, like you, that I was going to get out of it. I walked here from El Salvador, and Marcella and Rita walked from Nicaragua. We walked across the Sonora Desert. I've been walking half my life, and we're still not out of it, but we're on our way out. We bummed a ride on this side of the border, and here we are." He punched Julio lightly on the shoulder. "I'm going to get the hell out, too, Julio. Me and Marcell, and Rita, that makes six of us, eh?"

"Yeah, man. That makes six of us," said Julio.

"The men have to help make the coffin and dig the grave."

"Okay. I'll help." Mario and Julio walked back to the grave site where most of the men were digging. Two were putting the finishing touches on a casket made of two doors from shacks. Diego cut the clothesline from behind his house and coiled it to use to lower the casket into the ground.

Women cut flowers from their gardens for the grave, and those who had no flowers dug up wildflowers from the woods to plant on top. They gathered food from their shacks for Lavinia and Diego.

Sedar, Marcella, Lavina and Rita bathed Enrico's body and dressed it in his best clothes at Lavina's place. Lavina handed Rita the blanket from his sleeping mat.

"Take this to the coffin," she said. Rita took the blanket to where the men had completed the casket, and arranged the blanket in it. When she was finished, she went to the woods to pick some wildflowers for Enrico's grave, and Salvadore carried the casket to Diego and Lavina's.

Lavina got a tiny red bottle with a white rose painted on it from a chest that doubled as a seat. "This my mother gave me in Mexico. Perfume. I never use it. I save it for special." She dabbed a little on Enrico's head and hands and carried him outdoors. Laying him gently in the coffin, tears rolling down her face, she folded his arms and placed one hand on top of the other. Kissing him on the forehead, she whispered, "Good bye," and wept.

Everyone gathered around before they closed the casket.

"God bless, Enrico. God bless him," said Lavina, weeping softly. Diego, Salvadore, Mario and Julio carried the coffin to the grave site in the field followed by the rest of the farm workers. Diego, Salvadore, Mario and Julio lowered the casket into the ground as the others stood around the grave watching until they dropped the ropes onto the casket.

"I'm sorry this had to happen to Enrico," said Diego, grimly, his arm around Lavina. "God bless Enrico and everybody who helped us and none of the children play there ever again. Let Enrico's grave remind you. Now we'll pray the Lord's Prayer together." Everybody joined in.

Rita handed Marcella some of the flowers she'd picked in the field, and they threw them into the grave. The men shoveled the dirt over.

Salvadore made a cross and planted it in the middle of the gravesite. Someone in the camp had a can of white lacquer he used to paint it, each man with the knowledge that it could as well have been his son. Women from the community planted the mound around the cross with live petunias, zinnias, begonias, and asters, daisies and black-eyed susans. A woman brought a bucket of water for the flowers.

The crowd broke up, and everyone went home because dawn would come just as early tomorrow no matter how tired and grief-stricken they were.

Mario, Marcella and Rita took their bag of food from Sedar's and went to their shanty and ate voraciously without even speaking, they were so hungry.

"You go first in the shower, Rita," said Marcella. When she was finished she spread her poncho on the bare floor, happy not to have the stench from the filthy mattress that Mario had dragged away to haunt her dreams. Marcella took her turn, and opened her poncho in a far corner and Mario went last. He lay on his poncho beside Marcella in his shorts. The night was hot and sultry. She turned to him with a deep sigh.

"Life's going to be hard until we figure it out," said Marcella.

"It's worse than the desert," said Rita. "It's a different kind of hard."

"Don't look back," warned Mario. "It's history. Looking back is going back. Our challenge is all in front of us."

Rita fell asleep on her poncho, and Marcella snoredsoftly. Mario felt as though he'd just dozed off when Julio pounded on the door in the morning.

"Time to get up," Mario muttered, sleepily.

Rita woke, rubbing her eyes. It took a moment to remember where she was and why someone was making all that racket. Getting up, she went to the door and poked her head out. "We're up, Julio."

"The trucks'll be here in a half hour. Mama sent this over." He handed her a grocery bag.

"Wait a minute. Let me get you some money." She got three dollars out of her backpack and handed it to him. "Thanks, Julio. If we had to buy from Manuel, we'd go broke in two days,"

"I know," said Julio. Stuffing the bills into his pocket, he then disappeared into the fog.

Rita opened the bag and took out a jar of hot, black coffee, little packets of cream and sugar and three large burritos. They'd eaten so much so late the previous night that she wasn't hungry. Marcella took her clothes into the bathroom to dress in private.

Mario poured them each a cup of coffee, and Rita stirred cream and sugar into hers.

"This coffee's plenty strong and hot," Mario said, taking a sip. "Sedar knows what she's doing alright. I'll take these burritos with us for lunch." He made himself a small burrito for breakfast from the leftovers Sedar had given them the previous day.

Rita tried the coffee. "It's good," she said, making a face. The coffee jolted her out of her lethargy. "Hurry up in there!" She pounded on the bathroom partition.

"Use some patience, Rita," said Marcella, sharply.

"No more than seven minutes each!" yelled Mario, pulling on his jeans and tee shirt, "I'm going to drink your coffee, Marcella!"

"Don't even think that!" scolded Marcella, emerging from the bathroom dressed. She headed for the coffee and sipped it.

"Thanks, Sedar," she said.

"She can't hear you, Mom," said Rita, as Mario hurried to take his turn in the bathroom.

"You're not Sedar, so how do you know what she can hear?"

"She's too far away, Mom. Dad, did you hear Mom talking to you when you were unconscious on the desert?" asked Rita. The plywood walls were so thin she didn't bother raising her voice. She could hear every sound from the bathroom.

"Yeah," said Mario, from the bathroom. Rita heard the water splashing on his face.

"What did she say?"

"You're going to get well. Then she prayed, and said, God, make Mario well."

"Oh, right!"

Though the half hour to get ready passed in a whirlwind of chaos, they walked out the front door in good order, Mario carrying Sedar's ample burritos for lunch in his backpack. They walked to Manuel's in five minutes, where many of the other workers had gathered. Rita picked Julio out of the crowd, and he saw her at the same time and came to meet her.

"Hi Julio," said Rita.

"Hi Rita! It's a new day, eh? Maybe better. At least we know each other." Rita and Julio walked a little bit away from the crowd.

"Life's easier with a friend to talk to," agreed Rita, with a broad smile for Julio. "Thanks for the coffee. It got me moving. I'm really sorry about Enrico. It was awfully bad, what happened."

"It's not the first time, and Enrico won't be the last," said Julio, angrily. "I get so mad, I could kill somebody. Words can't say." A surly frown creased deep lines in his face making him look like an old man.

"I thought my dad would die on the desert. He got bit by a snake, and me and Mom had to kill birds to eat. He was out cold for days, and there was nothing we could do about it."

"Your dad told me we should stick together and talk about it," said Julio. "He was right, too. I was so mad I could kill someone, but after I talk to him, it lets up, and now I'm like before, just bitter where the killer instinct sleeps."

"When you get out of here, maybe the bitterness will go away, too."

"It makes it worse that I don't know how. How do we know we can get away if we don't know how?"

"They'll teach us in school."

"No, Rita. They don't treat us like the other kids. We're second class people in school."

"I'm going to look at it different," said Rita. "No matter how they treat me, I'm going to learn what I need, not what they want me to have. Everything I learn in school, I'm going to think, how I can use this to get out of here. When I know how things work, I'll see the way out."

"Let's make a pact," said Julio. "If you find the way to escape before I do, you'll show it to me; and if I find the way first, I'll show it to you."

"It's a deal," said Rita. "And we won't accept not finding the way. That's part of it. We will get out of here."

"Okay."

"Shake hands on it." Solemnly, they sealed their bargain. Julio held onto Rita's hand and pulled her close. He put his arm around her, leaning toward her. She felt his breath on her face and looked up into his eyes. He bent lower and they kissed. Julio's arms around her felt strong. His eyes were sincere, and she liked him immensely. Julio drew Rita deeper into the shadows behind the trees away from the others and they kissed and embraced again.

Salvadore and Sedar came walking slowly to the stop. "Did you sleep good?" Sedar asked Marcella. Marcella nodded, yawning. "Like the dead. Morning came too soon."

"It always comes too soon. You go home and cook and eat and go to bed, and it comes too soon again. I couldn't sleep. Enrico sticks in my mind. His parents didn't come today. Must be, they're gone. I don't know what I'd do if it was Julio."

"I never think that something that bad could happen to me," said Marcella. "I always know the best is going to happen. What you think makes it happen."

Sedar laughed. "You really think that? You never worry?"

"Not like that. I worry how I can make it like I want it to be. Like being here. I hate living in that dump, like some animal in a hole. I think about a house like I want, and how I could get to live there. I keep working my mind around that. My thought tries to run away to think about other things, like how Enrico died, and I have to keep dragging it back. It's very hard, but that's how I do."

"Do you ever think about getting a different job?" Mario asked Salvadore.

"You got to know someone," Salvadore replied, lowering his voice. "I'm going to get a job in a factory making windmills like my cousin. He'll let me know when, and then he'll pick us up. He lived here before us, and we took his place." Salvadore grinned his lopsided grin and a half-hearted laugh dribbled out the corner of his mouth. "Then I can make more money to send home to my younger brother. When I go, his family comes here."

"I know mechanics," said Mario, earnestly. "I can fix any car. I know how it works. How could I get a job doing that?"

"I don't know," said Salavdore. "That's why I'm here so long. Most come and go. All I know's my cousin."

"Keep me in mind when you get out of here," said Mario, as the truck pulled up.

"You might get out first," replied Salvadore. "Then you remember me."

More than fifty people had shown up, and half of them piled into the truck, including Mario, Marcella, and Rita. Packed in, Mario didn't get a seat on the benches on either side and had to stand in the middle. Another truck came right behind them for the others. The truck lurched, and Mario lost his balance and fell into the crowd. Someone else shoved him back upright.

"Hey, quit shoving!" yelled Mario, and everybody laughed.

They were driven to the orange grove, and a man with a straw hat handed out slings as each one stepped down from the truck. They said their names, and he checked them off of a paper attached to a clipboard. When Mario stepped down, the crew boss said, "Name?"

"Mario Dominguez." The man wrote in Mario's name at the bottom and put a checkmark beside it. He looked Mario steadily in the eye.

"You new here?" he asked.

"Yes," said Mario. The boss then asked Marcella's and Rita's names, and added them to the list before handing them their slings.

"Follow the last picker," he said, pointing after the woman who had preceded Mario. "Stop at the row after her, and start picking in that row at the top of the tree, every orange on the tree, one person to a row. You'll find empty bushel baskets next to each tree."

Mario, Marcella and Rita followed his instructions. Mario put his backpack by the first tree in the row and the sling around his neck, took his place on the ladder, and starting from the top of the tree picked oranges and put them in the sling. When it got too heavy, he climbed down and emptied the sling into a bushel basket.

After going up and down the ladder a number of times, his foot that had been bitten by the snake began to throb, and the throb soon turned to pain. Mario saw the woman's head in the next row appear at the top of the next tree, and his bushel wasn't even half filled. He tried to go faster, but before he was finished with his first tree, she was another tree ahead. Wishing he could stop and rest, he knew Rita and Marcella were wishing the same thing. Scorched by the sun, Mario felt its power that could be harnessed. He remembered something Marcella told him on the desert when the sun made him dizzy, and he had to get out of it.

"We don't know how to use the sun. Some day the energy from the sun will be used to run things like cars and trains. When you don't understand what something's for, it hurts you. But when you understand and use it, it doesn't hurt anymore." Mario knew how engines work. As he picked oranges, like tiny models of the sun, he thought about the energy that could roast ten million chickens at the same time or start combustion with a magnifying glass.

"I could make an engine that could run as long as there's sun," he said, to himself. While his hands picked and his body was tied to his singular task in the grove, his mind worked on the development of a solar engine that could power a car.

When the labor boss finally blew the whistle for lunch, Mario was picking from the ground, hot and tired and sweaty. As far as he could see were rows of orange trees and pickers.

Marcella and Rita walked over from their rows, and Mario limped back to the first tree in his row. He handed out the burritos and plopped down on the shady side of an orange tree, Marcella beside him and Rita next to her. Mario wolfed down his burrito without speaking. Marcella and Rita finished soon after Mario.

A water truck came down the center lane dispensing water, and Mario got up stiffly. Marcella and Rita stood, and everyone was given two quarts of water. They each drank as much as they wanted. Her muscles aching, Marcella fell backwards in the shade of an orange tree, stretching out. She closed her eyes but couldn't sleep. Everything ached. Rita and Mario followed Marcella's example. They had twenty minutes left to rest.

When he heard the foreman's whistle, Mario forced himself to get up. The pain in his heel had turned into a throb once more.

He knew how Marcella and Rita felt. Giving Marcella a hand, he pulled her to her feet, and they each took one of Rita's hands to help her up.

"Back to the salt mines!" joked Mario, pretending to break a chunk of rock salt with a pick axe. Rita gave him a weak smile, and Marcella returned to her row looking grim.

The afternoon dragged by in the blazing hundred and five-degree heat. In order to keep on picking, Mario had to think about something else. He thought about fixing the man's car on the desert.

When the foreman's whistle blew at last, they all walked back to the drop off point, Mario limping badly. Some of the workers made jokes about the work and the rich owners of the groves, but Mario, Marcella and Rita were too tired and sore to join in the laughter.

When the truck dropped them off that evening, Mario was first out, and he waited for Marcella and Rita. Rita looked for Julio, but he wasn't in that truck.

"Everything hurts," said Rita, as they walked back to the shanty.

"I know," said Mario. "I was doing the same thing."

"I like to complain when something hurts."

"Good. It lets it out a little. You don't have to go tomorrow."

"Why not? So we can stay in our new North American palace forever? I can play ring around the maypole with the babies and think about you and Mom on those ladders in the grove."

The middle-aged woman who lived next door came out carrying a baby about six weeks old in one arm and a shopping bag in her other hand as they passed her house.

"Senora, wait une momento," she said, stopping Marcella on her way to her shanty. Eight toddlers and infants played in the yard which had been fenced in with chicken wire. The back yard garden and a chicken coop were, also, petitioned off with chicken wire.

"Hi. I'm Riva," she said, handing Marcella the shopping bag containing eight ripe tomatoes, a dozen ears of corn, several pounds of green beans and a half dozen hard-boiled eggs. A dozen tortillas wrapped in plastic wrap were on top.

"Thanks a whole lot. I'm Marcella and this is Mario and Rita. It looks like you take care of the children," said Marcella. Riva nodded.

"Thanks," called Mario, shuffling past, his limp pronounced. "I have to keep going. If I stop here, I'll fall down, and I won't be able to get up. I'll have to sleep here."

"I know," said Riva. "I've been there, too. Go on."

Mario, Marcella and Rita continued on to the shelter with Riva walking with them. Mario went behind the dwelling and sat down, leaning against it. Rita turned on the water and went in to the bathroom to hose the sweat off. She was hot and crabby.

"It's hard at first. I give you seeds from Mexico, grow big corn, like mine," said Riva. Reaching into her pocket, she pulled out a brown envelope full of seed corn and handed it to Marcella. Don't plant it now, it's too late. Wait until April."

"Okay," said Marcella. "I can't say how much I appreciate this." They stood chatting as other workers approached Riva's home.

"Some of my friends coming to pick up their kids," said Riva. One child tried to go with the wrong mother, and Riva had to hold him by the arm to make him stay until his sister came for him.

"Someday I'll pay you back," said Marcella.

Riva shrugged. "Maybe, you. Someone'll pay me back, and maybe you'll pay someone else back. I never met the person again, who gave me the seeds, after she left."

A father came to pick up his child, and Marcella went to her shanty and dropped off the corn kernels in their envelope inside before taking the vegetables to the back of their shack as Riva talked to the worker about his daughter.

"More food," she said to Marcella and Rita. She left the bag and went in for their plates. Taking them out, she then put the vegetables on them and washed the beans and tomatoes with the hose. She sat down, leaning against the shack to snap the ends off the beans, and she could almost hear her bones creak.

"I will help you, because you're beautiful," said Mario, standing and bowing deeply. "But first...." He held the hose over his head and turned the water on, soaking himself. Then he squirted Marcella.

Laughing, Marcella wiped the sweat, grime and water off her face on her sleeve, but when she looked up at Mario, he wasn't laughing.

Mario hobbled to Mt. Garbage and came back lugging a four foot long board under one arm, a cinderblock in his hand and another cinderblock in the other hand. He hosed them off. Placing the cinderblocks three feet apart, he then bridged them with the board and set the plates on the makeshift table.

Marcella put eggs, tomatoes, tortillas and corn on the board. "From Riva next door," she said. She sat down with the vegetables and started cutting the ends off the beans with her pocketknife and threw the beans on one of the plates.

"These are good people here," said Mario, sitting beside Marcella, taking an ear of corn to shuck.

"We've always got something to be lucky about," said Marcella, with a smile for Mario.

Rita brought the plastic cups out and filled them with the hose. She set one at each plate, and sat next to Marcella, helping her with the beans.

"I guess this is a little more civilized than hunting up a wild turkey, strangling it with your bare hands and sleeping in a cave," said Rita. "It must be progress."

"You forgot my rabbit," said Mario.

When the beans were ready, they all loaded their plates and ate hungrily with their hands until they were sated. Marcella packed the remaining food back into the grocery bag.

A cooling breeze blew up before dusk. Not ready to get up, Marcella, nevertheless, inspired by the thought of rest with a roof over her head, dragged herself to her feet. She took the bag of food inside and placed it in the corner next to the bag that still contained leftovers from Sedar's offering.

Rita hosed off the plates, took a few swipes at them with the diminishing bar of soap and rinsed them. She then shoved the hose through the window. Marcella took it to shower, beginning the evening ritual.

Mario carried the plates inside, now limping badly. He took two aspirins from Marcella's backpack and put them in his shirt pocket, and Rita stayed outside to turn off the water. When Marcella was finished showering, she yelled, "Turn off the water!"

"No, wait," said Mario. "Can I come in?"

Marcella left the hose by the drain, and pulled the shift she'd brought to sleep in over her head. "Yes, Mario," she said. He went into the bathroom with his plastic cup.

"Would you fill this up?" he asked, and she obliged. He took the aspirin, and after that he made sure to always fill his cup when the hose was not in use. He went back out, turned off the water, and found Rita sitting, leaning against the back of the house. Painfully he sat down next to her.

"Everything's different here," she said, softly. "The desert's still at night and the stars are bigger and brighter. You feel different, you know?"

Music came from one of the shacks, and children playing in a field shouted, laughed, yelled and cried.

"I was too tired to notice," said Mario.

"Your foot hurts again, too. I can always tell. It doesn't get cold at night like on the desert. Here I keep waking up, because it's so hot. And you hear things."

"What things?"

"Night noises, little things that live in the grass and trees."

"Next," yelled Marcella, out the bathroom window. Mario turned the faucet on to take a shower. He went in and undressed in the bathroom. Working up a lather in the shower, he sang softly to himself. Singing lightened his heart and made him forget his foot. He'd picked up the words and tune of the Mexican folk song someone in the camp had been playing over and over. It kept going around in his head.

Leaving the hose running for Rita, he dried himself, and put on clean shorts. Mario added his dirty clothes to the small pile in the corner thinking they'd have to wash them tomorrow. Lying down on his poncho next to Marcella, he didn't have time to think a thought before he was sleeping soundly.

Last in the shower, Rita washed, dried as well as possible on the towel that was now very damp, and pulled a clean shirt of Mario's she'd adopted as a nightgown over her head. She hung the towel over the shower curtain pole and poked the hose out the window. Then she went out to turn the water off careful to replace the hose. The night was hot and still, and the smells of the camp were strong and unpleasant all mixed together; garbage and rot and improperly drained sewage sludge, sweat, clothes washed by hand and hung outside, a chicken someone had grilled outside, mixed with the pungent odor of garlic, onion and pepper as well as cedar and pine from a stand in the forest where migrants slept when the couldn't find indoor shelter. Though she was getting used to it, she sighed deeply, preferring the cold desert, and went in. When she unrolled her poncho and stretched out on it, she went to sleep immediately, listening to cicadas.

## CHAPTER SEVEN

Julio pounded on the door in the morning with another jar of black coffee and three enormous burritos made with meat and beans, peppers and onions and cheese. Marcella dashed for the bathroom, as Mario pulled on his pants and opened the door.

"Come in and help us drink this coffee, Julio," said Mario, taking the bag and handing Julio three dollars which Julio pocketed.

Wrapping in her poncho, Rita grabbed her clean jeans and shirt and crowded into the bathroom with Marcella, who was dressing. Rita had to dress in the shower stall, but she sauntered out of the bathroom dressed and combed with her teeth brushed five minutes later.

"Morning, Dad. Morning Julio." She greeted them, stretching casually. "I can't tell if I'm still sleeping or awake." Rita yawned and opened the door to get some air. The fog was dense and the temperature still stifling. She left the door open and hung her nightshirt and poncho on nails by the door beside Mario's and Marcella's.

Mario sat on a concrete block he'd carried in to sit on and poured the coffee, the throb gone from his foot. He gave Julio his cup and used a folding tin cup from his backpack.

Rita took her coffee and stirred in a packet of powdered cream and one of sugar.

"Hurry up and drink before your body quits being obedient and falls on the floor as good as dead," Mario said, trying the coffee and finding it great for waking up.

"My brain's gone already. It's only my body that's dragging around," Rita replied, making a bleary-eyed face and sipping her coffee.

Marcella emerged from the bathroom, laughing at Rita's efforts at comedy. Julio and Mario laughed as Marcella claimed her coffee, and the laughter revitalized them.

Mario put on his shirt and buttoned it and ducked into the bathroom, taking his coffee.

"I better get the hose and soak your head," quipped Marcella. "Then your brain can catch up with the rest of you."

"Never mind," said Rita. "It's caught up. The coffee did the job."

"Mama makes it like that," Julio said. "It's like dr...," he caught Marcella's eye. "It's like...."

"Learning how to smoke?" asked Rita, grinning at Julio.
Julio laughed. "Yeah, something like that."
Mario came out of the bathroom. "We need a wash bucket for the clothes," he said.
"I'll tell Mama," said Julio. "She knows what everyone needs when you get here, and she's got it."

Rita looked in the bags of food, and wrapped some pinto beans and cheese in a tortilla to eat. Mario and Marcella, also, took food from the bags.

"Help yourself," said Mario to Julio, handing him his plate but Julio didn't take it.

He shook his head no. "I already ate."

After eating and drinking their coffee, they walked slowly down the lane, Marcella and Mario a little distance behind Julio and Rita.

Julio took Rita's hand. "I got some books I bet you might like, Rita. Mama got them at a book sale at the library, four for a dollar."

"Did you read them already?" asked Rita.
"No, I don't understand them."
"What kind of books?"
"Science; come on over and see when we get back from the grove."
"Okay."
The trucks came and they wedged themselves in and were driven to the groves. Picking oranges all day, Rita thought about

Julio and his books. After work, this day was a little less grueling than yesterday. She stepped out of the van, hot and sweaty and tired, and Julio was waiting for her. Seeing him standing alone with his hands in his pockets, she forgot her misery. She liked the looks of him, tall and bony, with intense dark eyes and dark curls. She ran to meet him, and he smiled at her. Julio smiled so rarely that she knew he couldn't help it. He was as happy to see her as she was to see him. She slipped her hand into his, and they walked to his shanty.

"You remembered about the books," she said.

"I never say anything I don't mean. That's why I remember."

They went into Julio's house, and Rita followed him into a little cubicle with a cot. "This is my room," he said. He got down on his knees and reached under the cot for his books, pulled them out, and showed Rita the science books. "Mama thinks she can make a scientist of me." He grinned. "I don't know nothing about that stuff."

"I love science," said Rita, opening a biology book and reading over the table of contents. She leafed through the volume, reverently.

"You can have it," said Julio.

"I can pay you for it." She reached into her jeans pocket for two dollars, but he shook his head no. "I want you to have it. You like that stuff, and it's no good to me."

"Thanks, Julio! I'll bring it back after I'm finished with it."
"You don't need to."
"What are you going to be when you grow up and we get out of here?" asked Rita, sitting on the cot, holding the biology book. Julio sat next to her.
"Anything that's more exciting than a stuffy old scientist locked away in a creepy building. I want to buy a brand new car, red, and take you for a ride in it. I want to go to Los Angeles and get out of these stinking fields and small towns and see what's there."

Rita looked at him seriously. "What are you going to do to get the car?" she asked. "And to have money to buy everything you need?"

Julio mulled it over. "I never thought much about it, just that I got to do it. I guess I'll go to Los Angeles and be a cop, and when I bust someone and find out he's an illegal alien, I'll pretend like I never saw him." Julio laughed.

"You be careful, Julio. When you know what you want and go do that, you can live a happy life. What are you going to do to be a cop in Los Angeles?"

"I don't know that far ahead. This system cuts us out, Rita," said Julio, his face clouding in anger. "I hate this screwed up system. When Enrico died, it could be me just as well. Every day they're beating us up with our hands tied behind our backs. You got to fight back to go on living."

"We're outside the system, looking in at the party and the fun, and we don't know the way in," said Rita. "When we find the way, we can join the party instead of crashing it up."

"But then it'll go on and on and on. What about everybody else looking in? Too many die like Enrico when they're five years old or live like us now on a ladder and in a hole all their lives."

"When we get in, we have to find a way to open the doors. We have to make them understand."

Julio shook his head no. "They just don't know. Even those that don't mean no harm. I hate the system. I couldn't like you so much if you were one of them. I can't talk to anyone like I can talk to you."

"I like you, too, Julio. Come over even if you don't bring coffee in the morning, and we can walk to Manuel's together. I bet at school you can find out how to get to be a cop in Los Angeles."

"Sure, I'll come over," said Julio. "But I'll bring coffee, too. Mama makes plenty. Maybe you can go with me to L.A."

"Julio!" called Sedar, entering the dwelling. "Go out in back and pick some corn and tomatoes, would you?"

"Yeah. Mario needs a bucket to wash the clothes." He and Rita went into the living room, Rita carrying the biology book.

"Hi Rita," said Sedar. "I'm glad you came over. I wish Julio would read those books. Out back, Julio; you know where they are."

"C'mon Rita, I'll get you the bucket," said Julio.

"Thanks, Sedar," said Rita. She followed Julio to the back where Salvadore was hoeing between the corn rows. He and Rita exchanged greetings, and Julio found a stack of four large plastic buckets next to the house. He extracted one and handed it to Rita.

"Thanks, Julio. Bye, I'll see you tomorrow," said Rita, taking the bucket.

"Okay, Rita." He walked with her to the front with the book in one of her hands, swinging the bucket in the other, and Sedar appeared in the doorway.

"Why don't you stay for dinner, Rita?" asked Sedar. "It's good for you and Julio to have someone your own age to talk to. Julio don't like many kids his age."

"I have to go home now and help. I'll come another time."

"Come anytime," said Sedar, before retreating inside.

Julio took the book from Rita's hand, carried it, and they held hands intertwining their fingers. "I like you more than you know," he said, huskily. She walked with him to the side of his house, so they were shielded from view by a large camellia one of their predecessors had planted with the corn patch behind them.

"C'mere," he said, putting his hand on her back, pulling her close. He kissed her lightly and then longer with more intensity. He made her feel happy and delighted beyond the reach of poverty and pain in a way that she'd never known. She was suddenly special, and Julio was beautiful. For the first time in her life she felt like a woman. Though he made her want to dance and sing aloud, there was something about Julio that disturbed her deeply.

She drew back and looked into his eyes. They were shiny and large, and she felt like she could get lost in those bottomless eyes if she looked too long. "I like you, too, Julio. You're the first friend I made in America and the best friend ever. I like other people, but not like this. I have to go now." Julio handed her the book, and Rita ran home to help Marcella with the vegetables, but everything was almost ready.

Flushed, she paused at the door to catch her breath and set the bucket on the floor. She walked in not quite cool but in control. "Sedar invited me over to eat," she said, excitement in her voice. "She bought this biology book for Julio. She wants him to be a scientist, but he doesn't want to. He gave it to me."

Marcella leafed through the book. "It's a very good book, but I don't understand it. It looks really hard." She handed it back to Rita. "It's okay to go over for dinner," said Marcella. "I'm glad you got a friend already."

"Julio's very angry," said Mario, cautiously, picking up his dirty clothes from the top of the pile and dropping them into the bucket. "Don't let him make you angry."

"I don't know," said Rita, catching Mario's eye, her brow crinkling. "That's why I didn't stay. I like Julio a lot."

"You should go for supper," said Marcella. She took the bags of food and supplies from the shelter and went outside. Rita set her book on the floor and followed her with Mario, who took the bar of brown soap and his bucket of clothes. Marcella set the dishes and food on the table as Mario filled the bucket with water and began soaping his clothes.

"I'm a little bit afraid to stay at Julio's," said Rita.
"Why?" asked Marcella.
"I don't know," said Rita, unable to put her apprehensions into words.
"Then it's better what you did," Marcella said.
"It's good to hear you talking, Marcella. You never talk much anymore," Mario said, leaving his clothes in the bucket and standing beside her and putting his arm around her waist.

"I'm tired all the time. I never talk much when I'm tired."

"You walked all the way to California from Guatemala, and you were never too tired to talk."

"The desert and our purpose gave me strength. The orange groves take it all away."

"I know. I feel like that, too, but it doesn't change my love for you. It only makes it more." He drew her closer, and she turned to face him.

"I always love you just the same, Mario." She gave him a big smile, and kissed him.

"Ah, Marcella, my reason for taking another breath and staying on that ladder when I want to throw it." He rubbed her back, and she grabbed him around the neck and kissed him again.

Rita finished setting the table, her thoughts turning back to Julio "Tomorrow or one day real soon, I'm going to Julio's for supper," Rita said.

"That's good, Rita. You should go if you like. Do what makes you happy," said Marcella. She kissed Mario again, lightly on the lips and he leaned closer. "Let's eat and then we'll talk some more, all right?"

"Sure, I'm hungry." Mario let her go, and they sat down with Rita, who had already started eating.

"You give me back all the energy the oranges took away," said Marcella, putting food on her plate.

"Take," said Rita.
"Take away."
After they ate, Mario finished washing his clothes and hung them on a tree to dry. He then washed Marcella's and hung them. Rita came out with her clothes. "Want to do mine, too?" she asked.

"No," said Mario. "I'm tired of washing clothes. You can wash them."

"Okay," said Rita. "Then I'm going to read my science book outside. There's a little breeze out here, and it's too hot inside." Rita went in and got her science book. She took one of the turkey feathers that she'd saved from the desert because she thought they were pretty from her backpack. Going outside, she then settled at the makeshift table behind the shack to read. Before starting to read, she held the feather up to the sunset twirling it slightly so it seemed to change colors. Smiling, she then put it in the back of the book and started reading.

While Rita went out to study her book, Mario took Marcella in his arms, and they kissed for a long time, lingering for the fun of it, building excitement and drawing out each other's passion before spinning each other away to the land of the gods beyond the stars.

Rita read the first chapter and then went to Julio's and knocked on the door. Sedar answered.

"Can I buy or borrow some soap for washing clothes?" she asked.

"Sure, c'mon in. I buy soap from a store in Delano," Sedar explained, going to the kitchen. She scooped soap from a large box into an empty glass jar. "Soap powder is five pounds for a dollar, and the bars of soap five for a dollar. If you buy from Manuel, you pay five dollars for one pound of soap powder and two dollars for the bar of soap – same kind."

Sedar went to the bathroom and opened a cabinet. Sedar's house had indoor plumbing. She took a variety of personal items from a cabinet and threw them into a paper sack which she handed to Rita.

"Thanks Sedar, where's Julio?" asked Rita, taking the jar of soap and the bag.

"I don't know," said Sedar. "He'll be here when it's time to eat." Rita took three dollars out of her pocket, which she tried to hand to Sedar.

"I can't take it," said Sedar. "I owe too much from when we got here and everybody gave to us. I haven't paid all mine back yet. I've got something else for you in the kitchen." Sedar got down a box of cookies. "These are from the bakery in town," she said. "Take some."

"Okay." Rita took two oatmeal cookies wrapped in plastic

wrap. She went back to her abode munching on a cookie. Leaving the bag and jar of soap powder by the front door, she then went to the back and settled down with her science book until Mario came out to turn the hose on.

"That must be a good book," said Mario.

"Yeah biology; it's pretty interesting," said Rita.

He went back in and Rita heard the shower. He and Marcella came out in a little while and sat beside Rita. They finished the evening talking quietly into the night as the stars lit the sky, and Rita found Polaris. .

Rita was ready to go when Julio knocked on the door in the morning. He brought extra coffee, another bag of tortillas and tub of pinto beans, a half dozen tomatoes, and two large zucchinis from the garden plus the usual burritos for their lunch. Rita set the bag on the floor and rolled pinto beans into a tortilla. She put it on a paper towel and handed it to Julio.

"No, I already ate," he said, but he poured himself a cup of coffee. "Let's go outside." They went out and sat on the front stoop drinking coffee, and Rita ate. When Mario and Marcella came out, they all walked to Manuel's together.

"When do you get paid around here?" Mario asked Salvadore, as they boarded the crowded van. Used to the routine, his foot no longer bothered him until it was time to go home. He rarely limped.

"Saturday," said Salvadore. "But it won't be as much as you think."

"We picked a lot of oranges," said Mario.

"Not as many as you pick when you've been here longer, and Manuel takes some out for rent and water."

Mario frowned. "How much?"

Salvadore shrugged. "I don't know. We pay three hundred dollars a month for rent and he takes out some every week to make it come out right."

"But your house is twice as big as ours," protested Mario. "You've got water even and electric."

"He's always raising the rent. When we move out, he'll charge four or five hundred for ours because of all the work I did in it," said Salvadore. "My cousin connected to the water and electric before we got here. He paid two hundred for our place. When he comes to visit, we'll do yours, too. I don't know how."

The day rolled along almost exactly like yesterday. At work, Rita thought about Julio, and how much she liked him and wanted him to be what he wanted – a cop in L.A. Nothing had changed about the job or her lifestyle, but thinking of meeting Julio after work, she wasn't as tired.

Mario and Marcella dragged through the week, and Saturday came at last. Mario lined up, Marcella and Rita behind him, with other migrant workers at Manuel's shack to get their paychecks after work. Sedar was absent because she'd gone to Delano. Salvadore would pick up her check. Food supplies, a broom, sleeping mats, soap, candles, charcoal briquettes, lighter fluid and matches for Mario, Marcella, and Rita were on her list. The line moved quickly, and Mario's turn came.

"Yas still owe fer rent," said Manuel, between coughs. "An' yer water bill comes ta almost fifty bucks."

"Give me my paycheck!" demanded Mario, anger rising in his chest.

"Ya don't git the pitcher. Yas owe Mr. Painter, he don't owe yas. He give yas a job an' a place ta live. Yas got nudden! Yas use alodda water. Someone godda pay fer it. Here, take yer bill, and learn ta add." He shoved the paper in Mario's face. "Next!" he yelled.

Mario's face darkened, and his hands balled into fists. "How do you know how much water we use? You look in the window? Give me my paycheck!" he demanded, staring defiantly at Manuel. Manuel's cold return stare sent a chill up Mario's spine. Stifling a snarl of hatred, Mario drew back his fist, and Manuel braced for trouble.

Salvadore came and stood between Manuel and Mario, facing Mario. "Come friend. You don't want police. Come to my house. We'll have a beer and talk. Life's hard. I know. I was you last year."

CHAPTER EIGHT

Kate got to the newsroom early and dashed off an assignment on a police wrap up, so she could work on the project closer to her heart. Working from notes and her memory on a story about the Migrant Workers Union organizing orange pickers, she was interrupted by a phone call.

"Is this Kate?" came the voice.

"This is Kate," she replied, doodling on the notepad she kept on top of her desk.

"A boy died at the Painter Labor Camp," said the caller.

"Who's this?" asked Kate.

"I lived there. A boy died."

"What boy?"

"Enrico Mendez. He's buried in the field."

"At the labor camp?"

"Yes."

"How did he die?"

"An old shack caved in on him."

"I want to see the labor camp where he died and the grave. How old was he?"

"Five."

"I'll meet you at the news rack on the corner of Olive and Route 6."

"Across from the mill?"

"Yes."

"I'll go there now."

"I won't be able to get away until five." Kate underlined Enrico Mendez and wrote 5 o'clock on her note pad. She stuck her pencil in her hair over her ear.

"Okay, five. Goodbye."

"Bye, bye," she said, wondering if there was any connection to the Painter Labor Camp and the Horton Painter who had built an office building in Booneville that had collapsed, killing eight people and wounding eleven. One man lost his legs in the accident. Though the building had been built with inferior materials, Painter got off without charges, claiming innocence of the subcontractor's fraudulent license. Kate thought the deal reeked. No one accepted the subcontractor's bids after that, and he no longer had the opportunity to build. Her thoughts were interrupted by her managing editor.

"Who's got something for the front page?" yelped Ferrell, rushing down the aisle between the rows of reporters, looking at his watch.

Rarely still, Ferrell was always in a hurry. He walked fast, talked fast, drank fast, typed fast, smoked fast, and chewed gum fast the deadline forever looming overhead. Caught in a perpetual race against time, when he crossed the finish line, the clock was reset. His mind was a treadmill, and when no other part of his body moved, his foot tapped or his fingers drummed the desk.

"I've got number one for you," said Kate, her fingers flying over the keyboard.

"You mean that stale old farm worker hash? What did you get from your knock about town, Conrad?"

"Gee, Ferrell, not much," said Conrad, scratching his head. "The Fireman's Auxiliary is having a luncheon next week for...."

"Never mind, never mind. Doesn't anybody have anything?" The reporters looked at him blandly used to him avoiding Kate's stories for the front page whenever possible

"What's it about, Kate?" he asked.
"A demonstration,"
"Oh no, not another one," groaned Ferrell. "That's not news, and it looks like I'm damned well stuck with the shit. Victor!" he barked, at the photographer. "Pull a photo out of the file of some juvenile bracero. Be sure you get one with a big smile on his face, a kid."

"What for?" Victor stopped on his way to the darkroom with his rolls of film."
"To go with the farm worker number."
"No," protested Kate. "I have photos from the event."
"Of men at a demonstration?" asked Ferrell.
"Yeah."

"Not in my paper!" Staring at Kate, he yanked the partly smoked cigar out of his mouth and jabbed it at her, one jab for each word.

"Especially not on the front page."

"What's a smiling child got to do with the price of beans?"

"You weren't here when the migrant workers organized in the first place. You don't know what war is." Ferrell's beefy face reddened. "Blood flowed in the streets, and now they want to stir up more trouble."

"That's got nothing to do with my story," said Kate, mentally arming for battle.

Ferrell ignored her and rummaged through the photo file cabinet. He found an old photo of a Hispanic schoolboy, grinning under a wide-brimmed straw hat and headed for the composing room with it.

"That won't go," said Kate, snatching the photo from his grasp. "He looks like the winner of a junior high school 4H project."

"It's a fine front page picture," said Ferrell, snatching it back. He held it at arm's length, looking at it.

"Print my picture, Victor," muttered Kate angrily. Glancing at the large clock over Ferrell's desk, she then hurried to her computer and worked rapidly on the farm worker story, ignoring Ferrell, until a half hour before deadline.

"Did you print my picture, Victor?" she yelled across the newsroom.

"Yeah, Kate! Great picture!" Some of the reporters gathered around Victor to take a look at the photo.

"It's not going on my front page, Kate!" shouted Ferrell, steamed.

"You can't run a picture of a kid to represent a demonstration of grown men," argued Conrad, the city editor. "It doesn't relate." Turning back to his work, he muttered under his breath, "Get a brain."

"I can do whatever I want," said Ferrell.

"It doesn't go, Ferrell," put in Harry Rosenberg. He grabbed Kate's photo and stuck it under Ferrell's nose. Ferrell shoved it aside.

"This picture Victor printed is a perfect illustration of Kate's story. Look at the expressions. These men are getting fucked over, and it shows in every line of their faces."

"That's right, Ferrell," said Victor. "This is the picture that goes with the story."

"Forget it," said Ferrell, glancing at his watch. The newsroom was in chaos. "The picture of the kid runs." Ferrell spoke in his softest monotone intended to sound cool, reasonable and authoritarian.

"Did you like my story?" asked Kate, with a nasty smile and a voice like orange blossoms.

"It'll do in the absence of real news."
"It isn't there."
"What do you mean, it isn't there?"
"I killed it. It's nowhere but in my head."
"Are you crazy? A half hour to deadline, and it isn't there?" Ferrell's face turned scarlet and he jammed his cigar into his mouth.

"Not with a picture of a little boy. The story's got nothing to do with children at play. It's about adult men and women earning a living."

"All right, all right, put it back, for Chrissakes. I don't have time to argue with a goddamn...get the goddamn picture, Victor."

Harry stared at Sue Front, typing quietly at her computer. "What happened to you, Sue?" he asked, recalling the day when she, Kate and himself had stood the storms of Ferrell's wrath and conquered his demands to conformity to get the news that mattered into print for all to read.

"I'm busy," she muttered, without looking up.

"You're out of place groveling in the sewer of Ferrell's limited brain power," he growled.

Sue looked up at Harry, and her haunted expression told him his words came from ignorance, yet he'd not been able to gain her confidence. She quietly returned to pecking at her keyboard, ignoring the storm in the newsroom, and realizing his mistake, confused by her separation from himself and Kate, Harry left her alone.

Kate returned to her computer, typing furiously to get the story back in.

"What a miserable excuse for a newspaper," muttered Conrad, out of range of Ferrell's hearing. "If that guy's got a brain, I'm dog shit."

"He's got a hot date with his girlfriend on his lunch break," said Harry, not caring if Ferrell heard him.

"Where were you yesterday?" Ferrell asked Harry. "I don't remember what you were assigned."

"I was out delving into history."

"History's changing," said Ferrell. "We interpret it. It's what we say it is. We're creating history." His voice turned soft and low, as he stared at Harry.

"Journalism can't create history," said Harry. "People living their lives create history, and that's the way it'll always be. Say what you like, but that won't make it true."

"The media created the migrant worker's union with publicity, and it can uncreate it without publicity," insisted Ferrell, returning to his computer to edit a story for tomorrow's paper.

Kate filed Ferrell's statement in the back of her mind so she could answer it after she met the deadline. The story rapidly unrolled on her computer monitor, already composed in her mind.

"My story's up," she said, when she was finished. "And the Farm Workers Union was created by Cesar Chavez and his recruits, knocking on doors of farm workers all over California, when the only food they ate was handouts from migrant workers, and the only times they got to sleep inside was when somebody lent them a floor or a bed. It was the marches and steady painstaking organizing that built the union not publicity."

"I heard that Cesar Chavez lives in a mansion," said Victor. "It may've been true at the start, but they all get bought off."

"I was there, Victor. Go see his house in Keene for yourself. It's not as big as your garage," said Kate.

"Where do these rumors come from?" asked Victor. "You know where I heard that? From a Mexican bank teller with a thick Spanish accent."

"He heard it from a customer who heard it from someone else who heard it from someone else, but it's the kind of rumor that's deliberately planted to try to discredit a strong leader among his or her people. He wouldn't go along with some big money manipulators back east, and that lost him his preferred status with the media they controlled. The owners of our jobs aren't people like us. They're big time financiers vying for political power over large masses of people."

"He's a trouble-maker and a rabble-rouser, nothing more," said Ferrell, looking up from his computer. "He's one of those men who gets a kick out of stirring the pot and watching it boil, but when there's blood on the street, it's never his."

"Every troublemaker who starts a major movement shows us an error in justice," said Kate. "When he was thirteen, just beginning to think about making his place in the world, contemplating what it would be; and how to achieve it, a second mortgage on his parent's ranch in Arizona was foreclosed. The Great Depression was at its worst. A judge bought the land for next to nothing, and his family had lived and worked it when it was still part of Mexico.

"He had to quit school to do the same work he'd been doing on his own ranch for its new owner for not enough money to live on. He went from being a solid middle-class citizen to a worthless Chicano bum overnight. He paid his dues in hard labor. He'll be fighting the same battle the day he dies. When he's gone, someone else'll get jacked around by someone with the legal authority to screw him over and create his heir."

"That's a fair assessment of the system," commented Harry.

Ferrell hurried into the composing room, and Kate broke for a quick lunch before finishing an assignment for the next day. After lunch she worked steadily, and the time passed too fast. At quarter to five, she slipped out to meet her anonymous morning caller.

Driving to the rendezvous place, she then spotted her contact immediately. The migrant worker, in jeans and a loose fitting man's shirt, her sleeves rolled up, and her long hair hanging over her shoulders, was obviously waiting for someone. Kate pulled over, stopped and rolled down her window. The woman peeked in.

"Kate?" she asked.
"Yeah, now what's your name?"
"Emalina," she said, and went around to the passenger seat and slid in. She directed Kate to the orange grove, which was a good twenty minutes away.

"Turn down this lane," Emalina said, pointing out a direction. "It's about three miles down here." To Kate, all the narrow dirt lanes lined with orange trees looked exactly alike, thousands of acres that took up more land than some towns.

"Turn here, I think," said Emalina uncertainly. "I used to live in this camp, and I marked the way. But it's still hard to locate."

"How did you find out about Enrico?" asked Kate, making the turn.

"Word travels."

"Then you don't work out of that camp now?"

"No," she replied.

"How sure are you of your information?"

"I've got relatives. I've seen the grave."

Kate drove slowly, leaving a trail of dust that soon surrounded the car, and Emalina intently watched the trees along the side of the lane. She opened her window and leaned out, searching for her markers, and the car grew uncomfortably hot.

"There!" she said, pointing. "There's my marker, that red piece of yarn on that tree."

Kate strained her eyes looking for it and didn't see it.

"Now turn left here, and go until I see another one."
Noticing her mileage, Kate made the turn and drove on for a mile.

"No," said Emalina, grimacing. "Wrong way. Go back to my marker."

Kate turned around and waited for their dust to settle enough to see the marker before continuing.

"Here!" said Emalina. Sweat rolled down her face and neck dripping off her nose, and she took a rubber band out of her pocket and gathered her hair into a pony tail at the top of her head.

"Turn right and then take the first left. They move the labor camps after something bad happens. There's a lot of graves in these groves, and I'm not sure the Painter camp is still there."

"You don't mean Horton Painter, do you?" asked Kate, following Emalina's directions.
"You know him?" The woman was startled.
"I've heard the name. It is Horton, then?"
Emalina nodded. "He owns it. Here's the camp coming up," she said.

Kate approached the rows of shanties lining the dirt road, and drove slowly down one of the lanes at random scattering small children. Seeing a woman outside watering a showy camellia by the side of a shack, she stopped the car, took her camera out of the bag, and got out.

"Sedar," called Emalina. "Could you come over here?"
Sedar walked over cautiously taking in Kate and her late model Chrysler, gold watch and earrings, cotton business pants suit, and expensive heels suspiciously.

"I'm Kate," she said, extending her hand. The women shook hands with a firm grip. Since Sedar didn't volunteer any information, Kate continued. "I was told a child died and is buried here. I work for The Booneville Daily News."

"It's true," said Sedar, one hand on her hip. "We got rotten sewage, and the ground's soft and stinking in the low places. Enrico went through the floor of a wrecked house, and the rubble fell in on him. We couldn't dig him out in time."

"Didn't anybody report it?"

"We got no phone and no way to get anywhere. It wouldn't do no good anyway. They never come here unless someone gets arrested," said Sedar.

"When did it happen?" Kate wrote Sedar's name on her tablet and took notes, as more people came over to see what was going on. Soon a small crowd was gathered, watching curiously.

"A few days ago."
"Where do Enrico's parents live?"
"They're gone. Nobody knows where. Somebody else lives in their house. They used to sleep under the trees 'til Enrico's parents left. Enrico just got here the day before he died."
"Would you show me where Enrico's buried?"

"This way," said Sedar, and Kate followed her down the lane. A funky stench, still hanging over the camp from rain the previous night, assaulted Kate's nose. She picked her way through the field of slosh to the open area where children stopped playing baseball and Frisbee and came running over to see what was going on. The entourage walked to the farther field where Enrico's grave marked by the white cross and covered with growing flowers stood in front of the woods.

Kate photographed the grave, and the camp was alive with excitement as Rita approached Kate. "I heard you work for the newspaper," she said.

"Yes. Do you live here?" asked Kate.
Rita nodded.
"I'm Kate. What's your name?" she asked, surprised by the child's self-assurance and directness.

"I'm Rita. You can take a picture of the bathroom at my house if you want."

"That's an offer too interesting to pass up. Let's go have a look," said Kate. "First I need to see where Enrico was playing when he died."

"Right there," said Sedar, pointing to the wreckage. She led the way over and after Kate photographed the pile of rubble that killed Enrico the crowd proceeded to Rita's hovel. Kate snapped photos of other homes as she went.

Marcella was washing her clothes in the bucket behind the house when she heard the commotion in front and went to see what was going on. Mario was off in the woods with Salvadore showing him how to trap a rabbit.

When Rita got close enough to speak, Marcella asked, "What's going on, Rita?" But she was staring at Kate who stood out like the first lady visiting an Indian tribe.

"This is Kate, Mom," said Rita. "She works for the paper, and I told her she could take a picture of the bathroom."

"Can I take your picture?" Kate asked Marcella.

"Okay." Marcella smiled at Kate. Pushing her hair over her face, she turned her head away from the camera, so her face wasn't visible. Everyone laughed, and Kate snapped the picture.

"I was doing the laundry," said Marcella. "Excuse me." She turned and walked back to the bucket, and Kate and the others followed. Kate snapped a few shots of the laundry procedure with Mario's clothes hanging from the tree behind Marcella and her bucket.

Catching the hose running into the window, Kate shot that, too.

"No names, huh?" said Marcella.

"All right," said Kate. "Have you been here long?"

"No. Do you know...I mean...." Sensing alliance, Marcella was about to try to seek a clue to escape from the camps when she saw Sedar, behind Kate's back, shake her head no.

"What?" asked Kate, giving Marcella her full attention.

"Do you know if they're going to put this in the paper?"

"Yes, I am. Let's go see the bathroom, Rita." Rita led the way inside, and when she and Kate were in the shack, Kate closed the door on the crowd. Rita giggled.

Kate snapped shots of the bathroom and a few of the rest of the place.

Mario and Salvadore came across the field from the woods, Mario carrying a dead rabbit by the ears. Marcella and Sedar ran to meet them.

"There's a reporter in our house taking pictures," said Marcella. "She came because of Enrico." The four shouldered their way through the crowd to the door, and Marcella opened it. She, Mario, Sedar, and Salvadore went in, and Marcella slammed the door behind them.

Mario smiled at Kate and held up the rabbit. "We got dinner," he said. Kate snapped his picture, but not before he held the rabbit in front of his face.

"Did you know Enrico?" Kate asked, looking at each of the people gathered in the room.

"No," said Mario. "Julio knew him." He opened the door and shouted, "Hey! Where's Julio?"

"Here!" said Julio, fighting his way through the crowd to the doorway. "Hey, lady, are you going to put this in the paper?" Julio asked.

"Yes," said Kate.
"This camp's a high rent pigsty. Put that in, too."
"All right, can I quote you directly?"
"Just say, Julio says."
"Very well," said Kate, writing as he spoke. "Did you see what happened to Enrico?"

"Yeah; I was watching the little kids. Domingo was Pancho Villa and Enrico was one of his men. They met the Mexican Army on the border. That was the wreckshack. They had a shootout, and Enrico disappeared. The wreck closed over him right away, and I ran home for help."

Kate took down Julio's story.

"You didn't report it?"

"We got no phones and cars. How?" he asked, looking over at Kate's Chrysler.

"How much rent do you pay to live like this?" she asked.

"We pay $350.00 a month," said Mario from behind her.

"I've got lots of pictures of what you get for $350.00 a month," said Kate. That was more than she paid for her two-bedroom apartment with a full kitchen, dining room, central heat and air and hot and cold running water. "People will see."

"They don't care," said Julio, frowning angrily. "They think it could never happen to them because they're too rich and too good."

"Everybody doesn't think that," said Kate. "I don't."

Julio laughed. "You say that, but you never lived like this. I look at you and see it's true."

"All I do is write stories and take pictures of the way things are. You'd be surprised how hard it is to push things through the system, but I know what you're talking about."

"I bet you'd tell me the way out if you knew it; but you don't because you never been in it."

"I've never been in it," admitted Kate. "Can I take your picture, and put your opinion in my story?"

"Sure," said Julio. "Here it is." Turning his back, he walked away giving her the finger. Kate watched the crowd close around him, but not before he spit in the dirt. She faced the crowd from Mario and Marcella's door.

"I understand that people don't want their pictures and names in the paper," said Kate. "I'm not going to take anybody's picture or any names of people who'd rather not. Who can I talk to?"

Riva came forward. "You can take my picture if you want. I was born in California."

"Thanks," said Kate. "Would you stand apart from the crowd, please?" Riva stood in front of the crowd, and everyone turned or backed away except for several children, who wanted their pictures taken, standing beside Riva giggling.

Kate snapped several photos.

"Now they'll close the labor camp, and we'll all move on," said Riva. "When somebody gets killed and the news stays here, nothing happens. When they find out outside the camps, they close the camp. We go wherever we find work - picking and field work."

Kate took down her comments. "Does anyone else want to add anything?" she asked, looking into a sea of faces, some with sweat running off in trickles, some defeated, some angry, and none happy. She had, also, worked up a sweat in the stifling hovel. There wasn't the hint of a breeze, and the crowd was suffocating. She got a tissue out of her bag to mop her face, but it soaked through and turned soggy.

"Everybody's afraid of immigration if they say anything," said Riva, frowning, her head to one side. "I know this system. Manuel's calling his boss right now anyway. We're all going to move on, and everyone who's illegal is going to disappear in a hurry. That's almost everyone but me and my husband. Manuel's not going to move with us, so what difference does it make?" The crowd remained stone silent and angry, seething with no place to go with it.

"Never mind," Riva said. "That's all I got to say."

"Thanks," said Kate. She exchanged goodbyes with Rita, Mario, Marcella, Sedar, and Salvadore and handed Rita her card.

"If anything else happens you think I should know about, give me a call," she said. Rita looked over the card, eyed Kate not sure what to think of her, and pocketed the card.

"Let's go," Kate said to Emalina. "I've got enough." They walked back to her car, and got in. Parents grabbed their children away from the front of the car and lined the side of the road as she drove slowly down the lane.

"Who lives there?" Kate asked Emalina, nodding to the bright yellow shack.

"Manuel, the labor boss," she said. "He didn't come out. He didn't come out when Enrico died either."

"Then I'll go in." Emalina opened her window and rested her head on her folded arms.

Kate parked in front of Manuel's house, went to the door and knocked, but no one answered. She waited a few minutes and knocked again. Still there was no answer. She walked around to the side and noticed a ten year old Ford parked at the side of the house. Proceeding to the back, the scraggly dirt patch was as empty and absent of life as the rest of the camp was teeming. Kate returned to her car and drove away.

"How can I get in touch with you if I need to?" asked Kate. Emalina shook her head no. "I'm too young to die," she said. "It's too risky. If I'm seen in your car by the wrong people...." She made the motion of cutting her throat.

Kate drove back to town and dropped Emalina off at the paper rack across from the mill where she'd picked her up.

She stopped at the reporter's favorite place to get burritos in Tipton. The tiny one-room restaurant with a kitchen in back served the best Mexican food in town at the lowest prices. It filled a hearty appetite, and the cafe was always full of workers speaking Spanish. Cola and beer posters, christened with splotches of beer and grime, covered gouges on the walls. The small, square tables with plastic tops were carved and scratched with slogans, epithets, and hearts with names in them.

A chubby woman, who took Kate's order, Marita had a smile ready. Media people, who patronized the restaurant often enough to be easily recognizable, were treated kindly by the proprietors and help.

Kate noticed Sue Front sitting at a corner table alone. Dark circles under her eyes and her anguished expression, the evening shadows playing over her face, gave Kate a chill.

"I'll have one beef and one chicken burrito with guacamole and sour cream," said Kate.

"Un momento," said Marita.

While she was waiting for the burritos, Kate went to Sue's table and sat across from her. Sue had a diet soft drink in front of her and was playing with a taco salad. Kate estimated that she'd lost nearly ten pounds since she'd withdrawn from the rest of the staff, and she was worried about her. It seemed the more she tried to break through the wall Sue had built, since she'd covered the death of the governor, the further Sue withdrew into a shell that excommunicated her closest friends.

"Hi Sue. Come on over tonight. We've got to talk," said Kate, urgently.

"Sherman's waiting at home."

"He can come too."

Sue shook her head no, her cheek propped on her fist.

"Then why don't you go home and talk to him?"

"I can't talk."

"You can't go on like this. Have you looked in a mirror lately?"

"I don't know what to do...I...." Sue's eyes had never contained that look of desperation before she withdrew from her friends.

"Please, Sue. You're my best friend. If I couldn't talk to you about this job, I couldn't stand to be here. Nothing is so bad you can't tell me. Ever since the governor was killed...."

"You don't understand. I can't explain." Sue got up and rushed out leaving her drink and taco salad practically untouched. Though she'd always been self assured and aggressive before, Kate now sensed that she was ready to burst into tears.

"Here's burritos, Kate," called Marita.

Kate's went to the counter and paid her tab. There was no point in asking for extra hot sauce. Marita knew she wanted it, and she didn't even bother to check the bag. It would be there.

"Gracias," said Kate. "Adios."
"Bye bye."
Kate left with her burritos and drove home. Burt, her boyfriend's, car was in the parking lot. Always home first, he resented so much of her time going into her job. She took her briefcase and the bag of burritos and went in.

Eager to talk over the farm worker conflict in the newsroom with him, their evening conversations gave Kate insight. She'd learned that an idea that's wrong as a thought is often exposed as unworkable when debated or even just verbalized.

Burt was sitting in the living room reading the paper. He put it down and got up when she came in. "It's about time," he said, walking over to her and kissing her on the lips. "I wasn't going to wait past eight o'clock. I was just thinking about Chinese food. Good thing you brought burritos. I can feed my face instead of grousing about your hours." He followed her into the kitchen and got down paper plates and napkins while she put out the burritos and assembled the condiments in the middle of the table. Burt popped open two cold ones. They sat down to eat, and as Burt dug into his burrito, Kate said, "How did your day go?"

"The usual engineering stuff; I know you don't want to hear about my arguments with the city manager. Want a rough sketch of the blueprints for the new sewage lagoon, with a detailed blow by blow description of the pros and cons of the type of valve I've been fighting about all day?"

Kate laughed. "No, that's okay, Burt. I was just being polite."

"I don't care if you're polite or not, but I wish you were here."

"I know, but there's not enough time to do all my assignments and the more interesting stories I find on my own. Wait until Ferrell finds out his front page picture tomorrow is going to be of an illegal grave of a child on the property of his best friend. It's a good thing tomorrow morning's his golf day. Otherwise, it would be much more difficult to pull off."

Burt stared at her in alarm. "Why don't you find a job at another newspaper, Kate?"

"I can't."

"I don't think you see where you're going. You're fooling with people who have power to screw you to the wall."

"You're talking like you're on their side."
"I don't want you to be hurt. Let someone else do it."
"There's nothing I'd like better, but no one else is."
"What do you have to gain, what to lose?"
"We're looking at the same thing from different sides. It's my job. I'm beginning to see through the shiny facade of society into the blood in its veins, and it's polluted."

"You're making a mistake thinking you can do anything about it."

"I'm not trying to do anything about it but report it. It's the job of lawmakers to do something about it, but as long as no one brings it out in the open, they're going to ignore it."

"You always end our discussions with a diatribe on politics, and it's not my forte. Sherman called here looking for Sue. He's losing her to that job. The same thing's happening to us."

"That'll never happen to me. I talk to you and other people all the time. I just saw Sue in the Burrito Place, and she wouldn't talk to me. She won't talk to anyone. She can't handle the pressure, and she won't let anyone help her. I don't think there's any way any of us can make contact."

"You're her best friend. You're just going to give her up?"

"No, but I'm completely frustrated. How can I make contact with someone who walks out on me every time I try?"

"There's got to be a way."

"I'm swamped myself. If my load was a little lighter, I'd have time to give more thought to how to handle it and time to try on different solutions when the old attempts fail."

"You're too involved in your job, Kate. We haven't gone skydiving once this month, and the weather's been cooperative. You're losing your joy in living."

"I don't know how to make more hours in the day, but you're right. We worked so hard to get the plane. I don't want to sell it or let it turn to dust in the hangar. Go ahead and make the arrangements. My life is still my own." She gave him a smile from the heart. He was right. It would do her good to force herself to take a Saturday off. She'd gain a new perspective.

"And mine, as mine is yours," Burt reminded her. He wasn't smiling.

"I haven't forgotten. I know it seems that way. I need you, Burt, to pull me back from the brink. I'd get so lost in the work if it wasn't for you, I'd never do anything else."

"Good thing you've got me," he said. "Let's go to a movie and forget everything."

"Great."

The next morning in the newsroom, Kate gave her film to Victor. "We'll need this today," she said.

"What've you got Kate?" asked Conrad, who always stood in for Ferrell on his golf mornings.

"A dead child's grave in one of Horton Painter's labor camps. The other photographs will spice it up." Kate put her purse in her desk drawer, and sat at her computer. She got her notes out to start carving out her story.

"God, Kate, you're knocking on the door to real trouble. You know what's going to happen when Horton and Ferrell finish playing golf?" asked Conrad.

"They're going to have lunch at the country club, and then Horton's going wherever he goes and Ferrell's coming back here."

"You left out a step. The second the paper's on the street, Ferrell's going to pick it up no matter where he is, and he's going to be with Horton when they see it together. They're going to have apoplexy."

"Well, it can't be helped. They can hold each other's hands and have it together."

"When the shit hits the fan, I'm going to say you made me do it because we had nothing else for the front page but Myrtle Snodgrass's new baby."

"Hey, you want to put Myrtle Snodgrass's new baby on the front page instead of Kate's grave, go ahead," interrupted Harry. "You and Ferrell can take the double dickhead of the year award."

"What can I do?" said Conrad, shrugging. "I just work here. I don't have your balls, Kate."

The newsroom buzzed as the staff prepared the article and photos about Horton Painter's labor camp to take up the entire front page and half the back of the front section. Kate relaxed, writing her story without Ferrell's hot breath on her neck, and Victor chose the most descriptive of the photos. Kate wished Sue would comment on it or at least take a look at the pictures, but she sat at her computer typing, her eyes glued to the monitor, and Harry had to leave on the run to a bank robbery in progress.

After the story was written, Conrad edited it with a running commentary. "No kidding, a hose for a shower? This is incredible."

When Harry, the rest of the reporters, and Victor drifted back from lunch, the Boonetown Daily News was hitting the streets, and everyone in the newsroom found a copy at his or her desk.

"Nice work, Kate," said Harry, looking it over.

"Thanks," said Kate, pounding out her new jail number for tomorrow's paper. The tension of anticipation of Ferrell's entry into the newsroom was heavy until the storm broke when he burst in ruddy-faced and furious.

"If you have your jobs tomorrow Kate, Victor, and Conrad, it's not because I've got my way," he yelled. "I've already talked to our publisher about this. You just want to embarrass Horton because he's my friend. City Council's had a hard on for him since his building collapsed downtown, and smelling blood, you all want to be in on the kill."

"Richard will love it," said Harry, speaking of the publisher. "Don't you ever get here early enough to see him stop by Kate's desk every morning to ask her what trouble she's going to stir up? He gets a big kick out of it."

"It's news Ferrell," said Kate. "That's all I care about it. I don't even know Horton Painter."

CHAPTER NINE

Tired, as usual, when she got home from work at the labor camp they moved to after Painter's camp closed, Marcella warmed up tortillas and beans on the electric burner. They'd been at the new camp for six weeks and in addition to a tiny bathroom and kitchen, they had two rooms furnished mostly with packing crates. The family who preceded them had left suddenly, and they were heir to several pots and miscellaneous useful odds and ends; a can opener, two tablespoons, a kitchen towel, an old tin percolator that must have come from Mexico, and various plastic bowls and utensils. The labor camp foreman only charged them a hundred and fifty dollars a month, and their salaries were the same as they'd been at Painter's.

Hearing shouts and scuffling, Marcella ran to the commotion just in time to see Julio faced off with a young man she didn't know.

"Pedro!" shouted Julio, sneering.

"Don't call me Pedro. I changed my name to Blair. Call me Blair," yelled the young man, red in the face.

Julio laughed loudly, "Pedro you stinking bracero!" he shouted. "You're afraid to be Mexican, but I'm afraid of nothing, not even a stinking bracero named Pedro!" He shoved Blair hard enough with a punch to the gut, that Blair staggered back and fell down,

Leaping to his feet, Blair charged at Julio, shouting, "You're just mad because I won, and you owe me five bucks! You're not going to forget it either by calling me names."

Julio lunged at him, and Blair grabbed Julio in a bear hug. Agile, Julio loosened Blair's grip and wriggled away. As they faced each other again, Julio stabbed Blair in the stomach. He'd worn the knife in a sheath hanging from his belt at home taking great pride in it ever since Mario had shown him how to skin a squirrel.

Blood oozed out of Blair's body, staining his shirt and pants, as he fell to the ground, his face contorted in pain, and Julio sheathed his knife and started running.

Rita ran after Julio, crying. "Julio!" she called.

He turned and waved, shouting, "Go back!" Rita stopped, and he took off again. Rita ran after him. "Julio! Wait for me!" He turned again.

"Go back, Rita! You'll get me killed!" His expression was frightened, and even from the distance of fifteen yards, Rita could see the sorrow in his large dark eyes that seemed to take up most of his face. No tear stained Julio's face now. Rita watched him dart into the woods, tall and lank, broad shouldered, yet slender, black curls brushing his collar.

Sobbing, Rita returned to the gathering group and watched Marcella kneel beside Blair, taking his pulse. It slowed rapidly. "Don't stop," Marcella prayed. "Please, don't stop." In helpless frustration, she fought her own rising fury, blinking back tears. The crowd closed a circle silently around them, frozen like a still photograph.

Sedar broke through the crowd, tears staining her face, Salvadore right behind her. She sobbed hysterically.

"No! No!" she screamed. Salvadore held her back.

"Stop it!" he hissed in her ear.

Mario and Salvadore walked Sedar, sobbing uncontrollably, back toward her house, and Rita followed them, crying softly. When they passed the outdoor faucet, Mario threw some water in Sedar's face, bringing her to her senses.

Marcella left the dead youth to his friends and ran to catch up with Rita, putting her arm around her shoulder to comfort her.

"We've got to get out of here!" said Salvadore, fiercely. "There's no time. If the police come...."

"What can I do?" asked Marcella.

"Nothing," said Sedar, her tears flowing freely. "Only if we don't find Julio, and you see him somewhere, help him. He'll call himself Russ. We all made up names in case something happened. He wanted an American name."

"Hurry, hurry!" said Salvadore, dashing into the shack. "We've got to get clothes and food for the road."

Marcella, Mario, and Rita went in to see what they could do to help.

"Get Julio's backpack, Rita. It's in his corner, and put in clothes and food, as much as can fit," said Sedar.

Rita got the pack and stuffed in Julio's clothes. She left some space in the top and front sections for food; and in the kitchen, she put four packages of tortillas on top, a handful of beef jerky, some tins of fish, and three chocolate bars. She worked silently and quickly around Marcella, who was packing plastic bags with food.

Noticing some ball point pens in a plastic cup on a small pad of paper, Rita quickly scrawled, *I love you, Julio. Don't forget me and don't forget our pact.*

Taking off one of her earrings, she then pinned the note to the inside of Julio's backpack with it. She stuffed one of the pens and several sheets of paper into the little pocket in front and ran in the bathroom to get his shaver and a bar of soap, and pushed a towel through a loop over the top of the pack. She handed the pack to Salvadore waiting at the front door.

"Thanks," he said. "Hurry up, Sedar. Hurry, can't you?"

"I'm coming," said Sedar, zipping her backpack closed over a kitchen towel.

"We'll catch up with Julio," said Salvadore, throwing Julio's backpack strap over his shoulder. "I know where he'll go. We got a head start if they call the law."

Marcella hugged Sedar, and Mario clapped Salvadore on both shoulders. "Goodbye friend," said Mario. The men hugged each other.

Sedar leaned over and kissed Rita, hugging her close.

"I wish you could go with us," she said. Marcella put the bags of food down, and she and Sedar hugged each other close and took a moment to cry in each other's arms.

"Here," said Marcella. "Don't forget your food." Salvadore and Sedar took the plastic bags of food and ran out of the dwelling and across the field. Sedar's anguished expression burned into Marcella's memory. It would never come out.

"Come on Sedar, hurry up," said Salvadore a few steps ahead. He waited for her to catch up, and they disappeared into the forest on the run.

Rita threw her arms around Marcella, sobbing, and Marcella held her close.

"This is what we crossed the desert to escape," said Mario, distraught. "We can't run away from it."

"Julio will not get caught!" said Rita, through her tears. "He's clever and smart, and he knows how to make friends."

"We'll never know," said Mario. "We'll never see them again, and we'll never know."

"Julio will get away, won't he, Mom? Sedar and Salvadore will find him, and they'll make a way for themselves. I believe that. It must be true, huh Mom, if I believe it in my heart?" Rita asked through her tears.

"I don't know, Rita," said Marcella. "I don't know what's in Julio's heart. Let's go. We have something more to do." With Mario's arm around Marcella, hers around his waist, and her other arm embracing Rita, they returned to the bustle of activity in the camp.

A young woman, Canvita, thirty-three years old going on sixty, rocked Blair's lifeless body. "We escape together! We come all this way safe. At this camp, he fight with Julio all the time and now this!"

"We must call a doctor," said a man in the crowd. "The police will come."

"No," she said, "no policia."

"Jesus, help us," whispered Marcella. "What can I do?"

A woman in the crowd asked, "Got a shovel?"

"It's alright. They're already digging," said someone else. "We'll have a service tonight. Bring a candle."

Mario helped carry the body to Blair's house to clean up the blood and dress it in clean clothes.

Marcella returned to her shack. Rita had a cup of coffee in front of her, but she couldn't drink. Marcella poured a cup of coffee. "Do you want to go with me to the funeral, Rita?"

"No, but I have to. I'm not going to die like that. I swear it." Rita felt like her guts were being wrenched out. "They'll think I'm sorry for Blair, but I'm afraid for Julio."

Marcella pulled her chair close to Rita and sat down. She took Rita's hand. "This is the hardest part, Querido," she said. "I'll miss Sedar, too. Sedar and Salvadore and Julio and you and me and Mario, we're like one family. We couldn't have made it without them. We have to hold up now, and it will scar over as the days pass."

"I'll remember, forever," said Rita, sorrowfully.

"So will I," said Marcella. "Will you help me get ready for the funeral?"

"What should I do?"

"Get some candles ready. I have to take a shower and wash this blood off my clothes," replied Marcella, gathering clean clothes.

Rita cut a brown paper bag into squares and slit the centers. She stuck the candles through the slits to prevent hot wax from dripping on their hands when they were lit

When everything was ready, Marcella and Rita joined Mario and the crowd of campesinos at the gravesite at dusk with the candles. The homemade plywood casket was closed, and Canvita was all cried out. She stood dry-eyed.

"I had a speech, and I forgot it." Canvita spoke so softly, they could barely hear; and the still, silent evening was absent of sufficient breeze to flicker the three deep circle of candles.

"I knew Blair," said Jesus, stepping forward with a guitar. "He and Julio were my friends." At the mention of Julio's name, tears came to Rita's eyes. It felt like he was the one who was dead.

"We played cards, and sometimes I won but mostly Julio won. We were three good men, and Blair was sharp and clever, but Julio was young." His voice grew husky, and he blinked often. "Now one of us is dead and one gone." He started to sing and strum mournfully, a song he made up.

> *"One of my friends is dead*
> *The other gone away*
> *And I'm left to sing my song*
> *Alone at the end of the day.*
> *I don't know the way we came*
> *Or how to go alone I only know*
> *Life can't go on this way*
> *I'll still sleep tonight*
> *And wake tomorrow*
> *The candle man will turn my*
> *Sorrow into a memory some day."*

Canvita stepped forward then. "Gracias, Jesus," she said. "I remember now what I want to say. "Our Father in heaven, in the name of Jesus Christ, and in memory of the Virgin of Guadalupe, bless Blair, and give peace to his soul and speed to his journey. Be with us and with your people who feed each other when we're hungry. Have mercy on us, and give us strength to carry on."

"And let Julio get away," said Rita to herself. "Let Julio get away, let Julio get away," repeated over and over through her brain.

The men lowered the homemade casket into the ground, and each of the watchers threw in a flower, some of which had been picked in the field; wild daisies and black-eyed-Susans. Someone threw a tulip, and Canvita threw a dozen large zinnias one at a time. An unknown predecessor had planted them at her hovel, and they'd always given her pleasure when she went in.

Jesus strummed his guitar, tears rolling down his face.

The children stood with their candles burning until the hole was filled in by the adults and older teenagers. Those who had no shovel pushed the dirt over the casket with their shoes.

After the funeral, Canvita went to her best friend's house. The men and older boys who knew Blair took a bottle of whiskey to the grave for a night long vigil. The others shuffled to their trailers and shacks, some in families or small groups, talking softly, but the same thing was on all their minds. Who would be next?"

Marcella, Mario, and Rita went to their dwelling; Blair, Julio, Sedar, and Salvadore in their thoughts.

"My friendship with Julio started with death and ended with death," said Rita, unrolling her sleeping mat on the floor, and spreading her poncho on top of it. "He was my only friend."

"Death in the camps is like a disease that spreads," said Marcella.

"Salvador was my best friend, too. Someday you'll have another friend," said Mario. "Someday we all will." The silence of the camp was overwhelmed with cicadas outside, as each settled into memories of friends and the sorrows shadowing the camps.

The vans came the next morning. The oranges were waiting on the trees to be picked, but seven were missing; and their absence at the hand of violence that comes from inescapable tension of those who have no civil rights in a land of plenty and comparative wealth was a rock in Marcella's heart and a black cloud overhead that she feared would never drop its rain, and she immediately banished the unwanted sensation recalling the sunset over the desert.

Marcella's muscles were attuned to the hard, physical labor that was monotonously routine and her mind to death. The work took her body over until it acted like a machine. Thoughts of death were gaining momentum as she prepared her mind to endure the eternity that is the day under the sun, handling the pesticide-laden fruit.

While Marcella picked, she obscured the image of the funeral by picturing the house she wanted. She'd hang white cotton curtains in the kitchen. The living room would have a fireplace. She and

Mario would sit in front of it and make important decisions. Rita could study in front of it on chilly nights. Rita would have a room of her own and invite friends over, and Marcella and Mario would have their own room with a double bed.

She kept her daydreams active until she returned to the camp and prepared tortillas and beans for herself and Mario and Rita. When they were ready, she took the plastic plates and forks outside where Mario and Rita were sitting by an orange crate and talking.

"Here," she said, handing them each a plate. She went back in for hers and joined Rita and Mario, eating and talking. It was her favorite time of the day, and the first she could relax.

Tonight as they were eating, they heard a knock on the front door. They all started to get up, but Mario said, "I'll go." Rita and Marcella sat back down. Mario left his plate on the orange crate they used as a table and went around to the front. Rita and Marcella kept quiet so they could hear. It was the labor boss.

"You've got a school age daughter," he said. "School starts tomorrow, and she's got to go. It's the law in California." Hearing school mentioned, Rita ran to the front followed by Marcella.

"How does she get there?" asked Mario.

"Walk all the way to the end of the lane where you get the van to go to the groves and wait for the school bus at 8:30," he said to Rita.

"Okay," said Mario, and the labor boss went on to the next dwelling.

"At last!" said Rita, throwing her arms around Marcella and giving her a bear hug. Unable to restrain her happiness, she then hugged Mario and kissed him. "I was beginning to wonder if I'd ever get to go to school again!" They returned to the back to finish their dinner with Rita's excitement bubbling up as talk turned to speculation about Rita's school.

The next morning, Rita woke when the alarm clock went off, and waited for Mario and Marcella to finish in the bathroom instead of trying to jockey to be the next one in. She made the coffee and bean and cheese tacos for breakfast and burritos for their lunch. Taking a cup of coffee, she leaned against the wall, drinking it.

"What will you wear to school?" asked Marcella, biting into her taco.

"My clean jeans and shirt; I can't wait, Mom."

"You lost one of your earrings, but that's okay. It's what inside that will get you through, and that's beautiful."

Rita's brow wrinkled, and she frowned, looking down at her hands. "I pinned my other earring to Julio's backpack with a note. I think about him a lot."

"I do, too. I think about all of them. Today you'll have much more to think about. You'll learn about the government and how it works. Pay attention and do everything right. You can teach me what you learn."

"I'm going to learn everything."

"You must start making friends at school, Querido. It's not good to study all the time at your age, and to keep only Julio in your heart. You have to let it fade and go on with your life."

"If Julio just ran away it wouldn't be so bad. I'm afraid because he killed Blair. Do you know what that would do to a boy?"

"No, I don't know, Rita. But I know Julio, so I know it's very, very bad for him. Blair was his friend, and Julio was a very sensitive young man."

"He'll never get over it," said Rita. "That's why I'm afraid."

"To go on living, he will have to let it fade just as you have to," said Marcella.

Mario came in and took his coffee and tacos. "When I was much younger than Julio, I saw people I loved killed. That's why you didn't go out with him, Rita. I didn't want to kill someone because I saw death. Julio saw death too many times, too, but it defeated him. I'm still running away from killing. I can't stop until we can live and work without killing sneaking up on us. Many people never see death by violence. I want a life like that for myself and for you. We'll keep on running until we have it or we're killed, too."

Rita hugged Mario and kissed him on the cheek. "Maybe someday somebody will start a school that teaches you how to live without all the killing," she said.

"As long as there are people who try to force others to do something they will not, there will be fighting and killing," said Mario. "Want to trade places? You go to the groves and I'll go to school," he added, sitting on a crate and pretending like he was writing.

Rita laughed. "Sure, don't miss the school bus. Tell them your name is Rita." Mario and Marcella laughed, too, and finished eating and drinking their coffee. It was time for them to go to work.

"Bye Rita. Study hard and learn everything," said Mario.

"Don't get into any trouble," said Marcella.

"Bye, Mom, Dad." After they left for the orange grove, Rita washed the plates and showered and dressed. She felt like royalty going to school and not having to pick crops. Arriving at the bus stop early, she was the first one there. Two students close to her age came along to wait.

"Hi," said Rita, walking toward them, but they were so busy talking to each other they didn't see her, so she didn't go closer. Three young elementary children came along talking together, and they didn't speak either, so Rita waited alone, her heart aching for Julio to be there to speak to her. Right before the bus came two more young ones showed up, and soon there was a crowd of laughing, talking children. Rita stood back from the crowd, watching them still thinking about Julio, missing him and Sedar and Salvadore.

The American school was much like other schools she'd been to, except that the language was English, and most of the children and teachers were North American. She'd always loved school, soaking up everything she could learn; and now she had a singular mission in the American school, to learn the way into legitimate American society.

Rita was required to fill out forms, and nervously writing in her name and address, she thought, "Suppose they find out I'm illegal?"

She had to go to the nurse's office and was asked if she had standard immunizations. She shook her head no, and was told to wait at the end of a line for shots. She waited and was given several shots and an oral vaccine. She then made it through the paperwork. At recess, she stood back on the playground, and saw a girl who was standing apart from the other students. Rita went over to her.

"Are you new at this school?" she asked.

"Yes. My name's Juanita," she said. "What's yours?"

"Rita. I'm a farm worker."

"Are your Mom and Dad in The Union?"

"No. What's The Union?"

"My mom and dad are in it. That's why we live in a house instead of a labor camp. The Union makes the government provide houses we can buy."

"Oh!" said Rita, thinking about that. "Do you have to give the government any of the money for picking crops?"

"I don't know about that," said Juanita, giving Rita a strange look. "Why?"

Rita shrugged. "I just wondered how it works. I want to get a different job." She wanted to ask how to get legal but couldn't think of how to do it without giving herself away. If Juanita's parents were in The Union and could own property, they must be legal.

"I want to change the system," said Juanita. "Farm work is good work. We make them pay us minimum wage, like all the other workers in America. We're going to make them stop using the chemicals that kill us, and we get health care when we're sick. It's good to make your own living, but you can't be respectable when you're treated like dirt because of the work you do. I want to be proud of working to take care of myself. If I get another job some day, that'll be okay. But while I'm picking crops, I shouldn't be ashamed to do it."

"What about illegal aliens?" asked Rita. "They're not even treated like people."

"That's another thing we're going to change with The Union," said Juanita. "We're going to make them make the laws as forceful for farm workers as for doctors and bakers and manufacturers and everybody else. They pretend not to know that anybody's illegal, but those are the only people they can rob blind because they have no rights. The growers don't want to pay us minimum wages if they can make people work like slaves until they get caught in a crime, and then they go to jail or get deported.."

"I wonder how illegal aliens get out of their slavery," said Rita. "Do you ever wonder about things like that?"

"I was born in California," said Juanita. "I know that's how a lot of people get out of it. Anyone born here is automatically a citizen. Some come through relatives."

A dodge ball hit Rita in the back, and spinning around she grabbed it on the first bounce and ran to a circle of children with it.

"Come on, Juanita!" she called. "Let's play." Juanita joined in the game, and after recess, Rita went in with the other students and settled in for the afternoon's lessons...

When Rita got home, she washed her clothes for tomorrow and prepared dinner, guilty that her parents had to be working on the ladders while she was free to do what she wanted. They came in tired but anxious to hear about school. She told them about getting shots and filling out forms, about social studies and English and math, and about Juanita and The Union her parents were in. "Juanita says you should be proud of your work," she explained.

"I'm glad you've got a friend," said Marcella. "But I'll never be proud of this work. I wonder what my life will be like when I'm not picking crops."

"I don't see a way to stop working the crops. Not yet, I can't find out how. Nobody we talk to knows," said Mario, frustrated.

"I'm going to get a real job," said Marcella. "I don't know how, and I don't know what, but something good must happen."

"Why do you think so, Marcella? You always talk like that, and you convince me it's true, but on the ladder in the sun tomorrow, I think it's not."

"I'll make it true, don't you see? I have to believe it, so we can go to it. Otherwise, how would we ever get there?"

Mario laughed, like he always did when he didn't know how to answer Marcella. Then he thought of something to say. "This country is so rich. Every place you look, people are busy, and you see how they build things all the time. Yet, we get robbed every day by the labor camp bosses."

"Everybody is rich except illegal immigrants," said Rita. "I want to be a doctor. I want to learn everything so I can see how to get out of here. I've got these books." She showed Marcella and Mario her social studies, math and English books.

"Are there stores or places where you can buy the newspaper around school, Rita?" asked Mario.

"There are some stores you can see from the school," said Rita. "But you can't go to them. There's a big fence around the school, and you have to stay there all the time."

Mario reached into his pocket and got out a quarter. "Here's a quarter to keep in your shoe," he said, handing it to Rita. "If you ever get a chance to get a newspaper, buy one and bring it back."

"Okay," she said, putting the quarter in her shoe. "Dinner's ready. Let's eat." She finished setting the table and put the tortillas and beans out.

Marcella and Mario washed up and sat down to eat. "Rita this is very nice, but you don't have to fix dinner," said Marcella.

"I like to," said Rita.

"What a daughter I got," said Mario. "Stubborn as Liberty." He pretended to be riding the donkey across the desert, taking his hat off and wiping imaginary sweat from his brow, sending Marcella and Rita into fits of laughter.

After they ate, Rita sat in a corner of the two room dwelling with her new books to study. She stayed up until ten o'clock, and finished the assignments for the whole week.

Free from preparing the evening meal, Mario and Marcella went out for a walk around the camp, and returned to settle into their evening routines.

Rita woke up in the morning happy and excited. She hummed preparing the morning and noon meals for herself, Mario, and Marcella. After breakfast when Mario and Marcella left for work, Rita got ready for school and eagerly went to the bus stop with her new books. She approached students waiting at the bus stop who were about her age. A new boy was with them.

"I'm Rita," said Rita. "I'm in the seventh grade. I guess we're all going to ride the school bus together. What's your name?" she asked one of the girls.

"Cara," replied a girl about her age.

"I'm Liza, Rita," said the other girl, who was shorter than Rita and looked younger. "I'm in the seventh grade, too."

"I'm in eighth," said the boy. "I'm her brother, Warren. Hi, Rita."

"Hi," said Rita. "How come you weren't here yesterday?" she asked Warren.

"I played hooky. I hate school."

"The teacher sent a note to Mom and Dad that Warren would need an excuse to come to school," said Liza. Laughing, she rubbed her rear end, and Warren gave her a dirty look.

Rita and Liza compared notes and found they had gym and music together. They sat beside each other on the bus.

"How do you get to a store?" asked Rita.

"Dad thumbs a ride. He won't let me and Mom thumb, so we don't get to go. It's four miles to the highway, and then Dad and Warren hitch to Ranchville. It's five miles away. There's a great big grocery store where you can even buy clothes. That's where my clothes came from. There's a dollar store, too, where they've got clothes and shoes and towels, stuff like that. Dad goes on Sunday when he can."

"I wish I could go," said Rita.

"Me too," said Liza. "I like to go to school to get away from the labor camp. Warren goes hunting and fooling around in the woods, but I like school better than that."

"Would you ask your Dad if my Dad could go with him?" asked Rita.

"Sure, I think he'll show him the way, but they won't hitchhike in a pack. Nobody will stop."

"Just so he knows where to go," said Rita.

"When we go home, show me where you live, and I'll tell Papa."

"Okay."

The bus stopped at three more lanes to labor camps. Twenty minutes later it came to a halt at a suburban development for students to board. A mile down the road, it made another stop. The bus pulled into the drive in front of the school, which seemed to rise directly out of a corn field, and stopped for the seventh, eighth, and ninth graders to get off.

Liza and Rita parted company as they entered the building because they were in different home rooms, but they met up again in third period physical education in the gym. The teacher handed out price lists for gym clothes. Rita glanced at it, folded it, and stuck it in her science book. She had enough money saved to buy the articles at school. She and Liza walked to music together and spent the whole hour singing American songs from a song book. After music, they went to the cafeteria for lunch and met Juanita, who, also, ate with them.

Happy to be out of the orange trees, Rita found her attention drifting away as she became bored with the social studies teacher's droning voice. She knew all the answers to the teacher's questions from reading the books, and idled away the time by drawing in her notebook. After school, she found Liza on the school bus saving a seat for her. When she and Liza got off the school bus, Warren came over to talk to her.

"Want to come over?" he asked. "We can hang out in the woods. I got two cigarettes," he whispered in her ear.

"No," said Rita. "I have some things I've got to do. Liza, don't forget to ask your Dad, okay?"

"Ask him what?" asked Warren.

"None of your beeswax," said Liza. "I'll come and see where you live, so I can show Papa," she said. The three of them walked to Rita's abode.

"Bye Liza and Warren. See you tomorrow," said Rita.
"Bye," said Liza.
"What do you like to do?" asked Warren, following Rita up to her door

"Study these books," said Rita.

"You got to have some fun sometimes."

"Reading is fun for me. Do you know that every mineral in the ground is, also, in your body? I read it in my science book. Isn't that exciting? We're pieces of earth that breathe."

"Who cares?" said Warren. "Can I come in?"

"No, I have too much to do." He went away laughing, making curlicues with his finger around his head.

Rita thought about school as she washed her clothes from yesterday and hung them on a clothesline strung between two trees behind the shanty. She went inside to prepare the evening meal and set the table.

When Marcella and Mario came in, tired and brain weary from picking, Rita said, "I met a girl at the bus stop, Liza. Her dad thumbs a ride to town on Sundays. I asked her if he would show you the way, Dad."

"Good, you need school clothes; at least two slacks or a skirt and three or four blouses she needs, Mario."

"Yeah, I know," said Mario. "We all need stuff, Marcella, you, too."

"I'm not going to school though. Rita needs them now."

"How will I carry everything back?" asked Mario. "Maybe I'll carry shopping bags in each hand and line them up my arms." He walked around the room pretending to be loaded down like a pack animal making Rita and Marcella laugh. When Mario pretended to be something, he was very funny looking.

When they sat down to eat, Rita asked, "With all the millions of people in the world, why should one of them be me, Rita, with my flesh and bone and mind and thought and feelings? Why me, instead of someone else?"

"It's a miracle," said Mario.
"Do you think so, Mom?"
"Yes, no one else is just like you."
As they ate, Rita recalled a typical day in the orange groves. Bored with looking at the oranges against the bright green leaves, her attention had focused on her hands. She'd watched her brown, sun-burnt hands, swift at their picking, as though they were just any hands, not hers in particular; how fast they moved, how the veins stood out beneath the skin, how the fingers could fly. But when they stopped being just any hands, when she felt the connection of their movement to her volition, she felt like God in control of them. They could do whatever she made them do. They could hurt or they could help at her discretion.

She'd made them stop picking and start again. She'd clenched them so hard they felt like pieces of steel with soft coverings of flesh over them. She'd felt the skin of the orange with them and the texture of the leaf on the tree.

Today she'd used them to turn the pages of books, and for household chores, though she could've used them instead to smoke in the woods with Warren. Julio had used his to sink a knife to the hilt in the guts of his friend.

"The choice of what these hands will do belongs to me alone," she said to herself. She'd known since she met him that Julio was very angry. Julio wanted desperately to get even, and she wanted only to learn how to use the system to find her place in it and make it work for them.

"The legal Americans at school, who don't live in labor camps, take their riches for granted. It's because of this government. People who know how it works can do whatever they want to, whatever they can," she said.

"I don't know about that," said Marcella, finishing her supper and pouring the coffee. "Children who always lived here, don't know there is anything else, not from living it. Now you have new friends, a new life. You must be very excited about it."

"Yes, but I was thinking about Julio and how angry he was and how much I liked him. Mom, you make what you want to happen, and Julio couldn't do that. He could only let things happen to him. I'm going to be a doctor. That's what I'm always going to think about instead of how my heart hurts for Julio."

Taking her coffee and retreating to her corner, she then carefully read all the chapters of her subjects for the next day and checked her math. When she was confident that she had it all right, she put the school books aside and opened the biology book Julio had given her. It was much harder to read, and she started by memorizing the scientific terminology and definitions concentrating hard enough to forget her grief and anger.

As Rita studied, Marcella put two pounds of pinto beans in water to soak overnight, and Mario came in from washing their clothes outside in the bucket and hanging them on the line. They heard a knock on the door. Mario opened it, and Rita looked up to see Liza and a man standing at the door.

"Liza!" she said, getting up. Mario stood back.
"Come in," he said.
"This is my Dad," said Liza.
"Laredo," said Liza's father, shaking Mario's hand.
"Mario, and this is Marcella, and Rita," said Mario. He waved at Liza. "Hi Liza."

"Hi," said Liza.

"Nice to meet you, Laredo," said Marcella.

"I need to know the way to town," said Mario. "I bet my thumb will work as good as yours when I know where to go."

"I show you the way to the highway. Once you get there, go west, but you got to keep your eyes open. If you start talking to the driver, you miss it. I done that once. I walk two mile back. Ranchville ain't but a great big store on one side and a gas station and a couple little stores and a filthy laundry on the other."

"Great," said Mario. "Sunday?"

"Yeah, I go early, maybe bout ten. How's that?"

"Stop by for me. I'll be ready."

"Thing is we can't hitch together. No one will stop, they see two men together. Now that Warren's bigger, I make him go by himself, too. Then we meet up after we get there."

The plans made, Liza and Laredo left, and Rita returned to her books.

The week passed very fast for Rita. She purchased her gym clothes at school, and the labor camp boss distributed one notebook and a pen to each of the school children in the camp. Rita put pens and notebooks on her list for Mario. Marcella gave him another list, and he needed additional items of his own.

Laredo and Warren came over a little after ten on Sunday for Mario, and they started walking to the highway. As they hiked very rapidly without talking, Mario marked every turn on a topographical map in his head, and they came to the highway in about an hour.

Laredo stopped Mario at the edge of the trees with a hand on his arm, as Warren went to the shoulder and waited for a car to come by. Warren liked to get out of the labor camp without having to go to school, even if it was only for a few hours on Sunday, and he felt like a pack mule on the way back. Being first, he'd have time to hang out at the game arcade in the store before his father arrived.

"We'll wait back here until Warren gets a ride," Laredo said to Mario, out of sight of road traffic.

"I'll go last," said Mario. "I can find my way back so you don't have to wait for me when you get there."

"After only one trip; you sure? I don't mind waiting," said Laredo.

"I'm sure," said Mario. "Thanks for showing me the way. Are you in The Union?"

Laredo shook his head no. "You?" he asked.

"No," said Mario. "How long have you been here?"

"At this camp, you mean?"

"Yeah, and picking crops."

"I been here for three months, and I been picking crops twice that long."

"I wonder if it's hard to get citizenship. How would an illegal alien get out of the labor camps?" asked Mario.

"If I knew how, I no be here," said Laredo. "I try to get a job in a restaurant. You need papers; social security card and driver's license or green card. I run away when I find out. I got nothing. I come to visit American relatives, and they drop us off here."

"Other people get papers," said Mario.

A car stopped to pick up Warren, and Laredo said, "You can meet us in the cafe if you want."

"No, go ahead," said Mario. He got Rita's, Marcella's, and his own lists out of his pocket and showed them to Laredo. "Look at what I got to get. I might be there all week. Thanks for showing me the way."

"I like to help," said Laredo, and started walking to the road but turned back to Mario. "If you find the way to get papers, remember me," he called.

Mario nodded.

Laredo got a ride in five minutes, and then Mario hitched a ride. A young blonde woman stopped to pick him up, and he experienced a moment of extreme anxiety getting into the car. He'd expected a Latino or at least a man to stop. He started to get into the back seat, and the door was locked.

"Get in the front," she called, waving him in.

Mario got in, and she stepped on the gas, but slowed when she reached the speed limit. "My name's Kay," she said. "I always stop somewhere along here to pick up a hitchhiker. I know there's a labor camp somewhere in there, and that's probably where you come from, right?"

"Yes," said Mario. "Thanks for stopping."

"You're going to the shopping center, I guess?"

"Yes. My wife and daughter got a long list of supplies for me to pick up."

"Oh, uh huh." She got a pack of gum out, unwrapped a stick and stuck it in her mouth. She held out the pack to Mario.

"Thank you," he said, taking a stick of gum and chewing it. "I bet you never lived in a labor camp."

She laughed. "That's right, but I read an article in the paper about them. That's why I always stop to pick up a hitchhiker there. Sometimes they ask me how to get papers to get better jobs."

"What do you tell them?"

"I don't know. So many people have asked me, that I asked a lawyer at the courthouse where I work. He says you can't enter the country illegally and get legal. You have to get a resident's visa first before you come or manage to get yourself born here."

"That's impossible for some people," said Mario.

"You speak perfect English."

"I think there are people who get here first, and then get legal," said Mario.

"I'm sure you're right, but I don't know how."

It was approaching noon, when she dropped Mario off at the store. He hurried through his shopping tour, and coming upon a money belt that could be worn around the waist, he added three of them to his shopping cart. His pockets were beginning to bulge. He didn't want to leave his money unattended because their doors at the camps had no locks.

After making all his selections, he went through the check out line. "Can I trade in some tens and twentys for hundred dollar bills?" he asked the checkout clerk.

"Go over to the service desk," she said, pointing it out. "I don't keep hundreds."

Mario went to the service desk and traded in his smaller bills for hundreds. Next week, he'd bring Marcella's and Rita's bills and trade them for fifties and hundreds, too.

When he got home, Marcella and Rita were waiting to see if he'd gotten everything. Rita got new shoes, socks, two slacks, one skirt and four blouses.

"Thanks Dad. I'm rich," she said. "With all these clothes, I must be a princess." She tried everything on, and Mario and Marcella oohed and aahed over her appearance.

Delighted to be going to school, Rita and her studies became the center of interest and conversation around their home, and the days passed quietly with no wild disturbances in the camp. They all settled into their routines, and any day was every day until one Friday after work, the vans to the labor camp were met by the labor camp boss.

"We're not working tomorrow," announced the boss. "The work is almost finished here, but there's work cultivating grapes down the valley. Anyone who wants to work grapes, hang around after you get paid tomorrow. Only men can live in the camps, but there's enough clean up around here for the women who want to stay until another job opens up."

"Are you going to do it?" Mario asked Laredo.
"Yeah, I guess so. Got to do something," he replied.

CHAPTER TEN

Saturday morning when the women and men lined up to get their pay, the labor camp boss, accompanied by a stranger, stood on his front porch to make an announcement. "Any men who want to cultivate grapes, hang around after you get paid. This here's Gordon. He's going to tell you about the job." Gordon was tall, broad shouldered but slender and clean-shaven with a short neat haircut. He looked out of place in the labor camp in blue suit trousers and a white shirt, open at the neck, and rolled up sleeves.

The men and women milled around after picking up their pay. Mario and Marcella carefully folded their bills and put them in their inside pockets. They'd transfer them to their money belts later in the privacy of their homes.

Gordon remained standing on the porch, and the men gathered around the bottom of the stairs, while the women stood or sat in the shade of an oak tree to hear about the job.

"It looks like word all ready got out, that the labor camp in the vineyard only has facilities for men," he said. "The pay's higher for grapes then it is here. I heard forty dollars a day."

A murmur went up from the workers, and they began talking among themselves. "I heard that before," muttered a man in the crowd. "They always tell you too much. Forty means thirty or thirty-five if we're lucky."

"Wait'll the tortillas and beans and cot space get added on," said Laredo. "Take it down to twenty five."

"Free and clear?" asked Mario, shouting out his question

Gordon shrugged. "I got no details."

Mario knew that was his way of telling them it was a lie.
"Thanks," he said, acknowledging Gordon's confidence. "Where is there work for the women after they clean up here?"
"There will be more crop work in the area within a week," said Gordon. "There's enough here to keep them busy until it opens up."

"How far away are the vineyards?" Laredo asked.

"Ten miles at most.  If you want to cultivate grapes, the vans will be here at six thirty this evening.  Be ready to go to a different camp.  That's all."  He took a cigarette out of a pack in his shirt pocket, stuck it in his mouth and lit it.

The men mingled with the women waiting under the tree and began making plans.

As they talked, Gordon stood on the porch smoking, watching them carefully not as a group, but singling out individuals to watch one at a time.

"Warren, you have to stay," said Laredo.

"I'm not going to stay and work with women.  I'm going with the men," he said, indignantly.

"You'll have the most important job," said Laredo.  "You have to hitchhike to town and get a cell phone.  As soon as I can, I'll come back and get the number and give you a number.  You'll have to keep a list of where everybody is going to be.  After things settle out, we'll be able to find each other and take and send messages still."

"Okay," said Warren, the importance of his new responsibility a source of pride.

The camp residents hurried to their dwellings to pack and say goodbye.  When they dispersed, Gordon got into his truck, and the labor camp boss got in the passenger seat.  Gordon started driving slowly through the camp as the labor camp boss told him who lived where, and Gordon looked over each home.

His first trip took him from one end of the camp to the other.  Occasionally, he stopped to talk to one of the women or girls he saw outside.  Marcella was one of them.

"Do you like your work?" he asked her.

Looking over Gordon and his truck, she realized something unusual was going on.

"I like to make money," she said.
"Do you have any children?"

"One daughter."

"What are you going to do when this job ends?"

"Mario and I will find other jobs. We'll keep working in the fields until we can find work we like better." Gordon was impressed with her ability to express herself clearly. She'd appeared a cut above.

"What's your name?" he asked.

"Marcella Dominguez."

Gordon nodded, waved to her, and drove on, and the excitement of the move absorbed the worker's attention. Most of them ignored his procedure that otherwise would have aroused their curiosity. Gordon returned to the labor camp boss's house. "I need to see the work records," he said.

"Sure, c'mon in," said the boss. They went inside and an alcove in the front room contained a file cabinet and a desk. The boss pulled out the chair for Gordon to sit on.

"I want to see Marcella Dominguez's file first," said Gordon.

The labor boss got a folder out of the file cabinet and dropped it on the desk in front of Gordon. Gordon looked up Marcella's record, and saw that she'd never missed a day of work and rated a high output. He checked the records of several others, also.

"Does Marcella Dominguez ever give you any trouble?" he asked.

"Naw. She blends into the crowd."

"It looks like she's never sick?"

"If she is, she never said, never stayed off the job, so how'd I know?"

"Okay, I'll see you later."

Gordon left the bungalow, got into his truck and drove back to Mario and Marcella's dwelling. When he knocked on the door, Marcella answered. She stood in the doorway staring at him, cautiously waiting for him to state his business. Mario came and stood beside her. Rita ran around to the front from the back, where she'd been studying the science book Julio had given her, and stood watching.

"My boss needs a woman to do housework," he said. "You could do it. She lives north of Porterville, and I have to find the right person."

"I can clean a house," said Marcella, her face lighting up. "I did it before in...uh...I have experience."

"Where?" asked Mario. "How will I find Marcella?"

"Come on, I'll show you. Get your clothes and anything you want to keep. If you take the offer, you won't come back here." He said to Marcella. "We better hurry, if you're going to meet the grape worker's van," he said to Mario.

"Hurry up, Rita, get going, and pack your stuff," said Marcella. Marcella and Mario rushed inside, gathered their things and threw them into backpacks and plastic bags. Rita ran around to the back and retrieved her most precious possession, her science book.

"Look at all this stuff we've got," said Rita, folding her new clothes into plastic bags. "These books have to go back to my school."

"We can't take them back," said Mario. "Just leave them here." He sighed. "We're always running." When they were ready, they dashed out to Gordon's truck with their backpacks and bags.

Gordon was standing at the rear of the truck with the tailgate down. Mario, Marcella, and Rita unloaded their backpacks and bags into the bed. "Marcella and Rita, put your bags on this side, and Mario put yours on the other," he said. They did so, and Gordon then opened the back seat door and held it for Mario, Marcella, and Rita. They climbed in, and he reached in the front and turned on the air conditioner.

Before getting in, he buttoned his cuffs and the top button of his shirt, took a tie off a hanger in the truck, tied it around his neck, and put on a suit coat from the hanger. His style and demeanor was polished, even elegant, and neatly pressed clothes adorned the man distinguishing him from the labor camp bosses.

He drove to a mansion, stopped in front of a double garage down the hill from it, got out, and opened the door for his passengers. Leaning on the open door with his arm resting on top of it, he then waited for everybody to get out.

"Mary Griswold lives in that house," he said, indicating the mansion. "This used to be a garage, but it's been converted into a cottage that comes with the job."

Marcella looked it over. It was extremely different from anyplace she'd lived in America. It approached civilization. "This is fine," said Marcella, appraising the outside. Neatly painted, it looked like a cottage with windows and landscaping. She'd not have known it had ever been a garage if he hadn't told her. "Why did you pick me?"

"I can spot a good worker, and I looked up your camp record. Ms. Griswold wants a woman for her personal maid."

"How much does she pay?" asked Marcella.

"Eighty dollars a week...." Marcella caught her breath in surprise. That was more than twice she'd ever been paid before living expense deductions. "But you get room and board free. Griswold's leftovers are better than the middle class eats. Also, she throws in clothes and things she thinks you might want that she's tired of. Dishes, linens, things like that."

"Rita comes, too."

"Alright, but there's no work for her. She'll be going to school now anyway."

"How will I know where to go?" asked Rita.

"Your mother will have to ask at work tomorrow. I don't know. Marcella, you'll have every Sunday off," said Gordon. "A house job is nothing like the fields. This is a chance most farm workers never get. How many people lived in your camp, and how many of them have you known to get indoor jobs?"

"Take the job, Marcella," urged Mario. "I won't be too far away, and I'll come back as soon as I can. Maybe I'll get lucky nearby, too."

"I don't want us to be separated, but what else can we do?" asked Marcella.

"We'll be separated anyway when I go to the vineyards. You better take the job, and I'll work grapes."

"I'll take school any day," said Rita. "I'll miss you, Dad."

"Go up to the house at the back door at quarter to six in the morning," Gordon told Marcella. "We'll go from there." He took a key out of his pocket and handed it to Marcella. She held it in her hand staring at it.

Gordon laughed and gestured at the door.

"It's locked, of course," he said.

Mario took Marcella's hand, and they walked a little away from Gordon's truck. He hugged her to him. Putting her arms around his neck, she kissed him.

"This'll have to last for a long time," she said. He kissed her passionately wishing they had time for a decent goodbye.

"I'll be back on Sunday as soon as I can. If I can get back every week I will," said Mario.

"I love you Mario. Never forget that."

"You don't have to tell me, Marcella. You're with me everywhere I go, every breath I take."

"I know that," she said, grinning. "I just like to say it."

"I love you too, more than my life, my darling," he said. Their arms around each other's waist, they walked back to the car. Mario then hugged and kissed Rita.

As they said goodbye, Gordon took Rita and Marcella's backpacks and bags and placed them by the door to the cottage. "It'll take you six weeks to settle into your camp, Mario," said Gordon. "You won't be back here before that."

"Is there a phone where I can get in touch with Marcella and Rita?" asked Mario.

"Not in the garage, and you wouldn't call the house."

"I'll get back as soon as I can," Mario said. He turned to get into the truck, closed the door, and rolled down the window. "Look for me on Sunday, but maybe not right away. I'll have to see how it goes."

Marcella blew him a kiss. "Don't wait six weeks," she said. "I'll try for two weeks. Bye, Marcella. Bye, Rita."
"Bye, Dad."
Mario waved goodbye, with a sinking sensation in the pit of his stomach.

Marcella watched the truck driving away and felt like running after it. Since they'd met, she and Mario had faced the difficulties of their lives together. She felt like part of herself was driving away. Utterly dejected, she unlocked the door and carried her backpack and her other bags inside.

Rita followed her, also, loaded down with bags. "I know how you feel, Mom. I miss him already. Who will keep us laughing when everything goes wrong?"

"We'll be back together. We live for that," said Marcella, as they walked in. "Look, we've got cots with mattresses!" she said, dropping her gear and sitting on one to test it out. "And pillows! No more sleeping on the floor! I wish Mario would get a bed, too." She set the pillows against the wall and leaning back, she crossed her legs in front of her on the mattress. "Luxury!" she said. "Now I know we're in America."

Rita put her backpack and bags on the end of the other cot. She picked up one of the pillows. "Good for throwing!" said Rita. She tossed a pillow at Marcella, and Marcella bombarded her back.

"And taking your aggressions out!" said Marcella. "There's one!" She swatted Rita hard with a pillow. "And here's another. She hit Rita over the head with the pillow until feathers flew."

"This makes three and four!" said Rita, hitting Marcella back. They raged with the pillows until they could bear to go on with life without Mario.

A five drawer pine dresser stood against one wall with a mirror over it, and each cot had a one foot square end table beside it.

Marcella opened a sliding door to a three foot deep closet. Boxes of clothing and miscellaneous items stood along the inside wall. The single small window in the back wall of the room was stingy with light, but the larger two front windows, one on each side of the door let in more, and whitewashed walls brightened the space with the help of a five foot florescent light overhead. A tub with a shower, a sink, and a toilet were partitioned into a five square foot cubicle in the corner. Next to that was a kitchen sink in a cabinet with a cupboard overhead. A three foot high refrigerator stood next to it, and Marcella opened it and looked in. There were six ice cold soft drinks inside, and it had a freezer compartment with two ice trays. A small kitchen table with a chair on each side stood in front of the kitchen area.

Rita went into the bathroom and turned on the cold water tap. There was plenty of water pressure, and she tried the hot tap. After letting it run for a few minutes, she put her hand under the water and jerked it back.

"Hot water!" she yelled. "Mom! We got hot water! I'm going to take a shower!"

"Really?" asked Marcella. She walked into the bathroom and tested the hot tap. "Really!" she exclaimed, surprised. "I'm right behind you, Rita!"

Marcella emptied her backpack and bags, and put everything away. Using the top two dresser drawers, she left the bottom three for Rita. She set her personals on top. Her backpack, she hung in the closet with the distinct feeling of coming up in the world. The only dampener on her appreciation of her good fortune was that Mario wasn't there to enjoy it with them.

When Rita emerged from the shower, fresh and feeling good as new, she too unpacked. After arranging her things, Rita rested her elbows on the window sill and looked out at the mansion on the hill. "I'm never going to live in a house like that, not even when I'm a doctor," she said.

"Okay, because when you're a doctor, you won't be living in labor camps either."

Marcella took a turn in the shower. The luxury was so utterly enjoyable, she lingered until the water started to cool. Piling her hair off her neck and dressing, she then stepped out of the bathroom. "Maybe this place used to be a garage, but it sure is a little house now, and it's a lot better than the labor camps," she said "Now we'll see what the work's like and if they're really going to pay me what Gordon said. I never imagined, but now maybe it's true."

"Let's see what's in these boxes," said Rita, pulling one out of the closet and setting it in the middle of the floor. Marcella helped her haul the rest of them out.

As she rummaged through for useful items, Marcella emptied one box of bath towels, which were large and plush in comparison with the skimpy rags she was accustomed to. She held a soft yellow one against her face and then went to hang two in the bathroom, and threw the soggy one over the shower curtain pole to dry. The others she stored on the closet shelf. Rescuing dish towels and a dish cloth from a box, she hung them neatly in the kitchen area, and set the kitchen supplies in the cabinet beneath the sink.

Rita opened a box containing sheets and pillow cases. Marcella threw one set on her bed and one on Rita's.

"Don't you want any of those clothes?" asked Rita, holding up a white satin blouse with ruffles down the front. "You would look beautiful for Dad in this." Rita held it up in front of her, intending to keep it if her mother turned it down.

Marcella said, "No, I only wear my own clothes."

"Can I have it?" asked Rita.

"Why not? If you like it and feel comfortable in it, keep it." Rita tried it on and it was a little large, but she decided to save it for now anyway. She hung it in the closet.

Marcella found a hot plate and plugged it in to see if it worked. It heated red hot, and she set it on the refrigerator with the one she'd brought. "We can make coffee and warm food on these," she said. She'd brought her own sauce pans and can opener, so those items, she left in the box, but she extracted an old fashioned Corning percolator. "No more tin pot coffee, Rita."

"Mom, we've never been so lucky before. If you make all that money, and Dad makes a lot picking grapes, we'll be better off than all the people living all the time in labor camps like we used to. I'm going to find a way to get a part time job, too. We really will buy a house some day and even a car."

"Thank God, Rita. Now let's go find the town and the library and get a sandwich."

"Good," said Rita, eagerly. "The exploring part is fun. This is our first look at the real America."

"All of it is the real America," said Marcella. "Manuel's labor camp where we buried Enrico, and Julio killing his friend, that's just as much the real America as that big house on the hill like you're never going to live in."

"I just want to be ordinary real," said Rita.

"So do I. But everything we see and do and say and everything that happens is real. This is our real life, and though in some ways we're much better off, Mario isn't here. There's a hole in my heart until he returns. I'd rather be in a labor camp with Mario than here with all this luxury."

"I know," said Rita. "I wish we were altogether, too. But we can't be like that right now, so this is better than if we had to be in another labor camp, too."

Because she had a door that locked, Marcella put her money belt in the zipper compartment of her backpack, keeping out a twenty dollar bill. She folded it and put it in the inside pocket of her jeans. Seeing Marcella's new procedure, Rita, also, took a twenty, and stashed her money belt in her backpack.

Stuffing their dirty clothes and the wet towel into a pillowcase, Marcella said, "We'll find a laundry." She slung the pillow case over her shoulder and grinned at Rita. "Do I look like Santa Claus?"

Rita laughed. "Yeah," she said. If Mario had done that with his exaggerated expressions and gestures, she'd have been helpless with laughter.

They went outside and Marcella locked the door, standing on the porch briefly wondering which way to town. The sidewalk went in both directions, and they looked down the street one way and then the other.

"I guess this way," said Marcella, starting to walk west.

"Maybe we'll find out in ten miles," said Rita. Marcella laughed. "Do you want to try the other way?" she asked. "It's all right with me."

"No, because you're always right. How do you know?"

"You always ask me that, and I always tell you the same thing."

Rita sighed. "It's the same way I picked," she said.

Marcella saw an elderly American looking woman approach with a dog on a leash. "Do you want to ask her if we're headed for town?" she asked Rita. Rita shook her head no.

Marcella and Rita walked briskly, and after ten minutes, they saw a traffic light ahead and houses lined the street. A few more people were on the sidewalk. They came to a gas station with a little store. Marcella and Rita went in.

"Is there a laundry around here?" Marcella asked the man behind the counter.

"Yeah, straight on down Main," he said. "Two and a half blocks,"

"Thanks," said Marcella, and they proceeded to the Laundromat. A short chubby woman in an apron full of pockets across the bottom was wiping off the machines with a damp cloth. As Marcella started emptying her pillowcase into a washing machine, a man came in with a laundry basket full of dirty clothes. He threw them into a machine, went over to the attendant and got change, and Marcella and Rita watched him put four quarters into the slot and push the coins in.

Marcella got two dollars in quarters, and the attendant asked her if she wanted dimes for the dryer.

"Yes," said Marcella. She got two more quarters, fifty cents in dimes, and seventeen in bills. Marcella bought soap at a machine for thirty-five cents, and put four quarters in the washing machine and started it.

While she was waiting, Rita looked up the address of the library in a skimpy telephone book dangling from a wall phone by a chain. It was on Solingo Street.

"Where's Solingo Street?" Rita asked the laundry attendant.

"Go right out the door, and it's the first cross street," the woman replied.

While the clothes washed, Rita and Marcella went to the library. Rita took her time browsing and chose three science books. Marcella looked over the fiction section and selected a novel. They took the books to the check out desk.

"Can we check these out today?" asked Marcella.

"Sure, you need a library card," said the librarian, handing them each an application. They sat at a table to fill them out.

"What'll we put for address?" asked Rita.
Marcella looked at the card, blankly.
"What did you put on your school form?"
"Northside Labor Camp."
"Just write Main St., Ranchville, California," said Marcella. She filled out her form and signed her name. They returned to the check out desk, and the librarian glanced at the forms, and prepared library cards for them. When she handed them the cards, Marcella felt strangely excited. Though it wasn't an official identification that she could use to get a job, she felt like she was knocking on the door. Marcella and Rita checked out their books.

"I could eat a bear," said Rita.

"Me too, but first, we've got to put the clothes in the dryer. I saw a little cafe across the street from the laundry I'd like to try."

"Okay, Mom." They returned to the laundry and Marcella transferred the clothes to the dryer and put two dimes in while Rita looked over *An Introduction to Chemistry*.

"Let's go, Rita," said Marcella.

They crossed the street, went to the diner, and sat in a booth. The menus were on the table, and they looked them over. The waitress came to their booth. "Can I get you something to drink?" she asked.

"I'd like ice water," said Marcella.
"I'll have a root beer," said Rita.
When the waitress returned with the drinks and got out her order pad, Marcella ordered barbecued ribs, coleslaw, and fried potatoes.

"I'll have a beef burrito with salsa and corn chips," said Rita.

"Will that be all?" asked the waitress.

"Yes, thanks," said Marcella, and the woman bustled off.

"In America, you never know what's coming tomorrow," said Rita. "Not long ago we were scratching sand out of our hair, yesterday we picked oranges, and today we took hot showers, washed our clothes in a machine instead of a bucket, and borrowed books from the library. We had a nice walk, and now we're eating in an American restaurant."

"Yes, I heard life's like that in America. I don't know of another country in the world we could go from the desert to where we are right now in our whole lifetime. I knew America was different then anything we knew, but I didn't think it would be this different."

They chatted about the road they'd covered so far until the waitress brought their food. Eating leisurely, Rita loved having the resources to eat in an American restaurant.

After they ate, the waitress brought their check, and Marcella paid the tab. They walked back to the laundry, and folded the clothes. Marcella packed them into the pillowcase, putting her library book on top, and slung the pillowcase over her shoulder.

"Don't you want to put my books in there?" asked Rita.

"Only if you want to carry it; I got one skinny book. You've got a lot of weight there."

"No, that's okay," said Rita. They walked briskly, enjoying the exercise and returned to the garage at twilight.

"Rita, you put the sheets on the beds," said Marcella. "I'll put everything away. Then I'm going back to the store at the gas station to get something for us to eat tomorrow."

"I'll go if you want," said Rita. "It's not far."

"Okay." Marcella gave her a twenty dollar bill. "Buy tortillas, milk, cheese, eggs, salsa, meat, beans, and whatever you want."

Rita put the money in her pocket, made the beds and went to store as Marcella unpacked the pillowcase, put everything away, and arranged the kitchen area properly.

When Rita returned with the groceries, she gave Marcella the change and put the food away.

"Only one thing is missing," said Marcella. "I have all this to be grateful for, and one thing still makes me miserable. Maybe everything will never be exactly right."

"Yes, it will," said Rita. "That's what you always tell me. You have to keep thinking about how you want it to be."

"It doesn't work that way when you miss someone really bad," said Marcella. "I learn new things still, too."

"I miss him, too," said Rita, opening her chemistry book at the kitchen table.

Marcella got ready for bed and went early, anticipating a job out of the sun, reveling in the luxury of reclining on a mattress. She opened the novel and started to read it, but soon she was snoring lightly, the book closed on her hand. Rita took it out of her hands and put it on the night stand.

When the alarm clock woke Marcella, she dressed carefully, combed her hair, pulled it back, and held it in place with combs, nervous about going to the large, imposing mansion. Anxious to see the inside, she was, also, bewildered by deep animosity at this unusual opportunity as she walked up the hill and knocked on the back door.

CHAPTER ELEVEN

Mary Griswold had grown up in the high society of upper New York, an heiress of an American entrepreneur, a candy manufacturer. She'd attended exclusive private schools and the Northeast Business College for the wealthiest ten percent of America's children interested in carrying on family traditions.

Uncommonly intelligent and with a natural acumen, her primary interest was business. She was successful enough that she could afford to dabble in financial challenges, and when she heard of the sale of a hundred thousand acres of California orange groves, she had her legal staff investigate it.

"The price is unbelievably low," said her lawyer, Mabel Stewart. "And it's a great tax shelter. Most orange groves are owned by the upper crust for that reason. You need a shelter. An added attraction is that there's oil under the oranges that's being pumped now."

"Why is the price so low?" probed Mary.

"I can't find a thing wrong from a business standpoint. I'm sure you've read news reports about migrant workers. My guess is the owner wants to sell his labor problems. Picking oranges is mind-breaking work. Central Americans come from the south to work crops, but after they're here, they take restaurant and other service jobs, so there's a pipeline from Mexico to the orange groves."

Thinking about the proposition, Mary called a Florida orange operation to research domestic competition.

"We don't have any problem with California competition," said the grower. "I don't know anything about the California growing conditions, but an orange is an orange no matter where it's grown."

When Mary visited the groves, she saw no oranges ankle-deep in the rows between the trees. They had been plowed under for her inspection, and she saw only the oranges on the trees. But the low price nagged at the back of her mind. The seller put her suspicion to rest saying he was anxious to retire and join his children abroad. His holding were so vast that the oranges required too much of his time and attention.

"I've got such a long list of interested prospective buyers from back east looking for tax shelters and high profits that I really couldn't care if you buy or not," he assured her.

Mary closed the deal, but later discovered that she couldn't sell eighty percent of her oranges in the United States because of the Federal Marketing Orders that applied to California oranges but not Florida oranges. The groves had been dumped on her by someone looking for a way out of a bad investment.

The marketing orders originated during the Great Depression when owners of smaller groves needed price controls to keep their farms. If the market was flooded with multitudinous oranges for a dime each, nobody would buy the small farm yields at three for a dollar, and the small orchards would go bust.

California hadn't had a deep enough freeze to kill oranges for seven years, and since oranges can be stored on the tree and harvested at the most propitious time, the overabundance of California oranges made Mary's groves a losing fluke.

Adding to her problems, political action groups along the heavily populated seaboard were beginning to hold parades and demonstrations, saying poor people couldn't afford vitamin C while it rotted ankle deep in the orange groves. Consumer groups, also, demanded the sale of oranges at market value.

Mary tried to solve her orange problems with growing frustration that built to anger and began to change her personality from sweetly altruistic to grinchdom. "Load these goddamn excess oranges and ship them to California metropolises and distribute them free," said Mary. "Advertise big time. Shut up those agitators and their propaganda."

"We can't do that," said Stewart. "The Marketing Orders won't permit it. If people can get oranges free, it will destabilize the price of all oranges."

"Then build some packing houses in Mexico. Send this surplus south, and ship it back in cartons labeled in Spanish and sell it as imports."

"We can do that," said Mabel. "I'll set up the appropriate companies."

"What else can we do to offset these losses? I'm paying you, Mabel, to come up with some solutions. Do I have to think of everything?"

"No, I've given this much thought. Take out some of the oranges and grow cotton."

"Why?"

"You won't have to actually grow it, just threaten to. The government will offer you a large subsidy to not grow cotton because it'll disrupt the economy of the Southeast. That'll help offset your orange losses."

"Good Mabel; do whatever is necessary, and keep me informed."

"Very well, Mary."

Even instituting every new plan, Mary's large orange grove holdings continued to drain her bank account. She moved from New York to California to attack the problem from a legal standpoint, filing lawsuits in federal court challenging the marketing orders. The labor problems, she solved with relative ease. Her anger and frustration grew, as her more prosperous ventures had to support her orange groves. The tax write-offs didn't cover her losses.

When Marcella rang the bell at the back door of the mansion at 5:45, Gordon opened the door. "Come in," he said. "This way." She followed him to a door off the kitchen.

"Here's the women's dressing room," he said. "Find a uniform in your size and put it on. I'll wait out here." Marcella went in where two other servants were getting ready for work.

"Hello," she said. "I'm Marcella."

"Hi, Jenny here," said a tired woman nodded at her, twisting her long hair and sticking it to the back of her head with a clip.

"My name's Sylva," said the other woman. "Here's the uniforms. They're all lined up by size. You just have to find one that fits."

Marcella went to the rack and searched out a size eight. "Do you all like working here?" she asked, changing into black slacks and a white cotton tunic.

"It's better than the fields," said Sylva. "But it's not a real job. I want my own place so bad I about can't stand it." She lowered her voice to a whisper. "But there's a way out through this place. The woman who had your job got a job in another state. I'm doing my best. If you do real good someone offers you another job. You don't know how it works until you get the offer, but I've seen plenty go and new ones come. I figure it's about my turn next."

"Thanks," said Marcella, the first sign of hope lightening her heart.

"That's all gossip," said Jenny, tiredly. "I've been here for three years. I'm not goin' anywheres, that's for sure."

"When you leave tonight, throw the uniform in that laundry basket," Sylva indicated a large basket by the door, "and take a clean one tomorrow."

"Okay," said Marcella, looking in the mirror, combing a stray lock back. Hearing Gordon tap on the door, she put her comb in her uniform pocket and stepped out.

"This way," he said. Walking down the expansive hallway beside Gordon calmed Marcella's nerves. Despite his neat attire, polish, and formality, her instinct told her that he was a friend.

She took a deep breath. Her life from this point on could pass relatively easily with little turmoil or could be the next thing to torture, depending on the temperament, and personality of a woman named Mary Griswold.

"We'll start at the front entrance and tour the house, saving the dining room for last," said Gordon. "Griswold's on her way there now. She gets up at the same time every morning, except when she has company or is out the previous evening. The first thing she does is head for the dining room for breakfast."

They walked to the front entranceway. Paintings of western landscapes decorated the walls, and two arches led to the interior hallways on either side, a wide staircase in the center between them.

"We're going to the living room. Ms. Griswold does most of her entertaining there, a few people at a time. You'll see all the rooms, but you're not responsible for anything on this floor, except for on special occasions," said Gordon, his voice cold as marble.

They passed down the hall on the left to a living room, with a highly polished oak floor partially covered with a patterned oval carpet. All the furniture in the house was Georgian and genuine Early American antique. They moved into and out of the room at a quick pace, so Marcella hardly had time to take it all in.

"Here we have the library," said Gordon. They entered the large room from which glass doors led to a richly tiled patio surrounded by a garden with statuary amongst the trees and flowers. "We'll skip the dining room for now."

They proceeded to a spacious kitchen where cooks busied themselves with food preparation. Sylva was preparing a breakfast tray in the clean, quiet room.

"Mary's breakfast," she said to Marcella.
"I see," said Marcella.
Sylva winked at her. "You can use my kitchen anytime you want," she said. Marcella chuckled.

"Hello, Marcella, hello, Gordon," said Jenny.
"Hello," said Marcella.
"Hi," said Gordon.
"You're to prepare anything you want in the kitchen, or take anything you find already prepared. You eat in here on your lunch break," said Gordon. He opened the pantry. Cans, boxes, and jars of every food imaginable stocked the shelves. Gordon opened the doors to the refrigerators and freezer, so Marcella could peek inside. The kitchen was far better stocked than the stores she'd shopped in.

Under the stairs the length of the house, was a long room, with the door closed, which they passed by.

"What's in there?" asked Marcella.

"That's my quarters," said Gordon, leading the way through the back hall.

On the other side of the house, Marcella was shown a large ballroom which served for parties. "This room can be partitioned off with folding walls," said Gordon. "Ms Griswold is planning a big party here in six weeks. When she throws a party like that, everyone has to help."

"All right," said Marcella.

"Belle or Griswold herself will show you her quarters upstairs," said Gordon, as they returned to the dining room. They paused outside the door, and Marcella had a fleeting urge to run away.

"You'll do fine," whispered Gordon. He opened the door and went in, and Marcella followed him. He then stepped aside.

Mary Griswold was seated at the enormous dining room table alone. Her dyed light brown hair, waving over her forehead on the right side, was still held in place with yesterday's hair spray. She wore no makeup and was dressed in a blue satin bathrobe over white satin pajamas. With small hazel eyes and a high forehead, her narrow nose turned up on the end and her sparse mouth was drawn forward. She reminded Marcella of a little dog she'd seen pining wistfully out the window of an expensive automobile.

"Ms. Griswold, this is your new maid, Marcella Dominguez." Gordon presented Marcella and waited to be dismissed.

"Gordon!" said Mary, ignoring Marcella.
"Yes Ma'am?"
"I've lost more than a dozen employees in the past few weeks, and the price of bringing them over rises daily. I want a record kept starting this minute of the name of every hire with the date, job, salary, status, and reason for leaving. Nobody's to see it

but you and I. If someone doesn't show up one hour or one day, I want it reflected in this record. Understand?"

"Yes Ma'am."

"I want an immediate report on every one who takes off, no matter where I am, no matter what I'm doing. If you're negligent before I cancel this order, you'll be fired on the spot."

"Yes, Ma'am."

"You can go now."

"Yes, Ma'am." Gordon left the women alone.

"Marcella," she said, looking Marcella in the eye. "When you report to work, come here first. My personal maid quit yesterday, ran off with some local dipshit probably. I expect you'll always be on time, because I don't eat breakfast until you bring it. We're clear on that, right?"

"Yes," said Marcella.

"Yes Ma'am."

"Yes Ma'am."

"While I'm eating breakfast, you'll go upstairs and fix my bath, lukewarm with bubble bath, and put a magazine on the ledge by the tub. The magazines that came yesterday are in the rack in the foyer. Did you notice it?"

"Yes, Ma'am."

"Bring only one that was delivered the previous day, a fiction magazine preferably; otherwise, fashion or news. Leave the others for guests, or if you want any of the old ones, take them. Anything I'm finished with you can have if you want.

"Look through the drawers and take a peek in the closet, so you'll know where everything is. Clothing must be laid out according to what I'm going to do. Today, I'm going to a political meeting, and I want to present a highly professional appearance. A nice cotton business suit will do. Always select shoes that match the outfit, always. If you're not sure, Belle will help you today.

"After I leave, you'll change my bed and clean those rooms; tub, floors, everything. I can't abide dust, and that's your section of the house. I'll be out all day, so you can leave at two o'clock. Your schedule will conform to mine, but when I'm entertaining, you'll have more to do. Sometimes you might have to work late, but in that case, you'll have the next day off."

"Yes, Ma'am."

"You're to take all the food you want for you and your daughter but only what you prepare in the kitchen or what's already prepared. Don't take anything out to cook.

"I'm going to ring Belle. She's head of the household, but you won't have anything to do with her after today. She'll show you where you can find cleaning supplies, and that sort of thing, but I'm the only one to give you orders. You're my personal maid, and unless I tell you to do something, don't do it."

"Yes, Ma'am."

"Bring my breakfast now."

"Yes, Ma'am." Marcella left Mary Griswold and went to the kitchen.

"Here's her breakfast," said Sylva, indicating a covered tray on a cart on wheels. "Take everything off the tray and put it on the table exactly like it's on the tray. Make sure you put everything on the right side in the right order. She might die if you put the fork down next to the knife."

"I see," said Marcella, and wheeled the breakfast cart to the dining room. She set the breakfast in front of Mary, according to Sylva's instructions, wheeled the cart back to the kitchen, and returned to the dining room. A middle-aged matronly woman stood waiting beside Mary, who was eating.

"This is Belle, Marcella," said Mary. "Belle, show Marcella where everything is."

"Yes Ma'am," said the businesslike Belle. Marcella followed Belle upstairs and into Griswold's private quarters. Marcella noticed a fine vase on a corner table she thought could use some fresh flowers. Beyond the sitting room was the bedroom with a wall length cedar closet between containing four racks of clothing and four bureaus. The women went into the closet.

"Here are business suits, sportswear, casual clothes, and dresses," said Belle, indicating the garments with a gesture. "Underwear and fold ups are in the bureau drawers here, one for around the house casual, one for company casual, one sports and leisure, and one for formal." She opened the drawers one at a time, and Marcella dutifully peered into each one.

"She wears jewelry with everything," said Belle, pointing out the jewelry boxes. "Lay out jewelry with the outfit." Marcella opened the drawers of some of the four large ornate boxes on top of the bureaus to earrings, bracelets, necklaces, watches, rings and brooches for all occasions from tea parties to the courtroom.

"All her shoes are in these racks," Belle pointed them out, and Marcella noticed that though there were more shoes than she could wear in a month, none of them had a speck of dust on them.

"You're responsible for keeping everything stocked from detergent to hosiery and underwear." said Belle. "No one else is allowed in here. Before you run out of something, post a note on the bulletin board in the kitchen, and I'll order it. Always have plenty of extra. As soon as you open a new pair of hose, order another." Belle led the way out of the closet, and next to it between the bathroom and the clothes closet was a utility room containing a washing machine and dryer, cleaning supplies, and a hamper.

"Can I wash my clothes here?" asked Marcella. Belle gave her a horrified look.

"No! There's an employee's washer and dryer you can use off the employees dressing room. Always use that one. Don't use anything of hers unless she gives it to you or tells you to use it. Have you ever had a job with medical benefits?"

Marcella shook her head no, recalling Mario's snake bite and the labor camps. Medical benefit was foreign territory.

"If we get sick, she calls her doctor, and if we need medicine, she buys it. You don't ever work on Sunday, and usually you have Saturday off, as well." Marcella listened but wasn't sure she'd understood. It seemed doubtful that Ms. Griswold would care if she was sick or well, and Gordon hadn't mentioned Saturdays off.

"Here are sheets, towels, bubble bath, soap, and water softener. If you get it wrong, you'll hear about it right away, and you have to just stand and wait for her to blow off steam. It must be just so." She measured out the right amounts of water softener and bubble bath and threw them into the tub. Then she turned on the water.

"Feel the temperature, and get it just like that," said Belle. "Believe me she's fussy about things like that."

Marcella felt the water which was very hot.

"It'll cool to just right by the time she gets here," explained Belle.

"She said to get a magazine for her to read in the tub first," said Marcella.

"Alright; let's go get it. We probably won't talk again. She keeps her personal maid isolated from the rest of us," said Belle, leaving the water running.

"What happened to the last one?" asked Marcella, as the women walked down the stairs on their way to the front foyer.

"She took another job," whispered Belle, under her breath, straightening her apron. "It's the most common cause of people moving on."

"What kind of job?" Marcella whispered.

Belle shrugged.

"How do illegal aliens get legal?" asked Marcella, taking her life in her hands.

Wrinkling her brow, Belle put her finger to her lips in a sign to hush.

"Where should my daughter get the school bus?"

"How old?"

"Thirteen."

"It stops in front of the Convenience Mart a half mile down the main road at eight o'clock. She'll see the other kids waiting; anything else?"

"Where can my husband call me?"

"Not here."

"I can't think of anything else," said Marcella.

"Good luck then," said Belle. "Bye."

"Bye, Belle," said Marcella. "Thank you."

Marcella chose a fiction magazine from the section of latest arrivals to put on the ledge beside the tub for her boss. She took it upstairs and when the tub was full turned off the water. She set the magazine on the ledge of the tub.

Since the day was hot and muggy, Marcella took a beige linen two piece suit out of the closet. She matched it with a pale green cotton shell and green pumps and handbag. She laid out everything from hose and underwear to gold jewelry in the dressing room section of the bathroom. Then she went down to the garden to cut fresh flowers for the sitting room.

Mary had turned on the stereo, and was listening to chamber music in her bath when Marcella returned with yellow and orange chrysanthemums. Arranging the flowers and listening to the music in the pleasant room, Marcella then changed the bed and dusted while Mary was in the bathroom.

After Mary left for her political meeting without speaking to her again, Marcella left the stereo on. Cleaning the rooms was so much easier and the house so much more pleasant then the long tedious days in the fields that Marcella sensed the rougher existence already fading. She laundered the sheets, Ms. Griswold's robe and nightgown, clothes from the wicker hamper, and cleaned meticulously.

At noon, she decided it was time for lunch and went downstairs to the kitchen. Since Griswold wasn't there for lunch, the kitchen workers were fooling around, talking and laughing, but Jenny's silence made her stand apart from the others.

"Hi Sylva, Hi Jenny," said Marcella, taking out rye bread.

"Hi," said Jenny, her eyes tired and lifeless.

"Hey," said Sylva, bright eyed and vivacious.

Marcella opened the refrigerator and looked for something typically American to put on the bread, and took out ham, Swiss cheese, and mustard.

"You want to heat that up and melt the cheese?" asked Sylva.

"Sure," said Marcella. Sylva put the sandwich on a plate and stuck it in the microwave. She turned it on for a minute, and left the sandwich in until the buzzer went off. Marcella got the sandwich out and set it on the table in the kitchen. She turned the burner on under the tea kettle, and looked for a teabag.

"Here," said Sylva, "What kind?" She pointed out a variety of tea in a row of canisters, and Marcella took a pekoe tea bag and put it in the cup. When the tea kettle whistled Marcella poured hot water over her tea bag and sat at the table with it.

Sylva got a bag of chips, poured them in a bowl, took a jar of salsa out of the pantry, and sat down with Marcella. "It's better here than up on a ladder, no matter what your job is, eh?" She dipped a chip in the salsa and ate it. Marcella ate some of the chips, too.

"Yes, but I miss my husband. He's in a vineyard. Do you have a husband or kids?"

"Yeah! The kids are all in school. Domino's working grapes, too. He only gets over about once every six weeks, and we go to town with the kids before we spend any time alone, but I love it here. I hate the fields."

"I have a daughter, thirteen."
"She's got to go to school, you know."
"Yeah, she loves school. Where do you live?"
"I live in a house with four more servants and all our kids. It's behind this house. There are trees all around it, so you can't see it. We all have our own room and a dormitory for all the kids. She's a pain in the ass!" She nodded toward Jenny. "She's so tired all the time it makes me tired to look at her."

"Not having anything to do would make me tired," said Marcella. "What do you do when Griswold's not here?"

"I bring stuff. I've always got stuff to do. I write letters and read. Also, I got a stash of crossword puzzle books. That's why I talk better than her." She glanced in Jenny's direction. "She mopes. I'm so glad to be out of the damned trees like a monkey, that I keep a watch all the time how to go a little farther."

"I agree with you. This is much much better," said Marcella. "I wish Mario could get a job like this."

"Is that your husband or boyfriend?"

"Husband."

"It's next to impossible especially for a man. They never look at the men for domestic, like us."

"Do you get paid what they said?" asked Marcella.

"Yes. It's a fortune next to what I was getting in the labor camp."

Marcella ate leisurely, dawdling over a second cup of tea and a dish of vanilla ice cream, chatting with Sylva. She then made sandwiches to take back to the garage and put them in a paper bag with two bananas, a bag of cashew nuts, and a dish of sliced roast beef, mashed garlic potatoes and fruit salad with sour cream. She left the bag in the refrigerator, wondering if she and Rita could eat all that, and returned to Griswold's quarters.

Pleasantly full, Marcella worked alone and unsupervised in the quiet, clean, cool and well-lit house, and when she could find nothing else to do, picked up the fiction magazine Ms. Griswold had been reading, and read it until two o'clock. After one last glance at the immaculate rooms, she went to the servant's dressing room, changed her clothes and left the uniform in the laundry basket. Returning to the kitchen, she then got the bag of food from the refrigerator. Nobody was in the kitchen.

Stopping in the foyer to take a news magazine, with the intention of learning enough about the culture to come and go on her judgment and volition, she then went to her cottage, and found Rita reading at the table.

"Good afternoon, Rita," said Marcella, setting the bag of food on the table and taking a seat in the other chair.

"Hi, Mom," replied Rita. Using a turkey feather for a bookmark, Rita closed the book and set it on the small table next to her bed. She opened the bag, and looked in. "Someday, I'm going to figure out why what you think makes things happen," said Rita, taking a sandwich.

"If you know what makes something happen, you'd do better making what you want happen instead of worrying about why. Some things can't be explained with why," said Marcella.

"As soon as I think something, why comes with it."

"That's good for things that work that way, but you must recognize the difference. If you know the law, you can make a nice place for yourself. That's a why. If you don't know the law or how to find out about it, you're a step away from a good life. That's where we are now. In this country, there's only one law for everyone. They must teach it in school. That's how everyone knows it."

"Mom, we can be just as American as anyone who was born here when we get citizenship. Everybody, even the Indians who were here first, came from somewhere else, just like us."

"Yes, Rita. Most came to get away from something they couldn't live with, like we did. Nobody leaves a place where they're happy and doing as good as they can. Everything's not just as it seems though."

"What's not?"

"Wherever people live, they're still people. People are good and bad everywhere. It would be wrong to think that because we live in a good country, everything will be good when we get citizenship."

"It'll be better, because we can do what we want."

"Certainly, that's why we came. You can go to school tomorrow. You must be at the Convenience Mart, where you bought the groceries, at eight o'clock."

"Good. I'll be happy to get out of here for awhile. How do you like your job?"

"It's much better than the fields. The housework is no real work because everything's clean already. I just have to keep Ms.

Griswold's private rooms that way. My boss is nice to me, or else she ignores me, and she's the only person I have to deal with, so it's easy."

"I better go to the Convenience Mart and get a notebook and pen," said Rita. "I don't know if it'll be open yet when I wait for the bus."

"Is there anything else you need?"

"I don't know what else until they tell me, and the school loans you the books they want you to have. Mom, you know what?"

"What?"

"I can't wait for morning!" Rita hugged Marcella.

While Rita went to the Convenience Mart, Marcella stretched out on the cot with her library book, leaning against her pillows, and started reading *One Flew over the Cuckoo's Nest.*

Rita got back from the store, and they chatted the afternoon away. "Leave your clothes from today in a bag by the hamper. I can wash them at work. I'll take them every day, and we'll always have clean. No more buckets behind the shelter."

"Wow, we don't even have to go to the Laundromat any more," said Rita. "I like to go to town."

"You can go whenever you want, but you don't have to wash clothes," said Marcella. She sighed, thinking of Mario washing his clothes in a bucket.

Warming up the roast beef and fancy mashed garlic potatoes for dinner in the microwave, Marcella thought about Mario eating tortillas and beans. After dinner she took a shower and got ready for bed. She read her book until she fell asleep. Rita stayed up until midnight devouring her chemistry library book.

For the first time in America, Marcella jumped up eagerly, happy to get up when the alarm went off. She was first in the shower. When she came out, she made coffee, her first American habit, and breakfast for her and Rita.

They sat down to eat, and Rita was ebullient about starting a new school. "I'll clean up the dishes, Mom," she said.

"Thanks," said Marcella. "It's about time to go. I'll be a few minutes early, but that's okay. I can put our clothes in the washing machine, and talk to some of the others if they get there early. Good luck with your school, Rita. I hope you like it."

"Good luck with your job, too," said Rita.

Rita's first day of school the school staff was giving IQ tests, and after going to the office to register and get her books and class assignments, she was hustled into a testing room. She took the tests with no understanding of what they were for. They lasted all day.

Before leaving for the day, she was given her class schedule, and the classes were similar to the ones at the last school, but in a different order; science, math, physical education, art instead of music, English, and social studies.

Rita hurried home to get in touch with where the rest of the class was in each subject, do her homework, and go back over some of the material she'd missed. She opened the refrigerator first and got out a root beer and leftovers.

"Somebody here left these sodas for us like a labor camp boss never would," she said to herself feeling deeply appreciative of her new life. "It must have been Gordon," she thought. Her comparative ease made her sympathize with her father still stuck in the life she'd left behind, and she wished he could be with them.

The homework was very easy, and she whizzed through it before Marcella got home radiant with their clean clothes neatly folded in a nylon tote bag Marcella had been allowed to scavenge from the mansion, and another canvas bag full of broiled lamb chops and Greek salad with feta cheese and black olives. They now had brioche, pate and an assortment of tasty leftovers and drinks in the refrigerator to snack on.

"How was your new school?" asked Marcella, putting the food away.

"It's huge and spotlessly clean. There's a nice library, but I didn't have time to go in it today because we had to take IQ tests."

"What's that?" asked Marcella.

Rita shrugged. "I asked the teacher giving the tests, and she said it's to measure intelligence."

"How do you do that?" asked Marcella.

"They ask some pretty weird questions. They don't let you know how you did. They hire someone else to score them later."

Rita and Marcella passed the afternoons like an American woman and her daughter. They walked to the town and all around it visiting the parks and public buildings. They browsed through the stores in town to see what was there, but they didn't buy anything. Marcella stopped to look at cell phones and ask how they worked. She thought when she got paid, if she really did make as much money as they said, she would buy one for her and Rita and another for Mario so he could call them. If they ever got separated again, they could at least talk to each other.

The first week of Marcella's new job passed quicker than a single morning in the orange trees, and Marcella and Rita accustomed themselves to the new life which was so much easier and more prosperous than the old, but Mario was continually on Marcella's mind.

Friday, Rita went to school as usual, but in home room, Mrs. Ruther, her homeroom teacher said, "I've scheduled you for an appointment with the guidance counselor, Rita. You're to go there instead of to your first class."

"Yes, Ma'am," said Rita, going cold with fear. Her thoughts ran wild. *Have they found me out? Will I be arrested? Will I ever see Mom and Dad again? Will I be deported immediately or have to wait in jail? Will they arrest Mom at Ms. Griswold's and Dad at the camp?*

Rita's mind churned through all the possible terrors awaiting her, and she went to the guidance counselor's office close to tears. She waited on a chair outside the door for ten minutes in agony. A

Latino boy shuffled out, his head hanging, and Rita looked around to see if there was a policeman waiting for him with handcuffs, but she saw only school personnel and a few student aides.

"Come in Rita," said the counselor. Taking a deep breath, Rita held her head high and went into the office, steeling herself for whatever was to come.

"Have a seat, please," said the counselor, pleasantly. Rita sat in the chair beside the woman's desk a little more at ease. The counselor was happy; maybe it was good news.

"Your test shows an extraordinary Intelligence Quotient," she said. "Are the courses you're taking too easy for you?"

"Yes," said Rita. "They're very easy, but I study harder things at home. What is my IQ?"

"I'm not going to tell you. Where do you get the books?" Realizing that she wasn't in trouble, and the meeting was because of her test scores, Rita relished the conversation, completely relaxing.

"At the public library."

"I want you to take some courses at the high school that aren't offered at the junior high. Would you like that?"

"Yes," said Rita, eagerly. "I want to take some science courses. I got a chemistry book from the library. I'd love to learn things like that. I want to be a doctor."

"Then we'll talk about math and science courses that lead you in that direction."

"Math and science are my favorites," said Rita.
"What science course do you want to take?"
"Just one?"
"For now. One science and one math."
"Chemistry and geometry."
"Chemistry requires quite a bit of algebra. Have you ever taken algebra?"
"Just what I'm taking this year."
"Suppose you take first level high school algebra first. It will be much more difficult than the course you're taking now. If you try

another science course after you get the background algebra to make chemistry more fun, you'll be ready for it. High school chemistry is probably a lot more difficult than the book you got from the library. Next year, you'll be well prepared to take chemistry and geometry.

"Can I take biology? I've been studying it already."

"Yes, that will be fine. "I'll enroll you in algebra and biology. You'll have study time apart from the rest of the class, because these courses are tougher, and a student tutor from the high school will be available to help you if you want."

"Thanks," said Rita. "When can I start?"

"Monday; someone from the high school will come for you and walk you over to your high school classes and walk back with you."

"Thanks!" said Rita, thrilled. After her new schedule was arranged, she went to her English class exuberant. She wished she could tell Julio he was wrong about the schools. She breezed through the school day walking on a cloud. After school, Rita ran home from the bus stop and burst into the garage. Marcella looked up from the magazine she was reading, set it aside, and stood up.

"Mom! I'm going to take two high school classes! Biology and algebra!" She grabbed Marcella into a bear hug, and Marcella held her close. "It's because I got high scores on the IQ tests."

"Good for you! Maybe you'll be the one to find the way out for all of us. You have a good brain, but it's not just that. You use it the right way. Let's go for a walk to town and talk about it."

"Okay," said Rita. Marcella took some money, and they went for a long walk discussing the unforeseen opportunity.

"What's marvelous to me is that this could happen to an illegal alien," said Marcella. "They must not check out the students to see if you're legal. Still, there's going to come a time to get a job, you'll have to have papers."

"You don't."

"They must know I'm an illegal, and they hire me anyway. Probably as much as I'm getting paid, it's not as much as they would have to pay someone with papers. Those are the people who own the houses we walk past going to town. They drive cars. We're closer then we were on the ladders in the orange groves, but not yet close enough."

Marcella bought some zinnia and petunia seeds, a spade, and a hoe in town at the hardware store. She then stopped at a book store to buy a calendar. They returned home, and Marcella dug a flower bed in front of the garage. As she turned the earth over with the spade, Rita broke up the chunks with the hoe. Marcella made rows with the hoe, and she and Rita planted the seeds.

"These are for your accomplishment, Rita," Marcella said. "These flowers will sprout and bloom, and every time we come in, we'll see them. They'll make us happy, and we'll remember what they're for. I'm very proud of you."

"Thanks; you, too, Dad."
"For what?"
"My brains."
Marcella laughed. "Aw, I don't know if he heard you."

"I doubt it, but I'll tell him again when I see him," said Rita, giggling.

Marcella knocked all the dirt off the spade and hoe, went behind the cottage, and put the tools in a shed. They went in and washed their hands. Rita filled a plastic watering can from the shed with water and watered the seeds.

Hanging the calendar over her bed, Marcella then marked off the days since she'd seen Mario. She'd mark another one off each day.

After they ate, Marcella took a hot shower because it made her relax before going to bed. She opened her book with a deep ambivalent sigh. Bursting with pride in her daughter, and happy for her opportunity, she wished Mario could share Rita's good fortune.

While Rita studied her science books from the library, Marcella read another chapter in her American novel. Before going to sleep, she was struck with the realization that systems exist that some people never escape no matter where they live, and that one person can show many others a chance they would never have seen that could change their lives. Determined to keep her hopes and ambitions high, she remained convinced that it was impossible for anyone to escape incarceration in a miserable system who didn't know she could in advance.

Establishing a habit of reading at bedtime, Marcella determined to learn everything she could about America. Reading might show her a way into the mainstream, and it was free.

Though the days stretched into weeks much faster at Ms. Griswold's than they had in the fields, Marcella missed Mario badly, and found herself thinking about him when she wasn't talking to one of the other employees or Ms. Griswold or Rita.

"When do you think we'll get to see Dad again?" asked Rita, as Marcella was marking the day on the calendar.

"Gordon said about six weeks. It should be pretty soon," said Marcella, getting cantaloupe, milk, cheese, beans and tortillas out for breakfast. "When he comes back, we'll get a telephone, and then he can call us, and we can call him."

"I'm always worried about him because we can't see him. At first when everything was new and different, I didn't worry so much. But now I think about him all the time, you know?"

"I know," said Marcella. "But we have to keep putting it out of mind. Mario's all right. If he had bad trouble, I'd feel it even though we're apart."

Rita sighed. "I don't know why you say such things," she said. "I don't understand that."

"Someday you'll get married, and you'll be as close to your husband as I am to Mario. Then you'll understand."

"Humph." said Rita, doubting. "I can't put something out of my mind so easy as you do."

"You must, Rita. If you're going to be a doctor, you have to separate your worries from your studies and not let your worries in.

They'll sap your strength that you need for your work, and they won't do Mario any good."

Marcella's job generally went smoothly for the first six weeks, though there'd been a few bungles when she'd feared for her job. Most errors could be covered, but not all. As a joke one morning, Sylva prepared her own breakfast on a tray with a cover like Ms. Griswold's. She was always pretending to be the lady of the house, making Marcella laugh. Even the sober Jenny couldn't help cracking a smile at her antics now and then.

Marcella, breezing into the kitchen that morning, snatched the covered tray, as Sylva was looking in the refrigerator for the orange juice, placed it on the cart, and sailed into the dining room with it. When Sylva got her nose out of the cooler, seeing Griswold's tray still hot by the stove and hers gone, she went tearing down the hall after Marcella, but it was too late. She stood outside the dining room door cringing, waiting for Marcella to uncover the beef burrito with jalapeno peppers and a side dish of guacamole and another of sour cream and a dish of strawberries with cream.

Marcella confidently placed the utensils in front of Ms. Griswold, who was sitting at her place in her pink satin robe and slippers. Marcella then whisked the cover off the tray, and both women stared at the breakfast, Marcella horrified, Ms. Griswold livid.

"If this is a joke, it isn't funny!" she snapped, glowering at Marcella.

"Oh no, I'm so sorry, a mix up, ma'am," said Marcella quickly replacing the lid.

"I don't understand this mix up," yelled Griswold angrily. "No one else gets breakfast served in this house. Are you girls playing games in the kitchen or what? I certainly expect you to take your job more seriously, or don't you value it? You'd rather be back in the orange groves perhaps? Or are you so high and mighty now that you have an inside job that you'd rather go out in the world on your own and see what you can scrape up?" Every time she asked a question, Marcella tried to stammer out an answer, but her boss continued, giving her no opening.

After a ten minute harangue, Ms Griswold stood up and said, "Get this mess out of here, and bring me my breakfast now. And this better never happen again." She wanted to say, you're fired, but Marcella was the best personal maid she'd had, and she was reluctant to go through the procedure of finding another one that might not last the day.

Sylva darted back to the kitchen, and Marcella came flying out of the dining room with the cart. In the kitchen, Sylva had prepared a new breakfast so Ms. Griswold would get it hot. Picking up the tray as Marcella came running in pushing the cart, she didn't have to say a word. Her expression told Marcella how sorry she was. Marcella rolled her eyes at Sylva and removed her breakfast tray as Sylva placed the right one on the cart. When Marcella left Ms. Griswold pacified with her breakfast, she returned to the kitchen with the cart.

"Sit down," ordered Marcella tersely, her face a storm of rage. Sylva sat with a dejected plop. Marcella carried the tray over to her, took the silverware and napkin off the tray and set them in front of her. She then removed the cover and placed Sylva's plate on the table in front of her, gave a little bow and smile, and said, "I hope this is satisfactory, ma'am."

"It'll do," said Sylva haughtily, and Jenny howled with laughter.

With only a few scoldings from Ms. Griswold, and no serious breaches of confidence, Marcella was paid the amount she'd been quoted, and she saved every nickel. There was nothing she or Rita needed in the way of clothes, household furnishings, and food or luxuries like magazines, lotions, and cosmetics that she couldn't obtain as a job perk.

When she was ready to go out one morning, Ms Griswold tossed Marcella a large cosmetic bag full of cosmetics, nail polishes, face creams, lotions, and perfume. Some of them had never been opened. "I'm tired of these," she said. "See if you can find some use for them."

"Yes ma'am," said Marcella.

"Find me something else. I've been in this God forsaken California sun long enough to turn as dark as...you," Ms. Griswold said, handing Marcella a catalogue.

"Yes ma'am," said Marcella. After Ms. Griswold left, Marcella spent an hour browsing through it, and choosing different shades and products than those in the throwaway package, and tacked the list on Belle's bulletin board. Ms. Griswold displayed the same cavalier attitude about clothing, shoes, and linens. Fortunes in designer accoutrement were accumulating in the closet in Marcella and Rita's cottage.

The night of Mary Griswold's big party, which Gordon had mentioned the day she was hired, rapidly approached, and Marcella knew she'd be working overtime.

CHAPTER TWELVE

After Marcella and Rita were left at Griswold's, Gordon dropped Mario off at the labor camp. "Workers will be picked up here at six thirty to go to the vineyards," he said. "If you want to work grapes, be here."

"Okay," said Mario.

Mario balled up his dirty clothes, walked to the road, and hitched a ride to town. He purchased beef jerky, crackers, dried fruit, canned fish, tortillas, beans, cheese, salsa, and soap.

In the store, he saw a campesino take a bottle of cheap wine and put it under his shirt. As he tried to walk out the door with it, the manager collared him. Glancing up at the camera in the corner, Mario thought he was stupid, or he wanted to be caught to get a shower and a few meals in jail. His clothes were dirty and raggedy, and he smelled bad and was ungodly skinny.

"What's your name?" the manager asked him, waiting for the police, as Mario checked out his groceries.

"Juan Boleno," the man replied.

Mario left the store before the police arrived. The last thing he needed was to be anywhere there was trouble. He went to the dirty little laundry across the street and washed and dried his clothes and backpack. His backpack full of clean clothes, and his duffel full of food, he then hitched back to the grove and walked to camp. He had plenty of time to think about how much he missed Marcella and Rita and was waiting with Laredo and the other men when the buses arrived, some already half full, to take them to the new camp.

Mario was shuffled into one bus and Laredo into another. While he recognized a few faces from his labor camp, Mario didn't know any of the men by name. He took a seat near the rear of the van, and a labor camp boss went down the center aisle asking each of the new men their names and writing them on a sheet of paper. He stopped in front of Mario. "What's your name?" he asked.

"Juan Boleno." The alias popped out unpremeditated, surprising even Mario.

"Yeah." The man wrote it on his paper and put a check beside it. He asked the man in the seat beside Mario, "What's your name?" When the labor camp boss had all their names and got off the bus, it chugged down the lane with a loud belch of exhaust. Mario waved out the window to Laredo, who was waiting in a long line to get on another bus, but Laredo didn't see him.

"Hey! What's your name?" one of the campesino's asked Mario. "I'm Sherbolt."

"Mar...Juan. My name's Juan." Realizing that one of the others might know Juan Boleno, Mario then kept his mouth shut.

When they arrived at the camp, Mario was assigned to a barracks exactly like three others in a cluster. The long, narrow, stick frame structure with peeling paint was barely wide enough for two rows of cots with an aisle down the center. Four showers at one end of the long shed had drains in the floor beneath them and four toilets opposite.

When all the men were in the barracks, it was so hot and stinking that Mario couldn't stand to be in it. Leaving his backpack and duffel on his cot, he went outside looking for Laredo or someone he knew from another camp, but all the men were strangers.

The camp was surrounded by a variety of trees, and there were buckets, water spigots, bars of heavy duty soap, and hoses behind each barracks.

The men were herded into a chow hall for the evening mess, but Mario didn't feel like eating. He missed Marcella and Rita and felt out of sorts. Uncharacteristically crabby and angry, he'd seen no friendly face he wanted to talk to. When the men returned from chow, Mario took his backpack outside, and slunk away from the camp into the trees. Using his backpack for a pillow, Mario thought about the previous labor camps he'd lived in, and how the presence of his wife and daughter had made them tolerable. Memories of the friends he'd liked enough to last a lifetime loomed over him, and the speed with which they'd disappeared made him sick. He thought about this life in the great country until darkness fell, and looking at the stars in the silence of the night, the noise of the men in the barracks dim, he thought about Marcella until sleep overtook him.

Waking when the men trooped out for breakfast, he didn't go to the mess hall. He sat on a concrete block behind the barracks and opened a can of beans. He put his plastic plate on his legs and laid two tortillas on it. After emptying the can of beans onto the tortillas, he chopped a few slices from an onion and part of a jalapeno pepper into the beans. He added a slice of cheese and spoon of salsa to each one and ate his cold burritos. After showering in the empty barracks, he joined the other workers to wait for the trucks to the groves.

The labor boss came out of his little brick bungalow by the stop. "You'll be working for six weeks straight until we've got the soil prepared," he said. "You must show up here every morning for six weeks."

"I can't work on Sunday," said Mario.

"I heard it before. You got to go to church?" asked the boss.

A loud guffaw went up from the crowd of workers.

"I told my wife and daughter I'd come Sunday," said Mario.

"Then don't come back," said the boss. "More questions?" No one asked anything, and the heat seemed suddenly more oppressive. Mario got out his bandana and wiped the sweat off his face and neck. Two large trucks with rails around the beds pulled up, and the men were loaded like cattle and taken to the vineyards.

"What's your name?" Mario asked a burly giant beside him.

"Jose," said the man. He grinned at Mario but didn't ask his name.

"I'm Juan," said Mario, extending his hand, but Jose just stared at him grinning. Mario stuck his hand in his pocket. "Been working grapes long?" he asked.

Jose shrugged. "Yuh, gesso."

Mario thought Jose was uncommunicative because he had a speech impediment. The man was enshrouded in lonely isolation, and Mario felt sorry for him. When they got to the field, the trucks stopped, everyone jumped down, and they went to work.

Cultivating grapes was just as monotonous as picking oranges and Mario's back ached all the time. The days faded more slowly into weeks because he missed Marcella and Rita. The first week seemed like a lifetime, and the second stretched into eternity.

He had to eat in the mess hall sometimes, so he wouldn't run out of food before he could get to a town, and he begrudged the food bills. After Mario's food and shelter expenses were deducted, he made forty dollars each week. He was very surprised. Gordon had told him the truth. .

On Saturday, after Mario had been in the camp for six weeks, he saw Jose standing alone as usual. He'd noticed that Jose never lined up with the other men to get his paycheck. Overwhelmed with loneliness himself, he went over to Jose.

"How come you don't get paid after working all week?" Mario asked him.

"Owes ta mooch."

"What for? How much can a man owe to work all that time and get nothing?"

"Ya see." Jose laughed, making, a whuh whuh whuh sound.

"Don't you want to save some money and get out of here?"

"Wer' sh'ud go?" Jose shrugged his broad bear shoulders morosely. He had a nervous tic in his cheek and wore a gray pallor. Every so often his head jerked involuntarily, and his speech slurred, making him sound slightly drunk.

"Are you sick?" asked Mario.

"A liddle." Jose seemed unconcerned.

"What's the matter?"

"Wu'k g'apes ta mooch." Chuckling idiotically, he pointed to his head. "He'd allus hu'ts."

Seeing Mario talking to Jose, the labor boss barged out of his bungalow twenty yards from the barracks, and called Mario aside. He had a pistol stuck in his belt that Mario had never seen there before, and a warning shiver went up his spine.

"How come you don't buy soap and rent towels?" the labor boss asked belligerently.

"I brought my own." Mario's shoulders sagged, and his voice was as humble and whiney as he could make it.

"You don't like our beans and tortillas?" The man with massive arms and a large tattoo of a woman on his bulging biceps pulled the pistol out of his belt, examining it as he talked to Mario. His shirt, stuck to his body with sweat, was permanently stained under the arms. He wiped the perspiration from his face and neck with a red bandana and rubbed the barrel of the gun with the sweaty cloth.

"I can't eat much," whined Mario. "I work too much grapes. I take crackers and cheese everywhere." Shrugging, he tilted his head to one side. "It's special kind. When I eat too much other food, I puke. I got ulcers."

"You're not a trouble maker, are you?" asked the boss, looking down the barrel of the gun. He cocked it.

"I hate trouble," whimpered Mario.

"Good." The boss fired the gun into the ground once. "We don't tolerate trouble makers." Spitting in the dust, he then turned and sauntered to the house.

The camp without women and children felt like a jail cell without bars. When the others went to the mess hall, Mario remained in the bunk house. Thinking about Marcella, he filled his plastic glass with water, looked over his remaining stash of sustenance, and took two slabs of beef jerky and a pack of cheese crackers. Munching on the jerky, he then drained the glass, sat on his bed, and stretched out on his back.

He heard the men laughing and talking excitedly outside as they came from the chow building. Mario jumped out of the sack and went to see what was going on. Strangely happy, the men carried bottles of cheap wine. A full bottle in one hand, Jose guzzled from an open bottle in the other, wine dribbling down his chin, staining his shirt. An old, rusty truck with bald tires rattled down the drive, sending up billows of dust, sputtering and rattling. It stopped at the barracks.

Six young Hispanic girls in the bed of the pickup looked about Rita's age. Two could have been a little older, eighteen at the most. The driver got out and put the tailgate down, and the girls started to get out of the truck. Jose lumbered clumsily to the tailgate laughing. Grabbing one of the girls around the waist, he tried to pull her down. Screaming, she kicked him hard in the face until he let go, and the other girls, also screaming, climbed down from the truck on all sides, as the campesinos surrounded it. Mario realized the girls didn't know why they'd been brought there. Rita flashed through Mario's mind before the world turned red.

"Stop that!" he shrieked. Jose turned around in surprise; and charging to the tailgate, Mario punched him in the jaw. Holding his head, Jose staggered backwards and fell to the ground.

"Oooh," he moaned. Shaking his head and groaning, on his hands and knees, he couldn't get up. He collapsed in the dirt, and Mario leaped on him, but before he could start punching, two others pulled Mario off. Jerking himself loose, Mario turned and punched one of them in the stomach.

The girls fled across the fields as the campesinos fought, some trying to chase the escaping girls, the others stopping them from pursuing the girls.

The labor boss and two other men galumphed from the house, and Mario started running.

"Halt!" yelled the labor boss; and as Mario disappeared into the shadows of falling twilight, gunfire sounded around him. Feeling the volley whizzing around his head, hearing the whistle of the bullets, he first made it to the cover of trees and then dived, hugging the ground. When the shots changed direction, he got up and started running again. Running. Running away from gunfire from the time he was a small boy, running away through the desert with his wife and child, and now running, running with bullets still whizzing around his head.

"What did we walk across the continent for, for this?" he asked himself. The expressions on the faces of the children in the back of the truck, Jose's ham-like hands grabbing at the one who most reminded him of Rita, the leers on the faces of the others until he started the fight replayed in his mind.

Mario ran until he saw automobile lights along a road, but he stayed out of their range in the sheltering shadows of trees. By the time he found his way to the outskirts of town, it was late. The house where Marcella worked was easy to see from miles away because it was white, enormous, well-lit, and high on the hill. Music and activity came from it with many people coming and going. A uniformed servant brought cars from a parking lot to guests who were leaving. Some of the women wore long gowns, and the men wore suits.

Mario ran to the cottage, and tapped on the door, his lungs bursting from running so fast so far.

"Marcella! Marcella! It's me, Mario! Open the door," he gasped.

"Dad?" The door opened a crack, and Rita peeked out sleepily not sure she wasn't dreaming. When she saw Mario her eyes widened in astonishment. "Dad!"

Mario ran in, and closed the door softly behind him. "Where's Marcella, Rita?" he asked, still struggling to get his breath, his eyes wild.

"Mom had to work late. They're having a big party, and she has to help with it."

Desperately, Mario tried to collect his thoughts. He'd worked up a sweat running, but he felt strangely cool and detached. His eyes darted from one corner to the other, and he kept wiping his hands on his jeans.

"Dad?" Rita's small oval face was troubled. She knew something was wrong and the incessant fear of being found out that lived like a ghost haunting the back of her brain crept into her expression.

Mario looked out the back window. "What?" he asked.

"What are you doing here? What's wrong?"

"Trouble." He looked in the bathroom for another window, and finding none looked at the mansion out the only back window again.

"Bad?"

Mario paced the room, wiping the sweat off his face with his bandana, his mind churning through the fight. "Pretty bad; I can't go back. I knocked a man out. They shot at me."

"Where'll we go?"
"I don't know yet."
"Why did you hit him?"
"They brought some girls to the camp, about your age. Jose tried to grab one off the truck, and I hit him."

"Did she get away?"

"Yeah. They all got away, but I started a big fight."

"I'm glad." She hugged him, and he held her close, not wanting to let her go, a fear for her that he'd never considered clouding his mind. He let go of Rita and sat on Marcella's cot, trying to think.

"Will it be alright?" asked Rita, striving to stave off the unmentioned fear that had been nagging at her since they crossed the border that if they ran into trouble they'd have no authority to go to for help.

Looking at Rita's worried, trusting face Mario had never lied to her and couldn't bring himself to. Though he longed to relieve her anxiety, the day would come when she'd see through his lie, and what would she do then? What would he when she didn't trust him anymore?

"I don't know Rita. I just don't know. Let me think."

Marcella had been taking wraps all evening. Waiting in the foyer smiling, her feet and legs were tired from standing for a long time without a break. She felt like the smile on her face was only a picture as she greeted all the guests. If they had wraps, she helped remove them, listening to their conversations and turning them over to another servant to usher into the ballroom.

"It's harder every day to find decent servants, Senator," complained a pretty young brunette with large brown eyes to a much older man, as they entered the foyer. His brown curly hair was incongruous with his elderly, gray wrinkled face.

"I know, I know why we're so late, Natalie. We're lucky to be here at all, but let's don't bore our hostess with the sorry details." Marcella helped him out of his coat, thinking he must have come from a colder climate.

"Has the weather been fine in California?" asked the Senator, smoothing the hair on the side of his head.

Marcella wondered how much they paid servants. The young woman turned and looked her in the eye as Marcella waited for her shawl.

"Senator Bold!" called Kate, approaching the Senator and his aide. "I didn't know you were in town! What brings you to California?"

"Business and pleasure, my dear," said Senator Bold, posing for her to take his picture. Kate obliged.

"I'll take my own stole to the coatroom, I've some freshening up to do," said the young woman, and followed Marcella, who carried Senator Bold's coat. When they were out of earshot she caught up with Marcella and said, "I'm Natalie Clement. I'm Senator Bold's assistant. What's your name?"

"Marcella Dominguez."

"How long have you been here?" Natalie asked when they were alone in the coatroom.

"Six weeks." Marcella was surprised that the woman took an interest in her, and was immediately on the alert for her motives.

"Do you like working here?"
"Yes. It's much better than the fields."
Clement handed Marcella her wrap, and proceeded to the party on her own. Later, Marcella caught her staring at her. Clement whispered to Senator Bold behind her hand, and he stared, too.

Marcella rushed into and out of the coatroom with wraps all evening. When no one was coming or going, she stood by the front door waiting for someone to come or go. As Natalie Clement and

Mary Griswold passed near the foyer, Marcella heard a snatch of conversation.

"You never seem to have problems with your fine domestic staff," commented Natalie Clement.

"Nonsense! They take off the first chance they get, but they're innocent of the system and eager to make money. Illegal aliens will do whatever they're told. They're frightened and easy to intimidate because of the political nature of their survival." She pushed a pearl on her belt, and Gordon appeared at her elbow. She handed him her empty martini glass, and he left to refill it for the fourth time as the two women drifted out of earshot.

A little later while Marcella was waiting at the door wishing she could get off her feet for a few moments, Natalie Clement appeared in the foyer alone. "I must speak to you," she said softly and sailed into the coat room, Marcella following.

"How much do you make here?" Natalie asked in a low voice.

"Eighty dollars a week," said Marcella, matching the quiet of her voice.

"How would you like to make three hundred?"

Marcella thought she misunderstood. "Three hundred?" she asked, blankly.

"That's what I said."

"Close to here?"

"No, far away."

"I have a husband and a daughter, thirteen-years-old."

"You'll bring your daughter. She'll go to school. What does your husband do?"

"He's working grapes, but he knows all about cars. He can fix any kind of engine," said Marcella eagerly.

"We need mechanics. We'd start him at three hundred, also."

"I stay in the cottage," said Marcella. "I don't have a way to get in touch with Mario. I have to wait 'til he gets the day off and comes to see us."

Clement opened her bag and unzipped an inside pocket. She drew out her business card and snapped the bag shut. "Here's my number," said Clement, handing Marcella her card. "I'm a friend of Senator Bold's. Call me collect as soon as you know when the three of you can leave."

"Thanks," said Marcella, awed. She slipped the card into the pocket of her uniform under her apron and followed Ms. Clement out to the foyer, watching as she sailed into the crowd and stood with Senator Bold.

Spotting Kate monopolizing Morgan Bold, Mary pressed the pearl on her belt to call Gordon. "Who let that newswoman with the camera in?" she asked. "I didn't invite the media."

"I don't know. I didn't see her come in."

"Get rid of her at once!"

"Yes, Ma'am." Gordon went to the foyer. "Get the reporter's wrap. Griswold's orders," he whispered to Marcella.

Marcella caught Ms. Griswold's eye watching her. Her boss nodded yes to her, so Marcella went through her guest log to find the number on Kate's jacket, retrieved the wrap while Gordon waited, and handed it to him. She recalled Kate asking questions and taking pictures at the labor camp where Enrico died.

Gordon took the jacket to Kate and draped it over her shoulders, smiling. She frowned at him, and taking her elbow, he started walking her to the door. "Sorry you have to leave so soon," he said. Kate jerked her arm loose and was shown out.

The party wore on into early morning, and guests began to leave in a steady stream. Morgan waited impatiently until they were all gone to have Mary alone for a chat. Marcella listened from the front foyer, her feet and legs aching fiercely.

"You have to quit importing illegal aliens, Mary," said Morgan. "You can't imagine the flak I'm catching over this. Hire citizens and pay them minimum wage at least."

"You don't understand, Darling. I can't afford it. I've lost millions of dollars already. You should live here for a week, and you'd realize the impossibility of what you're suggesting. They're dirty, lazy animals and don't know the first thing about caring for themselves. They stink, lie, steal, and break everything. They disappear, like rats down a sewer, the first chance they get. That's to give you some indication of the magnitude of the problem. Americans won't do field work at any price."

"I'm sure you have your esoteric problems peculiar to your industry," said Morgan. "I'm not going to try to tell you how to run your business, but I'm having difficulty with my colleagues over illegal immigration."

"Darling, don't whine to me about your problems. We all have our crosses to bear," said Mary, crossly, her voice shrill. "Would you like a reminder of how much money I've put into your campaign? Adding what my friends in New York and abroad have done for you, your election wouldn't have been possible without my help."

Morgan shifted his weight uncomfortably to his other foot. "There are other constituents I owe. You know how politics works. I've done everything I can, and the flood from the south is drawing the attention of the whole world."

"You owe me your job." Mary laughed loudly.

"Don't go getting so crabby, Mary. We've been friends for such a long time."

"You've been friends with my purse for such a long time."

"I've got to be going," he snapped, turning red in the face. "I'll call you later when you haven't been drinking." He turned to go, but stopped when she said, "Change those damned marketing orders so I can get a fair price for my crops to at least break even, and we're in business."

Morgan turned to her with a long suffering sigh and sipped his drink. "That's out of my range, Mary. I'm not on any of the agricultural committees. I'm not even from California much less the San Joaquin Valley."

"Neither am I, Darling! I'm a New Yorker. I'm not taking a rest cure in this picturesque little hamlet!"

"Why don't you go back to New York and hire a manager to run the California show like everybody else?"

"Because I'm losing millions of dollars a year on those damn oranges!" she yelled. "I've got lawsuits going here. I need relief." She pressed the pearl on her belt to summon Gordon, and he appeared at her elbow with a martini.

"Is that a double? These taste like water." She handed him her empty glass and took the fresh drink.

"Yes, Ma'am, it's a double."

"Are other guests still milling around?" she asked.

"Natalie Clement's here waiting for Senator Bold. Everyone else has left."

Mary took a sip of the drink. "Take this and put some gin in it," she said crossly, handing the glass back to Gordon.

"Yes Ma'am," he said, retreating with the glass. He returned momentarily with another and handed it to her.

With the large room nearly empty, Griswold's loud, drunken voice resounded. "Get Marcella," she said. Marcella heard her and hurried in to see what she wanted.

"You can go now," Mary ordered. "Don't come tomorrow."

"Yes Ma'am," said Marcella, pondering what she'd overheard. After she left, the conversation resumed on a different note.

"You're drinking more these days, Mary," observed Senator Bold.

"Oh shut up, Morgan. You can be so goddamn condescending. I'm not through with you. Please wait upstairs for me, Darling."

"But...Natalie's waiting."

"Gordon!" called Mary. Gordon appeared immediately. "Send Natalie Clement home. Come right back." She laughed loudly as Gordon went out, but there was no pleasure in it.

"Do I have to tell you everything?" she asked, turning to the Senator. "You do remember where my bedroom is? Perhaps I can have a map printed up for you next time."

"I've got a meeting early in the morning," protested Bold, a whine in his voice as he glanced pointedly at his watch.

"No excuses. I'll have my driver take you wherever you want to go in the morning."

Morgan shuffled up the stairs, and with him out of the way, Mary turned back to Gordon, who'd just returned. "Gordie!" she barked, "Call your coyote, and get me six dozen IAs at once. And relocate the labor camps again."

"Yes Ma'am," said Gordon, watching Mary Griswold stumble up the stairs after Morgan.

It was nearly dawn when Marcella trudged back to the cottage on aching feet and legs, tired from working twenty hours with too few short breaks. Dropping heavily onto the cot in the dark and landing on a body, Marcella leaped up with a yell of surprise.

"It's me, it's me," said Mario, sitting up, startled out of his exhausted doze.

"Mario!" she said, joyfully. They embraced fervently their ardor rising and impossible to contain.

Rita turned over on the cot, her back to them; a lump under her blanket, and Mario took Marcella's hand and they went into the bathroom and made love as silently as possible. Marcella realized something was drastically wrong. When they came up for air, Marcella whispered, "Mario, what are you doing here?"

"We got trouble. We have to go tonight when it gets dark," he said, and went out and sat on Marcella's cot, his feet on the floor.

"Why?" She braced herself, and Mario told her what happened at the labor camp.

"God is with us," murmured Marcella. She kissed Mario on the lips.

Rita sat up, and leaned against the wall on her pillow, listening.

"I don't know why you say that, Marcella! The police will be with us if they find me."

"I talked to a lady tonight; Ms. Clement. She can get us both jobs, me in the house and you working on cars! They pay us each three hundred dollars a week! She was at the party Ms. Griswold doesn't know."

"They pay six hundred dollars for both of us?" Mario's jaw dropped in amazement. "Do you believe it?"

"Yes. I heard Ms. Griswold talking when she was drunk at the party. And when I started working for Ms. Griswold I heard many people she hires get away. Belle said they get other jobs."

"When can we go?"

"Right away; I have to call Ms. Clement. She gave me her card."

"The Virgin of Guadeloupe is with us," whispered Mario.

"Where are we going?" asked Rita. "Can I still go to my same school?"

"No. It's far away, but you won't have to pick any more crops. You'll only go to school and study and have an American life like other girls," said Marcella.

"What time do you have to be at work?" Mario asked.

"I don't go. I have to get some sleep."

"I'll make breakfast," said Rita.

"Just for you," said Mario. "I have to sleep, too."

Rita got up and took her clothes into the bathroom to shower and dress.

Mario flopped down on Rita's cot and was soon sleeping deeply as Marcella fell asleep on her cot.

Mario woke at noon and woke Marcella. As soon as she opened her eyes and saw Mario, she realized the importance of this day. She threw back the top sheet, leaped out of bed, and kissed and embraced Mario and kissed Rita. She was brimming with a joy and anticipation she'd never known.

Rita was sitting at the table, her notes spread out beside her, her algebra book opened in front of her, a turkey feather bookmark stuck in the back. Sipping a cup of perked coffee, she'd been working out a tough homework problem.

"I'll go to town and call Ms. Clement," said Marcella, gathering the clothes she wanted to wear. "Rita, you can come. We have to take the library books back."

"All right," said Rita, returning to her problem while waiting for Marcella to get dressed. She sipped her coffee, and when she looked at the problem again, the answer that had been so elusive before the distraction jumped out at her.

"Marcella, buy a newspaper, okay?" asked Mario, as Marcella took her clothes into the bathroom, and he followed her, closing the door behind him.

"Okay," said Marcella.

When Marcella was ready to go, she and Rita walked to town with the library books. They stopped at a phone booth, and Marcella went in to make her phone call. She rang, and someone said, "Hello?"

"Hello, is Ms. Clement there?"

"One moment, please. Who is calling?"

"Marcella Dominguez."

Marcella had a brief wait, and Ms. Clement picked up the phone. "Hello, Marcella. This is Ms. Clement," she said.

"Hello, Ms. Clement. I talked to my husband. We can take the jobs."

"Good. Meet me tonight at nine sharp at Flowers Cafe. It's at the Fountain Shopping Plaza. Do you know where that is?"

"Yes."

"Be ready to leave from there. You won't be going back to Ms. Griswold's."

"Okay, we'll be there at nine o'clock. Goodbye."

"Goodbye."

Marcella hung up unable to contain her excitement, and they continued to the library. "Rita, we're to meet Ms. Clement tonight about new jobs! We're going to be rich. Soon we'll be able to buy a house of our own!"

"Sure, Mom." Looking at the sidewalk, Rita kicked a stone as hard as she could.

"Aren't you happy? You'll have your own room, and we'll have a house with a garden. It's lots and lots of money, Rita, like everybody else in America!"

"That means another school," sighed Rita, angrily. "It's hard to go to a new school. Everybody already has friends. Every school is different. Some teachers hate farm workers. Some of the kids don't like me because I'm Latino. The stupid ones don't like me because I always know the answers. Sometimes I don't raise my hand because they're really mean. That's why I study, study, study, study. Every time I start to fit myself in, we have to move again. Every time, it's like moving to another world. Mom, what if they catch Dad?"

"We hope and pray, like always, eh? It's kept us safe so far. We have a lucky star. We have to believe in making it. We're not like people with money, who can pay their way out, or people with so many contacts, they can fake their way out. We can only believe that Mario will make it, that you and I will make it, because we have nothing else - only our belief. Don't you see, Rita? That's the thing that's paving our way."

"I believe," said Rita, her old determination renewed.

"There's a good side, Rita," said Marcella, as they walked. "We're going to be working for a United States senator. Maybe none of us will ever have to work crops again. Sometimes the greatest good fortune comes in a miserable disguise. If Mario wasn't in danger, he wouldn't be here now. Maybe Ms. Clement would've found someone else."

"Yeah, but here I'm considered brilliant. They do anything to help me. It's the best feeling in the world. I'm learning fast. I love this school. Now the other ones seem almost as boring as picking oranges. There's nothing to make you think. I know we have to go, but I don't have to want to."

"Rita, remember when we were on the desert, we thought we couldn't stand the sun another minute, and you got mad? You wanted to go back."

"I remember. I don't want to. I'm ashamed of the way I acted."

"We're still in forward motion. We can't rest yet. We're desperados, Rita. Until we find a way to be legal, we could be caught and deported at any time."

"I know. I didn't forget. I just wish it wasn't so."

"So do I, but wishing isn't enough. As long as we're alive, we have this chance to make our lives the best we can, and we owe it to ourselves to do that. Someone on this very ground we walk right now, who's long dead, did that, or this free country wouldn't be here for us to find a way into it."

"I believe that. I'm not here in this time and place for nothing. No one is."

"Did you hear what Mario told me last night?"

Rita nodded. "He told me, too."

"That could be you, Rita. Someone could offer you a job cleaning a house or working in a store for six or seven dollars an hour, and you could fall for it. If you got away, where would you go? If you went to the authorities or tried to get help, you'd be deported. We're in great danger until we're legal, or until other people believe, without question, that we are."

Rita sighed with the weight of centuries on her shoulders. "Dad, too; the police could catch him. It's a risky business we're in. Of course, I know we have to go. Of course, I know you can't go back. But I just wish we could stay somewhere!"

"Some day we will, Rita. Some day we will."

"Some day I will. I have to. When do we have to go?"

"We're going to talk to Ms. Clement tonight at nine o'clock. Mario and me will find out about our new jobs, and we'll ask about your school." Rita sighed with resignation.

They arrived at the library and returned the books. On the way back, Marcella bought a newspaper. Leafing through it, a drawing of Mario popped out of the back page at her. It looked just like him. Rita saw it, too. They exchanged guilty glances, and Marcella quickly folded the paper and tucked it under her arm. She and Rita walked as fast as they could without running to the cottage.

CHAPTER THIRTEEN

When Rita and Marcella returned to the cottage, Rita noticed the green sprouts of the flowers they'd planted poking through the earth. "Look Mom," she said, pointing at them.

"They'll keep growing, and we'll plant more when we get to where we're going. Soon it will be at our own house and not in front of a rich lady's garage," said Marcella, going inside. Mario was eating. Marcella showed him the article, and he gulped down his mouthful and read it out loud.

*A migrant worker attacked and killed another campesino in a fight at a labor camp last night. Juan Boleno is dangerous and may be insane. He killed Jose Encer with his bare hands in a sudden unprovoked attack. Boleno is wanted for questioning. Anyone who knows his whereabouts is asked to call the police."*

"Dios, Dios! I didn't give my right name!" said Mario. "What made me do that? The first time I didn't give my right name!" He jumped up from the table and threw the paper on the cot.

"Mario, we may use different names often," said Marcella, her eyes bright. "Sometimes we get caught up in the work and forget. We meet people and we forget. Rita studies and she forgets. I talk to Ms. Clement and I forget. We're fugitives, Mario. We must never, never forget. We must wear it in our hearts and make it a badge stamped in our brains."

"No, Marcella. We're people, whatever else we are, and we'll always be who we are. We'll live as good as we can, but we'll always be who we are."

"We're fugitives, Dad. We have no rights that can't be foreclosed if we're caught. Other people don't have to live like that. Someday, they'll open the borders, and there'll be no more fugitives, but today we're fugitives."

"Why do you say they'll open the borders, Rita?" asked Mario.

"Because I do nothing but read and study all the time, and I learn. The air is polluted with deadly chemicals, and they don't know if they came from one plant or another. They go where the wind takes them.

"The Love Canal contained poison that seeped into the water, and it flows beneath the ground to Pennsylvania and Ohio. It won't stay in New York. A bird carries a pesticide-laden seed from Alberta into Montana, and it grows a poison plant. Ideas, religions, theories, diseases, time, geography, everything ignores all borders. They're artificially created for defense and because there's money to be made.

"Only one time, I went to a football game because it was a special occasion, and we got out of class. My school played another school, and everybody went into a frenzy for our team to win. The kids in the bleachers were drugged on emotion. I could feel it penetrate my heart and mind, until I wished with all my heart that our team would win. I was us and they were them. But when the game was over, and I walked away, I couldn't tell who cheered for which team. Even the uniforms were the same; it was only the colors that were different. There was nothing between the winners and the losers but an imaginary line down a city street."

"Who won the game?" asked Mario.

"We did. I'm in special classes at this school for the brainy, Dad. It's very interesting. I was taking high school algebra and biology. I never got to do anything like that in my other schools."

Mario's eyes lit up, and he hugged Rita. "I'm so proud of you," he said. "You're learning so much so fast, faster even then the kids your age who were born here. That's the difference in you and Julio. Even if he was as smart as you, he could never get a chance like that because his mind doesn't think like that."

"There's a great difference between a free country and one ruled by dictators," said Marcella, who had been listening intently. "That's why there are borders. The dictatorship destroys everyone who disagrees, and the free country allows you to become what you can. It builds and creates."

"I meant underneath the governments of nations," said Rita. Marcella gave her a curious look. "Nature knows no government. It's ruled by another kind of law."

"Yes," said Marcella. "The law of the jungle. We conform to that law, but we, also, change it with a higher law."

"Only by the way we govern ourselves," insisted Rita. "Let me see you change the tide by making a law."

"That's what I just told you," replied Marcella. "In a free country nature is the only dictator, never a human being."

Mario came out of the bathroom, mugging at them, his face partly covered with shaving cream and his mustache half gone. Marcella roared with laughter and Rita lost control, looking at Marcella holding her sides, tears streaming down her face, rocking herself on the cot, or Mario, the corners of his eyes pulled down to the corners of his mouth, cross-eyed, his head turned pathetically to one side on a twisted neck.

Rita let her anger, hurt, and dismay out in a loud roar of wild laughter. Screaming with hilarity, she felt relief from the anguish that had been piling up inside. Distress of having to move at any moment; in the middle of a lesson she'd struggled to comprehend with a teacher who understood her plight, or a longed for friendship so close to bloom she could smell the flower, had been hanging over every word she spoke, every theory she learned, every equation she mastered. She'd move again and again and again. She'd have preferred to scream her rage, but it wasn't an option, so she was grateful for the alternative.

Mario returned to the bathroom and came out without his mustache, and Marcella and Rita recovered their sobriety.

"You look naked," said Marcella.

Mario rubbed under his nose and made a face. "I feel naked," he said.

"I have four hundred and sixty-five dollars in my money belt," said Mario. "How much do you have, Marcella?"

Marcella and Rita gathered all their money from their money belts and pockets, and Marcella put hers on the cot. She counted out eight hundred and twelve dollars, folded forty, and stuck it into her inside jeans pocket.

"I've got a hundred and five," said Rita.

"Here," said Marcella, handing her fifty. Mario gave her fifty more. Rita put all the big bills into her money belt, and kept two twenties in her pocket.

"Are you sure we can get these jobs, Marcella?" asked Mario.

"I'm sure that's what Ms. Clement said. I'm not sure it's true." Marcella frowned. "I have a feeling like something's wrong about it. It seems too good to be true; but this country has so many good things and so many rich people, maybe nothing's too good to be true."

"True or not, we have to go now," said Mario. "I want us all to have nice new clothes, Marcella. I want us to look nice, you know, American."

"We have enough money to buy all new outfits," said Marcella. "You too, Rita. You look fine in your school clothes, but you must choose and buy an outfit for yourself."

"Yes, I agree," said Rita, excited at the opportunity.

"Do I look like this picture?" Mario held up the newspaper sketch next to his face.

Marcella laughed, shaking her head no. She made a mean, nasty face at Mario. The drawing had a fierce and desperate expression, and the mustache made Mario look older and macho.

"No, Dad," said Rita, "especially when you smile."

Mario pasted an exaggerated grin on his face, making Marcella and Rita laugh again.

"You look very, very young," said Marcella, "like Rita's older brother." She'd never seen Mario without his mustache.

Each one carefully sorted out what to take and packed their backpacks, not like Enrico's or Julio's parents, but leisurely. Shouldering their backpacks, Marcella, Rita, and Mario left the garage behind. They walked to the mall, and Marcella stopped at the fountain in the center of it. "This is a good meeting place," she said. "I'm going to buy my outfit, and I'll meet you both here." They said good-bye and separated to purchase their American clothes.

Rita went into a boutique specializing in junior fashions. She bought a swirling orange cotton full skirt, and peasant blouse on sale. In a discount shoe store she found a pair of beige slippers with low heels and a bag to match that set off the outfit nicely and found a beige wallet for two dollars. After taking all the tags off in the restroom, she changed clothes, put her old ones in the bag, and transferred a twenty from her money belt to her purse.

Popping into a fast food restaurant on her way to the rendezvous point, she then went to the order counter. "I'll have a small pizza with pepperoni and a root beer to go," she said.

"It'll be ready in ten minutes," said the clerk. He looked at her lasciviously, and she ignored it, not permitting the insult to gain ground. "I need all my resources for things that count," she said to herself.

When the pizza was ready, she took it to the fountain and sat on the edge of it to wait for Marcella and Mario. Rita was eating lunch when Mario showed up in casual cotton slacks and a polo shirt.

"Hey, you look more beautiful than any other American teenager," said Mario, grinning. "How do you like my new self?" He modeled his outfit, turning to one side and then the other with his nose in the air and a different expression for each swivel, making Rita laugh.

"It's the same old self," she said. "Just the wrapping is new."

Sitting next to Rita, he helped himself to a piece of pizza. "I know you really liked your school. You were doing well, and you'll do well again."

"I know, Dad. I just hate moving so much, you don't know."

"Yes, I do. When I was your age, I lived in four different countries. My life's been like this from the time I was born. Running away from the war. Running away from the labor camp. Running away from your garage cottage. I want to stop. I want to never have to run again. I want to never move a single step except by choice, because there's some place I have to go, not someplace I'm driven from."

"Dad, I'm not going to be like you. When I'm grown up, I'm going to stop running, no matter what they do to me or to you. I'm going to break this chain, even if they kill me."

"You scare me when you talk like that, Rita. I don't understand you."

"Sometimes I don't understand myself, but I understand that."

"I wonder what's taking Marcella so long." Mario looked at his new watch."

"Oh," said Rita. "I wish I'd thought of that. How much was it?"

"Three dollars; about as much as your pizza."

"Maybe Mom got caught."

"Don't say that, Rita."

"Why isn't she back then?"

"I don't know, but she'll come."

"I always worry every time someone's late or doesn't show up."

Mario's attention was attracted to a beautiful, young woman walking rapidly toward them. His eye involuntarily picked her out of the crowded mall. She wore white slacks and a navy blue tank top, her short hair curled around her face, and he felt a strong attraction to her. Ashamed and confused by his disloyalty to Marcella, he quickly looked away.

Rita stared into the crowd; and following her gaze, Mario stopped on the same woman again. It was Marcella! She'd gotten a haircut. Marcella stood out of the crowd, like a diamond in a coalmine. Taking her in from the curly dome to sporty sandals, against the other shoppers, there was not much difference in clothing, hairstyle, even her new handbag was almost exactly like a dozen others. Mario's heart skipped a beat. He stood up.

"We look just like Americans," said Marcella, joining them. Her curls gleamed with a blue-black sheen, like the feathers of a raven. Her eyes looked larger, her chin firm and determined, her face less round. She looked older and sophisticated. Mario noticed that other men looked at her like they hadn't before.

"Where's Marcella? Where's my wife?" asked Mario, looking all around, anxiously.

Marcella and Rita laughed. "You better get a haircut, too, Mario," Marcella said quietly. Her mouth smiled, but her eyes were serious.

"Yes. I better. Wait here a minute. There's something more important I have to do first." He ran off, and Marcella sat beside Rita to wait for him. He returned in ten minutes with a bag. He took two pairs of sunglasses out and gave Rita one pair. The other pair, he put on before handing Marcella the bag. Marcella got a man's baggy plaid, cotton shirt out of the bag and a large pair of owl-like sunglasses. Laughing hard, she removed the tags, and put the shirt and sunglasses on. The shirt hung to her knees, and the sunglasses took up half her face.

"That's better," said Mario, feigning a sigh of relief. "You look like a picture in a book," he whispered in her ear. "You don't look like my Marcella. I got a new woman. I don't know what to do."

Laughing, Marcella pecked him on the cheek. "I'll show you later," she whispered, taking off the shirt and glasses and stuffing them into the bag.

"What?" asked Rita.
"Let's go get our hair cut," said Mario.
"No, my picture wasn't in the paper. I'm going to keep my hair," said Rita. "I'll meet you in the Hair Care."

Mario and Marcella strolled back to Hair Care like Americans who weren't on the lam.

Rita entered the drug store and went to the hair aisle. She chose a pony-tail holder and on an impulse picked up a pack of bubble gum in a display by the cash register as she waited in line to pay. On the street, she stuck a chunk of bubble gum in her mouth, and was soon blowing bubbles.

Taking her improvement project supplies into a bathroom in Bornnmans Department Store, she then experimented with different hair styles. The one she ended with drew her hair into a pony tail high on the back of her head with a few curly wisps hanging loose around her face and ears. Unzipping the outer compartment of her backpack, she removed the cosmetics she'd brought from Ms. Griswold's expensive collection. Carefully applying powder, lipstick, and a little blush, she then dabbed perfume on her wrist. Standing back, she tossed her head, pleased with the effect.

Rita walked into Hair Care, blowing a large bubble. She stopped short when she saw her father in the chair. With shorter hair that covered his head with tiny curls he looked much younger than he did after shaving off his mustache. Only the rough, sun-weathered leather of his skin betrayed his age and background.

Holding a hand mirror to see the back of his head, Mario's eye was drawn to a jaunty American teenager entering the salon blowing a bubble. Absent-mindedly, he watched her sit next to Marcella, who was reading a magazine, and say something to her. Marcella leaned toward her, and the teenager turned her head. The bubble went back in her mouth, and Mario saw that it was Rita.

"Holy tornado!" he mumbled, under his breath, getting out of the chair, and going over to Marcella and Rita. They stood up. "First my wife goes away and now my daughter. What have you ladies done with them?" he asked. They walked out of the shop laughing, and waited outside for Mario to pay his bill.

Leaving Hair Care full of high spirits, Mario caught up with Rita and Marcella on the sidewalk. "These are our disguises, and we'll fit into them, but we'll never forget who we are," he said, seriously.

A skinny campesino in raggy filthy jeans and tee shirt, slinking along with a bottle in a brown paper bag, reminded Mario of

Jose Encer and Juan Boleno. "I killed a man, Marcella," he said, suddenly grave. "He worked in the fields all his life. He had nothing to live for but to get drunk and forget his misery with a bottle and a little girl who was in the same trap. It could've been me if I had no place to go. The pesticides made him crazy. Sometimes he couldn't remember his name, but he still knew he was a man."

"There was no time for thinking about that when you hit him, Mario, only for action. You helped another campesino out of her nightmare," said Marcella.

"Everything that happens means something," said Mario. "You're right, Marcella. Jose died, but the other men knew, when I hit him, that what they were doing was wrong. Something changed, but what I did is starting to sink in."

"Dad, that girl is happy for what you did. She'll never forget it. You changed her life and all of the other girls. You gave them a chance. Jose would've died, even if you didn't hit him. Men don't die from a punch in the jaw."

"But it brought us so much trouble. Now if I get caught I go to jail or death instead of getting deported."

"It won't be the first time someone got in trouble because he did what was right," said Marcella. "Leave it with the snakebite. You're the one who's always telling us...."

"Sure," said Mario, grinning. He looked like a schoolboy, and the direction the conversation had taken made Marcella feel like a mother hen.

"I feel like an animal sprung from a trap," she said. "America likes us!"

"I'm glad to be out of the trees," said Mario, "and away from dust and pesticides and men shooting at me. I can breathe without coughing, and I don't have to pretend to be screwball. Are you hungry, Marcella? Rita and I had pizza, but I'm still hungry."

"Yes," said Marcella. "Here!" She stopped at a fast food fried fish chain. They went in, and Rita bought hush puppies and ice water, and found a table near the window, so she could watch the people go by when Mario and Marcella's conversation descended to the mundane, as it always did. She sat facing the window, and Mario and Marcella soon joined her with fish lunches and took seats opposite each other.

A policeman stopped outside the window, and Rita thought he was looking at them. She resisted an urge to smile and wave at him. He pulled a handkerchief out of his pocket and mopped the sweat off his face and neck.

"I have as much right to survive on this earth as he does," said Rita, to herself, pretending not to notice him enter the restaurant.

"This restaurant is exactly like the one in Nogales," said Mario. "They're all the same."

"No," said Marcella, playing along. "What do you mean? Only the food is the same. These tables are white plastic, and the ones in Nogales looked like wood."

"I meant the food," said Mario.

"Let's go to a movie," said Rita. "Do we have time?"

"Sure," said Mario, looking at his watch. "We've got time. There's a double feature. I saw it when we went by. One's called *Escape From Babylon*."

"Sounds right to me," said Rita. "What's the other one?"
*"An American Ace On A Foreign Adventure."*
Rita laughed. "It must be in the two dollar theater," she said.
"There's a genius among us," said Marcella.

When they finished eating, they walked to the theater at the mall to wait out the two hours until they had to meet Ms. Clement. Mario lost track of his troubles in the cool, dark theater, where everybody was anonymous, their minds devouring the same distraction that enveloped him into the mass and leveled them all. He looked at the glowing dial of his watch often. At quarter to nine, he tapped Marcella on the arm.

"It's time to go," he whispered. Marcella nudged Rita. "It's time to go." Mario followed Marcella and Rita out of the cool theater into the dry, hot night. He couldn't stop looking at Marcella. He looked as different to her as she looked to him, and Rita tripled the effect. They'd crossed the line of back breaking, heart-wrenching struggle for the basest of survival to the magical world where poverty and war and misery are illusory.

Wordlessly, Marcella and Mario walked arm in arm, Rita beside Mario. They rounded the corner, and Marcella saw Flowers, the trendy upbeat cafe that played classical jazz softly enough that people could hear one another talk without raising their voices. She'd passed it on her way to the low cost boutique where she'd purchased her American clothes.

They entered the restaurant stepping on spongy maroon carpeting, and foliage separated the dining areas into cubicles of privacy. A hostess appeared in front of them.

"Are you Marcella?" she asked Marcella.
"Yes," said Marcella.
"Are you sure?" asked Mario.
She smiled at him flirtatiously.
"This way," said the hostess, briskly. Marcella, Mario, and Rita followed her to Ms. Clement's booth. The surrounding ferns, ivy, and philodendron, the avocado trees artfully intermingled with live bamboo gave an unworldly, jungle-like aura to the surroundings.

The hostess waited for them to sit down, handed them dessert menus, and disappeared. Ms. Clement stood up, and they all remained standing shaking hands all around.

"Mario, Rita, this is Ms. Clement I told you about," said Marcella.
"Hi," said Rita.
"Good evening, Marcella, Rita, Mario," said Ms. Clement.
"Good evening," said Mario.
"Please have a seat. I was just having a cup of tea and a piece of pecan pie." Ms. Clement sat down, and everybody else sat, too. Marcella, Mario, and Rita opened their menus and looked them over. "I know what I want," said Marcella. Ms. Clement folded Marcella's menu, and put it aside. Mario and Rita folded theirs too

and placed them on top of Marcella's, and the waitress appeared with an order pad and pencil.

"I'll have coffee and New York cheesecake," said Marcella.
"Chocolate cake and milk," said Rita.
"Key lime pie and a El Toro," said Mario.
"We don't have much time," said Ms. Clement, getting down to business. "There'll be more time on the other end for questions. I've arranged jobs for you, Marcella, and Mario in New York. Rita, you'll be going to school in New York, like you've been doing in California." She paused, waiting for her words to sink in.

"New York?" exclaimed Rita, incredulously. "Did you say New York?"

"Yes, I said New York," replied Ms. Clement crisply.

"We're going to New York!" exclaimed Rita. "All the way across the continent!" And then she started laughing, unable to contain her excitement. "And to think, I didn't want to go!"

Marcella looked from one to the other, trying not to show her confusion, and then she laughed with Rita. "See! It's not the end of the world, after all!"

"No," said Rita. "It's the very beginning of my life, Mom!"

Mario's jaw had dropped open, and he gaped from Marcella to Rita and back, his expression running the gamut of amazement to disbelief. "What jobs?" he asked.

"I understand that you know all about automobile engines," said Ms. Clement.

"Yes," said Mario. "I know everything about them. I can fix any engine for a car."

The waitress came with their dessert, and Rita was almost too excited to eat, but she had grown accustomed to adjusting herself to the flow of events no matter how bizarre or unexpected, so she forced herself to eat as though she'd been told she was going back to Mary Griswold's garage. Once she got started, the cake was delicious.

"You'll be a mechanic in New York to help maintain a fleet of cars on Senator Bold's estate. For this, you'll earn three hundred dollars per week. Marcella, you'll be working in the kitchen on the same estate. You'll, also, earn three hundred dollars per week."

"No more fields!" said Marcella.

"No more fields, no more crops," said Ms. Clement.

"Where will Rita go to school?" asked Marcella.

"One of the best junior high schools in the United States, The Lincoln School for Gifted Children."

"Where in New York?" asked Rita, thinking she could get lost in the variety of it, yet maintain her identity. She could be friends with everyone who wasn't hostile and beholden to none. In New York, she'd use everything she'd learned in the labor camps to get to her destination, and when she achieved it, she'd help anyone moving in the same direction.

"You'll be working and going to school in a U.S. Senator's hometown upstate," said Ms. Clement.

"That's where we were going," said Mario, "to New York."

"Well," said Ms. Clement, "in that case, your schedule just got moved up a little. Finish your dessert. I'm to drive you to the airport. Your flight leaves at midnight."

CHAPTER FOURTEEN

Kate found a note from Harry on her desk when she arrived at work early. *A man was killed at Labor Camp 14 last night. Ferrell's got a number in this morning's paper.* Reading the article and looking at the accompanying police sketch, she recognized the drawing.

Kate got in touch with the medical examiner. "This is Kate Dolore. I'm calling about Jose Encer who died last night at Labor Camp 14. What was the cause of death?" she asked

"Massive heart attack and stroke caused by nervous and circulatory systems damage from pesticides. He inhaled the toxins too many times; these chemicals are powerful. They go through the skin as well as directly into the lungs. Kicks in the face, and a blow to the jaw set off the attack."

"Are there next of kin?"
"Not listed."
"Thanks."
"Bye."

Kate then called Kevin Sidon, her best contact at the police department, at home. The phone rang three times, and she was resigned to talking to the answering machine when Kevin picked up the phone.

"Hello," he said, his voice deep and drowsy.

"Hi Kevin. This is Kate. I hate to bother you before you've even had time for coffee; but don't get crabby, it's urgent."

"There's nothing I can do about the crabby, Kate. I'm not all together yet. I don't know why in hell you couldn't wait for a decent hour. Do you know what time it is? Damn pushy woman!" she heard him grumble under his breath.

"Ah, deadlines!" apologized Kate. "They make me the most unpopular person of all my friends. The death at labor camp 14 last night, what do you know about it?"

"Can't say much on this one," irritation remained in Kevin's voice. He sat up in bed.

"Is the department investigating or are there arrests or an official search for the fugitive?"

"No. You know how the D.A. feels about farm workers. Unless there's some political advantage, why waste the taxpayer's money?"

"Where's the camp?"

"I don't know the location. The report says camp 14."

"What did witnesses say?"

"They all say what the labor boss tells them to say. There was a fight and the labor boss came out shooting. The suspect ran away. Could be we'll find his body in the groves this morning." Kevin got out of bed in his shorts and put on his robe. He carried the phone into the kitchen and started the coffee.

"Did they search the groves for his body last night?"

"Kate, how many times have you talked to the chief and seen the cartoon on his door?" Kevin referred to a hand-drawn caricature of a monkey with the head, feet, and hands of a campesino. In a straw hat, his head was tilted back; and bellowing in rage, he was shaking a short-handled hoe in his right fist. "They're hoping one of their bullets found his heart or his head and he bled to death."

"What was the fight about?" Kate took notes as Kevin talked.

"Girls were brought to the camp for a party, and this guy went berserk and started the fight. No one knows why."

"Anything else I want to know?"

"Yes, the man who started the fight isn't Juan Boleno. He's in the county jail. Nobody knows who was using Boleno's name."

"Thanks Kevin, bye."

"Bye Kate. Next time don't wake me up."

"Okay, I hope not." Kate hung up and called Fernando Rios, her overall guide and main contact in farm worker affairs. Fernando answered his phone.

"Hi Fernando, this is Kate. Did you hear about the death at camp 14?" she asked.

"Yes," said Fernando. "I worked with Jose several times years ago when I was in the fields. He worked too long in grapes. They're lethal. You want to know what happened? I can tell you what happened. To keep the campesinos in line and cash free, they round up young Hispanic girls from various camps under the pretext of hourly wage work and take them to the men's camps for unpaid prostitution. They charge the men's accounts, but the girls never see the money. Since the man was new, he didn't know the routines. When you hear about it, you go nuts, but when you see our people preying on their own like that, you lose everything. I'd bet my bottom dollar, whoever the guy is, he's got a daughter, or maybe one of the girls was his daughter."

Kate stopped doodling. "No clues to the fugitive's identity?"

"He just got to that camp six weeks ago. I don't know anything about him. Nobody does. Inside news travels pretty fast, but this man kept entirely to himself. Management had him pegged for a trouble maker. He brought his own food and soap and towel, so he knew the ropes and wasn't going to be had."

"I want to drive out to the camp and see who I can talk to before the workers go out to the fields this morning."

"Okay. Pick me up."

Before going to the newsroom, Kate stopped by Fernando's office. He came out of the low nondescript storefront building as soon as she pulled up at the curb and got in the passenger seat.

"Good morning," she said.

"Hello, Kate," said Fernando, buckling his seat belt. The usually talkative friend was silent, and Kate knew something more disturbed him then the business she'd come on.

"What's wrong besides this death at the camp?" she asked.

"Your story," he said. "Usually you don't make accusations like that without at least talking to someone from our side. Nobody's been charged with a crime yet."

"It wasn't my story. I didn't hear about the death until I read it myself."

"I noticed it didn't have your byline. Who wrote it?"

"I suppose the police chief called the editor and gave him the item. I think anyone else in the newsroom who heard of it would've told me. Why didn't you call me?"

"I tried to get a message through, but you weren't at your desk. I don't like to leave a message. If I don't talk to you directly, I'm not sure you get it. There's where you turn, next stop sign." Fernando directed Kate to camp 14, and as they got out of the car, the labor camp boss came out of his house with a rifle, wearing reflective sunglasses.

"No visitors, no troublemakers," he said, loosely pointing the gun at Kate. "You're on private property. You're trespassing."

"I'm Kate Dolore with the Boonetown Daily News," said Kate, fishing in her purse for her wallet with her press ID. "I have a few questions about the man who was killed here."

"Clear out," he ordered, raising the rifle and clicking off the safety. Farm workers, who had been approaching to meet their rides to the fields stopped and watched, but nobody stepped forward.

"Let's go, Kate," said Fernando. "No good fooling with this."

Disappointed at being so rudely turned back, Kate got in the car, and Fernando slid into the passenger seat. She started driving back to town.

"Let's stop for coffee," said Fernando, disgusted. Kate pulled into a roadside diner and they went in, got coffee to take with them, and returned to the car.

"Are you going to keep on covering farm workers?" Fernando asked and took a sip of the hot coffee. He looked worried.

"Yes," she said.

"I hope that's true, but I know you're not in charge."

"We've done all right so far. Don't worry," she tried to assure him. Driving to Fernando's office, she then dropped him off and went to work.

As she walked to her computer, Ferrell stared at her crotch seething with combative hostility, warning her of a storm coming. He'd usurped the offensive, and she was braced for trouble.

"I've got the front page all planned, Kate. No farm business. Zilch. We've got legitimate news; the murder of a woman and a toxic leak. This is heavy stuff. I'm putting some of the men on it. You're out of your league with politics and the hard stuff that takes more sensitive handling. You're too brash, Kate."

"I'm pretty inexperienced compared to you," agreed Kate. "I've got to admit, I'm not fully fledged yet. I've probably got fifty years before I'm really tooling."

"You're headed in the wrong direction. Take your head out of that warm, dark place."

"He knows all about warm dark places," muttered Sue, at her computer. "That's why he's such a shithead."

"Speak up, Sue!" said Ferrell, going to her desk. "What did you say?"

"I said that some of us know more about warm, dark places than others  It all depends on our experience," she yelled.

"I've had enough of the under the breath mutterings around here," said Ferrell, loudly. "If anyone's got anything worth saying, it's worth speaking up and being heard. Otherwise, keep it to yourself." Leaning on Sue's desk, he stared at her, though she continued working as though he wasn't there, and he returned to his computer.

Kate wrote a brief story about her attempt to interview witnesses to the death at the labor camp and being driven off at gunpoint. She included the coroner's report on the cause of death of Jose Encer and waited for the paper to come out with considerable anxiety. When she read the story in print, with her byline, her heart sank.

*The man who killed his friend with his bare fists at Laber Camp 14 is armed and dangerous. The men were fiting over the Farm workers union. The union originated in the capital of California, San Francisco. Jose Encer was beaten to death by Juan Boleno as other workers cheered him on because Encer said he woud not join the Union.*

She'd be discredited before the people who knew. Looking up from the newspaper, she saw Ferrell staring at her, smiling. Punching up her story in the computer, it had been replaced by the one in the paper with her byline. She had no written record of it. Glancing at Sue, Sue gave her a knowing look.

*He's screwed over Sue's stories in some way, too. There's a reason for her refusal to speak of it. She knows something I don't, but I've got to make her see the importance of sticking together,* thought Kate.

"What's the meaning of this, Ferrell?" demanded Kate, taking the paper to his desk, pointing at the item furiously, trembling in anger.

"A good question; that's pretty poor work, Kate," said Ferrell. "Brush up on your spelling and usage, and straighten out your facts."

"I didn't write this tripe!" she growled, crushing the paper and throwing it on his desk.

"I've heard better excuses from my five-year-old grandson, and he has a better handle on his temper. You can do better than that. Who did write it?"

So angry she couldn't think, Kate walked quickly out of the office and down the sidewalk. She couldn't prove that Ferrell changed her story. Returning to the office, she pounded out a filler piece and left as soon as possible, stopping in Tipton for a drink. Sue came in, and when she saw Kate, she turned to go.

"Sue, we've got to talk. This can't wait," said Kate.

"Can't," said Sue, pausing with her hand on the door. "You've got to trust me. I'm in deeper than you."

"We must talk! We need a lawyer!"

"You're going to get us both killed. Back off."

"What are you talking about, Sue?" demanded Kate, in frustration. Shaking her head no, Sue ran out

Kate purchased her drink and returned to the office. Sitting at her computer, she heard a sudden noise behind her and jumped. Ferrell had crept up on her silently and was standing right behind her.

"Why are you sneaking around like that checking up on me?" she asked.

He went to his desk and didn't answer, and she decided to change her approach.

"Guess who's in town, Ferrell?" Kate asked, conversationally with no trace of anger in her voice.

"Your cousin from back east with six kids," said Ferrell, sarcastically, shuffling through some papers on his desk showing no interest.

"Morgan Bold."

"I know that, of course. I thought you were going to tell me something."

"I've got something I've got to check up on. See you in a little," said Kate getting up to go out. She didn't have to leave the office, but wanted to think out of Ferrell's range.

"I'm playing a little golf today. You won't see me until later."

"Oh, but today's not your golf day, and you always play early in the morning."

"It's whenever I want it to be."

Kate sauntered slowly out the door. Out of Ferrell's view, she dashed to her car, raced home, and grabbed one of Burt's sport's coats and his golf cap out of the closet. Pulling on the jacket, she then stuffed all her hair under the cap. She borrowed his golf bag on wheels from the closet, got in the car, and sped to the golf course. She arrived at the green before Ferrell, but there was no place to park where her car wouldn't be seen. Driving down a side street, she then parked in the suburbs, put on her opaque dark sunglasses, and dragging the bag which was on wheels ran back to the clubhouse.

Skulking in the shadows of the clubhouse behind a blue spruce tree, she heard a car pull into the parking lot. Men's voices approached, and Ferrell's was instantly recognizable. Morgan Bold was with him and a man Kate didn't recognize. Satisfied that she hadn't been seen, Kate remained motionless.

They entered the building, and she slipped unnoticed into the clubhouse and pretended interest in a golfing attire display, hiding behind it, listening to their conversation as they signed on for eighteen holes.

"The illegal element is certainly overburdening our little towns in the valley," said Ferrell. "You make the laws in Washington, but we have to pay for them here."

"It's a real paradox," said Bold. "Natalie was just complaining yesterday that we can't get anybody reliable and efficient for domestic work in New York, and in California you have such excess of cheap labor."

"We don't want it; we're stuck with it, and the crime and riffraff that comes with it."

"I saw the article about the Painter Labor Camp, and I've just gotten on a committee that can do something about it. I'm working on legislation to alleviate the problem. The suffering poor have been heavy on my mind, since I read that article." Bold wagged his head, sadly. "This is America, after all, and a news syndicate could easily pick up a story like that and really tarnish our image."

"I see the direction you're heading in, and I'm not interested," said Ferrell. "I'm not going to be in this business much longer. It produces too much tension. My doctor and my wife have been harping on me to retire. I'm leaning more toward some political appointment, not as much stress as this, something of a diplomatic nature." Ferrell glanced at his watch, forced by habit.

"Ah, how we all love respect," sighed Morgan, thinking over Ferrell's needs. The men, having signed in, strolled casually to the door, and Kate meandered to the other side of the exhibit, staying out of sight.

"Something in California, I suppose?" asked Morgan.

"Yes. I'm an information specialist," said Ferrell. "I've dealt in information all my life, and I'm not moving. All my friends and most of my family are here."

"I've always thought we need a federal information liaison officer here," said Bold. "I'm sure it could be arranged, Ferrell, but you have to deliver the goods first." Their voices drifted away as they went out to play, and when they were out of her range, Kate returned to her car. She left Burt's golfing equipment, cap and jacket in the trunk of her car and returned to the office.

After checking Senator Bold's financial disclosure statement, she found that he paid no social security tax on domestic staff. His New York properties were worth millions. She couldn't guess the extent of his other American and European real estate, and that empire had to be maintained. Also, she suspected that it was much vaster than the records showed. Experience told her that much of it would be listed in names other than Bold's.

She'd seen Bold and his aide, Natalie Clement, whispering, eyeing Marcella at Griswold's party, and until today she hadn't a clue to what Morgan Bold was doing in town.

As she thought over the conversation she'd overheard, Sue walked in and went to her desk. Sue appeared haggard with dark circles under her eyes, her face tense and drawn, and her eyes too bright. Her haunted expression looked like she was trying to emerge from hell and couldn't quite make it.

"Sue," said Kate, quietly, getting up and going over to her desk. "Let's go out and have a cup of coffee. I've got a problem, and I need help bad."

"Can't," muttered Sue.

"I'd help you. This is a free country. You can do whatever you want."

"No, I can't." She shook her head.

"You're going on the sky dive aren't you?"

Sue looked up at Kate and smiled for the first time since before the governor and his aide were killed. "I wouldn't miss it," she said. "I need a break, too."

Returning to her computer, Kate then began hacking out an assignment from her notes. Several hours later Ferrell walked in.

"Senator Bold didn't have time for eighteen holes?" asked Kate.

Ignoring Kate, Ferrell stopped at Sue's desk. "You're not generating much these days," he said, his tone taunting. "Go cover this building demolition this evening." He handed her a paper with an address scrawled on it. "If you can't think up any copy to go with it, at least get a few pictures. I'm sure you can handle that," he added, sarcastically, glancing at his watch. Obediently, Sue opened her drawer to get her purse and camera.

"Send a photographer," called Kate, appalled that Sue didn't put up a fight. "I need help with hard news. I've got it coming out my ears." Angry with Sue, Kate felt like shaking her awake.

Sue ignored her. "Thanks, Ferrell," said Sue, meek as a lamb. "Just what I need to keep me busy and earning a paycheck." Ferrell went to his desk and sat down at his computer, and Sue glowered at Kate. "Take it easy, Kate," she mumbled, under her breath. "I've got as hard as they come." Taking her camera bag and slipping her note pad into her purse, she quickly left the newsroom.

"What's she onto?" thought Kate, thoroughly exasperated. "She's sure not working with anyone in this newsroom."

Kate called Senator Bold's office to find out what he was doing in his committees and identified herself. "I need copies of all his legislation regarding Military Armaments Regulation and Housing and Human Services for starters," she told his aide.

"I'm sorry. Military Armaments Regulation is highly classified information, and he's new to Housing and Human Services. The only legislation originating in this office is still in the draft stage. He won't let it out until it's ready."

"When will it be ready?" she asked.

"Give him a couple of weeks at least.

"Thanks," said Kate, "Could you send me the first draft?"

"I'll send a press release when it's ready. The Boonetown Daily News?"

"That's right. Address it to me, Kate Dolore. Thanks." Kate hung up. "This could be the hookup, armaments," she thought. She called the newspaper's attorney and spoke in the low monotone that shielded her words from other sharp-eared employees.

"I can't get any information from Senator Morgan Bold's office on legislation he's worked on regarding Military Armaments Regulation," she complained. "He claims that it's all classified."

"What are you looking for? We can sue him for anything that's not classified," said Cornelius Denet, the lawyer. "The Freedom of Information Act gives us an opening."

"I suspect there's a connection between investments in arms sold to Central American countries and illegal immigration from Central America to the U.S.," said Kate, fishing. "I want to find out if he's using national security and the Military Armaments Regulations Committee as a cover to reap personal profits by investing in companies that manufacture armaments. I, also, want to find out if he's acquiring cheap labor by human displacement war creates. I don't believe all his investments are listed on financial disclosures. He can make up corporate names from here and other countries to hide behind."

"I'll see what I can do and get back to you."

"Thanks," said Kate. Hanging up, she prepared to leave the newsroom, but Harry Rosenburg charged in red-faced, waving a rolled up newspaper, and she stayed to see what was going on.

"Where's my story about the school board taking *The Grapes of Wrath* and *Of Mice And Men* off the library shelves?" he demanded, furiously.

"It's not running, Harry. We're going to talk about it," said Ferrell.

"How is anybody going to know it?" demanded Harry.

"Nobody needs to know. Nobody's interested in that kind of stuff anymore," said Ferrell, rubbing his chin. "It's old fashioned. There's a whole new creative journalism opening up, and we're part of it."

"Who's going to replace Steinbeck in this new creation?" Harry yelled, his color deepening to near purple. "Roger Rabbit?"

"You don't have to worry about that anymore. I'm taking you off the school board, Harry. I was talking to the superintendent of schools this morning, and we decided it would be better this way. When items of public interest come up, Ms. Fargo will give you a call."

"Bullshit!" shouted Harry, enraged. "I don't give a flying fuck what Ms. Fargo wants us to know! I'm going to the school board and report what happens. If the only thing we print is what they want us to know, they can do whatever they want, make Steinbeck a nonperson. And if some other local bunch of mini-dictators cooks up a deal with you to decide anyone with Aids or any group out of favor should be rounded up and separated out of sight, who would have to know? Somebody might get upset, God forbid, and they can give us a fucking jingle on the telephone if it's anything we might be interested in?" Harry pounded the rolled up newspaper on the desk.

"Screw you, Ferrell! My mother died at Auschwitz! They did research on living human beings, and there was an article on the wires a few weeks ago, that didn't sink in until just now, about results of experiments there on freezing living human beings being released to drug companies now! People won't stand for your stinking trip, Ferrell! Won't stand for it! I'm going to cover the school board and print the goddamn articles if I have to make flyers of the news and hawk it on Main Street for a nickel a shot, or tack it on the telephone poles with the circus posters!" Harry threw the newspaper at Ferrell and stalked out of the newsroom. He stalked back a few minutes later, trembling with rage.

Ferrell turned his back to the newsroom, facing his computer, and began editing a story. Harry stood behind him, not an inch away, a smoldering tower of fury. Kate went and stood next to

Harry. Sue stood next to Kate. Conrad and Victor came and stood on the other side. The sports team crowded around them, and all the reporters from the family and style sections gathered, making a semi-circle around Ferrell's desk. Managers and secretaries and clerks and accountants and ad salespersons drifted in from the office, and presspersons and a delivery girl, and proofreaders and layout people from the composing room, because news travels faster in a newsroom than anywhere else, and everybody who hadn't heard Harry's argument heard about it.

Ferrell continued pecking at his computer as though seventy people weren't crowded into the newsroom around him, waiting. Without turning around, he said, "Okay, Harry; your story will be in tomorrow's paper." Nobody moved.

"You can go on covering the school board for now," Ferrell said, in his practiced, reasonable monotone. Harry turned to go to his desk; and after separating to let him through, like the Red Sea after Moses' challenge to Pharaoh, the crowd broke up.

Kate went home and found Burt in the kitchen making tuna fish salad sandwiches. "We're eating light today," he said. "I'm keeping slim, and so are you." Kate kissed Burt, and stashed her briefcase in the closet. Joining him in the kitchen, she then got a cold beer out of the refrigerator and sat at the table as he took a salad out of the refrigerator, and put out salad dressing. He sat down across from her with a soft drink.

"I expect that Morgan Bold and Ferrell have a conspiracy going, but I need more solid evidence," Kate said.

"You make some pretty bold assumptions about people."

"I've been kicking around on this job long enough to separate the legitimately concerned and dedicated from the greasy, and Bold and Ferrell are slippery as they come."

The telephone rang and when Burt answered it, there was no one on the other end. "That's the third time this evening," he said, frowning. Kate dropped her fork and bent down to pick it up, as a large rock crashed through the window. She'd have been hit in the head if she hadn't bent over for the fork. Glass shattered all over the table, and Kate jumped up, backing into Burt who was already on his feet.

"I'm on somebody's shit list," she said, trembling.

Burt balled up his paper napkin and threw it in the mess on the table. "Do you ever consider taking up a quieter vocation?"

"Don't bother me," she replied irritably, going for the broom.

"Let's clean up and go out to eat," said Burt, brushing Kate's broken plate into the trash with paper towels.

"Okay, no point in helping them out by eating glass. But I better report this first. I want everything in the record." She called the police on the reporter's line, and got the dispatcher, who she knew and spoke to often. "I have to make an official report," she said. "I got a rock through my window just now, aimed at my head. I dropped my fork and bent over to pick it up just in time to avoid being killed or brain damaged."

"Someone will be right over," said the dispatcher.

"Thanks," said Kate. By the time the policewoman arrived, Kate and Burt had cleaned up the mess around the rock, but they hadn't touched the rock. It remained on the kitchen floor, and the officer squatted, got a pair of tongs out of her briefcase, picked it up with them, and placed it in her evidence case.

"Do you have any idea who might have done this?" she asked.

"None," said Kate.

"Could it have been a kid's prank?"

"I doubt it."

"Who's got it in for you?"

"Hard to say," said Kate. "I cover the news; maybe someone I talked to last year was offended then and in the meantime lost their job or met up with some grief and is looking for someone to get back at. One thing you learn in this business is that people are funny that way."

"Well, here's my card," she said, getting one out and handing it to Kate.

"I've got your name and number," said Kate, taking the card anyway. She showed the officer to the door. "Thanks for coming so quickly. It makes me more secure," she said.

Burt finished cleaning up the mess where the rock had landed and hugged Kate. "You can't imagine how much I worry about you, woman," he said.

"Yes, I can," she replied. "If you had to look at Sue every day and see what's happened to her, you might even go mad."

"We'll forget all our troubles on the sky dive next weekend, leave 'em on the ground. When we get down, we'll feel like new people."

"I need the distraction," said Kate. "I need relief from work." She and Burt embraced, comforting each other.

"I never thought I'd worry about a woman as tough as you. That's what I love in you."

"Don't then. It won't help a thing."

"But Kate, this is seriously dangerous. You need a break, and I need more of you. Is the sky dive on or off?" Burt's brow furrowed into a frown.

"It's on, but I can't get Ferrell off my mind. He's such weasel."

"He couldn't have had someone throw the rock through the window, could he?"

"Yesterday, I'd have said, not a chance. Today, I don't know. Everyday, he lets something slide about his prejudice against Hispanics. He had some rough times when the union was organizing, and he's never had to suffer discrimination. The way he treated the death in the labor camp, though, shows him at his pettiest. His attitude toward me is openly hostile. I'm in over my head. I don't know how to handle it."

"I knew it, Kate. I'm scared for you and Sue, too."

"I'm only beginning to find out what she already knows, but she won't let me in on it. Why? It makes it seem like she's on his side, yet I know that's impossible."

"How so?"

"She goes along with everything he says."

"She must have a good reason. You know she'd talk to you if it could help either of you. Frankly I'm worried about you, Kate. You can't see yourself. You don't know how you're changing."

"I know. I'm worried about all of us, you, too, because you're my man."

"C'mon," said Burt. "Tell me in bed."

Kate took off her shoes and walked out of the room, down the hallway, and upstairs, leaving a trail of clothing along the way. She walked slowly, turning occasionally to watch Burt following. Since he was laughing, she maintained a sober expression taking in his body, finding delight in it, and in her rising desire.

Letting her eyes linger on his physique, she wished he'd take off his clothes. She stopped; waiting. She wanted him to know how she felt without telling him. Laughing, he took off his shirt and let it fall on the stairs. She felt like she was seeing him for the first time, his chest, his shoulders, the rectangularity of his shape, the shape of his mouth. She proceeded up the steps and suddenly ran to the top, and he ran after taking the stairs three at a time.

It was her turn to laugh, but now he stared straight into her eyes without the slightest trace of amusement. She waited for him to take his pants off, and when they were both naked, she put her arms around his neck, and they kissed. He was hard, and his thighs and chest strong. His need excited her, and the love she felt for him made her want to give him pleasure, to hold nothing back; and she could feel in his embrace his love for her. It was the depth of her emotion that grabbed him that way. It came from admiration of the way he conducted himself on a daily basis, on a deep respect and trust like she'd never had for another person besides herself.

She kissed him hard, and deep and long, and pulled him in feeling herself surrounded by the strength of his arms, the firmness of his muscles beneath the skin, his hands on her back and sides. The need of him brought an unsurpassable joy, because he was there with her at this moment in this union and for this her world was made. Thought abandoned her, and the physical thrill where he entered her body was superficial in comparison to the depth of emotion opened on the invisible plain. An electrical charge went up her spine and hit her in the back of the head and the explosion scattered the stars. When she came down to earth, he was still inside, waiting for her and for those few moments it took to get hard again, and Kate was not a separate entity, but part of him, transformed by her love of him, and each time was better than the last reaching deeper and higher on the emotional ride, until there was nothing else in the world but one being. When they were finished and spent, they fell asleep in each other's arms.

CHAPTER FIFTEEN

When Mario, Marcella, and Rita got off the plane and walked up the ramp to the airport in Greenbrier, New York, Marcella was disoriented with jet lag. "Nothing seems right," she said, half asleep, looking around in confusion at the bustle of travelers.

Before Mario could answer, a woman approached them and asked, "Marcella, Mario, Rita Dominguez?" In gray slacks and a red silk blouse with a long, gold chain around her neck, a gray wool vest hanging to her knees, and rhinestone jewels dangling from her ears, a halo of reddish blonde hair frizzed around her head.

"Yes," said Mario, extending his hand.

"I'm Margie Parks," she greeted them, ignoring Mario's hand. He, Marcella, and Rita felt the insult. "I'm to help you adjust to New York." Her voice was sharp and clipped and hurried. "Come with me," she ordered, hurrying down the concourse. Mario, Marcella, and Rita followed.

Mario stopped to buy a newspaper on the concourse, but Parks didn't wait, so they had to run to catch up in order not to lose sight of her.

"She's in a big hurry," said Marcella, irritably, as they trailed Parks to her car in the parking garage. Opening the trunk, she then tapped her foot impatiently while they set their backpacks in it. She slammed the trunk, and they climbed into the back seat. Margie Parks leaped into the driver's seat, fastened her seat belt, and before they all had found their seat belts, she took off.

When they were buckled in, Marcella took Mario's newspaper and opened it, because she was getting irritated with Parks. Glancing at the front page, a photo immediately caught her attention. A thousand people were lined up to apply for two hundred jobs at a new restaurant soon to open in New York City.

"Why are we so lucky to get this chance?" Marcella asked. "There are so many people looking for jobs."

"We're not in New York City, and all those people have to pay social security tax and income tax and state tax. You're very lucky to have important friends. You must be happy for that and not ask too many questions. I'll take you to one of my boarding houses where you can stay for a week. For the three of you, it'll cost five hundred bucks, but I make the employer pay it. If you stay after your first paychecks, you must pay it; but a house for you to rent will be ready by then." Parks talked extremely fast, and darting through the parking lot and into traffic, she drove like she talked.

"What is social security tax?" asked Marcella, eager to gain information.

"You'll make a lot of money, so you can save some for retirement. It's money taken out of paychecks by the government and given back when people get too old to work. You'll get to keep all your money."

Mario took in the New England city in silence as they passed shops, apartments, and office buildings. Traffic whizzed by on both sides, and Parks didn't stop at yellow lights. Mario flinched when someone missed hitting them by a hair.

"Everyone's in an awful hurry," noted Rita. "The air's damp and heavy. Look at the high fence around that school, just like California. Are they afraid someone might escape?" Mario and Marcella laughed, and Margie scowled.

"The only fences at your school are around ball fields and tennis courts," said Parks, lighting a cigarette. Rita rolled her window down, and a blast of cold air hit her. Mario coughed, and Rita was cold with the window down. She rolled it up leaving a space at the top for the smoke to get out.

Swerving to avoid a car pulling out from the curb, Parks nearly hit one in the left lane. The driver blasted the horn and his passenger shouted. "Get a driver's license, you stupid son-of-a-bitch!"

Rolling down her window, Parks shot back, "Blow it out your ass, sweetheart!"

"Can we get other jobs, too?" asked Marcella. Parks screeched to a halt, the drivers behind her braking to avoid collision, blasting their horns. Turning, she stared Marcella dead in the eye.

"No, you can't get another job!" she snorted. "Your employer paid a thousand dollars air fare for the three of you. You don't have to pay taxes. You do want these jobs, don't you? Or should I drop you off right here and tell Senator Bold to eat the loss?" Under the reddish gold halo and jewelry and silk, Marcella sensed the instincts of a barracuda.

"No," she replied. The woman's sharp disgust, as though she thought Marcella stupid, added to Marcella's consternation.

Rita gaped out the window, overwhelmed at the speed of New Yorkers, speechless with elation. "I wanted to come to New York, and here it is. I can't believe it's me. It seems like a dream, and I might wake up." Rita felt like she was conquering Mount Everest.

Margie Parks' wild ride, jerking suddenly to stops, and starting with screeching tires seemed normal in the rush of traffic. They careened at hair-raising speed from traffic light to traffic light with Parks glowering at Mario in the rear-view mirror from time to time.

"No one in New York is happy," noted Marcella, studying the faces of the hurrying people they rushed by.

The car in front of Parks stopped at a light, and slamming on her brakes too late, she slid into the rear of it. No one got out of either car, but the other driver gave Margie the finger and sped away when the light turned green. At last, Parks stopped in front of a large boarding house.

"This is where you're staying," she said, getting out of the car and going around to the trunk as Mario, Marcella, and Rita piled out. "I'll pick you up here at eight o'clock sharp tomorrow morning. Marcella and Mario will go to Bold's estate and Rita to school."

Out of the car on the sidewalk Mario, Marcella, and Rita shivered with cold. Parks opened the trunk so they could get their backpacks, and as they proceeded up the walk with them, her car jerked forward into traffic, forcing cars behind her to hit the brakes hard. The blare of horns added to the medley of street noise.

By the time Mario rang the doorbell, Rita's teeth were chattering and they all had goose bumps. A short, slight, poker-faced woman with square bifocals answered the door.

"Dominguez?" she asked, starkly frugal with words. Mario nodded.

"Follow me." She walked briskly inside and up the stairs with Mario, Marcella, and Rita following in single file. "The rent is five-hundred dollars a week in advance. Yours is paid this week," she said, talking very fast as they went. Opening the door to a large room with varnished wood floors furnished with one double bed, a chest of drawers, and table with four chairs, she took a step back. Mario, Marcella, and Rita trooped in, and saw through an open door an adjoining smaller room, barely larger than a closet, that contained a single bed. A small desk in the corner had a telephone on it, and seeing it, Rita's eyes opened wide. "A telephone!" she said, and running to it, she picked up the receiver.

"You have to dial nine to get a dial tone," said the landlady, standing in the doorway. "Local calls are included in the rent, and that's the only kind you can make." Rita hung up, not knowing anyone to call, but determined to try it out later. There was a bathroom with a shower stall, toilet, and sink between the two rooms.

"Laundry's downstairs behind the stairs we walked up," said the woman, glaring suspiciously at Rita, who was too thrilled with being in New York to be intimidated. "It costs four quarters for the washer and two for the dryer. There's a change machine." The landlady waited a few seconds to answer questions, and when no one asked any, she stepped out of the room, closing the door, her footsteps softly retreating down the hall.

"A double bed, Marcella!" said Mario, pushing on the mattress, testing it, and Marcella dropped her backpack on the floor and flopped down on it.

Mario emptied his backpack on the bed, and shaking some of the wrinkles out of his clothes; he then folded them and put them in a drawer.

"Everything's happening too fast," said Marcella, irritably. "I don't like this. My brain's still up in the clouds somewhere. I'm all out of sorts. I hate to fly."

"At least we're in New York," said Rita, exuberantly. "I like New York." She went into her room and looked around. "My life gets better every day," she said, putting her clothes away. She changed into jeans and tennis shoes and socks, and hung her backpack in the closet, before bouncing on the bed, testing it.

"Let's walk the cobwebs out," said Mario. "I know what you mean, Marcella. I feel like that, too." He laughed weakly. "We'll walk it away."

"I'm going to take a nap," said Marcella, sitting up to take off her sandals. Dropping them on the floor, she then lay on her back and covered her eyes with her bent arm. "I don't want to go out."

"We'll see you when we get back," said Mario. He leaned over and kissed her. She grabbed his head and kissed him hard before turning over on her side to go to sleep.

"C'mon Dad," said Rita, opening the door, impatient to walk in New York. She and Mario went outside.

"We need to find a store where we can buy jackets before we turn to ice," said Mario. They walked very fast because they were cold and soon began trotting slowly to work up some heat.

"It looks like down that street would be more stores," said Rita, suggesting a different direction. "There are a lot more people, and look, a whole line of traffic lights." They turned and kept trotting until they came to a store with sweat suits, jogging shoes, and jackets hanging in the window.

Going in, they then browsed, but everything was too expensive, so they stayed inside only long enough to warm up and went on to the next one.

The third store they entered was more to their liking. They tried on jackets in their price range. Mario selected a blue one for himself and a red one for Marcella. Rita chose a warm fleecy yellow water-proof jacket. After they bought them, they put them on, and Mario carried Marcella's.

"That's much better," said Rita when they went back out. Comfortable now, they walked aimlessly around the city, chatting and commenting about the sights; the river that ran through town, the large lake they could see in the distance with green mountains rising behind it, and the shops close together with architecture much different than California's. All the houses and shops were at least two stories high, and many had covered front porches. They were all different.

Walking for several hours and covering most of the downtown area, wore Mario out, and Rita was starved. "Let's get something to eat," she said.

"Yeah," said Mario. "I'm hungry, too." They stopped at a diner, and ate. Mario took a hamburger and French fries with him for Marcella.

They walked back to a park with a river dividing it and sat on a retaining wall to watch some children fish. Noticing a girl about her age, who looked at her and smiled, Rita waved. "Hi," she called.

"Hi," the girl returned the greeting, waving back.
"Dad," said Rita, "New York's going to work for us."
"We'll see," said Mario.
Rita got up and stretched. "Let's go back to the bookstore," she said. "Now that we've been all over town, that's where I want to go."

Mario, affected by jet lag and amiably disconnected from anything resembling volition, agreed. He drifted with Rita back to the bookstore, and found a large section of maps. After studying them, he selected a map of Greenbrier and the newspaper. When he went to check out, Rita was right behind him with a best-selling novel.

"What?" asked Mario in amazement. "No chemistry or advanced calculations?"

"I'm not going to buy those books. They cost too much. I'll wait until I find a library. Tonight I'm going to read what everybody else here is reading. I want to see how they think."

"Hmm," said Mario.

When they returned to the boarding house, Marcella was sleeping soundly, and Mario hung his jacket and Marcella's in the closet. With Rita soon absorbed in her novel, he read the paper and then studied his map.

Marcella woke up still crabby. She ate the food Mario had brought her, but was completely out of sorts, and couldn't think. "I can't wake up all the way," she said to Mario. "I hate New York."

"I brought you a jacket," said Mario, getting it out of the closet and handing it to her. "Rita and I got one, too."

Smiling, she took the jacket. "Thank you, Mario," she said, trying it on. She turned this way and that modeling it. "Just right."

"Goodnight Mom and Dad," said Rita. "I'm going to bed and read my new book."

"Goodnight Rita. You wanted to come to New York, and here we are," said Mario.

"Goodnight Rita. I hope you sleep well," said Marcella.

Rita went into the bathroom and took a shower first so she wouldn't clog the bathroom early in the morning. Then she went in her room and closed the door wanting to shout for sheer joy at walking into a room of her own. She threw herself on the bed and turned around in it before getting up to get her book. There was a lamp on a table right beside the bed so she could read comfortably. "I might as well be the queen of England," she said to herself. "What more could anyone want?"

Before going to bed for the night, Marcella closed her bedroom door and climbed into bed with Mario. "I always dreamed of this luxury," she said.

"Oh Marcella, Rita was so right. We're in New York going to new lives. Imagine, me a mechanic. Can you believe it? I thought this would never happen when we lived in the labor camps, and then after I killed Juan. Everything we heard about this country being great and wonderful and good; it's all true. Where else could I be running from the law one day and here in a bed in our room the next?"

He kissed Marcella on the mouth.

"I don't know," she said. "Something is wrong. I don't know what."

"Not now, it's not," he said and kissed her fear away. They made love in the large, soft, roomy bed, but long after Mario went to sleep, Marcella remained wide awake. She dozed off a few hours before it was time to wake up and get ready to meet the dragon.

Margie Parks showed up on the dot with a sharp toot, and Marcella looked out the window. "There she is," said Marcella disdainfully. "I can't stand that woman." She noticed a dent in the right fender that hadn't been there the previous day, and started to open the window to holler down at her not to blow the horn again, but Mario held the window closed.

"We better just hurry up and go," he said. "What would we do if she left without us?" Mario grabbed his backpack with his map in it, and they all put on their jackets and ran down the stairs, and out the door. The back car door hung open, and they piled into the back seat. Margie Parks had just lit a cigarette, and the car smelled like stale smoke, but now Mario could crack his window at the top so the smoke could go out without them freezing.

"Watch the way I'm going," said Parks, who took off before Mario got the door closed. He slammed it on the fly, and Marcella glowered at the back of Parks head wishing to land a good punch in the curly halo of reddish gold curls. "I have a bus schedule for you, but some of Bold's staff ride bikes to work. That's an option." She handed the bus schedule back to Mario.

"Rita will walk to school," announced Parks, her voice crisp with authority.

Relegating the bus schedule to his backpack, Mario then took out his map. When Parks drove into the parking lot of the red, brick school building that took up the whole block, and parked, he marked the location on his city map. He then folded the map and returned it to his backpack.

"Come on, Rita," Parks said, getting out of the car and opening the back door. Marcella got out to let Rita out, and started walking with Rita, who trailed Parks.

"Wait here," Parks ordered Marcella. She hurried Rita into the building, leaving Marcella to return to the car fuming. She got in and slammed the door.

"I hate that woman!" raged Marcella. "That's my daughter! Margie Parks shouldn't be taking her to her new school. I should take her, or she should go herself, like always."

"She's used to bossing everybody around," said Mario.

"I don't think we have to do what she says, Mario. I'm going to tell her next time."

"No, Marcella. We don't know anything and she knows everything. We don't even know where the jobs are."

"She shouldn't be taking Rita to school! Margie Parks is not her mother!"

"Sshh," said Mario. "Here she comes."

"I don't like to sshh about my own daughter," said Marcella, furiously.

"You're the one who told me, Marcella. Never forget that we're fugitives. It won't always be like this...."

Marcella motioned with her eyes to Parks opening the car door. "What a great town this is," Marcella said, poking Mario in the ribs. "Don't you just love it, Mario?"

"Yup. I can't wait to see the auto shop. That's for sure."

Margie Parks drove to Bold's estate, slowing and waving at an iron gate where a guard sat in an entrance booth. The guard waved at Parks, smiled, and picked up a telephone as they passed. The high iron fence went as far as Mario could see in either direction, and a bike rack full of bicycles stood along the outside of the fence.

Inside the grounds, the estate was manicured with gardens like those he imagined would surround a palace, and Mario's eye was drawn to a forest in the distance. Before he could see more, Parks stopped in front of the garage.

"This is where you get out, Mario," barked Margie Parks.

Mario got out of the car, and Ms. Parks proceeded slowly and cautiously down the road. A tall, slender, Latino man came out to meet Mario. He wore a faded red baseball cap and overalls over his jeans and shirt. Mario would never see him without the baseball cap. His eyes were sad and his face frozen in a perpetual frown. He looked like one who has forgotten how to smile. Mario smiled when he shook his hand with a strong, firm grip which the man returned, but still he didn't smile. His face lacked expression. Sensing his sadness, Mario thought some profound tragedy had befallen him. He felt the fellow's alienation.

"I'm Mario."

"I know, Mario," he spoke softly. "Let's go in." They went inside, and the man said, "I was expecting you. I'm Marco. I'm to show you your job. The shop has everything you need, and if you want something that isn't here, it'll be ordered." He opened the door to a closet with six uniforms hanging in it.

"These are your uniforms," said Marco. "Take them with you when you leave. You must always wear one to work." He turned back to the shop. "All the tools are on this side, except for heavy equipment. Here's the screwdrivers, wrenches, socket wrenches. He named the tools as he pointed them out, and many items were in drawers and cabinets which Marco opened to show him.

"Okay," said Mario, who didn't know the names of some of the items. "I won't remember everything though."

"I know, but I have to show you just this way." He lowered his voice and spoke in a monotone. "The only thing *we* can do *our* way is the work on the engines because *they* don't know how." With his eyes, he directed Mario's attention to a television screen in the corner of the shop.

"I don't understand," said Mario confused, his gaze flicking to the silent screen and back to Marco.

Ignoring his comment, Marco said, "I'm rebuilding the engine for this car. You can tune up the car Senator Bold drives and change the oil. I'll help you if you need it. He has a favorite Lincoln."

"That white one," guessed Mario, gesturing to a white Lincoln parked along one wall of the shop.

"Yes. After you finish the tune-up, until more maintenance comes in, you'll work on whatever you want. Come over here, would you?" Mario followed him to a bulletin board, trying to comprehend what he was saying, but it made no sense. What did he mean, work on whatever you want?

"This is a schedule, and you must always check it first to see if there's any new work posted for the day before you do anything else," continued Marco. The only work posted was the tune up, oil change, and maintenance check on Senator Bold's Lincoln.

"I can do whatever I want when there's nothing new on the schedule?" asked Mario, thinking he had misunderstood. Marco nodded yes.

"I'll get to work on an engine I design myself?" asked Mario, incredulously. A vision of his solar engine appeared in his mind; the parts, how they'd fit together, how the battery would fire the generator, how to focus and collect the energy through a tempered thermapane hood with built in magnifiers to concentrate the energy into a narrow beam.

"I'll need a forge and tongs and goggles," said Mario, staring at Marco, incredulously waiting for him to tell him where he was going wrong. He expected Marco to burst out laughing at his joke at any moment. "I'll need sheet metal and special glass."

Marco handed him a pencil and a small notebook. "Make a list. I'll order everything," he said. Mario stared at Marco, dumbfounded

"I can't believe this!" Mario's voice rose to a squeak and shook with excitement. "Do you understand, Marco? What I do here after I finish the routine work can change the world, not only with new things, but with how things are done? The day before yesterday I was working grapes, and my lungs burned from the chemicals. They were on fire, Marco. Did you ever work grapes?"

Marco nodded solemnly, and leaned over an engine. He didn't look at Mario. "Everyone here worked fields in California," he muttered, running his words together, making them hard to understand.

Mario was dying to break into his native Spanish to try to figure out what Marco was so reticent and angry about, but he dared not. As he was pondering what to do, Marco muttered, "Speaking Spanish is not allowed."

Mario took one of his uniforms into a bathroom and dressing room and changed into it, and hung his clothes in the closet. He went over to the Lincoln to start work on the car, and as he worked on the engine his imagination was fired with the one he'd build. Anticipating dealing with the problems, he had to stop thinking about it to ponder his partner's aloofness.

"My wife got a job in the kitchen," said Mario. "We just came from California. I got a daughter."

Marco's glance flicked to the television and back to his work, but he didn't say anything.

"Are you married?" pressed Mario.

Again Marco glanced quickly at the television. He nodded yes. "Pretty soon, we'll go out for a break. We have to wait until it's time. We can't go whenever we want," he said.

Mario thought Marco meant, *we can't talk whenever we want.* Falling in with Marco's brooding silence, Mario lost himself in his job, relating the workings of an engine to the sun as a fuel source; but when Marco suggested they go out, he was happy for the chance to make a friend.

As soon as they were outdoors, Marco lit a cigarette and offered Mario one. He declined. "You have to be careful what you say," Marco said in an undertone outside.

"Why?" asked Mario.

"You can't believe at first. You have to be here a little while. If you stay, we'll talk a little," said Marco, adjusting his baseball cap.

"I love mechanics. I hate fields. Why would I go?"

"Just wait," said Marco, ominously. He smoked a cigarette in silence and Mario was relieved to return to his job, but Marco's peculiar attitude and brooding silence nagged at the back of his mind.

Margie Parks had driven Marcella down the road which wound through gardens planted with stately trees and shrubbery. They passed a fish pool with a large fountain in the center. Statues of Greek gods and goddesses lined the approach to the house, and a serene-looking forest could be seen in the distance. The Georgian motif of several buildings within a quarter mile radius blended with the architecture of the main house and surrounding gardens.

Ms. Parks stopped at one of the back entrances to the mansion, and Marcella was overwhelmed with the grandeur of the estate. "You can get out here," said Ms. Parks.

"How will I get home?" asked Marcella.

"Just go, and don't ask so many questions. You'll see," she snapped, flicking her wrists at Marcella as if she were shooing a dog.

Marcella got out of the car, slammed the door hard in her irritation with Parks treating her like an imbecile, and went into the mansion. She was met by a slovenly young woman, who had a fat rear and pendulous bosom that heaved when she walked, at the kitchen worker's entrance. The woman constantly scratched her face or her crotch, and an unlit cigar, barely larger than a cigarette stuck between her lips at the corner of her mouth. It sounded like there was a war going on inside

"Greetings," she shouted, to be heard over the noise from the kitchen. The cigar forced her mouth into a weird twist when she spoke and threw her face off balance.

"Good morning," yelled Marcella.

Handing Marcella a plastic bag, she showed her a dressing room and bathroom for servants off the kitchen. "Put this on!" screamed the woman, out of the corner of her mouth. "Take your clothes home when you go."

She indicated a larger plastic bag with a half dozen uniforms folded inside. "Take those uniforms, too. When you get your uniform on, come out to the kitchen, and I'll give you some onions to chop." She pushed her thick, hair out of her face, revealing a scar from her eyebrow to her ear.

The sudden display of the wretched scar was a shock to Marcella, but she quickly recovered. "I'm Marcella," she shouted.

Nodding, the young woman then closed the door to the dressing room and yelled over the television blaring in the kitchen, "I'm Elena." Leaning closer to Marcella, she shouted in her ear. "This is not a good place to talk about your family or yourself or anything important." Marcella thought Elena was loud and brash and rough, but she welcomed the opportunity to converse with someone she might be able to trust who knew more about the system then she did.

"Why don't you turn down the television, so we can hear?" asked Marcella, loudly. "I'd like to get to know you all."

"No one who can turn the television down cares what you'd like," she yelled. "It has no volume control, no channel selector."

"Are we the only women here?" asked Marcella. "I thought all the kitchen workers would be women."

"Don't think," shouted Elena, her eyes downcast. "Please try not to think." Elena went out of the dressing room, slamming the door behind her, and Marcella was grateful that it shut out a little of the noise. She changed into the uniform and went into the kitchen dismayed that she had to listen to a war blaring on television.

Elena showed her a work station, where there was a paring knife on a counter and a cutting board. She dumped a peck of large white onions out on Marcella's work space. "Peel and chop," she screamed. Marcella began peeling and chopping the onions. Her attention was drawn to the thirty-eight square foot television screen where she saw a man ram a bayonet up another man's rear disemboweling him, and she got dizzy and struggled not to puke all over the onions. She quickly looked away and studiously refrained from looking at the screen again.

When she finished chopping the onions, her eyes and nose dripping, Marcella washed her face and hands. Elena had a peck of potatoes ready for her to peel. Some of them she set aside. "These are for French fries," she shouted and held up a French fry cutter.

"First you must take a fifteen minute break," yelled Elena, her hands on her hips, the cigar dangling from her mouth. "Would you like water, or coffee, or tea?"

"I'll take my break with you," said Marcella, wishing to make a friend on the job.

"It's not allowed. You have to take it now. Sit down." She pulled out a chair at the table. "Coffee or tea?"

"Tea." Marcella left the knife on the cutting board and sat relieved to get off her feet. Elena got a mug out of a cabinet, put a teabag in it, and poured hot water from a kettle on the stove nearest them into it. She brought Marcella the tea and went back to her work station. The break gave Marcella the opportunity to look over the other employees.

A tall, fat salad man moved like a robot, his brown eyes glazed. He never looked at the television or any of the other workers. His eyes were fixed on the vegetables he worked with.

The pastry maker's every move was short and jerky, and like the others, his eyes were attached to his work, shutting out all other activity.

Another man, much older than the others, worked on a sauce at the stove. His movements were, also, jerky and automated, his eyes glassy.

They must have been slicing vegetables and preparing food for so long, Marcella thought, that it was completely automatic, like picking oranges. Marcella was saddened with Elena's remoteness and the isolation of the others. When the migrant workers in the fields had the chance to be together, they laughed and joked, or fought and told each other stories, no matter how miserable the work was. In the absence of the only sociability she'd encountered in America, her suspicion and fear rampaged.

These workers reminded Marcella of beat dogs. Profound misery had settled over the silent workers, and the television broadcast now described a hideous crime. Marcella was forced to listen to the grim details, and she dared not look at the screen. This kitchen made Griswold's job seem like a peaceful retreat, and she had a fierce longing in her heart to flee to Sylva and Jenny and Gordon and Ms. Griswold.

In twenty minutes, Elena came over to Marcella. "Break's over," she shouted, and Marcella returned to the potatoes. Elena then tapped the salad man on the arm to get his attention. She jerked her head toward the table, and he got himself a cup of coffee and sat down. Each of the kitchen workers waited until Elena told them to take a break before taking a turn to sit down. By the time everyone was finished with breaks, Marcella was almost through peeling potatoes. The time went so slowly, Marcella could hardly stand it. Her back ached, and she kept stopping to rub it. Her feet and legs hurt from standing. In Ms. Griswold's kitchen, the workers often peeled and cut up vegetables sitting on a stool, laughing and exchanging stories about their families and field jobs and bosses. She felt a tap on the shoulder and whirled around.

"Lunch time," Elena shouted and waddled off to the pantry, Marcella following. "Here's our food for lunch," said Elena, pointing out a shelf. "Make whatever you want, but you only got a half hour." Marcella made a burrito and a cup of hot tea, but she didn't have time to finish the tea before it was time to go back to work. The noise she'd endured all morning made her head pound, and she'd do just about anything to escape for even a few minutes.

"Tomorrow, I'll bring my lunch and go outside to eat," she shouted at Elena.

"Not allowed," Elena yelled back, shaking her head no.

Glumly, Marcella took up her station on her feet in the same space, making bread dough. The day seemed eternal, and the incessant noise of the television, lurid details of carnage and mayhem wore Marcella's nerves to the nub. "Where do they get that stuff?" she shouted, at the kitchen crew in general, loud enough to be heard over the racket. Elena's expression permeated with doom warned her to be quiet.

Hating the indignity of violation of her mental space; the ability to think what she wanted and ponder her problems and those of her family, and even the freedom to daydream were wrested away by the television.

Marcella longed to walk around or sit down. When she was finished with the bread dough, she sat down at the table, even though it wasn't break time, to relieve her aching back and sore feet.

"No!" hollered Elena. "No breaks outside the schedule."

Jumping up, eyeing Elena resentfully, Marcella returned to her work station to find her next assignment, muffins to be put together, mixed, and baked.

Understanding of her fellow workers glassy-eyed lethargic, automated movement brought uneasy dread. If she stayed there long enough, she'd get to be just like them. After the mid-afternoon break, she could hardly wait for the oppression of the kitchen to end.

Marcella looked at the large wall clock for the fourth time in ten minutes, thinking surely at least a half hour had gone by. When a bell rang signaling the end of the working day, Marcella rushed out of the kitchen, forgetting her street clothes and extra uniforms. Hurrying through the hallway to the back door, she caught the eye of a woman on the night crew coming to work. Marcella stopped facing the woman, who, also, stopped to look at Marcella.

"Marcella," said Marcella.

"Mareno." Mareno was large and fat and sloppy and fiercer than Elena. Her button nose was surrounded by bulging, fat cheeks, and her scowl could have frightened a whole crew of Elenas. Her mouth turned down at one corner, and she didn't need a cigar to distort the line of her chin and jaw. She'd walked crookedly, with a lumbering gait, her right shoulder lower than her left, and her expression was terrifyingly mean. Instead of the utter submission of abject defeat the other workers displayed, was a spark of defiance in her eyes from the darkest ring of hell. No sooner did Mareno show Marcella that glittering speck of fight, than she immediately concealed it. Her eyes glazed over. She threw her head, like a horse that would not break, and Marcella caught sight of an earplug in her ear when her hair flicked back for an instant.

"Thanks," thought Marcella. She took Mareno for one who refused to capitulate to the environment of the kitchen, and that gave her hope.

Marcella shuffled out the back door with the rest of the kitchen staff and onto a shuttle waiting for them to board. A burly security guard with a pistol in a holster was ensconced in the front seat behind the driver. A radio blared so loudly that no one tried to speak. Marcella plopped down on one of the seats with a sigh of relief, her back aching, resting her tired feet on her heels. When they were all seated, the shuttle rolled on to the gardeners shack, and the gardeners boarded. The next stop was the garage where Mario and Marco got on. Mario blew Marcella a kiss, making her smile, and sat in an empty seat near her, carrying his uniforms.

The bus stopped at a bus stop outside the main gate, and all the workers filed off the shuttle. A city bus rounded the corner and lurched along immediately. Some of the workers took bicycles out of a bike rack and pedaled away.

CHAPTER SIXTEEN

"At last, we can talk," said Marcella, taking a deep breath, waking from the nightmare of her working day, as the bus stopped in front of them. The other side of the iron fenced mansion grounds was such a relief she wanted to cry.

"We're going to 18$^{th}$ and Fitch," called Mario to the bus driver. "What bus should we take?"

"This one," he said. Mario and Marcella boarded the bus. "I'll let you know when we get to 20$^{th}$ and Fitch, and you walk two blocks over," said the driver.

"Thanks," replied Mario. He and Marcella got a seat together. The bus was silent of artificial noise, but Marcella could still hear the television screeching in her head.

"I hate that place, Mario. I've never been in such a place," said Marcella.

"They are rich, rich people, Marcella," whispered Mario. "We never saw people live like that, but here they do."

Marcella shot him a fighting glance. "It's an awful place to work," she said, still talking too loud and angrily. Strangers turned to stare at them, and Mario pulled his hat lower over his face and slouched down in his seat.

"Let's talk about it when we get back," he said, in an undertone.

Marcella sighed loudly. "I don't care who hears!" she said, but she crossed her arms under her bosom and didn't speak anymore until the driver yelled, "20$^{th}$ and Fitch," and they got off the bus.

"This is the best part of the day," she said, as they started walking to the boarding house. Walking was a great pleasure after confinement at the noisome work station all day and it relaxed her back and legs somewhat.

"Why?" asked Mario, in surprise.

"There's no noise or screaming or zombies," she said. Listening to street traffic, two men yelling at each other and a dog's continuous barking at them from a park they were passing, Mario gave her a strange look.

"We can't talk at work. There's too much screaming from the television, and we can't turn it down," she explained, turning into a drug store on the corner. "I have to stop here." Mario went in with her, and Marcella purchased a plastic box of earplugs. Mario bought the paper, and they stopped at a sandwich carry out shop for food to take back.

Passing a city park with benches, trees, and flower gardens with a path winding through it, Marcella held Mario's arm and stopped to watch children play and shout in a corner fenced off with swings, sliding boards, and sand boxes. It occurred to Marcella that Rita's zest for new and interesting things was caused by her different beginnings. "Rita will never think like the children in that playground when all of them are grown, even if she makes much more money," she said.

"True enough," agreed Mario.

When they arrived at their rooms, Rita was sitting at the table looking over her new school books, thinking about all the knowledge she was going to cram into her brain.

"Hi Mom! Hi Dad!" she said, getting up. "I've got a great school." Rita moved her books from the table, and they all sat around it to eat, Mario flashing Rita an understanding grin.

"I've got a great job, too," he said. "I love it."

"Good for you both," said Marcella, unable to appreciate Rita's excitement and Mario's sociability. "But something's very wrong." She sat down and took off her shoes. Stretching her legs, she then massaged her foot. "Really bad wrong."

"What's wrong, Mom?" asked Rita, deflated by Marcella's lack of interest, a silent prayer in her heart that the something wouldn't force her to leave yet another school before even one semester was completed.

"Something at work I can't figure out. Tell us about school."

"It's the classiest school in the world, and I can take geometry and biology and chemistry. I get to use a laboratory for experiments. The school has a great library. Every book I need is there."

"It sounds like a good school," said Mario.

"I have a bad feeling," said Marcella, greatly dejected, as they ate their sandwiches.

"Look in the paper at what other people pay mechanics helpers and kitchen workers to start, Marcella. We could never make as much money as we'll make at Bold's estate," said Mario, mystified at Marcella's attitude.

"Just think, when we got to the first labor camp, we couldn't even leave it. Now we have money; we can buy things," said Rita. "I can go to school. We can walk around in New York wherever we want to go and buy jackets and sandwiches. We're already living like human beings."

"I don't like Margie Parks. I don't like to work in that place. Why is the money so much there and not in the ads in the paper?"

"Because Senator Bold is rich," said Mario.

"But we're not. Why do they want us, who don't know anything here? They have money to buy whoever they want, who was born here and knows everything, the best cooks and mechanics in the world."

"Don't worry all the time. It'll be alright," said Mario.

Marcella stopped complaining so she could finish eating and studied the ads in the paper. She then threw her trash in the waste basket and made an appointment to see a house for rent. "Let's go see this three bedroom rambler with kitchen appliances," she said, thinking maybe if she could make something better in her life, she would be able to stand working at Bold's estate tomorrow.

"Okay!" said Rita, enthusiastically. She wanted Marcella to cheer up. "My homework can wait for that."

"I'll go," said Mario. He located the street on his map. "It's only seven blocks. We can walk."

They found the address with no trouble. The brick house was in a neighborhood similar to the boarding house and appeared in good shape. They went to the door and were met by the real estate agent who was selling the house. He showed them through the house. "It has new paint inside and out. It costs $650.00 per month to rent," he said.

"We'll have plenty of money for this house," said Mario.

"Here's an application," said the agent, tearing a form off a pad of them. In a suit and tie, he appeared as respectable as Manuel had been sleazy.

"We'll take this application home," Marcella said, glancing over the space for references, and bank account. "Do all landlords want references?

"We do. They don't have to be from this town, just so they're not relatives. We do check references."

"I like the house just fine," said Rita. "I can have the middle bedroom, and we'll have one extra."

"Thanks for showing us the house," said Mario. "We'll talk it over and let you know."

"Call me at my office. Here's my card," said the agent, handing Mario his card. Mario slipped it into his shirt pocket, and they left, stopping to take another look from the outside before walking back to the boarding house.

"We'll have to get references from the people we work with now," Marcella said. "But I don't think we should ask Ms. Parks."

"We'll ask the people at work," said Mario. "But I don't know if it can be that easy. We can't get a bank until we get paid. We can't get paid until we've done some work. Can illegal aliens have bank accounts?" he asked.

Marcella sighed in exasperation. "We'll have to find out, Mario. You ask in the shop. I can't talk in the kitchen."

"It's hard to talk to Marco. Something terrible happened to him. He's a haunted man, and he doesn't talk."

"Ask him anyway."

When they got back to the boarding house, Rita went to her room and closed her door to do her homework in the privacy of her own room.

Marcella took a hot shower trying to unwind, but her muscles still ached, and she couldn't completely relax. Mario went out to get them each a beer, but decided a bottle of champagne would pick up Marcella's spirits. To his chagrin she was sound asleep snoring loudly when he got back.

The next day at work, Mario said, "Marco, I want to rent a house. I'll put you down for a reference, eh?" Marco was always grim, but needing a reference and a friend with the information to get by in the unfamiliar city, Mario was determined to get along with him. Marco shook his head no. Mario buried his anger and confusion in work on the engine. The migrant workers had helped each other whenever they could. He studied Marco's face, trying to figure him out, and Marco directed his glance to the television but Mario didn't look at it.

On her way into the kitchen, Marcella put her earplugs in, but was disappointed that they didn't shut out the sound, though they dimmed it. Marcella couldn't yell over the din of the television to Elena. Her throat was irritated from trying to communicate yesterday. On her break, Marcella wrote Elena a note. *I'm going to rent a house. Can I put you for a reference?* Taking the pencil from Marcella, Elena wrote, *No* on the paper and handed it back. Marcella felt like she'd been slapped. It seemed like the work in the kitchen would never end, and when she and Mario boarded the bus to go home at the end of the day, they compared notes.

"These workers are not like the field workers," said Mario. "Marco won't give me a reference." At work, he'd tried to tune his naturally friendly personality to accommodate Marco's non-communicative demeanor without success. Snubbed, he loved the work itself and could forget Marco's coldness in working out the problem with an engine. Even Marcella's reticence couldn't dampen his enthusiasm for the work and his dream of the solar project of his own design.

"Elena, too," said Marcella, taking out the note and showing it to Mario.

"We need them," said Mario. "I don't understand."

"Sedar or Riva or Sylva or Jenny would've given me a reference," she said. "I keep telling you, Mario. Something is very bad here. We don't know what it is yet, but everybody else knows."

"No, Marcella. Don't try to make it bad for all of us because you don't like it," said Mario, her incessant foul mood beginning to affect him. They returned to the boarding house, and Rita was there studying.

"We couldn't get references to rent the house," Marcella said to Rita, who studied her expression thoughtfully.

"Ms. Parks said a house would be ready for us in a week," Rita reminded her.

"I know, Rita," said Marcella, aggravated. "I don't trust Ms. Parks. I don't trust Natalie Clement and my stinking job. That's why I wanted to find our own house."

They ate dinner together that evening, and the week passed rapidly for Mario and Rita, one day flowing smoothly into the next as they adjusted to their new situations with relish, but Marcella's unhappiness grew.

A hard time getting up in the mornings added to her miseries with longing to turn over and escape into sleep. She forced herself to put her feet on the floor, get dressed, and go to work on the bus with Mario, but the days were interminable, and she could hardly put a complete thought together in her mind, even when she was at home with Rita and Mario. The television wars, the screaming and killing and mayhem even haunted her dreams. When she left Senator Bold's kitchen in the evening, her head pounded from the pestilent din of the television, and she came to depend on aspirin more than food. Losing her appetite, she, also, lost weight.

One evening when Marcella and Mario arrived from work, the table was set with a repast fit for the senator himself.

"Mom, look!" said Rita, who had gone to a supermarket on the way home from school and purchased an already prepared chicken that had been roasted on a spit in the deli section and smelled heavenly. Worried about her mother, she'd, also, bought coleslaw, three bean salad, and a braided bread from the bakery, thinking if Marcella had something different to eat, her appetite might return.

"Querido, you didn't have to do that," said Marcella, smiling at Rita, and hanging up her jacket.

"I know, Mom," said Rita, beaming with pride.

That's great, Rita. Thank you so much," said Mario. "I'm tired of sandwiches, too. This smells great. Roast chicken. I can tell by the smell it's better than your famous chef of a father's roast rabbit."

Rita laughed loudly, and Marcella laughed with them and sat down at the table. "I feel like a spoiled child from a very rich family," she said and burst into tears.

Rita and Mario waited for her to quit crying.

"I don't know what we can do, Marcella. We can't go back, can we?" asked Mario.

"No. I'm sorry," she said, sniffling and blowing her nose in her napkin. She smiled at them. "I didn't want to do that. I wish you could see my day."

"What do you want to do now?" asked Rita, trying to be helpful.

"I don't know, Rita. If I only knew. Let's eat!" said Marcella, her hand shaking as she took a piece of chicken. They all dug into the extraordinary meal vigorously, and the spirit of Rita's care infected them all with good humor. It helped Marcella get through the week until Friday, but every night, she lay staring at the ceiling mentally replaying what she'd heard on television, trying to put it out of her head and unable to.

"Today's payday," said Mario, at breakfast Friday morning. He poured himself another cup of coffee, fairly dancing around the table, filling Marcella's and Rita's cups jubilantly.

Marcella laughed bitterly. "I remember the first time we went to get our paychecks in this free country."

"I guess that's what they mean when they say, someday you'll look back and laugh, when something bad happens," said Rita. "Remember the first time you got your paycheck at your last job? We were so happy and surprised."

"I forgot that one," admitted Marcella.

"My job's so good, and Rita's school, too, something good is going to happen for you, too, Marcella," said Mario. "We'll go places where other people like us are - like to church. We've got an opening. Now we'll find the way."

"If I can't get out of there soon, I'll jump right out of my skin, Mario. I can't stand it!" said Marcella. She, Mario, and Rita finished breakfast and put on their jackets. Rita walked to school and Mario and Marcella took the bus to work. Mario was eager for his first payday, but even getting paid couldn't ease Marcella's sullen hatred of her job.

When Mario walked into his shop, he first hung his jacket in the closet. "Good morning," he said to Marco.

"Good morning," mumbled Marco. Marco unlocked a drawer in his desk in the corner and got out two checks. "Here's your paycheck," he said, handing Mario one check and putting the other in his pocket. Mario looked at the check for a hundred and fifty dollars and, his expression betrayed his outrage as he tried to hand it back, but Marco didn't take it.

Mario's anger was building rapidly, and in order to assuage it, he turned to the tools, got a wrench to start an oil change to involve his mind on an opposing course, but he couldn't make the emotional switch. He returned to Marco and tried to give him back the check again. "This is wrong," said Mario, scowling angrily. "Take it and make it right. It's supposed to be three hundred dollars."

"I know," said Marco, looking Mario in the eye and speaking softly. "They told me the same thing when I came here years ago." He showed Mario his check. It was for a hundred and fifty dollars, also. "I only hand the check out. It's in the drawer on Friday. There's no one to complain to." Marco glanced at the television for the hundredth time that week as always instead of answering Mario's question, making Mario so mad he wanted to bash in the screen with his wrench. With Marco standing in front of him, the urge to bash in his face instead was so strong, he started to raise the wrench, but something in Marco's eye stopped him, and he dropped the wrench on the floor. A flash of Blair's death in the labor camp traversed Mario's memory, and he put the check in his pocket, trying hard to stifle his antagonism. He wanted to leap on Marco and beat him to a pulp, and he knew it wasn't his fault.

"Don't let them make you angry," Marco said, his voice a low monotone.

"How?" asked Mario, furiously. Marco's clear eyes showed no anger or malice, but something smoldered deep behind his mask that Mario hadn't seen before. Both men turned to their work, but at their break outside, Marco slipped a scrap of paper into Mario's pocket. An address was scrawled on it.

"I work there at night," whispered Marco. "I can get you a job, too. No one they hire works out, and they need help. But you have to wait till someone quits. Don't come until I let you know. Otherwise, I can't help."

Mario was surprised at the sudden offer of help. He'd thought Marco didn't like him. It made him feel easier about working with Marco, and his anger abated. They were in the same situation, and Marco knew much more about how to handle it than Mario. "Where can I get a bank and cash this check?" he asked.

"Go to this credit union." He reached into his back pocket, pulled out his wallet, and handed Mario a card from his credit union. "It's like a bank. They will cash your check because it's from Senator Bold's estate. But don't try to open an account, not yet. You need a social security card." Mario took the card and read the address. He could stop there on his way home. He knew where it was. He rode passed it every day on the bus.

"How can I get a social security card?" he asked. "Do you have one?"

"Wait," said Marco and went back into the shop.

"This isn't right!" Marcella shouted at Elena, in a fury, when she got her paycheck for a hundred and fifty dollars. She yanked the plugs out of her ears. "I'm supposed to get three hundred!"

"I know!" Elena yelled back. "They tell me the same thing in California. I find out when I get here, too. I only find the checks in this drawer on payday. There's no one I can talk to about it."

"Here!" said Marcella, shoving the check into Elena's apron pocket. "You're the boss! Make it right!"

Opening the drawer she found the paychecks in, Elena yelled into it, "Marcella's check is wrong. Fix it!" Throwing the check in, she slammed the drawer. Following Elena and looking over her shoulder when she passed out the other checks, Marcella saw they were all for a hundred and fifty dollars. Before slipping her check into her jeans pocket, Elena held it up in front of Marcella's eyes. It was for a hundred and fifty dollars.

Throwing her arms up in the air, Marcella yelled, "Why don't we all...."

"Yooow," yelled the salad man, and the other kitchen workers contributed to his yell, drowning her out.

"No!" screamed Elena in Marcella's ear, making her ear ring. Marcella jumped back, covering her ear. "You don't understand. Don't let them make you mad, or you'll see what's worse than working in this stinking kitchen!" Elena's horrified expression stopped Marcella cold. She tried to open the drawer to retrieve her check, but it was locked. Elena unlocked the drawer, and handed Marcella the check. Snatching it, Marcella then pocketed it.

Seething through the long day at work, chopping the endless pecks of vegetables and shelling beans and peas, Marcella wished the screeching television was in reach. The clamor seemed to settle in her back and legs and feet pain and headaches and make them worse. She was being taken over by the violence she couldn't tune out. In the afternoon, making the bread dough, she imagined bashing the television in with a meat cleaver regardless of the consequences; but she couldn't reach it. Nevertheless, her wrath and resentment surged, and she hurled an egg at it which broke and ran down the screen. Greatly relieved, she threw another and another. Everyone in the kitchen stopped working and stared at her in horror. Defiantly, she hurled more eggs. As the workers went about their business, the raw egg dripped down the screen and hardened.

When the shuttle stopped at the shop that evening, Marcella knew as soon as Mario boarded by the expression on his face that his paycheck was, also, wrong. She'd gotten into the habit of saving a seat for him, and he sat down next to her.

"We have to get off at the next stop, Marcella. Marco told me where to cash our paychecks." She kept silence until they got off the bus at the credit union.

"My paycheck's wrong, and I know yours is, too," she said, still simmering, as they crossed the street and went into the building. They stood in a line with many Hispanics and waited to cash their checks. No one in line appeared happy or even approachable.

"There's Marco," said Mario. "I better go speak to him." He walked over to Marco standing in another line. A fat ugly woman was right behind him. Mario tapped Marco on the shoulder, and Marco looked at him.

"Hi, Marco," said Mario.

"Hi," said Marco and turned away, and again Mario had to restrain himself from attacking him at that insult. Mario went back to Marcella utterly confused, furious, and dejected. She glared at Marco darkly though he didn't bother to turn around to see where Mario was going.

"I saw that," said Marcella. "These workers are crazy and nasty as pit vipers. Don't they know we're just like them?"

"I don't understand," said Mario, still seething. "He told me where I could cash my check."

"There's Elena right behind him," said Marcella, pointing her out. "But I don't feel like talking to her anyway."

After they cashed their checks and were back on the street, Mario looked up at the white clouds, and the sky looked bluer than ever. The leaves on the trees were bright green, and the brightly colored nasturtiums in the flower beds lightened his spirits. He leaned over and picked two nasturtium leaves and ate them, their spicy taste and fragrance tickling his senses. The nature around him was so different from that of the desert and the Southwest, yet in a thousand years it would be pretty much the same, and it gave him a sense of stability. In some ways he was just like the sky and the trees and the flowers. He thought about the Virgin of Guadalupe telling him to go north when he was a little boy, and put his arm around Marcella's waist and hugged her.

"Hey, Marcella," he said. "We're in New York. We have money in our pockets and money in our money belts. We came with nothing and we got new clothes and jobs even if you hate yours. We sleep in beds now. Let's go to that big market. They'll have better prices than the little store on the corner."

"Okay," said Marcella, smiling at Mario. "I can live like this until we escape because I don't care about all this money and stuff we got in America. I got you, Mario. That's what I live for." He kissed her and the remnant of his anger dropped away.

They went shopping and bought two beers, a root beer, tortillas, cheese, beans, rice, coffee, and some fresh fruit and vegetables to take back. Stopping at a carryout, they then ordered tamales and enchiladas to go. The walk to the store and restaurant worked some of the kinks out of Marcella's back. "I'm going to walk home," she said. "I feel better with that little walk."

"Okay," said Mario. "I like walking better, too." He carried the two bags of groceries, and when Marcella didn't demand to take one of them, he knew her discomfort was severe. He could still feel her anger beneath the pleasant facade and it made him recall Marco's warning. "The first thing we must do is not get mad," he muttered half to himself thinking about Marco's calm, self-possession, though he'd suffered the same robbery.

"Not get mad?" shouted Marcella. "I'm mad, Mario! Why not get mad? I want to kill them all like Julio killed Blair! That's how mad I am, Mario!"

"We should've known New York would be no different," said Mario. "We have no right to believe those liars. Then we wouldn't get so damned mad." Wrestling with fierce anger, trying to reassert itself, Mario saw a large advertisement on a pole with a ladder half way up the pole. "Watch this, Marcella!" He set the bags at the base of the pole, and leaped for the ladder but missed. Falling on his seat, he got up rubbing his rear and snuck a glance at Marcella. The scowl began to give, so he tried again and this time, he grabbed the ladder, got his legs wrapped around the pole and slid down.

Marcella smiled her old happy Marcella smile, so he jumped up on the pole, shinnied part way up, leaped for the ladder and grabbed it. Swinging from the bottom rung, he had no where else to go, and hung there ten feet above the ground pretending to be afraid to let go. Marcella laughed hard, and several other pedestrians had stopped to watch his antics. They laughed, too. With a larger audience then he'd intended, he let go with one hand, scratched his side with his great ape impersonation and dropped to the ground, with all the anger laughed out of Marcella.

When they returned to the boarding house with food and drinks, Rita was full of news from school, as Marcella set the table, and Mario put the food out. They ate listening to Rita's stories from the other side.

As they finished eating, their first visitor knocked on the door, and Rita answered it. Margie Parks breezed in past Rita without waiting to be invited. "I have good news," she said, bubbling with cheer. "I've found you a beautiful house to rent - only five hundred dollars per month."

Mario felt like leaping out of his chair and punching her in the face. Squeezing his aluminum beer can into a ball under the table he pictured her lying in a puddle of blood on the floor.

"When can we see it?" asked Marcella, calmly, knowing there wasn't a woman alive who couldn't sense her hatred.

"Right now; come along." She bustled out and down the stairs and out the front door, like a mother hen, with Mario, Marcella, and Rita grabbing their jackets and falling in behind her.

When they reached the car, Margie Parks opened the front door on the passenger side. "You can get in front," Parks chirped to Mario. Pretending not to hear, Mario left the door hanging open and got in the back with Marcella and Rita.

"Close the door, would you Rita?" asked Ms. Parks.

Rita pretended not to hear and turned to Marcella. "I guess we're finally going home," she said. Marcella smiled at her.

"Looks like it," said Mario.

"Someone get out and close the door!" barked Ms. Parks. No one budged. She lit a cigarette and smoked half of it, tapping her fingers on the back of the seat before getting out, slamming the door, and returning to the driver's seat. "I have to fill in a report about your attitudes and suitability for these jobs," she warned, sternly. "Cooperation counts highly with Senator Bold, and, unfortunately, he's had employees that haven't lasted two weeks."

"Where did they go?" asked Marcella.

"Back to Mexico or wherever they came from," she said, testily taking off with screeching tires. No one spoke, and she turned at a gas station on the corner of a row of tawdry shops in a seedy neighborhood onto a block with houses lining both sides of the street.

Despite her rage, Marcella was anxious to see the house. Peeling paint, sagging porches, and fallen gutters marked the neighborhood, and some of the houses were boarded up. Parks stopped in front of a house, shaded by a maple tree with little islands of grass showing through the crabgrass and bare earth. One of the wood front steps was broken, and a shutter hung from one hinge.

As they got out of the car and followed Parks inside, Marcella said to herself, "I can plant flowers in front. Mario can fix the house." The house was furnished in used discount store. Large mirror tiles on one wall reflected the living and dining rooms. The two bedrooms and bathroom, also, sported wall mirror tiles. The rent wasn't much lower than for the pretty, well kept rambler they'd looked at when they were counting on the promised salary, but at least Rita would have a separate bedroom.

Looking out the kitchen window, Marcella noticed the back yard was more than large enough for a vegetable garden. She turned on the stove burner and it came on immediately. Opening the refrigerator, the light came on inside, and the freezer compartment held two ice trays full of ice. Off the kitchen was a laundry room with a washing machine and dryer.

"Everything works. Here're the keys," said Margie Parks, handing them each a key. "The rent is due on the first of each month. Give your cash or check to Elena or Marco. They'll leave it in the drawer for the landlord."

"Somewhere is a mistake," said Marcella, struggling to keep her wavering voice steady. "Ms. Clement told us in California that we were to get three hundred dollars every week."

"No, my dear; you're the one who made the mistake. Ms. Clement told you three hundred for the family. That's what they always pay," burbled Ms. Parks.

"Marcella isn't wrong," said Mario. "I was there in the restaurant. I heard with my own ears."

"I heard, too," said Rita. "She said three hundred dollars each."

"You misunderstood. You heard what you wanted to hear." Ms. Parks looked at her watch. "I have another appointment in a few minutes. If you hurry, I can give you a ride back to the boarding house to get your things." She fluttered to the door.

"We don't want you to give us anything," said Mario, angrily.

Ms. Parks shot him a poison-tipped dart of a glance, her jaw clamped, and hurried to the door. Mario started to follow her, his reason a gutted castle in flames. He was consumed with the intention of strangling her to death.

Marcella stopped him with her words. "We can take the bus," she said softly, her eyes catching his, arresting his anger.

Parks slammed the front door on her way out. Grabbing Marcella and holding her in his arms, Mario buried his face in her neck, missing her long hair that used to cover him, and she embraced him. "Thank God, I got you, Marcella. There's something to thank the Virgin of Guadalupe for." Feeling a pat on his shoulder, he then included Rita in his embrace.

"You too," he said to Rita.

"We get so mad because every word that comes out of their mouths is a lie," said Marcella. "We'll save some, even if it's just a little every week, and we'll get out of here. They don't want us to know what's going on, how the system works. If we knew, we could get away. It's stupid, what they're doing. Can't they see they'd be better off with us contributing honest work instead of driving us to escape the system?"

"They're not stupid, Marcella," said Mario, solemnly. "They know something we don't that we need to function, and they're very clever. They're liars and lawbreakers, and they know how to keep us from reporting their crimes so we work for them like slaves for subsistence."

CHAPTER SEVENTEEN

Morgan Bold had been the governor of New York for eight years before his election to the U.S. Senate. He'd been a senator for fifteen years. In that time, he'd acquired considerable wealth. His investments leaned heavily toward real estate. One of Bold's most valued assets was a newspaper columnist, Lyman Mills Jr. Personally, he thought Lyman had been in the business so long he was easy. Bold had worked hard to cultivate Lyman, holding parties regularly to make him feel important after Lyman obliged him with favorable press. Bold, in turn, gave Lyman information and access to other information that no other journalist was privy to, giving him extraordinary status with his peers.

"Washington?" said Bold, to his secretary in his office in the mansion. "Get my little friend on the phone. I need to get an idea out and accepted in a hurry." Washington, a slender, efficient middle-aged woman, never laughed at Bold's jokes or made suggestions. She carried out secretarial duties like a soldier in battle, and she went home to her family at the end of the day, forgetting the office existed. Washington put aside the legislative bill she was editing, and dialed Lyman Mills at his office.

"Senator Bold is working on important legislation, Mr. Mills," she said. "He needs the expert opinion of an intelligent political analyst before he can proceed. Can you come over this morning?"

"I'll be there in about an hour," Mills said, his importance varnished to a high shine. He took a sip of skim milk from his glass on his desk.

"Good. See you then," said Washington. She buzzed Bold on the intercom. "Mills will be here in an hour," she said.

"Good, Washington," said Bold, and continued outlining the assignment he had in mind for Mills until he showed up.

"How are you this morning, Mrs. Washington?" asked Mills.

"Fine thanks, Lyman. Go right in. The senator is expecting you. It's a sticky number he's working on. If the public got the wrong impression, it wouldn't go far. It needs the delicate touch of a master's hand," said Washington, softening him up.

"Sure," said Mills. "I'll see what I can do." He tapped on the senator's door and walked in. Morgan got up from his desk and greeted Lyman with a handshake.

"Let's go back to the temple of the gods," said Bold, clapping Mills on the back and opening the door to his private computer video room. He went to the bar, poured Mills a glass of skim milk and handed it to him. Picking up the remote control, he flicked on monitors to the auto shop and the kitchen. The new kitchen girl caught Lyman's attention.

"You've got a new potato peeler," Mills said, singling out Marcella, but the screen's blurry. Bold backed up to a clear screen, and stopped at the point Marcella picked up the first egg to throw at it.

"Ah ha ha," chuckled Lyman. "You got one with some spirit left in her."

Backing up again, Bold zoomed in on her face, and they watched her as she worked. Then he enlarged the view to take in Marcella in her workstation. Lyman let out a low, long whistle. "I like her," he said. "I like her a lot."

"Solve my problem, and you've got her," said Bold. The men sat in two armchairs, facing each other with a checkerboard on a small table between them, and Lyman waited for the problem to unfold, sipping his skim milk.

"Your last number on finance was absolutely brilliant, Lyman. I envy your genius for analysis. If I could think like that, everybody would be coming to me for advice," said Bold, setting up the black checkers.

"Which column was that?" asked Mills, beaming. "The one that knocked Haman off his feet?" Sipping his milk as if it was potent, he laid out the red checkers. Haman, the Secretary of the Department of Education, Senator Bold had learned through his spy system, had been planning to challenge him in the next election. Haman was smart, persistent, and Senator Bold knew he'd keep trying until he broke through, so Senator Bold had unleashed Lyman on him. Using their alma mater, Greenbrier University tactics, unpleasant things began to happen to Haman's son.

First an item in a gossip column in the secretary's hometown appeared in the newspaper. It read; The Secretary of Education, Mort Haman's son was arrested last night for possession of cocaine and is suspected of dealing it.

"Not true," protested young Haman, a graduate student, in a letter to the editor which was published with a picture of young Haman. He was unshaken in his avowal that he never used illegal drugs. Later he was stopped while driving and his car searched, but no cocaine was found, yet, innuendos and open accusations surfaced again and again.

At the university in Texas, young Haman's college friends talked about little else until he got sick of hearing about it.

"I don't want to talk about it," he said to one of his friends. "You know me. We go out together and party together. Have I ever used drugs?"

"Your friends don't care about that slop," said his friend. "Come to my party Friday night. We'll relax and forget it." At the party, he was offered a snort of cocaine, and young Haman immediately left asking himself, "Who are my friends?"

*Mortimer Haman's son, who claims to never use dope, attended a party last night where cocaine was injected into veins. Our innocent young people are being poisoned slowly by these dealers*, stated a column written by Lyman and inserted in his syndicate's Texas paper. Shaken but sure of himself in his innocence, young Haman called his father.

"The news media is accusing me of using drugs, and I don't, Dad. Even my friends are beginning to act strange. Why don't I sue them for libel?" he asked.

"They'd get worse. They'd drive us crazy. Public officials almost never win a lawsuit for libel against the press. They're allowed mistakes in the case of public officials because they have deadlines to meet, and their job is to keep us honest. We're fair game. My attention has been drawn to the news reports, Son," said Haman Senior, on the phone from Washington.

"But I'm not a public official."

"Those vultures don't give a hot damn about that. Their intention is to screw me, and since I'm clean as a whistle, they're trying to get to me through you."

"You know it's not true, Dad."

"I know. The senator is making up lies because he's desperate, and I'm going to challenge him in the election. It's one of his typical smear campaigns. They're going to continue to try to get you to use it. Can you handle it?"

"Of course, I'm not going that way, but I'm not sure how I'm going to handle it," he said nervously. "I'm constantly on guard. I'm not used to living like this. Finals are coming up. If I allow my attention and energy to be drawn away, I won't pass at the top of my class. I've been working on it too long and too hard to let up."

"Well, keep up the good work, but they're not going to back off," said Haman Sr. It's Bold's way of telling me if I back off from the challenge, he'll leave you alone."

"Stick, Dad. Don't let him use me to blackmail you. They can't prove that I'm doing something I'm not."

"I've seen it happen, Son. Be careful."

"I intend to do that. Bye Dad, and good luck. Win and we'll be through with these terror campaigns. As soon as finals are over and I have the time, I'm going to sue their pants off."

"Good luck, Son. You have my full confidence. You can't miss. Bye."

The pressure increased. *Young Haman's girlfriend reported finding marijuana seeds at a small gathering of friends at Haman's apartment, and a Grand Jury is being formed to investigate Haman's attachment to the underworld,* proclaimed the gossip column. Two weeks later Haman Sr. read the final item about his son in the gossip column.

>*Would-be law school graduate with highest honors, Mortimer Haman Junior, killed himself with an overdose of cocaine the evening before graduation.*

Haman Sr. knew his son had been murdered. Deeply grieved, he couldn't deal with his guilt. "If I hadn't challenged Bold, my son would still be alive, graduating with highest honors and moving on to a brilliant career," he said to himself. "I'd still be the Secretary of Education positioned to retire with full retirement and benefits in two years." As it was, he'd used most of his financial resources in the campaign; and his friends, who opposed Bold's tactics, had thrown so many of theirs into his campaign that he couldn't quit and leave everybody in the lurch.

After an analysis by the crime lab, the "marijuana seeds" turned out to be ordinary poppy seeds used in cooking, and people who'd attended the party recalled eating sandwiches made with poppy seed rolls. No one in the underworld who knew Haman could be found, and the grand jury was quietly dissolved, but after the young man's death the media lost interest.

Then Haman's wife was photographed at a party. Greeting a male associate with a hug, as she greeted all her guests, a photograph was taken. When it appeared on the front page of the paper, the couple appeared to be in a close embrace, and the photo was doctored to make the expressions passionately stupid. The caption under the picture implied that they were having an affair, and Faith Haman was driven to distraction.

The coup de gras was Lyman Mill's accusatory syndicated editorial, involving an incident that occurred when Haman was twelve years old. *Has Mortimer Haman covered a life of unsavory connections with an interest in the public good in order to prey upon ordinary people from the time he stole his first bicycle as a teenager?*

Lyman's column read as though he were Saint Peter fighting the power of evil in high places. Haman recalled the incident the article referred to. He had bought a bicycle when he was twelve years old with money he'd saved from a paper route and mowing lawns. When he left the store with it, an alarm went off, and he was stopped by a security guard.

"Where's your receipt?" the guard had asked. Haman couldn't find it.

"I paid four hundred dollars for this bike," he said. "Maybe I dropped the receipt. Let's go to the clerk I bought it from. He'll remember."

"Yeah, let's just do that," said the guard, "and don't think you're going anywhere else." Insulted, Haman confidently walked with the guard back to the bicycle department, pushing the bike.

"Tell him I bought the bike," he said to the sales clerk he'd handed four hundred and fifteen dollars, including tax, to not ten minutes previously.

"What bike?" asked the man, staring at him blankly.

"This bike!" said Haman, indicating the bike he'd wheeled back through the store. He was beginning to sweat. "It was four hundred dollars, a special sale. There wasn't one on the floor," he said, turning to the guard. "He had to go back to the stock room to find it."

"There's a whole row of them behind the bikes that aren't on sale," said the clerk.

"You're lying!" said Haman, so angry he couldn't think.

"Why would I lie?" he asked, staring at Haman with wide-eyed innocence, stepping over to the aisle where the bikes were on sale and pointing out the row of bikes. The clerk, Haman, and the guard looked at the bikes with a large sign in front of them in plain view.

"That sign wasn't there before!" protested Haman. The guard grabbed Haman by the arm and walked him to the office in the rear of the store. In a blind panic, Haman put his hand in his pocket, looking for something to wipe the sweat off his brow, and pulled out four hundred dollars worth of coupons. The store gave coupons for the purchase of particular products that could be collected and used as discounts for other purchases. The clerk had tried to avoid giving him the coupons, but he'd insisted. Haman's coupons were proved to have come from the clerk's cash register, but the guard had not even made his call to the police before the truth was established, and the store manager had apologized profusely, realizing the possibility of a lawsuit.

That his son could be murdered with cocaine, his wife slandered and driven half crazy, and Lyman Mills could report on the bike incident, which had never even made it to a police report, forty-eight years later gave Haman pause. As the accusations, which were impossible to refute but caused public scandal increased, Haman's confidence in his ability to unseat Bold wavered followed by a collapse in his self-confidence. Like all powerful prior reformers challenging Bold, Haman had retired from politics.

"I need advice on a very delicate matter, a proposal I'm seeking for the public good," Senator Bold said to Lyman, making a move that invited Lyman Mills to jump him. "Look at this article." The senator handed Lyman a story about the closing of the Painter Labor Camp and studied the board. Then he jumped Lyman twice. Lyman waited to make his move until he looked over the article.

"People shouldn't have to live like that in America, ever, should they?" asked Senator Bold.

"No one should have to live under those conditions anywhere," agreed Mills, going for the bait, laying the paper aside. He sipped his milk, making his move. "Still, it would've taken an enormous dent out of Horton Painter's holdings to repair that shantytown," he said, looking the senator in the eye. "And you know how hard we all have to work for our money." Senator Bold's next move allowed Lyman to maneuver him into losing two pieces and gaining a king.

"There must be a way to improve these properties, so they can be sold at a profit, wouldn't you say?" asked Senator Bold.

"I have the perfect solution," said Mills, making the obvious move. "You asked for my advice, and here it is. Pass a law that repairs of shabby properties come out of taxes. I have a reputation for looking after the interests of the poor. I'll plant the seeds of change in my column."

"If some radical upstart looks too deep, my chances in the next election wouldn't be worth much, you know." Pretending to be distracted by the importance of the conversation, Bold didn't block his previous error, leaving Lyman's advantage wide open.

"I have a lot of clout in my business. Don't you worry about that. It's not like the old days when every rabble rouser who came down the pike had a voice." Lyman jumped two of the senator's men and claimed his crown. He was then in position to easily corner and jump Senator Bold's remaining pieces off the board.

"Another game?" asked Lyman, the victorious.

"No, no, I don't seem to be in top form today," said Senator Bold, scratching his ear, satisfied that the wheels were sufficiently greased. "There's just one other thing, Lyman. Do you have any idea how much money our friends, yours and mine, are losing on their California citrus crops?"

Mills sipped his milk. "You know, Morgan, we've been over this. I'm going to try to think of a new angle, but I've tried before and have been unable to do anything about the marketing orders. Every time we turn up the heat, they replace someone in the Agriculture Department. Their committees that regulate the citrus sales have power that we haven't been able to touch."

"Think of something," snapped the senator. "That's not a good answer."

"I'll try, but don't count on it," said Mills. "How many times have we tried before? Some sacred cows don't fall."

"Bullshit."

Mills shrugged. "I'll try. If you come up with any angles to work from, let me know. In the meantime, don't forget our current bargain. I expect to have a new date the day my column breaks." He stood up to go to his office and work on it. "Goodbye, Senator," he said.

"Goodbye Lyman. I'll be watching for your column," said Senator Bold, showing Lyman out of the temple of the gods, and the senator's top form immediately surfaced. He went into his office and called his secretary.

"Washington, Babe, scout me more cheap real estate, low-income housing in need of repairs, and do it on a dba basis. Thanks, Babe."

"Very well," said Washington. "How much property do you want?"

"As much as you can acquire."

"Very well, anything else?"

"Hire a general contractor; make sure it's one of our associates, to supervise the rebuilding of property you buy."

"Very well. Bye."

"Yes, Lyman is necessary," said Senator Bold, to himself, remembering the bad rap his father got from the press for being a slum landlord. He'd been ordered to clean up his tenements by the court, and it had cost the old man plenty. He'd inherited his father's appreciation of wealth, but he had to laugh at the old fart, always thinking he was getting there with his penny-ante real estate. He wished the old man could see him now. He'd have the last laugh on the old bastard.

## CHAPTER EIGHTEEN

"I'm going to find another job," announced Marcella, angrily as she, Mario, and Rita finished dinner at their house after work.

"How are you going to find a job, Marcella?" asked Mario. He thought about the job Marco had mentioned but was hesitant to bring it up until he heard what Marcella had to say. He'd always been honest and straightforward with her, but now she was a woman on the edge, and he was afraid. He didn't know how to handle it.

"I don't know how, but I must get out of there," she said. "They watch everything we do. Maybe that's why we have all this stuff."

"What do you mean...how watch?" Mario got up and pulled the curtains closed. Lowering his voice, he glanced furtively around the room.

"I don't know how."

"Then why do you say such things?" asked Mario, his tension building.

"Do they have TV on where you work?"

"Yes, but I don't pay attention. I'm working on my engine all the time. I love to work in mechanics. We must put the money behind us. Here is better than the fields. Where could I work in mechanics? Huh? Tell me that. I'm building a solar engine, Marcella! It'll make the air clean. I hate the fields. I never want to go back."

"I hate that place, Mario! I can't stand to go there! The fields are better. Ms. Griswold's was paradise if only you could be there compared to this place."

"Where else can we go? Where? Where?" He threw up his hands in despair.

"I'm afraid! I don't know why. Something very, very bad is happening. I feel it in here!" She jabbed at her heart.

"I don't understand you, Marcella!" yelled Mario. "We worked and planned for a chance! We sweat blood to get here! We lived for this, studying English and tramping on the desert all night with Rita from the time she could walk.

"We run and hide like dogs! We pick and scavenge and sleep in the dirt for this, and now you don't want it? What can I do?" Mario put his hands on his temples and held them out to Marcella in a forceful gesture as though he was throwing his thought at her. "Look at my hands, Marcella!" He held them out in front of her, and taking her hand, he opened it and ran his fingers over her calluses. "Even Rita, we have hands like this, and they can do many things besides pick, pick, pick."

"I hate Bold's kitchen!" she yelled, unrepentant. "They have TV on all day at work, and it isn't real programs. It's awful horrible stuff; people screaming and fighting and killing each other in gruesome ways. I don't look, but I have to hear. It's so loud, you can't talk. All the workers look like zombies, and that's why. I can't stand the sight of a TV, even if it's off!"

Tired of arguing, Marcella grabbed the newspaper and sat down with it, but reading an article disturbed her even more. "Look here at this newspaper article," she said. Mario and Rita gathered around her. "Look here about this." She read slowly. *A fourteen-year-old Latin American boy was shot in the back by a law enforcement officer in El Cajon, California. His eight-year-old brother is being held in the county jail with deportation proceedings pending. The scavengers crossed the border illegally and stole food and clothes. They were searching for their parents who crossed with coyotes three months previously. They said their parents were supposed to contact them immediately and send for them, but they never did. The boy who died was playing with a toy gun the officer thought was real.*

"How come this was not one of us shot in the back? How come these things happen every day, only to other people, but we're so lucky?"

"Because we came by ourselves; we didn't depend on coyotes," replied Mario.
"Then read this," she demanded
"I'm tired of reading," he replied exasperated and fatigued

with their fighting.

"This is the last one for today. You won't read. There's no way I can get you to believe what I say. You always used to read the paper, and you believed me before."

Mario let out a deep sigh of frustration. "I still believe you," he said, taking the paper. "I believe you're afraid, and you don't know why. It's a scary thing, what we did, but you'll see. It'll be alright. But you're right. I was the one who always read the paper, and now I never do. I'm not looking as hard to get away as you because I like the work and you hate it."

Mario read the article she showed him about a new type of engine being designed by scientists at Greenbrier University. He frowned. As he read the description, the lines on his face tightened with his grip on the paper. He jumped up, shaking it furiously.

"How could they know this?" he shouted in a rage, slapping the paper with the back of his hand. "This is my idea! It came from my head with my hands shaping new parts on a forge! Nobody could know this!"

"That's what I'm saying and saying and saying. Something is wrong, and it's something very, very bad."

Mario stared at Marcella and thought about his engine and where he was designing and developing it. Why would they give him everything to build such an engine as he was doing?

"The TV," said Mario. "That's why Marco looks at it every time I ask him a question! The image and sounds are transmitted on radio waves. The TV is at the shop, so someone can watch us. Images and sound travel just as easily either way. The TVs at work are eavesdrop monitors."

"Gosh," said Rita, aghast. "I'm glad we didn't get a TV. Now I don't want one. I'm going to tell my friend at school."

"Don't tell anyone," said Mario. "Your Mom was right. If they know we know, I don't know what they'll do to us."

"The people who know us would read a story like this in the newspaper," said Marcella, straightening it out and pointing to the article about the boy who was shot in the back.

"Then what are we going to do?" asked Rita.

"Think," said Mario. "Canada is not too far away."

"Maybe it'll be the same," said Marcella. "It might cost too much to live there. How would we get jobs there any easier than here?"

"Until we find the way out, we'll do exactly what we're doing and pretend like we don't know. If they steal my engine, they steal my engine. Our lives are more valuable."

"I don't know what to do," said Rita. "We're in real trouble."

"Study," said Mario. "That's how you've always handled it, maybe that's why. Study is what will get you through. We have to rely on each other, but we must, also, rely on ourselves."

"I'm going to my room then. That's exactly what I'm going to do - study," said Rita, grateful for a retreat from the tension of too much togetherness.

"Rita, before you go to your room, I want to talk to you," said Marcella. "We never talk anymore."

"What, Mom?" Rita was happy that Marcella wanted to talk. She'd been so angry all the time that Rita found herself hibernating in her room more each day. Marcella was no longer fun to be around.

"When I was your age, I was interested in boys more than books. Don't you ever want to go out with the other children? Who's your new friend at school?"

"Margaret. She's real smart. She wants to be an engineer. She likes to study, too."

"Not all the time. It's not good at your age."

"My world is not like the other kids," said Rita. "I want only to get out of this mess and into their real world. I want this for myself and Julio because he was the best friend I ever had. We made a pact to escape, and I'm going to keep it. Wherever he is, he's going to keep it, too. I don't want to make another friend like Julio until I don't live in a place where we might be murdered or captured, but where we can come and go like every other kid."

"I understand that, Rita. Can you bring your friend, Margaret, over sometime to study?"

"Usually we study at the library."

"Are you ashamed of our house?"

"No. It's a dump, but I don't care about that. You're changing, Mom. You're mad at me and Dad even, and we didn't do anything."

"I'm sorry, Rita. I don't know myself what I can do about it, except to get away from Bold's. I'll find a way."

"I have to study," said Rita. "I like talking to you when you're not mad. It's like it used to be when we crossed the dessert and worked the crops, and we trusted each other and depended on each other."

"Thanks for telling me your true thoughts like we've always done," said Marcella. "I was never afraid on the dessert. Even in the labor camps, I hated to be there, but I wasn't afraid. We were going to a better life. We were making it happen. Here I'm afraid because there's something very bad happening to me, and I don't know what to do. I want to run away, but there's nowhere to go."

"I hope it'll be okay, Mom." Rita put her arms around Marcella and kissed her before going to her room and closing the door. She opened her chemistry book and had to forget everything else to concentrate.

"Marcella, you and I never talk since we got to New York either." Mario rested his hand on her shoulder, and she moved away to clear the table.

"I can't. I can't explain," she said softly. Looking down at the plate, she picked it up. "Something so bad is happening to me. I don't know what to do. It's the job. I've got to get away."
Covering her face in her hands, she burst into tears. Mario had never

seen her cry before they got the jobs at Bold's, and he was at a loss of what to do. Again he tried to comfort her the way he always had. He put his arms around her, but she drew away. He glanced around the room, trying to think of something funny, but nothing came to him.

Sniffling loudly, she blew her nose and wiped her face. "I'm sorry, Mario. I can't help it." Silently, Mario helped with the dishes. When they were finished, Marcella settled into a comfortable chair with a novel from the library.

"You never used to read much," said Mario, missing the time he was accustomed to spending with her after work.

"Stories written here about people who live here will help me know how they do things," she said.

"I thought our lives would be better here, Marcella. Maybe it's no better anywhere." Mario got ready for bed restlessly. He felt the crack in his bond with Marcella widening. They'd always come to an agreement on every matter of importance, and the unimportant faded into history, leaving little noticeable trace except for the minute influences that molded each of their viewpoints. He felt it most painfully when they were in bed which was only to sleep since moving to their house. Marcella, who had so freely shared his anguish and his joy, was building a resistance to being close to him.

He took a shower and went to bed, waiting for her. She'd always wanted a bed, and they'd joked before about what it would be like to have a room of their own with a double bed in it. Brooding, he couldn't think of what to do about her. Her reticence aroused a terrible anxiety, and caused a need that had been absent when he was confident of his relationship with her. They'd spent many long hours talking quietly, intimately sharing each other's hopes and fears and dreams, sometimes silly, sometimes serious, but now everything was different.

He watched her come to the bedroom and get ready for bed, watched her brush her hair, thinking of what it felt like on his cheek, on his hand. He decided to wait awhile tonight. Try something different. Try not to rush her, but the need of her, his love of her, and her physical beauty made trying a plan nearly impossible, and though contrivance would reduce both their pleasure, relief was necessary. He had to get back the wholehearted unrestrained love, the delight she found in him that had carried them through hell. She came to bed, and he felt her tension.

"Good night, Mario," she said.

"Good night, Marcella. I love you." Listening to her slow, regular breathing, he tried to think of a new approach. He had no experience in dealing with the woman beside him who felt like a bomb about to detonate if he couldn't defuse it. He tried to move closer, to take her in his arms, like he used to, but when he touched her, she sat up suddenly, with a sharp cry, cracking him in the mouth.

"I'm sorry," she said, touching his lip gently. "I was half sleeping. You woke me up. I'm sorry."

He sat up, and putting his arm around her, he took her chin in his hand and kissed her. She pulled away.

"I can't."
"What's wrong?"
"The television at work - I keep seeing and hearing the hatred, the crime, the filth that people do to each other here. It makes my blood go cold, Mario. It's something being done to us in the kitchen on purpose. If you come and see, look at the kitchen workers when they leave - they're not even people. That's how I'm beginning to feel." Marcella started crying, and Mario got her a glass of water and got back in bed. She drank it and put the glass on the floor.

"I need you, Marcella. You're driving me crazy. I need you. I don't know how to talk about it. We've never talked about it. Do you still love me?"

"I'm sorry. I love you more than my life. You're part of me. But I have to get away from work."

"What can I do to help you? What can I do?" asked Mario, desperately.

"I don't know. I love you just the same, but I don't know." She turned to him to comfort and relieve him, but her pleasure wasn't in it, and Mario went to sleep a worried man.

At work the next morning, engrossed in his engine, Mario hadn't paid much attention to the television. Minding his own business, ignoring Marco's incomprehensible sorrow, Mario had tightened each bolt of his engine, picturing each step, forging the parts, working it until it fit the image in his mind. When he was working, he'd thought of nothing else, but knowing that someone was stealing his labor killed his inspiration, and he lost his joy in his work.

Pondering the turn of events, unable to concentrate, his attention drifted to the television. He watched two men playing checkers, carefully noticing their faces and movements. Their lips moved, but the sound was so low, he couldn't hear what they said. They were intrinsically different from him and Marcella and Rita. He attributed the differences to those of wealth and class, but looking more carefully, he saw those differences were vague, like shadows, in comparison to a much deeper divide he couldn't identify. "The one on the right is Senator Bold," he said to himself.

"Go back to work," muttered Marco, under his breath. "It's important."

"Is that Bold?" whispered Mario. Marco nodded.

Halfheartedly, Mario turned back to the engine, but he couldn't bring his attention to focus on it. Again, his attention drifted to the television. Unmistakably, beneath the men playing checkers was another image, though it was vague. At first he couldn't tell what it was, but studying it, he realized it was a man and a woman having sex in bed; and then he saw that it was Senator Bold. In a flash of comprehension was the knowledge that the woman was Marco's wife, Mareno when she looked young and beautiful. He thought about the other women working on the estate, and how they seemed to deliberately make themselves ugly. He looked at Marco then, the jut of his chin, the set of his eyes, the determination in his shoulders, the defiance in his movement. He knew why Marco only glanced at the television to indicate it but never watched it, and taking one more glance, he determined that he would never watch it again either.

But what he saw transfixed him with horror. The images that had been superimposed were gone, and he saw Rita sitting naked on the toilet in their bathroom followed by clear as life movies of him and Marcella in bed. He felt like the top of his head was coming off driven by a volcano within.

Marco moved in front of the television blocking his view, caught his eye, and shook his hand in a firm grip. "Stop it," he mouthed. "Stop it. We're all going to get away," he voiced, and Mario had to read his lips to make out what he was saying.

The instinct to survival came to Mario's heart, and he turned back to the engine, his mind and heart racing. Staring at the engine, he didn't see it. The rest of the day he pretended to work, going through the motions. Marco, understanding what was happening to him, gave him many small menial jobs; changing oil, a routine tune-up on an older Lincoln, replacing parts.

Before leaving the shop for the day, Mario concealed a hammer on the inside of his uniform. He didn't speak to Marcella when they got off the shuttle, and she'd had such a horrendous day that she was happy to be let alone to seethe in silence.

Mario had a job to do and wouldn't rest until it was finished. They got on the bus in silence and rode to their stop in silence. When they got off, Mario stalked to the house that no longer felt like home, but more like an animal cage in a zoo; Marcella beside him. He looked calm on the outside, but there was a raging fire within.

"What's the matter, Mario?" Marcella asked. He didn't answer.

"Mario, what's wrong? Mario?" She half ran to keep up with him, a man possessed. Entering his house with a grunt of rage, he ran to the mirror in the living room, striking it with the hammer until it cracked and then splintered, as Marcella stood in the doorway watching, stunned. This Mario was a stranger.

Rita ran out of her room to stand beside Marcella, watching, too flabbergasted to speak.

He continued his frenzied whacking until the mirror shattered. The sound of hammer swacking against glass, the glass cracking, and then tinkling to the floor, gave Mario immense relief as he forgot himself in his systematic destruction of the mirrors. Hammering again and yet again, leaving the glass all over the floor, he then proceeded to another room, splintering the mirror, grunting and groaning in fury.

Slivers and chunks of glass clung to his hair and his clothing and covered his shoes. He went on to the bathroom and then Rita's bedroom.

Whack! He now held the hammer with both hands, swinging his whole being into each blow, letting the wrath and humiliation, the shame of himself and his wife and daughter being treated like animals, his wife's forced emotional separation from him by the abuse at her job, the theft of his idea, run into each blow of hammer on glass. He imagined Bold's face, and the faces of the other men he'd seen on television in the shattering mirrors; and he wished the blood trickling down the broken mirrors to be theirs instead of his.

"Someday," he vowed, between grunts of rage. "Someday, I swear it will be their blood; and mine and the blood of those I love will stay with us; and the two can never mix because our blood is water and theirs is oil!" He moved on to his and Marcella's bedroom, gasping for breath, hammering again and again, the veins standing out on his temples, sweat pouring off him.

Thwack! "That's you, Bold." Thwack! Thwack! "You, Clement!" Thwack! Thwack! Thwack! "That's all of you who looked through that spyglass!" he shouted. Thwack! Thwack! "Pigs! Filthy pigs!" The words came out as little more than grunts.

Marcella silently followed Mario, staying out of the range of flying glass, with a broom and dustpan. Rita walked behind Marcella with the trashcan. Marcella returned to the broom closet for a bucket and mop and scrub brush when the mess under her feet turned bloody. She sympathized with Mario's fury, and she, too, felt relief from her own building tension. If she had another hammer, she'd have helped him.

Rita, in the strange state of unforeseen circumstances, went into the kitchen to prepare the evening meal, listening to shock after shattering shock of hammer blow on glass. Mario's groans and utterances sounded more like those of a dying animal than her father.

His rampage continued until there was nothing where the mirrors had been but blank walls, marred and broken in places by the hammer and broken glass; and he was certain the microscopic cameras were pulverized.

Mario took a shower, making the water cold as ice, and stayed in it until the blood stopped flowing from his superficial lacerations, and the slivers of glass were all washed out.

Marcella cleaned the house stunned into silence, and Rita finished preparing dinner. When the tortillas and beans and salad were on the table, and everyone was ready, they sat at the table together.

"Don't ask," growled Mario. "Just don't ask. I'm almost a man again. Almost."

"I understand," said Marcella.

"I don't," muttered Rita. She'd always been included, and her outside status was a knife in her heart. For once she was afraid to ask, multiplying the unfamiliar sensation by a hundred. The father and mother she knew had never demonstrated violence, and the adults she was sharing this meal with were unknown. She ate on the edge of tears.

After dinner Marcella and Mario stayed in the kitchen to clean up, and Rita, forcing back the tears trying to flood through the dam of her control, immersed herself in algebra, emerging to get a soda when mental fatigue set in. She heard Mario talking, as she entered the kitchen.

"They watched us through cameras behind the mirrors," muttered Mario. "And they put it on TV at work. I saw it - us making love in bed - Rita naked in the bathroom. Who else saw, I don't know."

"The kitchen workers are beaten up and mutilated on TV," said Marcella. "That's why I hate it and don't watch."

"What are we going to do?" asked Rita, from the doorway. Included by her knowledge of why Mario had smashed the mirrors, her self-confidence returned as quickly as she'd faltered.

"I don't know," said Mario. "What do you think, Marcella?"

"I don't know either. We don't know why, how can we know what to do? We ate the snake on the desert, but we knew why. Mario got sick, but we knew why. We crossed the desert, but we knew why. Because we don't know why, we can't make plans to help ourselves. We're like animals in a trap. We have to find out why they do these things."

"I have to fix the walls," said Mario. "They might send us back now."

"Don't talk like that, Mario. We never gave up yet. Don't give up now. We always wear our money belts so we're ready to run."

The next morning, Marcella set the breakfast table in silence. Mario started the coffee wordlessly. Rita prepared three grapefruit halves and set one at each of their places.

After filling the bowls with steaming oatmeal, Marcella sat down. She ate hastily, silently, sneaking furtive, meaningful glances at Mario and Rita, fearful that Mario or all of them might be arrested for Mario breaking the mirrors.

"We'll be all right," whispered Rita, under her breath.
"Mi Dios!," said Mario, "Deliver us from evil."
"God go with us," said Marcella.
"And with New York," added Rita.
"And with America," said Mario. Mario finished eating in silence and went outside to sit on the front stoop with his coffee.

"Let's go sit with Mario," said Marcella, going out. Rita left the dishes in the sink, refilled her cup, and took it out to the porch. She sat with Mario and Marcella.

"Marcella," said Mario. "Do you think people are different here?"

"No, Mario. They're no different. When we left our countries, we took a chance. We were desperate. We did the right thing. Here we found the bad behind the good of having a place to live. There are millions of people who live here in private houses. Some day, we'll be like them."

"There must be freedom and justice with law," said Rita, putting her cup on the step and resting her elbows on her knees. "It must be here. I learned it in school. The whole world knows it. The whole world can't be wrong."

"The Virgin of Guadalupe told me to go away to the north when I was just a kid," said Mario. "There's an angel watching over us. Remember on the desert when we talked about going back?"

"Yes. I'm glad we didn't. You were right. You can't go back. We're on the road that starts in the womb. It only goes one way," said Marcella.

"I'll finish the dishes," said Rita. "I've got time." She took their coffee mugs inside, and Mario and Marcella went to the bus stop and caught the bus to Bold's.

Mario couldn't concentrate on his job. Smoldering beneath the noncommittal expression he forced to hide his feelings, the scheme of the engine, which had been a labor of love, was lost to the bitterness he didn't know how to cope with.

"Where can we go from here?" he asked himself. Without the creative genius to spur him, he resigned himself to working on conventional engines. Every time the creative spark returned, at the sight of his unfinished project in the corner, the disgust with his situation and helplessness to escape it shut him down. The eager joy with which he'd looked forward to work turned into monotony, and Marco's sinister hopelessness oppressed him. After work, he talked to Marcella on the way to the house he no longer considered home.

"These people are powerful, Marcella. I never thought I could be this scared of anything. You never know what the rules are or when they might change them or what might happen. The law doesn't apply to us. There's no justice we can appeal to."

"We have to wait and watch for an opportunity. If we can keep making money and saving some, we'll find a way out," said Marcella.

"We pay rent and buy a few clothes, but we never save enough because everything costs so much and something happens. We have to spend."

"Our chance will come. You told me yourself, Mario. Senator Bold is against the law, too. There must be many people who want him to get caught, maybe who are working on it right now. A person that vicious is not only after us. We're caught in his web because we crossed his path. He must have many enemies among his own people."

Mario laughed, bitterly. "He makes the law, Marcella, but he has so much money that he doesn't have to live by it. I hope you're right, though."

As they rounded the corner to their house, Rita bounded down the sidewalk to meet them, her ponytail flying out behind her.

"I got a job at a fast-food restaurant after school!" she said, unable to contain her excitement. "I'll be able to help us save! It's more than minimum wage, and it's at a Fishermans!"

Marcella stared at Rita. "The same chain Fishermans we stopped to eat at the day we left California?"

"Yes."

"That's great," said Mario. "You can save it for things you need." Mario remembered the address of the work place Marco had given him, as they walked down the street to their house. It seemed like he'd been waiting a long time for Marco to call

"Many people know how we got here, and there are many more like us than we'll ever know," said Rita. "We don't know who they are; maybe the family next door, maybe the man across the street, maybe the bus driver. They come to get away from a place they can't live, and some employers forget to ask for your identification. My friend at school got a job at a fast food restaurant. She said they'd hire one more without a green card. I'm going to work there."

"That's what I'm going to do," said Marcella. "I have to find a way. You give me hope, Rita. If you can do it, I can, too."

"Marco works at night washing dishes. He can get me a job at the same place," said Mario. "But I have to wait until someone else leaves."

Marcella looked at him quizzically, sensing that something had changed between them. "Why didn't you even tell me?" she asked.

"I don't know. I don't want to do anything to make things worse between us. I don't know what to say anymore, what to do."

"We can't let them change who we are," she said. "Mario, you said we'll always remember who we are."

"Remembering who we are is easier than being who we are. I'm afraid because of what they've done to you, Marcella. I've never been afraid before. I don't know how to handle it, but Marco knows. I watch him, and I'll learn."

"Then Rita and I will have to learn from you," said Marcella. "I'm glad you told me Marco can get you a job." She smiled at Mario, shyly, almost like when he first met her, and his heart leaped.

CHAPTER NINETEEN

Morgan Bold read Lyman Mill's syndicated column in *The Greenbrier Daily News.* It would appear in thousands of newspapers across the United States and some abroad. It would be available to everybody who subscribed to the Internet. He folded the paper and tuned in the kitchen staff on the closed-circuit television with his eye on Marcella. He had a passion for hot-blooded Hispanic women. "I'm in love," he stated, matter-of-factly, and called Parmado, the head houseman, with his beeper. Ten minutes later, Parmado appeared in the temple of the gods.

"Yes, Senator Bold?" he asked.

"Get the new woman in the kitchen, Marcella Dominguez, and take her to my bedroom," he said. "Stay there on the other side of the door until you hear she's subdued. When I leave, get her cleaned up and installed in the guest room. Call Lyman Mills, and tell him his reward is ready."

"Yes, sir," said Parmado. He left Bold and assembled three additional housemen.

"Bold wants Marcella," he said. They exchanged meaningful looks with semi-veiled eyes, careful at hiding their disgust. They followed Parmado through the storage room adjoining the kitchen. He stopped briefly at a cupboard and grabbed a navy blue tablecloth, and concealed it under his suit coat. Though no word was exchanged, the others read their leader's action.

They followed him to the kitchen where Marcella and Elena were cutting up vegetables at different stations. The other kitchen workers stood at their respective stations involved in different tasks. One of the large, burly housemen stood in front of the doorway, his arms folded across his chest. Three others approached Marcella, one from each side and one from the rear. Sensing them closing in, she whirled in time to see Parmado, out of view of the television screen, throw a tablecloth over it.

"Stand back!" she shouted, slashing at the first to come near. Her knife found its mark, and the men suddenly turned on each other punching and pushing each other, grunting and groaning.

"Run," yelled Elena, "yanking the earplug out of Marcella's ear. "You're the target! Get out! They're risking their lives to give you cover." The knife still in her hand, Marcella dashed out of the kitchen, down the hallway and out the door, heading for the woods.

Elena jumped into the melee, kicking and flailing wildly, followed by the other kitchen workers.

"Goddamn it!" shrieked Bold, when the screen went black. He pounded on the monitor and then shook it. "What's the matter with this fucking equipment? It works perfectly until you're counting on it!" He heard the sounds of a great battle. "She must be fighting hard," he said, his eyes glazing over.

Parmado poured cooking oil on the floor, causing the housemen and kitchen workers to slip and slide all over the kitchen, and leaped back into the fight. When the kitchen was a shambles, and Marcella had enough of a head start, Parmado pulled the kitchen alarm. The housemen then found their feet and chased Marcella, but she was nearly to the forested area behind the mansion. Elena pulled the tablecloth down and crammed it behind the stove for later removal.

Breathlessly, Marcella ran down a trail in the woods. Hearing a dog loping behind, she turned as a large German shepherd leaped for her arm. The animal had mange, and its ribs showed through skin that hung, like a loose glove. Its eyes cloudy, it let out a vicious snarl. She slashed the side of its face, and it ran away whining, leaving a trail of blood. Marcella picked up speed, as more dogs came from different directions. One bit her on the calf, and she turned around slashing. Her knife caught the top of the beast's head, and it retreated with a howl of pain.

She shouted and brandished the knife; and hearing another dog from the rear, she was forced in another direction. She could run only a few yards at a time before she felt the breath of dogs behind her and had to turn again, yelling and slashing to hold them at bay. Making her way slowly, she developed her technique, shout and brandish fiercely, turn and run until dogs were close enough behind that she could feel their breath; and turn on them again to stop them, so she could run again. The starving dogs soon grouped, and she was no longer surrounded. The taste of blood and the excitement of beasts in a pack drove them.

Marcella fled onto a narrow overgrown trail down a steep hill, where they'd have to follow in single file or two abreast. She came upon an adit deep in a ravine, and ran for it. She heard the pack behind her and turned in time to see the dogs only a few yards behind. Picking up a large rock, she hurled it, catching the lead dog in the head. He fled, an unholy howl rising from his bowels, and two dogs followed him. The others stopped where they were, barking and growling savagely.

Stepping through the entrance to the mine, Marcella felt her way along the cold, damp wall deeper into the shaft, and the dogs stayed whining and snarling at the entrance.

The housemen returned to face the consequences in Senator Bold's office.

"She got away, Sir," said the disheveled Parmado, his hand wrapped in a bloody dishtowel. "She had a knife, and she's strong. She threw oil on the floor, and it was hopeless."

One of the others with a bloody sleeve studied his feet; his hands clasped behind his back, his shirt tail out, and tie askew. Another limped; all of them were scraped and bruised.

"Does anyone else have anything to say?" asked Bold, tight-lipped, his eyes narrowed to slits of rage.

"You can't stand on the floor, Senator," whined the man with the limp. "Even the kitchen workers are down. I fell over Parmado. He was already on the floor. They're all still tangled up in a pile down there. We're lucky to be out of there."

Bold looked at the monitor unhappily. "The power went out on the monitor," he said. "It's back now." Feeling the loss of his long anticipated afternoon sport, his rage surfaced. "What kind of men are you?" he snapped. "One little woman's too much for you to handle? Find her first, and bring her back. Then go get yourselves cleaned up and respectable. And get the video staff in here to find out what the fuck is wrong with this monitor. Get it fixed before anything else."

"Yes sir," mumbled Parmado, and the housemen shuffled out to carry out instructions.

In his rage at the monitor suddenly going blank, and not supposing she'd have made it out of the door, Bold hadn't thought of tuning in to the forest. He now flicked on the forest channel, and caught views of the excited dogs, some of them bloody.

"Gone!" he muttered, cursing his luck. "Too bad, just the kind I like." He decided to let Parmado and the rest of the houseboys search in vain. The dogs would surely have killed her by now. Randomly he changed the channels to view his staff, searching for a replacement for Marcella, but the anticipation of excitement was absent. He'd wanted the one that got away, and the other's looked like hell spoiling his appetite. He drank a shot of scotch and then two more, and got in a car he drove himself. Leaving the estate, he went for a drive to try and cool down. When he returned, he called Margie Parks, his conventional girlfriend, to come over..

Mario had a hard time concentrating on his work, assiduously avoiding the television. Marcella and his need of her, and their changing relationship, was on his mind all the time. Since he'd smashed the mirrors, he'd felt violence building inside, and he knew it connected to Marcella's reticence in bed. Sneaking a glance at the television, he saw a man in a business suit with a glass of milk sitting at a desk, reading a newspaper. Marco was out of the shop, driving a car to hear what was wrong with it, and in a sudden passion of pent up hope, Mario addressed the television, and the man looked up from his paper.

"I'm a poor man," said Mario, earnestly. "I had nothing but Marcella and Rita before I came here. Now we have the money from our work and the things we bought with it. We're simple people, ordinary people who want only to get away from killing. Everybody in the world knows this is where you get a chance to make your life the way you want it. We want only to be free, like everybody in this famous country. We're good people." His rationality broke through his foolhardiness suddenly. "Dammit!" he cursed in frustration, under his breath, throwing down the rag in his hand and picking up his wrench. What had he done, talking to the TV like that? Some bad damage?

It seemed like the day would never end. He looked at his watch every few minutes. Finally, it was time to go home. When he got on the shuttle, Marcella wasn't on it. He sat next to Elena, Marco right in front of him. Marco turned to look at Mario.

"Where's Marcella?" Mario shouted in Elena's ear, as the minibus lurched forward.

"Wait'll we get off this friggin bus!" she shouted back.

Mario got up and ran to the front of the bus. "Where's Marcella?" he yelled at the driver. "My wife! Where's my wife?" The driver shrugged, and the security guard in the front seat stood up, his hand on his holster. He shoved Mario into the seat behind his.

"Where's my wife, Marcella?" demanded Mario, jumping up. The security guard cracked him in the jaw with the butt of his pistol, knocking Mario back down in the seat, and he rode the rest of the way, dazed, dabbing at his bloody jaw, staring at the man's hand on the pistol butt.

When the bus stopped, Mario was the first one off. Marco ran after him and jumped down to the pavement. "You better come to work tonight," he said. "You've still got the address?"

"Huh?" said Mario, unable to tune out his fears for Marcella.

"If you want the job, come tonight. Otherwise someone else will get it."

"My wife," he said, as Elena got off the bus.

"Tonight," said Marco, and quickly walked away. As he stood there in confusion, his jaw on fire, Elena appeared at Mario's elbow.

"Marcella escaped this morning," Elena told him. "The senator sent his housemen to take her to one of his bedrooms, and they helped her get away. She ran to the woods before they knew she was gone. You can't go there. You'd be arrested and deported before you could holler."

"What can I do, Elena?" Mario was frantic.

"I got a idea," said Elena, taking a small notebook and pencil out of her purse. She wrote the name, *Anita* and a telephone number.

"This is a lawyer. When somebody gets away or gets arrested, she can find out what happened. She knows how. If nothing can be done, she tells you what's what. Don't tell anybody. They don't like her. They look for how to get her because she helps us."

"Thanks," said Mario, slipping the paper into his shirt pocket with a shred of hope.

Mario had missed his bus, and Elena's bus stopped. She boarded it and was gone. Mario started walking home, his hands in his pockets, his shoulders slumped. He stopped at the first phone booth he came to and dialed the number Elena gave him. A woman answered. "Anita Sale's office."

"I must speak to Ms. Sales."
"This is her assistant, Carrie. Can I take a message?"
"No. It's urgent. I must talk to her...please!"
"One moment." Carrie, buzzed Anita. "Another urgent, and this one sounds desperate," she said.

"I'll take it," said Anita, and picked up the phone. "This is Anita, but my phone's tapped. If it's urgent, can you come to my office?"

"Now?"

"I have a full house." She glanced at her appointment book, and finding no hole, she saw a place to take ten minutes from each of two back to back appointments. "Tomorrow at six thirty?" She spoke slowly and deliberately. She'd taken many cases that other lawyers avoided. Because of her choice of cases, she remained on the poor side of middle class despite dazzling success. Her reputation was formidable.

"Yes," said Mario.

"I'll write you in as urgent." She scribbled urgent on her tablet underscoring it heavily. "Here's my address," she said, and read him the address.

"Thanks," said Mario. "Thank you." He fumbled for the pen and paper he always carried and wrote down the address before hanging up.

Anita went out to Carrie's desk in the lobby. Bending over Carrie, she spoke quietly in her ear. "Six thirty tomorrow has no name but urgent," she said. "He'll have to make up a name to get up here. Squeeze him in."

"Sure," said Carrie, writing urgent on the line above six thirty.

Mario went home utterly dejected.

"Where's Mom?" Rita asked him, anxiously. "How come you're so late?" The expression on Mario's haggard face told her their worst fear had materialized. The constant threat of such an emergency broke into reality like a rush of water breaking down a dam too weak to contain a raging river.

"I don't know," said Mario. "Something bad happened. Elena says she ran away."

"What'll we do, Dad?" Rita threw herself into Mario's arms, weeping softly. He held her close.

"I don't know. I got a lawyer who'll maybe tell us tomorrow."

"My school books didn't say all these things will happen here," said Rita, composing herself and drying her eyes. "Mom was right. There's something very, very bad. I want Mama back."

"Me too," said Mario.

"I'm scared, Dad." Rita's face was pale as death. She sniffled loudly and wiped her eyes. "Not like on the desert. Then I knew we'd make it. I knew the desert. I knew walking. I read about New York in a book, and I thought I knew about it. What I knew was nothing."

"No, we didn't know. But if we did, we'd still come here. There are good people in New York. We got hooked up with the bad, because we're desperate, and we don't know the ways. We'll see the good, too. Do you have to watch TV in school?"

"No, hardly ever. They don't have it in the classrooms. Sometimes we watch a movie in connection with what we're studying or a special made for school program on the television in the library or the auditorium."

"That's a relief."

Sick inside with worry and fear for Marcella, Rita started crying again.

"It's all right to cry, Rita. I feel like crying myself."

"Can we go outside for a minute? I'm afraid to talk."

"Sure." His hand hanging loose on Rita's shoulder, they walked outside.

"I'm supposed to go to work tonight, but now I can't go, Dad," she said, drying her eyes. "I have to wait for Mom."

"It's better if you go because when there's nothing you can do, it's important to keep on. I have to go to work tonight, too. Marco told me today."

"I'll go to work then. Maybe Mom will be home by the time I get back."

"Sure, Rita. Let's eat first, do you have time?" Nodding, Rita felt like she was standing on the top of a mountain that was cracking from the bottom and would soon fall and swallow her up. They went inside, and she warmed up the beans and rice and tortillas as Mario set the table, but when they sat down to eat, she had little appetite. She could tell that Mario wasn't hungry, but he was eating anyway, and she forced herself to eat, too.

"I have to get ready to go meet my friend or I'll be late," she said after they ate.

"Go ahead, Rita. I'll clean up the kitchen." Rita got ready and went to work. When he was finished in the kitchen, Mario showered and dressed in his best slacks and shirt and found the street for the restaurant on his city map before leaving the house.

Needing to keep moving, he was driven to walk the four miles at a brisk pace. There were other restaurants on the block, and he got out the paper with the address to check it. The restaurant he was looking for was The Cannery. It appeared classier than any restaurant he'd been in except Flowers in California. When he went in, a bright cheerful hostess approached him briskly in a suit and high heels carrying a menu. "Table for one?" she asked.

"I'm supposed to see about a job in the kitchen," said Mario, nervously. "Can I speak to the manager?"

"Oh yeah, they need another dishwasher. Just a minute." She disappeared and returned with the manager who was almost running.

"Can you wash dishes?" the manager asked.
"Yes," said Mario.
"Come with me," she said, and Mario followed her through the kitchen and into a large dish washing room. Marco was shuffling dishes into the dishwasher, but he didn't look up.

"We're desperate, as you can see," she said. There were stacks of dirty dishes on the stainless steel counters and more tubs full stacked on the floor. "One guy just walked out, and a woman never showed up. Can you start right now?"

"Yes. How much does it pay?"

"Six dollars an hour," she said. "Marco," she barked. He looked at her not slowing in his work.

"Yes ma'am?"

"Show him the ropes, and don't let him leave without stopping by the office for the paperwork"

"Yes ma'am," said Marco as she hurried out.

"There's the aprons," said Marco, indicating a tree by the door where plastic aprons hung. Mario put one on and started emptying bus tubs and stacking dishes for Marco to put in the dishwasher; all the plates on one pile, bowls on another, glasses in racks. Marco rinsed them with a hose hanging over the large sink and put them in the dishwasher. Mario deftly shuffled the dishes into the stacks as fast as a dealer deals cards, the practice at quick hand work from the fields coming to his aid, and the stacks were soon three feet high.

"How can I do paperwork?" asked Mario, softly enough not to be heard outside the room, but loud enough for Marco to hear over the clatter of plates.

"Use this name and social security number. A friend of mine went back to Mexico." Marco reached into his pocket and got out a scrap of paper which he handed to Mario with the name, Jorge Manales on it and a social security number. He grinned at Mario, the first time Mario had seen a crack in the grim concrete face. "That's only for this job," he said. "You'll get a permanent name and number later."

Mario glanced at the name and number and shoved the paper into his pocket with a glimmer of hope in his heart. "Where could Marcella go?" he asked, stacking the dishes rapidly as bus boys and bus girls continued to bring in more tubs of dishes. He worked faster and faster to keep up. Mario emptied a half full plate into the garbage can, which was already nearly full of food.

"I don't know," muttered Marco, in a low monotone. The loud rock and roll music piped into the kitchen and the continuous clinking of dishes covered their voices. "My wife didn't get away, Mareno. Elena's the only other woman I heard of escaping, but she didn't get away from the estate." He shoved a rack of water glasses into the dishwasher and slammed the door.

Shocked at the waste of food, Mario scraped some barely touched plates into the garbage can, and started to put the unopened packets of butter, cream, and jellies aside to take with him, but Marco shook his head no. Mario hated to dispose of them in the garbage, yet he saw the wisdom of not risking being caught with restaurant food out of the restaurant.

"She's smart, Elena," said Marco, loading another rack with glasses. "She's been at Bold's longer than me."

Mario's mind swirled, and his jaw ached. "I can't think," he said, organizing the salad plates, dinner plates and bowls into stacks, throwing the flatware into another rack.

"Keep calm. It's most important to keep calm," said Marco, under his breath. "We can't leave until Bold Done Day. Everything must be just right."

Mario stared at Marco without comprehension.

"Pretend I'm not telling you anything," whispered Marco, urgently, making a racket with the dishes. "We could be watched right now. We don't know."

Mario scraped and stacked, pretending to be calm, but his heart was thumping, his mind racing with meaningless disconnected images.

"We're only waiting until we have passable identifications for every one of Bold's employees and all our children."

"What do you mean?" Mario paused, the scraper in his hand.

"Keep working. You can't show them anything. Nothing is different to our tormentors. This second is just like the one before you knew."

"I've got to learn to be like that," said Mario, to himself, scraping dishes rapidly as Marco's words began to sink in. "What is Bold done day?" he asked.

"The day we all escape. We're going to put the power out, and take over the mansion," said Marco. Mario tried not to rattle the plates any more than he'd been doing and kept his hands steady.

"You're going to be a cable cutter. We're going to interrupt public broadcasts and get our message about Bold's slave trade through."

"What about when it's over?" asked Mario.

"We'll have our identifications in our pockets. With them, we can get driver's licenses and passports. I already have my papers, but we have to all go at the same time. We think only of success. We even dream about it. Escape is our second goal. First we have to stop Bold's network and make it public with our own broadcast from his shop." Throughout his explanation, Marco's expression didn't change.

"How do we get equipment to make a broadcast?" asked Mario, starting a new stack of plates. "It costs very, very much."

"The film's already composed. We stole a television camera piece by piece, a lens here, a shutter there. We put it all together. We cut a few feet of film here, a few feet there, they all splice together bit by bit, piece by piece, years of work. We work always, never stopping, thinking of freedom to live like any other person without fear."

Mario nodded as the plan took root in his mind. "But they have guns," said Mario, gingerly touching his jaw where the guard slugged him.

"We have anesthetics," said Mario. Mareno works part time in the Greenbrier University Hospital in the day. She's on the night shift at Bold's." He grinned again.

"Oh, I see. Do you know who helped Marcella?" asked Marco.

"Everyone there?" asked Mario.

Marco shook his head no. "Parmado. He's the head of the housemen. When Bold's not there, Parmado copies his videos We have everything on video. Parmado knows everything about electronics. He knows scrambling devices and techniques. He's our technical expert."

"I never thought we could do this."

"You're with us then?" asked Marco.

"Yes! Yes!" Mario could hardly contain his excitement at this news, as all the tension of hiding out, the uncertainty of the fugitive that lived like a ghost under his skin, felt like rolling out of him in a tidal wave of hope and good will.

"Start getting the things you need for your job. Don't go buy everything at once. One at a time, and make it look like you need it for something else; cable cutters, a spade you can take apart and carry in a briefcase, black briefcase, black clothes, everything black so nothing shows at night, black duffel bag."

Mario nodded as he worked.

"Go to church, the little, white clapboard one on July Street at Sixteenth. I don't go, but one day I will, and none of us knows what Sunday it'll be. If you go all the time, it won't look like we're meeting there."

"I understand." Mario grimaced to hide his smile. He worked side by side with Marco hustling the dirty dishes to the stacks for Marco to load into the dishwasher until one o'clock. Though the restaurant closed at midnight, the dirty dishes had started tapering off by eleven o'clock. When Mario mopped the floor, wiped his plastic apron dry and hung it up, he was a jumble of suppressed emotion, every nerve taut. He prayed that Marcella would have found a way to get him a message. Though he was happy for this new chance, he was still distressed at Marcella's absence, also.

"Bye Marco," he said and started to leave the restaurant by the alley door, and Marco grabbed him by the arm.

"No matter how tired you get, no matter how bad things go, you must not forget anything," he said. Mario looked at him in a daze, his eyes glazed, longing for sleep.

"We have to go to the office, and get your paper work done. It's nothing, a few signatures."

"Okay," said Mario, nodding. He followed Marco to the office. Only a night manager was there doing paper work from the day's business. Marco didn't say anything to him. He walked over to a hanging file on the outside of his door, took out some forms, and handed them to Mario.

Mario got out his pen, and to his horror, he couldn't remember his name or number. He had to get out the scrap of paper Marco had written them on and copy them onto the forms. When he was finished, he handed the papers to Marco, and Marco slid them into another file on the back of the door. Both men went outside.

"There's my bus. See you tomorrow," said Marco, then running with the speed and agility of a gazelle to catch the bus that had stopped at the corner.

Watching him in admiration, Mario then waited fifteen minutes for his bus and rode it for two blocks from his house and got off. Turning onto his street he saw a light in the window, ran home, and bounded up the front stairs, hoping against hope that Marcella had come back. He dashed in and ran to his room which was empty, and he looked in on Rita. She was curled up in her bed, and he didn't disturb her. She'd be exhausted after work and may have had a hard time falling asleep; let her sleep.

Before going to bed, he found July Street on his city map and marked out the way to it in his mind. It was only six blocks from his house. Mario went to bed and couldn't sleep or think. His mind was as unruly as it had been since Marcella ran away. He got up and got a beer.

"There was a time, we'd have thought we already made it if we could get a beer from our own refrigerator," he said to himself. He drank it and two more before going to bed. He dozed and woke, dozed and woke, and kept reaching for Marcella in his sleep. Once he heard a scratch at the window. Leaping out of bed, he ran to it and looked out, but it was only a cat.

Too soon, dawn came creeping like a thief into his window, and he stretched, got up, and made the bed. Going to the kitchen to put the coffee pot on, he then found that the coffee was already made. He poured a cup and took it back to his room to drink while he dressed more spaced out and scattered than before, and the coffee didn't help.

When he returned to the kitchen, Rita was eating a bowl of cereal with milk and drinking coffee. "There's no word of Mom," she whispered.

"Let's take our coffee outside," he said, and gave her a wan smile. Rita's face brightened, her eyes wide with hope, but he shook his head no. Again she was crestfallen. She finished eating while he piled pinto beans with rice and cheese onto a tortilla. He wrapped his breakfast in a paper towel, and they both carried their coffee outside, and sat on the front stoop.

"No word?" she asked.

Mario shook his head no. "But I'm going to a lawyer tonight who can maybe find out. We're going to get away."

. "Get away? What do you mean?"

"I learned at my job last night. I'm a dishwasher. My partner in the shop is, too. Everybody at Bold's is going to have identification. That's what we're waiting for. When we all have it, we're going to take over the estate and run with legitimate identifications. We have to start going to church because the signal to put the plan into action is Marco going to that church on Sunday."

"Wow!" said Rita, jumping up, her eyes shining. Mario stood, too.

"But what about Mom? How will she ever find us?"

"We'll find a way to get in touch. One thing we know is that she can't go back to Bold's, and she can't come here. I know Marcella. She's going to find a way to get in touch with us, and we have to find a way to get in touch with her."

"How are we going to escape when we have identification?"

"I don't know the details yet. We must do everything we always do, so they don't suspect. Are there any other kids in your class whose parents work at Bold's?"

"Just Margaret who helped me get the job."
"Don't talk about it to anyone, not even her. Can you do it?"
"What else can I do?"
"Nothing. Blow the escape plan for all of us. Was Margaret at school when you started?"
"Yes. She's been there for two years."
"Then she already knows the plan, and she didn't go blabbering it to you."
"I won't mention it. When do we start going to church?"
"This Sunday. Tell your boss, you're very religious. Your parents make you to go to church."

"Suppose they don't give me the time off?"

"It's only an hour. If they don't give you the time off, you have to quit."

"Okay."

"I've got to hurry. I'll be late tonight, because a lady who works with Marcella gave me the name of a lawyer who knows how to find out if she was arrested or picked up or hurt and taken to a clinic or hospital unless she gives the wrong name. At least we'll know more than we know now."

"Okay, Dad. Good luck. Do you work tonight?"

"Yes. I have to go every night. They only have two people. I'll come home first. Bye." He leaned over and kissed Rita on the head. "Thank God we still got each other," he said.

"Thank God," said Rita.

Mario got on the bus and went to work apprehensively thinking they knew he knew his house was watched because he broke the mirrors. He got off the city bus, waved at the guard at the iron gate and boarded the shuttle. It idled for a few minutes waiting for the next bus. Workers on bikes came rolling along sporadically, parked their bikes, and boarded.

When the bus arrived, Elena and the rest of the workers from the bus climbed into the shuttle. The shuttle lumbered off with a loud fart and Mario and Marco got off at the garage. Mario went in sweating in anxiety, not daring a glance at the television. Marco's calm exterior gave him the courage to keep on working as though it was just another day.

On his break, Mario took one of the cigarettes Marco offered him, and it made him dizzy, but he smoked it anyway. He still couldn't think the way he always had. The day dragged by in slow motion. Daring not mention the escape plan, his curiosity about how they were going to carry it off was nearly intolerable. The only things he needed to talk about, Marcella and the escape were the only two things he couldn't mention.

When the shuttle stopped in front with no fallout from the catastrophe that befell Marcella, he took a deep breath and got on.

The guard eyed him warily, his hand on the butt of his gun. When the shuttle stopped to let the workers off, Mario started to walk over to Elena, but she put her finger over her lips and hurried away.

Mario's bus was right behind it, and he got on to ask where to get the bus to the address he had for Anita Sales office. The bus driver told him to wait for the 55 bus which would be along in five or ten minutes. Mario got off and waited until the 55 showed up. He rode it to the stop right across from the large building that housed Ms. Sale's office. Getting off the bus, he steeled his nerves to enter the modern upscale building that took up a whole block.

The friendly guard in the lobby smiled at him. "Want to sign in, Jack?" he asked. Mario went over to the registration desk, picked up the pen, and signed Jorge Manales.

"Where are you going?" asked the guard.

"Anita Sales office. I have a six thirty appointment."

"Hold on a minute, Mr. Manales," he said, picking up the phone, and Mario braced for a quick sprint out the front door. "I have a six thirty appointment for Anita, Jorge Manales?" He hung up. "Go on up," he said, nodding at Mario.

Mario took the elevator up, and locating Anita Sales's suite, he then entered her office lobby. A woman behind a desk glanced at the appointment book as he entered. Another man waiting to see Anita drummed his fingers on the arm of his chair, impatiently.

"Jorge?" asked Carrie, looking up at him.
"Yes." Mario tried to smile, but it refused him.
"I'm Carrie. Anita's not here, but she'll be in any moment."
Mario looked around the packed room for a seat, but they were all taken. Clients sighed, looked at magazines, and fidgeted in their chairs. He stood against the wall. A woman in jeans and a denim jacket entered soon after Mario. "Good evening," she said to Carrie.

"Good evening," said Carrie. The woman got a magazine from the coffee table and stood next to Mario with it.

Carrie dialed Anita's home phone, waited what seemed an interminable time, and got no answer. She hung up and called another lawyer down the hall. Mario took a magazine from the coffee table, listening to Carrie.

"Hello, Aubrey? This is Carrie. Anita's got appointments waiting, and she's not here."

"I just got in," replied Aubrey. "I dropped her off at her house not ten minutes ago. She had to pick up a brief and her car. She can't be more than a few minutes behind me," he said.

"Thanks, bye," said Carrie, and hung up. "Anita will be here any moment," she announced. The clients shifted around and muttered.

Mario tried to read the magazine, but he couldn't concentrate. Fifteen minutes went by.

Distressed at her partner's tardiness, which had never been Anita's habit, Carrie went into a private office and called Aubrey back. "Aubrey, she's still not here. I'm going to move all the appointments back a day and go to her house."

"Something's very wrong. She said she was coming straight here. I'm going to call 911. I'll go as soon as I do and meet you there," said Aubrey.

"Very well. Bye."

Carrie returned to the waiting room. "I'm sorry, Anita's been delayed," she told the clients. "I'll get you all in at the same times tomorrow and move her tomorrow's appointments back all the way to Sunday."

"I can't make it tomorrow," said a client. "I'll have to check my schedule and make another appointment."

"All right," said Carrie, making a note of it. "Anyone else?"

Nobody replied, and the clients shuffled out, one lady grumbling about having to take time off work again, and another commiserating.

When only Carrie and Mario remained in the office, she got up preparing to leave, and Mario said, "I gave the wrong name."

"I understand," she said. "That's why we have the music so loud. It helps camouflage conversation. You're not the only one, but if you speak very softly in a monotone, you won't be understood."

Mario followed her instructions, and imitated the way Marco always spoke to him. "My wife and me work at Senator Bold's estate. We're illegal. She ran away because they tried to rape her. She's missing, and I don't know how to find her. She'll be afraid to come home or go back to work. They watch us all the time through TV."

"Write both your names here," she said, handing Mario a pad of paper. "Come back tomorrow whenever you can. If she uses an alias, do you have any idea what it would be?"

"Maybe the first name of a friend but not the last name," speculated Mario. "Maybe Sedar, or she might call herself Sedar Salvadore."

"Any other names you want me to check?"

"That's the one she'd use. Thanks," said Mario. He wrote down Mario and Marcella Dominguez on the tablet.

Ushering Mario out, Anita than locked up and dashed for the elevator.

Mario returned to the street and stopped at an electronic store to pick up a cheap cassette recorder and a tape before taking the bus back to his neighborhood. He stopped at the hardware store, went in and purchased a spade that unscrewed for easy disassembly and a pack of vegetable seeds. When he got home, Rita had dinner ready.

"I'm going to plant beans and squash in the back yard," said Mario, showing Rita the seeds. He turned on the recorder to cover their conversation and spoke quietly in a monotone to Rita. "Speak very softly, and they won't hear us over the music. Any news?" She shook her head no.

"You?" Rita asked. "What about the lawyer?"

"She didn't show up. I have to go back tomorrow."

Nodding, Rita gave a little smile and sat down to eat. "I got more hours. I go to work right after I eat."

"Good," said Mario. "It's better to have something to do." He sat down with Rita, and started eating.

"I have studying, but I can't concentrate like I used to. I keep thinking about Mom. Work at the restaurant's easy. I don't have to think."

"It's the most important to keep on holding to what you want to do, like studying, when it's the hardest."

"Why?"

"Because then you know you always can. It's the difference in doing what you want and giving up because it's too hard."

After dinner Rita went to work, and before going to the restaurant where he worked, Mario went to the back yard and planted the seeds. He then washed his hand, disassembled the spade, tucked it away in his closet, and headed for the restaurant.

At work, Mario first put on his plastic apron, and started stacking dirty dishes which were overflowing their boundaries again. "I got the spade," he whispered to Marco, but Marco shook his head no and clamped his mouth shut. Mario knew that meant he wouldn't talk about the escape plan.

"We have to wait. There's nothing else we can do," Marco said, fiercely. Mario forced himself not to mention Marcella or the lawyer, because it showed Marco his worry. He needed to practice being like Marco, so Rita would have an example, too. He appreciated having something to do and it seemed a great bonus that it was a paying job. He'd go nuts if he had nothing to occupy him but thinking about Marcella all night. When he got home exhausted, Rita was studying.

"Don't you ever sleep?" he asked.
"I try," she said.
"Good night, Rita."
"There's nothing we need to talk about?"

"No, you?"

"No."

Mario kissed Rita and went to bed. He slept deeply, not dreaming, his body at the point it shuts down of its own accord against any will or outside force, until the alarm clock went off. He felt like he'd only closed his eyes a minute ago. He and Rita went through their morning kitchen routines with the cassette player blaring the oldies tape, *You've lost that loving feeling*, at top volume, so they could talk.

"I'm going to put an ad in the paper," said Mario, accustomed to speaking in a low monotone, practically in Rita's ear. "It will just say, Julio, meet Snakebite at Fishermans. She knows you work there. That might be where she tries to make contact with us anyway. She'll know the message is from me, and she'll go there. She'll look in the paper because we read it and talked about it."

"If she can get the newspaper," said Rita. "I can put the same message up on store bulletin boards."

"Okay," said Mario.

As Mario waited for the bus, his attention was drawn to the headlines of the newspaper in the rack. *LAWYER ANITA SALES FIGHTING FOR LIFE AFTER ATTACK.* Dismayed, he bought the paper and read the first paragraph of the article. *Two lawyers associated with Anita Sales interrupted an attack on her in her home at 6:40 p.m.yesterday. Sales is now fighting for her life at City Hospital with multiple concussions and broken bones. The assailants, six men wearing ski masks fled when a law partner and friend arrived at her house to find out why she hadn't shown up at her office for her evening appointments.*

The bus stopped and Mario got on, but the spirit went out of him, and his heart sank. He wanted to show the article to Marco, but something told him to leave the paper on the bus. Thought deserted him. Going to work in a daze, he struggled though the morning like a man trying to walk through a pot of glue until he and Marco went out for a cigarette break.

"Elena told me about a lawyer. I went to see her, but she's in the hospital," Mario muttered. Marco handed him a cigarette.

"I saw the paper, too," said Marco, lighting his cigarette and handing Mario the plastic lighter. "I prayed you wouldn't bring it."

"I'm catching on. I wanted to bring it. I'm going to put an ad in the paper," said Mario. Marco nodded. "Are you going back to the lawyer's office?" he asked.

"Yes," said Mario. "There's still nothing we can do but wait for the rest of the identifications and pray for Marcella and Ms. Sales."

Marco nodded his agreement, and he and Mario went back to work after their break. Mario worked on a job Marco gave him. He had no heart to work on his solar engine.

After work, he bought another newspaper while waiting for the bus, and went back to Sale's office at six fifteen, not daring to hope. A college student was at Carrie's desk, and Mario scribbled Marcella's name on a scrap of paper. Under her name he wrote: aliases she might use and handed it to him.

"I checked this name, Sedar, and Salvadore," he said, somberly. "She's not dead. She's not in custody. She hasn't been arrested or shown up at any hospital or clinic. There's nothing official. If she isn't using a different name, she's not in the system."

"That's a great relief. Does it have anything to do with this?" Mario held up the paper with Anita's picture on the front.

"I don't know," the man said. "Is there any reason it would? Do you have any high connections or involvement with people in power or criminals? Drug dealers?"

"No, nothing like that, but we're illegal aliens and we work for Senator Bold. We're the next thing to prisoners."

"Senator Bold may be a connection. It's something to go on. For now I have to close the office and go to the hospital. Anita's still critical."

"What can I do?"

"I'm not sure. The only advice I can offer is to wait until your wife contacts you and put messages in places she'll go - supermarkets, a newspaper she reads with the number of a friend for her to call if she can't call you. I'll keep a lookout, and if anything happens such as an arrest, police report, hospital or clinic appearance, or if I get a message by the grapevine, I'll call you."

"Grapevine?" asked Mario, frowning, recalling picking grapes.

"A message transmitted by word of mouth."

"Thanks," said Mario. "I don't have a phone. I'll stop by here?"

"That'll be okay. We're going to take turns being here for Anita's clients until she's back as often as we can, but it would help if there was some place you could be reached. The office will be locked up for large blocks of time."

Mario's mind flickered over the possibilities, and he shook his head no. "What could happen to Marcella?" he asked.

"Does she have much money with her?"

"A little."

"My guess is she's hiding out and using another name. She may be gone to a nearby town to let the smoke clear before trying to contact you. There's a lot of ways she could get a job to make money like babysitting, companion to an elderly homebound person, or any work in someone's private home. Individuals usually don't think of going through official channels to hire help for jobs like that."

"Okay," said Mario. He left the young man in the lawyer's office and went to the newspaper. Directed to the classified sales department, he then purchased an ad to run in the personal messages section. It read: *Julio meet Snakebite at Fishermans.* He paid cash for the ad to run for three days.

Stopping at a store on the way home, he then purchased a black jacket, a black cap, and black gloves. When he got home, he scanned the classified ads carefully for a message from Marcella, but didn't find one.

After school, Rita printed index cards with the message: *Julio meet Snakebite at Fishermans.* She took them to the grocery store, drug store, convenience market, and a discount department store, and tacked them to the bulletin boards. Every day at work, she waited for word from her mother. She hoped that even if she didn't show up, she'd find a way to get her a message there or leave a message for her on a bulletin board.

At dinner time, Rita turned on the cassette to the sweet strains of Tony Bennett 's, *I Believe*, and was careful to speak softly, "Dad, I got a B on my physics test. It was an important one. I'm slipping." She sounded like she'd flunked out of school, and her head was not as proud and high.

"That's fine, Rita. You don't have to be perfect all the time. Make up your mind to get an A next time," said Mario, lowering his voice. "We don't know that Marcella's not free, trying to get in touch with us. We must hold to that hope. The more we worry, the worse we handle all our affairs."

"I know that's true when you say it, but it's different to keep on acting like it's fine when it's not. What can I do?"

"What would Marcella say?"

"She'd say I must pray and believe that God will make it true."

"Did you do that?"
"No. I forgot."
"Let's do it now."
Rita took Mario's hands in both of hers. "Our Father, let me keep my balance and get high grades so I can be a doctor, and bring Mom back to us," said Rita. They repeated the prayer together with Mario substituting Rita for me and Marcella for Mom. As much as Rita tried to believe with all her heart that it was true, it was not as easy as when Marcella was with them. She wasn't sure.

"Something prevents her from getting in touch," said Rita. "I put ads in all the stores that have bulletin boards. Maybe she'll see them."

"She'll get in touch with us when she can find a way. I just thought of something else, Rita. We must try to separate ourselves from this crisis. Think of it as training to be a doctor."

"That's a better help. I don't understand Mom's faith. It worked for me when she was here. I understood it then, but now I understand what you're saying much better, and I'm going to try to separate myself from Mom being missing. After all, that's what has always gotten me through the toughest places. I escape it all in studying." She looked up at Mario and smiled.

"One more thing," said Mario. "When we get Marcella back, you're going to go on with your life. How you handle it through this is where you're going on from. We don't know what she's going through. The stronger we stay, the better we can help her. What would she think if she got through hell and I was out panhandling hiding out in a park somewhere, and your grades were so low that there was no way into medical school?"

"Thanks, Dad."

On the way to the church on July Street on Sunday, Mario saw a woman that looked like Marcella from the back. He ran up to her, but when she heard his footsteps and turned around, it was a stranger. He waited for Rita to catch up, and they arrived at the church with a plaster statue of the Virgin of Guadalupe in front. It reminded him of the Virgin of Guadalupe in El Salvador when he was a boy struggling with his conscience for understanding of his situation. This statue had pristine gleaming paint, no chips, and the building it stood in front of was immaculate. Gazing at the statue, he knew he'd done the right thing in coming to the United States, though now he was less certain of the outcome.

Mario took off his hat, and they went inside. He bowed his head in the chapel and prayed for justice and his family's reunion and escape, especially for Marcella to be all right, and for Rita and him to carry on with their lives.

"God, let us find Mom, and let the escape plan work, and give me the faith to prevail," said Rita, to herself. The prayer brought back her and her mother's one time prayer when Mario was sick on the desert, and Marcella's absolute certainty that it was answered. Rita took Mario's hand.

"We have to say this together," she whispered, with renewed assurance, "Bring Mom to us safe, and we have to know it'll come true." Holding hands, Rita and Mario repeated, "Bring Marcella, Rita said Mom, to us safe," and Mario felt he could bear up for the duration if God was with him.

When the service was over, Rita said, "I like this church, Dad."

"It's a good church," said Mario. "We should come every Sunday to show our thanks for my better job and your job and pray for Marcella's return."

"Okay. I'd like to come back."

"I've got to stop on the way home. I need a duffel bag like Marco's to carry my work clothes home in. I'm the only person on the city bus in a uniform. When Marco leaves, you can't tell he's a mechanic." They stopped at a department store, and Mario bought a black duffel bag for the cable cutters.

When Mario went to work the next day, there was something different about Marco. He was less morose, but though Mario could feel the difference in his mood, no trace of a difference showed in his face or movement. Unobtrusively Mario, in a state of high alertness, noticed everything in the shop. The only thing different was that Senator Bold's white Lincoln was parked in a different place. There must be some significance to this because Marco never made a move that didn't mean something.

They went out for the morning break, and Mario asked, using his soft monotone, "Why?" Marco replied in a whisper in his ear, "The panel covering the electric works is behind it. Look for a white line."

After the break, Mario walked between the Lincoln and the wall. The car blocked the view of the panel covering the wiring to the shop from the television screen. Scanning the paneling, he saw the board with a white chalk mark on the bottom and knew the line he'd someday cut was behind that particular board. He counted how many boards from the corner it was in case the mark got erased.

Returning to his work, as though nothing was different, he had to work extra hard at showing no trace of emotion because he'd picked up Marco's ebullience.

CHAPTER TWENTY

The Cloudhawk's smooth takeoff into the clear sky on a sunny, cloudless day contrasted drastically with the turbulence of its occupants. With the self confidence of a hundred and six flights behind her, Kate was an expert pilot.

Burt, Sue, and Sue's husband; Sherman were geared up for a sky dive, but the emotional flight of joy and adventure that always accompanied ascent was damped down by Sue's black mood.

Kate recalled the loose merriment of their previous airborne adventures; the laughter, the jokes, and her exuberance as the earth fell away. She sneaked a look at Burt in the seat next to her, hoping to find relief from the intimidation of Sue's misery, but Sue's irritable mood pulled all their best feelings into its black cloud.

Kate caught a glimpse of Sue in the mirror, sitting on the floor of the two-seater behind Burt, her elbows resting on her knees, her head in her hands. Her helmet lay on the floor beside her, and her long hair was caught up on top of her head in a loose bun.

Looking out the window, the airport, automobiles, buildings, and railroad tracks looked like toys with a gray tape unraveled for the road. Miniature forests lined the railroad tracks and scattered over the hills. A blue ribbon snaked from west to east, and the scene reminded Kate of the train display she and Burt laid out every year under the Christmas tree. Lake Larchmont might have been a swimming pool or the roof of a doll's house. Only the tunnel for the train was missing, replaced by a trestle over the river.

"You look like a doomed city, Sue," said Kate. "It's bad enough in the newsroom, but up here, for God's sake?"

Saying nothing, Sue sighed and looked out the window.

"I can smell that black mood prowling around you, and it's sheer hell not knowing what's going on," persisted Kate.

"Kate can help, Sue. You've got to let us try, at least," said Sherman, sitting on the floor behind Kate.

"I never shut you out like that, Sue!" said Kate, her anger and the tension from the newsroom spilling out in a torrent. "It's not natural! We've been friends for so long. Whatever Ferrell's done to you, he's on my case, too. I'm right behind you. We've got to confide in each other and stick together."

Sue kept her face turned to the window, looking out, and Kate couldn't see her expression.

"It's got to do with the governor getting killed by the train. That's when you started acting strange," said Kate.

A loud sigh came from Sue who studied the sky as though searching for something lost.

"No, Kate," said Sherman, somberly. "Sue disappears for three or four days at a time and comes back exhausted."

"Traitor," said Sue, shooting him a dagger.
"I feel like the betrayed," said Sherman.
"Next time, I'll rent a balloon to jump out of. There's not as much hot air in that as there is in here," griped Sue.

Kate laughed and the tension let up a little.

"You've got to let us in on it, Sue. If not me, someone. I'm watching you die little by little," blurted out Sherman. "Can't you see the sheer torture you're putting me through, or don't you care?" Sue didn't reply.

"You don't trust me anymore," said Kate. "I'm worthless to you. It's not as though I'm not in serious danger. I'd never leave you out on the limb like that, Sue."

"Kate!" said Burt. "That's enough. Don't we all come up here to leave the ground behind? Sue as well as you?"

"She didn't leave it behind!" Kate's escalating anger rose with her voice. "She brought it along! She's losing weight, and you should see her at work. Whatever is eating her is changing her personality from a tough-minded, analytical partner to a meek, obedient little pet lamb."

"That's true at home, too, Burt," said Sherman. "You hate to see someone you love turning into a...."

"Talk about changing personalities," said Burt, reasonably. "I've never heard you talk about someone present as though she wasn't here."

"Look at her!" yelled Kate, her voice shaking. "She isn't here! Are we talk...."

"We can bail out pretty soon, Sue," interrupted Burt. "At least, you'll have a few minutes of freedom in the air. When we hit dirt, I'll help you escape to Tahiti," he turned to wink at her.

"Fake me a passport, and I'm on my way," said Sue, solemnly.

"Why a phony passport? What's wrong with your real one? Who's on your case?" demanded Kate.

Sue heaved a deep sigh. "You don't have the built-in radar to know when to lay off! You act like a hound dog howling after a rabbit," said Sue, sharply.

"If you escape to Tahiti, what about me?" asked Sherman, pushing his glasses up with his index finger. His nose was fairly flat below the bridge and flared out suddenly in the middle, and his glasses had a tendency to slide down to the fleshy part. "Can an environmental engineer find work in Tahiti?"

"I wish I could lay on the beach and let the waves wash over me until all the garbage is gone, and I feel human again," said Sue. "I wish I could quit my job and go away. I wish...wish...wish I'd never gotten involved." She buried her face in her arms folded over her bent knees.

"I love you, Sue," said Sherman, in an unguarded instant of intense feeling. He scooted across the floor of the craft and sat beside her. "I see something happening to you, and you shut me out when I should be of some use. I'm helpless as a baby, and it's awful. If it's dangerous to you, I should have an equal share. Put yourself in my place."

"There are worse things than not fair," said Sue.

"You keep saying the same thing." Sherman didn't try to hide his exasperation. "Sure there are worse things than death. There are worse things than losing weight. There are worse things than feeling bad all the time. There's worse than any of us know, but it doesn't answer our helplessness."

"All right!" yelled Sue, standing up suddenly, holding onto the back of Burt's seat. "I can't stand it any longer! I can't stand what's happening! If someone told me the story I'm about to tell you, I couldn't believe it, but I'm at the end of my line. I must speak or I'll go mad. I go to a house near Greenbrier, New York in the country. It's in the mountains. You remember, Sherman. You went with me once."

Kate looked in the rear view mirror, and six amazed eyes watched Sue, upright of posture, speak in a strong unwavering voice, her personality suddenly flowing into her from outside with great force.

A sudden roar of thunder interrupted her soliloquy, and jagged lightning flashed around the craft. A black cloud rolled out of the north, engulfing the Cloudhawk. The sky turned pitch black and hail pounded the aircraft.

"What the hell!" yelled Kate. "We're losing power! We've lost power! The emergency system isn't functional! "Bail out!" she screamed, leaping from her seat and opening the door manually.

She jumped and falling free for an instant, then pulled her ripcord. Looking for the others, she saw only two chutes in the black clouds and driving rain. Catching a draft a distance from the Cloudhawk, she caught a glimpse of Sue's white jump suit and pink parachute hurtling to the ground. Her chute wasn't opening. A strong gust carried Kate out of the turmoil, and she saw Dan and Sherman maneuver their lines to blow clear, too. She watched the craft in the storm in amazement. The sky was clear all around the storm engulfing the Cloudhawk. The craft exploded and caught fire, the fragments raining to earth, as Kate floated down in the same weather she'd ascended into, watching the sphere of fire and fury.

A shadow of oppression hung over Kate long after Sue's funeral. When she got home one evening, a stranger was waiting in her apartment with Burt to speak to her. They both stood up as she entered the living room. "Kate this is Ike Bailey with the FBI," said Burt.

"I've got some bad news," said the agent. "Would you like to sit down?"

"Yeah, you have a seat too, why don't you," asked Kate, flopping into a chair. "Let's see your ID."

The FBI agent walked over to her and displayed his badge. "I'm going to record this conversation." He got a recorder the size of a cigarette pack out of his briefcase and switched it on. "Sue Front may have been murdered," he said.

"Oh my God," groaned Kate. "Does Sherman know?"
"Yes," said Bailey.
"No!" said Burt, leaping to his feet, confused. "We hit a storm. We all had to jump."
"The line was cut on her chute inside the pack," said Bailey.
Burt sat next to Kate, and they stared at Bailey, waiting for him to continue. There was a long pause. Agent Bailey addressed Kate. "Do you know who wanted her dead?"

Kate shook her head no. As much as she hated Ferrell, she couldn't believe he'd have Sue killed. She reeled through stories Sue had worked on and couldn't think of anyone who would want to kill her.

"I don't know," said Kate. "She was on the edge, but she wouldn't talk about it. She was terrorized, and she was onto something. After the governor died in the train crash, she started to change. She used to be open and outgoing with me and the other reporters, but she turned into a recluse."

"Then you think her death may be related to her work?"
"I'm sure of that," said Kate.
"Her husband agrees with you. Did she mention anything about going to New York for two or three days at a time?" Bailey asked.
"She said something to that affect right before the storm on our fatal flight," said Kate. "But we were interrupted by a storm."

"I've got a few questions about the explosion of your Cloudhawk," Baily said. "The engine was hit with a remote controlled laser. It's not something the local police department has access to. Also, the plane was bugged."

"So, what are you going to do about it?" asked Kate. At last she might have help from someone who knew how.

"Find out who's responsible. I'd like your version of what happened that day."

"We went up like we've done a hundred times before. I was piloting, Burt next to me, Sue and Sherman on the floor in back. The Cloudhawk's a two-seater. Sue, Burt, and Sherman were going to jump. The sky was clear and blue, and suddenly a storm was all around us, and the plane went haywire. The engine quit, the door jammed, and I had to open it manually. We all jumped. I got clear of the plane on a draft and saw Sue plummet like a rock. Burt and Sherman got clear, too. I saw the plane explode, but the storm was only surrounding the aircraft. Everywhere else was clear and blue."

"Who could've sabotaged your plane?"

"Ferrell Sinker could've wanted to, but he wouldn't have access to that kind of resource, a remote controlled laser. I can't imagine the immensity of what we're involved with."

"Do you think someone wanted to kill you and got Sue Front instead?"

As Kate pondered the question, Burt said, "Yes. Someone threw a rock through our window. If Kate hadn't dropped her fork and bent down to pick it up, she could have been killed or seriously injured. It would have caught her in the head."

"Someone could be gunning for me, but I have no idea who could have done that," said Kate. "Don't think I haven't given it serious thought. Sue was covering Hurly before he died with his aide in the train crash, and I think she was onto something relating to that. But I don't know anything about it. I wasn't in trouble with anyone but Ferrell as far as I know. But it's because he doesn't like my coverage of the farm workers organizing. It's something we fight about in the newsroom."

"Any specifics?"

"Not evidence that would stand up in court, but Ferrell Sinker acts strangely in my presence. Sue said he was on her case, too. I believe it involves Sinker and Senator Morgan Bold. Ferrell's been tampering with my stories. He outright fictionalized one and substituted his tale in my computer. I'm sure he intimidated Sue in the same way."

"Why?"

"If I only knew! I first thought it was a personality clash. He's one of those guys who thinks the women in his life should be cooking his dinner or making his bed. It wasn't until I realized that I was under attack, and Sue too, that I even suspected how much deeper it is. I believe he's got some deal cooked up with the New York Senator Bold, possibly involving illegal aliens or weapons."

"What else are you into?"

"You probably read the paper. Farm workers and other things of interest I hear are the only things I generate myself. Everything else is assigned."

"Give me a direction," persisted Bailey.

"I don't have anything solid. I hate to speculate without some sure backup."

"What do you actually know?"

Kate laughed bitterly. "Not nearly as much as you with your investigatory resources. Otherwise I wouldn't be in this ridiculous position."

"Are you afraid?"

"Yes. So what can I do about that?"

"Quit."

"I have to pay the rent and eat. Do you think I could get a job bagging groceries?"

"We have a secret witness program if you come clean with everything you know and suspect, but you have to give up all your contacts."

"I'm not dead yet. Thanks anyway."

"Then we're finished for now," he said standing. "I'd appreciate it if you wouldn't let the word out just yet that Sue Front was murdered."

"I know how to keep a secret," she said. She and Burt stood, and started walking Agent Ike Bailey to the door. "In this job, Mr. Bailey, you never really know who you might have offended. I believe that Ferrell Sinker and Morgan Bold are behind this. The high tech killing makes it seem like the only possibility. But I never know who I might have offended. There are surely large corporations that operate in secret beyond the reach of the law that have a financial stake in what happens, and every statement that appears to be fact has an opposite side."

"What do you mean?"

"Take the orange marketing orders for instance. Thousands of people in California make a living on oranges, and the health of the local economy is heavily dependent on agricultural crops. But at the marketing order hearings, where the decisions will be made, the pro marketing orders side calls in all their big guns. The top experts from major universities and institutions parade by and testify under oath why these orders are necessary. Every one from the poor suffering farmer struggling to hang on to his livelihood to the millionaire making a killing on investments has the opportunity to put in his two cents worth.

"Then the growers and consumers organizations who want to get rid of what they refer to as a relic from the Depression parade just as impressive and qualified array of experts who say exactly the opposite with just as many hard fact proofs. No matter how you present the issue, there are going to be those furious enough on both sides to take you outside the city walls and stone you to death, or quietly hire a gun. Add to that the battles from the beginning of time between labor and management, and you get an even clearer idea."

"You mean someone you don't even know you may have offended could have hired someone to try to kill you or Sue Front?"

"It's possible. Like I said, I think somehow Sinker and Bold are involved because of Sinker's strange behavior at work, and there's definitely some connection between him and Morgan Bold. I want to be very clear though, that I'm not sure. That's all."

"Don't hesitate to call me if you get onto anything substantial," said Ike Bailey, and he left.

Kate closed the door, and she and Burt walked back to the living room. "Murder," said Kate. "I can't believe it. Murder."

"I'm going over to Sherman's tomorrow," said Burt, glancing at his watch. "It's too late now. Can you get away?"

"I'll have to," said Kate. .

Burt called Sherman. "Sherman, an FBI agent was just here. We heard that Sue was murdered. I'm so sorry. Can Kate and I come over tomorrow night?"

"Yeah," said Sherman. "I could sure use the company. I'm taking the day off tomorrow. I can't gather my mind around this."

In the newsroom the next morning, expecting no cooperation but hoping to pop some clue out of him, Kate started a peaceable conversation with Ferrell and steered it around to Sue. "What was Sue onto? You knew more about what she was doing than anyone," she asked.

"I don't know, Kate. She was always stirring things up. Sue and I never had any kind of professional relationship. She did as she pleased. I couldn't assign her anything she couldn't sniff out on her own."

"You were a personal friend of the governor's, weren't you? Could it have anything to do with the train wreck that killed him?"

"Half the town was friends of Gregory Hurly. I doubt there's a connection. Your friend was killed in a plane crash, straight and simple." Ferrell's voice took on the tone of a lecture. "You don't understand how the real world operates, Kate. You're a hopeless idealist. Your work would be better if you could overcome that and adopt a more realistic attitude. That's all there is to it...deals that turn wheels, and other considerations have nothing to do with it. You made a bad judgment, flying in a storm, and now you're looking for a place to lay your guilt."

"Sue discovered something dangerous, and she didn't want to involve anyone she knew. You were the only one who could've demanded to know," Kate insisted.

Ferrell started laughing. "Where have you been for the past six months? I couldn't talk to her. I've been a hard-assed newsman all my life. I don't understand the bleeding heart syndrome. This world is a jungle. If the kind of fights that go on in the jungle are too tough, she should've taken up knitting instead of newspaper work where you're right in the thick of it."

"Sue was as tough as they come."

"Why don't you take a little more time off, Kate. You look tired, and you're not completely together. You've got vacation coming to you," suggested Ferrell, kindly.

"Take a vacation yourself if this is getting to be too much for your delicate system," she retorted. Tuning him out since she was getting nowhere, she then plugged herself into her computer and worked steadily, catching up on assignments.

After work, Kate went to Sherman's apartment and rang the bell. He answered the door. "Come on back," he said. "I'm trying to figure out what to do with Sue's things. Burt's already here. Want a drink?"

"I'll get a beer," said Kate, heading for the refrigerator. The sink was full of dirty dishes, and the counter splotched with crumbs from various sources and a glob of potato salad that might have been dropped last week. Slipping and nearly falling on a pickle slice, she then picked it up and threw it in the garbage. She got a cold one, noticing that the refrigerator held plenty of beer, several bottles of wine, a shelf full of diet soda, a few bagels, ham, Swiss cheese, and several pints of salad from the deli section of the supermarket.

Taking her beer back to the bedroom, she realized that she had almost as much cause to worry about Sherman as she had for Sue, though in a different way, and easily made the transfer. Sherman had made very little progress. He was starting to hang clothes he'd laid out on the bed back in the closet.

"Should I run those down to the salvage box?" asked Kate, stopping him.

"Oh, is that what you do with them?" He went out of the room and returned with a roll of black, plastic bags and began putting the clothes into them. Kate opened a bag and helped while Burt stood watching. Sue's death had left Sherman mentally adrift.

"Do you want any of these clothes or jewelry, Kate?" Sherman asked her.

"Sue's clothes would be too small for me. I'll look over the jewelry if you don't want to save it or have some of the jewels reset. It's valuable. You might want it later after some of the grief wears a little thinner."

"Alright, take whatever you want, and I'll leave the rest in a drawer. If I still don't know what to do with it in a year, I'll ask you again," said Sherman. "Thanks for taking care of me, Kate. I'm not used to it, but I appreciate it. I'm in unknown territory."

Kate chose a gold bracelet. "I'll keep this as a reminder," she said, putting the bracelet in her bag. "What was Sue going to New York for?" she asked. "I wondered where she was several times over the past year. She never spoke of it, and when I mentioned it, she'd pretend like she didn't hear me or walk out on me."

"She went to a house in the mountains, and I insisted on going once. I hated the place. It was oppressive. I was only there part of one day, and I had to leave. Sue started meditating shortly after Hurly and his aide, Morrie Phillips, were killed. That's all they did there. I'm sure that caused the change in her personality. She lost her inner fire. I complained, but she insisted that her feeling for me hadn't changed. She was becoming more self-controlled in everything she did."

"That's, also, about the time she became secretive about her work, but I thought it was because Ferrell tried to spike everything she did," said Kate. "They were at opposite poles politically, and he's sexist."

"I tried to get her to quit going to New York," said Sherman. "That started whatever finished with her death."

"Meditating is something people do to relax their minds and relieve stress. It couldn't connect to violent death," said Burt. "Maybe she was doing something else in New York."

"I'm trying to establish connections," said Kate, closing a bag with a twister. "The Cloudhawk was sabotaged. Clear weather was forecast, and it was clear everywhere except over us." She started on another bag, as Burt carried the full one out to the hallway.

"True," agreed Sherman, putting another armload of clothes on the bed, and contemplating the closet shelf.

"Who were those people she meditated with, Sherm?" asked Kate.

"I don't remember much about them." He took a long swig from his diet soda. His face had rounded out, and his tendency to overweight was becoming a battle. He had steadily taken on weight as Sue lost it.

"Let's go to New York, find the house, and see if the residents can enlighten us," said Burt.

"I'm game," said Sherman. "They gave me the creeps though. They went into a trance. I went out for a walk in the woods to get away from them. When I got back, late in the afternoon, they hadn't moved an eyelash."

"How many were there?" asked Kate.
"Four."
"Are you sure you can you find the place again?" asked Burt.
"Yes."
"Sue started getting crabby and withdrawn at work after Hurly and his aide were killed," said Kate. "Did she mention the train crash that killed the governor to you?" Kate closed another plastic bag with a twister and tore another bag off the roll. She scooped up an armful of clothes from the bed and put them in the bag.

"Yes. Right after he died, she said it wasn't an accident. She said he was too smart to leave a planning session with a lot of community leaders, and get drunk, and run his car into a train," said Sherman, taking boxes off the closet shelf and placing them on the bed. He pushed his glasses up. "Later she wouldn't talk about it at all."

"Hurly had a reputation for carousing," said Burt, leaning against the doorframe.

"He was very clever. An enemy tried to plant that idea, and he turned it into a kind of down home, Stonewall Jackson image, and let it ride, instead of fueling it with denial," said Kate. "I don't see how he'd have had time to get drunk though. The accident happened about fifteen minutes after he left the meeting."

"I can down four double shots in fifteen minutes," said Burt.

"Yeah, if you're trying. But why would Governor Hurly leave a meeting clearly designed to polish his public image, down four double shots and try to outrun a train?"

"Sue covered every public event the governor attended," said Sherman. "She said she never saw him drinking or drunk. He was friendly and easy-going."

"Ferrell's the only one who could've nipped that rumor off, and he didn't," said Kate. "He probably started and nourished it. Did Sue keep any computer files at home, Sherm?"

"Not since she started fading. She worked on her computer at home before that, but I don't know what happened to those files. I wanted to see what I could turn up, but there's nothing here. How about her files at the office?"

"Ferrell wouldn't leave anything incriminating himself or useful to us in her computer. I can't even hold onto my own files in their original accuracy, and I'm alive and fighting back.

"The most significant thing Sue covered before Hurly's death was Hurly, and after that she couldn't get any action. The rest of us stopped trying to help her get stories into print, because it was impossible, unless they were about the dog catcher making his quota. Ferrell's using the same tactic on me, and I have to find a different approach than the one Sue used."

"I certainly hope so," said Burt. "We know where that goes." They worked steadily cleaning out the closet and refreshing themselves with an occasional beer late into the evening. As they stayed and talked, Sherman began to deal with his grief.

"We'll go to Sue's mountain retreat this weekend," said Sherman, lining the last of the plastic bags up in the hallway. "You'd never find it without me, and I about can't stand it around here without Sue."

"Excellent idea! I'll book a flight Thursday night. Kate, you'll have to take Friday off," said Burt.

"Good. I wish I could take the rest of my life off."

"Don't you have to ask your boss?" asked Burt.

"Ferrell will be so overjoyed not to have to put up with me for one day he'll have a party or go hog wild at lunch and get wiped out. One of the reasons he takes a morning off for golf once a week has got to be so he won't have to fight with me. We can drop these clothes and things off on our way out, Sherm," said Kate.

"Thanks. I'll help you carry them out to the car."

They each grabbed two bags and stuffed them into the trunk, and returned for more. When all the bags were loaded, Burt said, "I'll call and let you know what time, Sherm." He slammed the trunk.

"See you Thursday night then," said Sherman, leaving them at the car and returning to his apartment.

CHAPTER TWENTY ONE

Kate, Burt, and Sherman arrived in Greenbrier, New York early Friday morning and Kate rented a car. The day was as rejuvenating as the one on which they'd started their fatal skydiving venture. Kate followed Sherman's directions through a small picturesque New England town and into the foothills of the mountains. The scenery and climate were invigorating after the California sun.

"Stop somewhere so I can buy a flashlight and some food," said Sherman.

"Sure," said Kate. She pulled into the first shopping center she came to with a grocery and hardware store in Apple Valley. "I can handle the food."

"I'll go with Sherman," said Burt. They separated to purchase supplies and regrouped at the car. Kate took three cold drinks out of the grocery bag and put the rest of the groceries in the trunk. Sherman took the flashlights with him so he could load the batteries.

"It's remote," he explained. "I'd hate to be caught there after dark without a light."

Kate distributed soft drinks, and they set out. As they approached the mountains, the spectacular bucolic landscape with steep, green slopes rising on either side of the valley and high peaks covered with forest beyond enhanced Kate's cheer, yet Sue's absence kept the dark questions persistently nagging in the back of her mind.

"I can see why Sue liked to come here," she said. "This country is a welcome change. If it wasn't for our circumstances, I could almost relax."

Burt chortled at this. "If you ever actually relax, it'll be because you're dead."

"My brain's always on the move," she replied. "It burns up energy when I'm sitting still. That's why I eat more than you and you're the one who gains all the weight."

"All my weight is in my brain, lightweight," said Burt. "Sheer intellect."

"Yeah, asleep in a bed of muscle, bone, and fat."

"Come on, you guys," said Sherman. "You sound like a couple of second-graders. Follow the signs to Iroquois Lake." Kate followed the signs, wending her way deeper into the mountains, passing the lake.

After they'd been driving about an hour, Sherman said, "Turn here," at an unmarked, easy-to-miss road. Kate turned off the highway onto the narrow, country road snaking up the mountains. She had to slow down to stay on her side. As they ascended, spaces in the thickly forested area provided glimpses of magnificent scenery. Spires of dense thickets of evergreen, oak, and silver maple penetrated the clouds below them. As they passed the clouds, landscapes of high peaks and valleys opened to their view.

"Move over to the center," said Burt, in alarm, leaning toward her. "You're going to topple us off this ridge if you get one inch closer to the edge."

Kate giggled. "The road's going into one lane. There's nowhere to move over to. Do you want to drive?"

"No. Are you sure we're going right, Sherman?" asked Burt.

"There can't be two roads like this," said Sherman. "I asked Sue the same question several times before we got there."

Eventually, the road broadened slightly, and they began a descent down the other side of the mountain.

"Watch carefully," said Sherman. "Slow down. The lane to the house is easy to miss. It's hidden in the trees. There!" he said, pointing. "Stop, stop!"

"Where?" asked Kate, braking carefully.
"You just passed it."

Kate backed up cautiously and found the lane that curved at an angle, almost parallel to the road, before cutting to the right. She turned onto it.

"This lane is obscured by the way it's laid out," said Kate, foliage brushing the car on both sides of the rugged trail.

"There's nothing here, Sherman," said Burt. "You've got us off on a wrong turn."

"That's what I thought when I came here with Sue. This is the right way," Sherman assured him.

A mile into the woods, they came to a great meadow with a thicket of towering evergreens, ancient oaks, and maples clustered in the center.

"The house is hidden in those trees," said Sherman.

Kate drove to the end of the trail, and brought the car to a halt in a gravel parking lot with weeds poking through. She got out stretching. Leaving the keys in the ignition, she noticed a peculiar absence of sound; not a bird song, not the rustle of a leaf, not a cricket or cicada. The noise they made getting out of the car was magnified by the extreme stillness of their surroundings. A chill racked her spine.

"Don't forget to take the keys," said Burt, anxiously.

"Why? A fox might sneak them out of the ignition and make off with them?" She left them in the car. "That house is haunted," she said, shivering. "I can hear my bones rattling."

Burt put his arm around her, laughing. "You can't believe that nonsense, Kate." Shaking him off, she was irritated by his certainty.

"There's a strange feeling to this place," said Sherman. "I noticed it when I was here with Sue. Everybody was talking and eating when we arrived, so it wasn't the silence then."

"The only strange things are you two. Ghosts vacated my life with Santa Claus," said Burt.

"I didn't say it was ghosts," said Kate. "I said it was bad

vibes."

"You said it was haunted," said Burt.

"The place feels abandoned," said Sherman.

"Yes, that's it," said Kate, as they walked around the red brick house with off-white shutters and a rust colored tin roof. It had a stone chimney built into one outside wall, and a brick chimney stuck up from the center of the roof of the well-maintained building.

The house in the trees and the field around it were encircled by the forest which encroached on the irregular border about fifty yards from the house. A strong scent of honeysuckle came from the dense woods.

Kate walked a little way into the forest along the first trail she saw behind the house. A thick layer of pine needles carpeted the woods, and following the trail to a mossy rock inviting her to sit down, she did. She had a magnificent view of mountain peaks. Taking a deep breath, she then exhaled slowly. A brilliant yellow primrose, catching the sunlight through the leaves of the tall trees, caught her attention. Gazing at it, she felt something move in her head, and for a split second, she was not altogether there. Shaking her head, she let it pass.

Looking down, she was shocked to see the rock she was sitting on perched on the edge of a cliff with a sharp drop off. She couldn't see to the bottom of it. Fighting intense vertigo, Kate felt a compulsion to jump, as though pulled by an invisible force. She leaped back off the rock in alarm. "How could I have avoided noticing that?" she thought. If she had stayed on the trail, not watching where she was going, she'd have walked right over the edge!

As she quickly returned to the meadow, sunlight flickered over the wooded hills, a brown and purple rocky canyon, and steep nearer valley, which was highlighted with patches of brilliant red poppies. Burt and Sherman were standing at the side of the house talking.

"Don't ever go out there in the dark," she warned, pointing. "There's a sudden drop off. Come on, I better show you."

They all walked back to the precipice, and contrary to her premonition of death, when she was alone, peace settled over Kate. The first trace of contentment she'd experienced since Sue's death came from her heart and pushed out until she was enveloped in it. She felt like her, Burt, and Sherman were three yolks in the same egg, a mood of exquisite pleasure and well-being.

"The way the house and gardens are situated in front of this cliff causes confusion. Obviously, it was deliberately built that way," said Burt, frowning.

"I don't like it any better now than I did when I was here with Sue," said Sherman, glancing down into the abyss. "You're right, Burt. This appears to be deliberately set up. Any of us could've walked down this trail and off the cliff," said Sherman. "Let's go back."

Walking back to the clearing, they then stopped at a garden which had been planted and heavily mulched but had not been harvested, and rows of shriveled plants with dried beans lay exposed to the sun.

"Strange that birds didn't get at these beans," said Kate.
"Strange that we haven't heard a bird," said Sherman.
"There's bound to be an explanation," said Burt. "Maybe someone died in the house."
Sherman laughed. "That's an explanation?" he asked. "Sounds like ghosts to me." Pushing up his glasses, Sherman walked with a perpetual slouch, cultivated from a rebellious childhood when he was told daily to straighten up and fly right. His whole body shifted from side to side as he went, and he kept his hands in his pockets. His extraordinarily large brown eyes peered from behind thick rimless glasses in a steady gaze that held their object, which startled anyone meeting him for the first time because they attested to a clear, solid self-confidence that betrayed his loose, casual posture and slouching jaunt.

"Some ways, this place seems like a bit of paradise, but where are the rabbits and groundhogs, and all the little critters that eat garden vegetables?" asked Kate.

"Hiding out from the spooks," said Burt. "Where else?"

"You're cute," said Kate, as they returned to the house. Kate walked the wide-board oak porch which wrapped all around the house with Burt and Sherman, resisting an urge to press her forehead and nose to the window and peek in. A thin veneer of dead leaves and dried forest and meadow sediment covered the porch displaying no tracks but theirs.

They entered a large mudroom containing tools; a long handled axe, several handsaws, lanterns, and fishing and camping equipment, but the door to the kitchen was locked. Burt felt a surge of delight. Before teaming up with Kate and moving to the city, he'd loved working in the woods, hunting, fishing, and camping. Now he had little time for these escapes.

"We'll try the front door," said Kate. They trooped around to the front of the house, and Kate knocked on the double front doors, not expecting an answer. She tried the door, and it swung open. She stepped in.

"Hello!" yelled Burt; he and Sherman following Kate in. "Anyone home?" He got no answer.

A coat tree stood empty in the foyer on the black and white checkered tile floor, and they took off their jackets, hung them, and proceeded to the living room to the left of the foyer. Off-white walls were bare of ornaments, and the floor was carpeted in cushy dark forest green. The focal point was a large stone fireplace built into the stone east wall. A gun rack on the adjacent wall held four rifles. Facing the fireplace was a six-foot mustard yellow sofa flanked by an armchair on each side.

To the right of the foyer was a spacious dining room with a redwood picnic table in the center and eight chairs around it. The roomy square kitchen was behind the dining room, and next to that was a hallway between the living room and dining and kitchen side. A small bathroom and shower stall was behind the kitchen. An arched doorway opened to a large cedar paneled room with a highly varnished cedar floor which ran the width of the house and thirty feet deep.

"It smells good in here," remarked Kate, shivering in the cedar room.

"Yeah, but it's cold and drafty," said Burt, studying the ceiling, where the cold air came from. This room was bare of furniture. An earthen fire pit, lined with rocks and enclosed on three sides by fireproof glass was vented by stovepipe through the ceiling in the center of the room. The wall facing the forest was cedar to a height of three feet, and glass to the ceiling, affording a fabulous view of the mountains. Smoothly varnished, the floor was reflective as glass, and Kate restrained an urge to take off her shoes and feel the bare, warm-scented floor beneath her feet.

"This is where they meditated," said Sherman. "They had a fire in here and sat around it. They looked like logs. Even Sue didn't look like Sue. Can you imagine what it would be like in this ungodly stillness with your spouse and four strangers, sitting like the living dead?" Sherman shivered, pushing up his glasses. "They didn't speak after we filed in here. They were off on some star and didn't even hear me go out. If you think the silence is sinister now, you should've been here when they were meditating. It was quieter than quiet. They could've been relatives. There was a sameness about them."

"Sounds pretty weird. When we get back home, can I borrow Sue's address book?" asked Kate. "If any of them are in it, I'd like to give them a call."

"I looked and they're not listed."

"This place is cut off. There's no exit or entry except the road we came on," noted Burt.

"There's another road I found on my hike," said Sherman. "It cuts into the main road a few miles down the slope, and it's in about the same shape as the one we drove in on."

Kate went into the kitchen and flicked on the light switch. Lights came on with an initial outburst of a motor, like a riveter in a holy shrine. The generator in the cellar then faded into a dull hum. The counters and appliances were covered with dust.

Burt and Sherman entered the kitchen. "I didn't know a place as remote and isolated as this existed in this country," said Burt. "That noise sounded like a generator in the basement. There's no electric line to the house. I'll test the water." He took a drink from the tap. "Fresh as a mountain spring," he pronounced.

Kate quenched her thirst, also. "Undoubtedly, it's mountain spring water," she agreed. "As beautiful as it is here, a person could go nuts. Every time I turn around, I get confused."

"Let's eat. Then we can make a fire in the pit, meditate, and see what we flush out," said Burt.

Sherman laughed loudly, shoving his glasses up with his index finger.

"I'm not making concessions to ghost theories," said Burt. "I was referring to legitimate meditation. I did some research on it. There's nothing to it. You sit with your eyes closed in a comfortable position without moving or talking, and don't think."

"Don't think?" asked Sherman.

"That's what he said," said Kate. "Burt, you always know everything, and you're always wrong," said Kate. "It's only in your organized mind that everything goes by the book and fits into categories."

"Bullshit. You just love to argue," retorted Burt. "The whole idea of meditation is to empty your mind of thought. Peace is then supposed to come in."

"Look who's talking about picking a fight. You should run for Congress."

"Come on you two. This gets old," said Sherman.

Burt went out to the car and brought in the groceries. Kate and Sherman were waiting for him in the dining room, and he sat down, put the bag on the table, and took out paper plates and food.

"Maybe after we eat when we start meditating we'll pick up some feelings hanging around," said Kate enthusiastically.

Burt laughed. "Feelings don't hang around, Kate. They're created by the person feeling them. When you don't feel them anymore, they're gone."

"There's a lot we don't know about emotions, parapsychology, UFOs, all that business," remarked Sherman, opening a container of macaroni salad and spooning some onto his plate.

"If we pick up anything that we can all agree didn't come from any of us, I'll believe that feelings can separate themselves from a person and hang around," said Burt, laughing, as he fixed his plate. "Even if it was true, and I'm not conceding the possibility, that still wouldn't prove anything about Sue's death."

"You're so damn smug, Burt." said Kate, frustrated with his skepticism. "I went into a public lounge with nobody in it once, and there was a feeling of grief. I suddenly got so depressed, I almost cried, and it wasn't my grief. Someone, who was having a bad time, must've left right before I went in."

Burt laughed. "Everything has a logical reason. Take a card trick, for instance. When you know how to do the trick, it makes perfect sense, but for the person being fooled, it's spooky."

"What kind of a freak would play a trick to kill a person?" asked Sherman.

"A person with a problem," replied Kate. "Someone Sue could hurt by something she knew."

"Sue was always interested in the philosophic, like how thoughts originate," said Sherman.

"They come from the things our senses take in," said Kate, "and how we process them to order our lives."

"Yeah, but I meant the things we pick up without knowing it. Maybe if we try to put ourselves in her place, we'll have more success. She could perceive things she couldn't before joining this group, and that's why her personality changed. She was unnaturally cold and aloof before she died. I hoped for a transition back to the Sue I fell in love with. That Sue was a warm, loving woman who cared for all life. It's only beginning to dawn on me what this business did to our relationship," said Sherman.

"Sue stumbled onto things that led to big breaks, and she never knew how she happened to be in the right place at the right time," said Kate. "Or she'd say something that elicited a revelation from someone who'd rather kept a tighter cover. She started meditating to get a handle on what was happening, not the other way around."

"Spending enough weekends here could cause drastic change in a person," said Burt. "She didn't hear the city sounds or argue with the editor or run down leads."

"She quit acting like a reporter after Hurly and his aide died," said Kate. "I can't figure out how that connects to this place. I feel like I'm in the last century." Kate finished eating, and put her trash in the grocery bag. "The silence has the most sinister effect on me," she added. "At least, we're making a little noise." She pushed her chair back and got up from the table. "I'm going out to gather wood for a fire."

"I'll chop some," said Burt. "I need the exercise." He put his trash in the trash bag, and got his jacket from the foyer. Unlocking the kitchen door, he then walked out to the mudroom, took an axe, and tromped out relishing the cold, mountain air, the woodsy smell of pine and deep forest.

The altitude made him slightly short of breath when he began chopping wood; nevertheless, he was invigorated. The air was cleaner, fresher, and he fancied himself a lumberjack. The old days of his bachelorhood hiking and camping away from the pressures of his job and civilization flooded his soul and renewed his energy, giving him an exhilarating sense of conquest.

Skydiving had let much steam off and moved his focus of activity from the mountains, but immersed in the forest, his love of the wilderness overcame all competition. Watching the chips fly, feeling the energy coursing through his muscles, the pull against his torso, gave him a jolt of subtle pleasure; and in it, he forgot his worry about Kate and anguish over Sue's death.

The steady thunk, thunk of his axe could be heard at the lodge, as Kate went back for some larger logs she'd seen stacked below the cedar room and brought an armload in.

Sherman took the trash bag back to the cedar room, threw it in the fire pit, and went out to pick up tinder and kindling. He gathered as much as he could carry, and seeing Kate bringing another armload of wood, he went in and started the fire.

Sherman got a good blaze going, and placed three logs on top. The wood soon caught, taking the chill out of the room.

"That fire and my full stomach are going to put me to sleep," said Kate, taking off her jacket and sitting as close to it as she could. "It's so cozy." The blaze sent eerie shadows flickering over the walls and ceiling. Watching the mesmerizing fire, Kate pictured Sue in her mind's eye. In her vision, Sue's mouth moved as though she was trying to tell her something.

"What?" Kate asked. At that moment, a moan came from below, starting with a low vibration, and grew into a terrifying howl. Kate's eyes popped open as the sound increased in volume and resonance. Surrounding the house, it seemed to come from the ground and all sides at once. Tension from within built as the inhuman wail became a frightful tortured shriek that enveloped the room, mingling with her breath and invading her lungs. She was being crushed by it. Gasping, she grabbed her jacket and jumped up.

Kate and Sherman tore out of the house and dashed for the car. Kate stumbled, unable to see clearly in the thick fog that had crept over and now covered the mountain. A faint glow came from where she thought the car was parked, and she made for it, Sherman on her heels.

When Kate and Sherman stumbled into the car, Burt was already in the front passenger seat with the inside light on. Before Burt could lean over to open the driver's door, Kate was half way into the car. Sherman leaped into the back, slamming the door.

Kate started the car and sped down the narrow lane in reverse, unable to see in the thick fog. The lane was unlit, and the mountains at night were too dark to see the trail, but she felt the tires in the ruts and gripped the wheel loosely, letting the ruts guide. She backed onto the road, and careened down the curving lane for several miles, fog obscuring her vision.

"Stop!" screamed Burt. "Stop! Stop! Stop!"

Jolted to her senses, Kate slowly braked, controlling an urge to stomp on the pedal, and brought the car to a halt.

"Jesus," she whispered, "sweet Jesus." They sat silently, listening to themselves breathe, staring into the foggy night. Kate opened the door, her heart in her throat, her hands trembling. Hugging herself, she was extraordinarily cold and shivering. She got out of the car.

"Where are you going?" asked Burt. His voice quavered, and he cleared his throat.

"To see where the edge of the road is, so I can tell if there's room to turn around without driving over it." Kate laughed, nervously. Her mouth was dry, and she was soaked with perspiration.

"I'll go with you," said Sherman, taking two of the flashlights, which he'd left in the car. He pushed his glasses up, and met Kate in the glare of the car's headlights. They used the flashlights to find the edge of the road.

"There's room to turn around with three or four maneuvers," estimated Kate. "Could you stand at this edge with the light to mark the side of the road?"

"Sure. Good thing we can't see how close we are to the edge of the mountain. I'd die of fright."

"I understand," said Kate. She walked back to the car and slid into the driver's seat. "What could have happened to Sue?" she asked, maneuvering the car around with the aid of Sherman's light. "What in the world could it be?"

"I don't know. Aren't you scared, Kate?" asked Burt.

"Yes."

When the car was heading in the right direction, Kate waited for Sherman to get in and drove back slowly and carefully, unable to find the lane to the house. She stopped.

"I won't see the entrance in the dark. We better get out and walk until we find the turnoff," she said.

"We'll go," said Sherman. "C'mon, Burt." He handed Burt a flashlight. Burt and Sherman walked slowly along the edge of the road for ten yards until they came to the lane to the house. One of them stood on each side with a light, and Burt waved at Kate with his light to proceed. She drove very slowly and stopped for them to get in at the path.

"We could leave the car here and walk back," said Sherman, getting in. "I can't see anything in that fog."

"You could walk back," said Burt.
"Alone?"
"Kate will protect you. I'll drive." Burt laughed at his joke.
"I'm in the ruts," said Kate. "I can't see either." Kate allowed the car to roll along, goosing the gas pedal occasionally to prevent coming to a halt and stopped in the parking lot.

They all got out and advanced cautiously on foot with their flashlights, the house looming over them cheerless as a tomb, the double doors to the entrance gaping open, like a hungry shark's mouth moving in on food. Dead silence, marred only by their rubber-soles on the ground, was more ominous in the cold, dark night then beneath a sunny sky. After the howling tension that drove them to flight, the stillness seemed to conceal something sinister, more terrible for its unknown and unnatural character.

Kate laughed suddenly, and Burt and Sherman jumped.

"What did you do that for?" asked Burt in annoyance.

"To break the ghastly silence. I'm not afraid of it." Her voice echoed unnaturally loud, and she swallowed the lump in her throat.

"Maybe we should walk faster," suggested Sherman, picking up his pace resolutely. Kate and Burt fell in step. They marched up the front stairs and into the house, leaving the doors open behind them.

"When can we come back?" asked Kate.

"Let it rest two weeks," said Burt. "We'll have a four day weekend, and I can take comp time if necessary."

"Sherman?"

"Suits me. I've got plenty of leave accumulated. All I do anymore is work."

Burt put the fire out and found a bucket in the mudroom to carry the ashes. He soaked them and dumped them outdoors into a barbecue pit. Sherman carried out the wood they hadn't used. He swept and mopped the area, leaving it as they found it, and Kate wrote a note:

*To whom it may concern: Sue Front is dead. Her husband and two friends came to talk about her unusual death. We're coming back in two weeks, on the 24th. If you can't meet us, please leave a note telling us how to get in touch with you. Yours truly, Kate.* She placed a business card beside the note, as the men came in.

"The fire's out," said Burt.

"I'm ready to go," said Sherman, putting the broom and mop away.

"It doesn't seem so spooky now," said Kate. "It's kind of nice with the light on. Do you think...."

"No," said Burt, walking out to the front porch. Kate and Sherman followed him, and Sherman pulled the doors closed behind them.

"I'll drive back," volunteered Burt, getting into the driver's seat. When everyone was in, he started the long drive to the airport.

"I don't know what could have caused that gruesome howling," said Sherman.

"It sounded like an animal in horrendous pain," said Kate.

"Maybe it was," said Sherman, "a large animal, like a bear dying some grotesque death in a trap. It had to be fairly large to make such a noise."

"I felt pressure, though," said Sherman. "I felt like I was breathing something in, a living substance that could squash the breath out of my lungs."

"Yes, now that you mention it, there was a definite pressure. Did you notice it, Kate?" asked Burt.

"Yeah, that's what was so scary. I've never known of anything like it. It felt like it had volition and was trying to suffocate me."

"Don't be surprised if I conveniently break my leg and can't go next time," joked Burt. Kate and Sherman laughed, their self-confidence returning as they increased their distance from the house.

CHAPTER TWENTY TWO

The social worker turned the radio on again, and Anita turned it off again.

"The radio is very helpful, Miss Sales. Believe me I've been through this more times than you have." Officious, Mrs. Piper's bleached blonde beehive bobbed on top of her head, making her look taller and weightier than she was. Her presumptions, and the loud, sure voice with which she declared them, like Moses just down from the mountain with the law engraved, heavy in his hands, irritated Anita to the point that if Mrs. Piper declared a blue jay to be blue, Anita would've felt compelled to argue the point. She'd corrected Mrs. Piper on her name, Ms., not Miss so many times, that Mrs. Piper won.

"How many times have you been hospitalized after being assaulted?" asked Anita, sarcastically.

"No, I mean helping other people in trouble."

"If I need your help, I'll let you know."

"Perhaps you'd rather listen to another station? Why don't you select the station?" Mrs. Piper stood back from the radio, a twitch in her right eye, magnified by her glasses that always distracted Anita.

"I'm not going to listen to the radio. It can't be good for you to impose yourself on innocent people who aren't in a position to fight back just for money."

"You're hurting yourself more than you realize. The radio brings you back to the present when your mind starts to drift." Mrs. Piper sighed, with a heave of her heavy bosom, her demeanor sagging under the weight of Anita's recalcitrance, with her most condescendingly concerned expression. "Here's the number for Social Services." She handed Anita her card. "Don't hesitate to call. You won't have to talk to me. I'll assign your case to someone else if you like."

"That's gratifying to know." The card passed through Anita's hands on its way to the trashcan. "Bye bye," said Anita, wishing she'd leave.

Heaving one last profound sigh of concern, Mrs. Piper took her cue, and Dr. Lapere came in soon after. "I came to release you," he said, cheerfully.

Anita asked a question she'd been nurturing since regaining consciousness, postponed to the last opportunity for fear of the influence of a negative answer. "Is it likely I'll fully recover my mental acuity, Dr. Lapere?"

"It's hard to tell. Many people fully recover from severe trauma." His foot on a stepping stool by the bed, he rested his arm on his bent leg. "You're at an advantage, having complete recall up to the time of the break-in. If you return to your house, your memory might be jogged. That could spur a quicker recovery."

"I'm glad I don't have to go back. Lon Dedaman and Carrie found me a smaller cheaper place. I can live on my savings until I reorganize myself. My house is rented out."

"Yes, I know. You told me that." Dr. Lapere straightened up.

"Oh, a lot?"

"No, three or four times." Anita's somber expression changed to a frown. Closing her eyes, she concentrated on having told Dr. Lapere that Lon and Carrie found her a smaller, cheaper place and she'd rented her house. "I'm never going to tell him that again," she vowed to herself. "In fact, I'm never going to mention it to anyone again."

"Don't worry so much. The more time that goes by, the better you're likely to be."

"Are you sure I won't deteriorate?"

"It depends, quite a bit, on your attitude. Everybody's different. You're lucky to be alive, and you've always had good sense. Tell yourself that you're going to make a full recovery.

Never tell yourself the opposite. You can actually talk yourself into your cure or your doom."

"Yes."

"The last thing you remember still is the knock on the door?"

"Yes. I went to answer the door. The next thing I knew I was here."

"I'll want to see you in my office in two weeks to make sure that back is healing properly. That's the only physical residue."

"I doubt I'll need this cane in two weeks."

"Don't give it up if you need it. There's no good in discarding it too soon. You can actually hurt yourself trying to be brave."

"I'm not one of those."

"Good luck, Anita." Dr. Lapere smiled, shaking her hand.

"Thanks, Dr. Lapere. I'll see you next time." Going to the phone as Lapere left, she couldn't recall her boyfriend's number.

"I'll have to call information," she said, but she couldn't recall that number either and dialed the operator. "What's the number for information, please?" she asked. Anita felt stupid, but she adopted unshakable faith that she could talk herself into full recovery. "I know I'm really bright," she reminded herself. The operator interrupted her musing with the number which she wrote down. She then called Lon, and expecting her call, he answered almost immediately.

"I'm ready to go home Lon. Can you pick me up now?"

"I'll be there in twenty minutes."

"Bring Carrie."

"Sure. Bye."

"Bye."

Rummaging through her purse, Anita couldn't find her small notebook she'd been using to take notes on things necessary to remember. She searched the bathroom, and finally found it in the drawer of the nightstand with a tube of lip balm.

She rubbed in a cosmetic base and dabbed on some powder that Carrie had brought her to cover the scars on her face somewhat. The bruises had faded entirely. She felt the ridges on her head, where the stitches had been, forty-three on one side, nineteen on top, and a few scattered over the other side.

Her hair had never been so short. That's what made her look different, she decided. Yet, her eyes were different, too; pale, the brown seemed to have washed out.

She paid attention to the little things; putting the compact in her purse, going through the drawers to make sure she hadn't left anything, actions she used to perform without thinking, because these were tripping her up.

At the door to her room, with her small suitcase, she had to stop and think which way to go. The first four or five times she'd walked to the lobby, she'd ended up at the entrance to the operating wing instead of the elevators. Then she'd gotten off at every floor the elevator stopped at and had to wait for it again to get to the lobby. This time, she made the trip perfectly.

Thinking about her successful law practice made her feel like crying. She'd been self-sufficient all her adult life, and now she had to practice to get from the fourteenth floor to the lobby. She waited only a few minutes before Carrie and Lon walked in.

"You look great, just like the old Anita," said Lon, with a broad grin. He hugged her close, and Anita drew away but managed a trace of a smile.

"Welcome back to the world, Anita," said Carrie, hugging her.

"I'm glad you two could come," Anita said, genuinely happy.

"How are you?" asked Lon, putting his arm around her. She moved away, and he frowned.

"Okay in some ways. It's depressing to realize how much I've lost in memory and mental capacity. How much of it I get back depends on my attitude they say."

"Anyone would be bitter," said Carrie, happy that Anita was finally going home. She'd missed her at work, keeping the office barely alive, and she hoped and prayed for a complete recovery.

"I suppose so," said Anita, uncertainly.

"Do you want to go to your place or mine?" asked Lon.

"Or mine?" asked Carrie, noticing her friend's insecurity, so different from the aggressive lawyer she'd once been. She made a mental note of finding a way to help Anita retrieve the certainty that accompanies a dynamic personality.

"Take me to my place. I want you both to be there when I see it and take the first walk through."

"We couldn't get all your stuff in," said Lon. "An awful lot is still at your house."

Lon drove, and Anita sat in the back seat with Carrie, gazing absent-mindedly out the window, watching the inner city of shops and businesses fade into a residential section. She was in a different part of town than her house.

"This apartment is farther from my office," noted Anita.

"It's a comfortable neighborhood, though," said Carrie. "Rents skyrocket as we get closer to your office."

They arrived at the building in a changing neighborhood, which looked as though it had been prouder at one time.

"This is the best we could do with the budget you limited me to," said Lon, sensing her disappointment.

"We did the best we could," echoed Carrie.

"Thanks. I appreciate your help, both of you, more than I can say," said Anita, smiling to show she meant it.

Lon drove through the security gate and parked on the asphalt lot behind the seven-story building. Seeing her car, Anita got out of the car, hobbled to it with her cane, and searched her bag for her keys.

"The car keys are in your apartment," called Lon.

"Why didn't you tell me before I got all the way over there?" she asked, walking back.

"How would I know what you were going to do?"

The old, red brick wall of the building had rows of sash windows, many with flowers in window boxes. An alley behind the parking lot separated the property from the back of a dilapidated building that had once been another apartment building but now stood vacant. A quick glance showed the rest of the alley to be lined with the backs of buildings in various states of repair. Green trash collectors marked the end of each property. She paused, staring at one of them.

"You don't take the garbage out," said Lon. "There's a chute, and the building has a janitor."

"How did you know what I was thinking?" asked Anita, picking up her pace, struggling with irritability, Carrie following behind.

"You've been staring at the receptacle."

"Oh, I'm sorry."

Lon sighed handing her the keys to her apartment.

"Don't they give you two sets?" asked Anita, brushing off his attempt to take her arm, as she limped around to the front of the building with the cane.

"They gave me two sets. One's at my place. If you lock yourself out or need me to get something...."

"You'll have to bring them over. I don't want anyone to have keys to my place."

"But I have keys to your house."

"You do?"

"Don't you remember?"

"Of course, I remember."

"So, should I keep the keys?"

"No. I don't want anyone but me to have keys."

"Why? Someone else should have a key in case of an emergency."

"No. I don't know why." She couldn't control her antagonism, and the conversation ended.

The building was landscaped with a large juniper on one side of the porch and a yew on the other side. A row of trimmed hedges bounded the property.

Climbing the four stairs to the front door brought pain to Anita's back. Leaning heavily on the cane, seeking a more comfortable way to maneuver, she winced.

"Here, let me help you," said Lon, taking her arm.

"No." Anita gave him a little push and nearly lost her balance, pain shooting through her back.

"What's the matter with you, Anita?" he asked, irritated.

"I can't stand being this helpless," she said angrily.

"You never objected to my help before."

"I've never been so miserably unable to take care of myself before. You can't imagine. There's no worse situation in the world." In the presence of Carrie and Lon, Anita's loss of mental agility disturbed her much more than when she'd remained under the protective wing of the hospital.

"When you're completely well, maybe things will be the same as they used to," said Lon.

"When I'm completely independent, it'll certainly be a change for the better," said Anita, making an effort to sound more agreeable.

"They haven't made one scrap of progress in finding out who attacked you or the motive," said Carrie.

"Maybe we'll figure it out," said Anita, relieved that Carrie wasn't taking care of her, too.

The front of the building was much more appealing than the back. It had cheerful shutters, and was extremely well kept. The fronts of the houses and apartments lining the street looked like those of a very nicely kept village. It seemed to Anita a facade, and she thought she was only a facade of herself.

Going inside, the interior of the building was in better shape with unmarked paint and fresh wallpaper. While the paintings on the walls were not masterpieces, neither were they dreary. A painting of modern dancers brought a peculiar feeling of deja vu.

Lon touched her arm, and Anita moved on to the elevator. The three of them rode it up to her floor, and when they got off, walking down the corridor, she was flanked by Lon and Carrie. She paused at the door to her apartment.

"Go ahead, open it," urged Carrie, eagerly.

Anita unlocked the door and led the way in. The large foyer led into a living room with a hallway behind it. The cheerful room had a picture window from which she could see the city street in the all- residential area. There was little traffic, and she liked being able to see who was at the front door from the window.

Her end tables stood on each side of the modern sofa, the wool carpet in front of it with two occasional chairs at one corner of the carpet, facing the sofa. The walls were painted white. Twenty-foot-high ceilings made the room seem even larger than it was, and the antique brass chandelier lent an artistic touch.

"You remembered that I hate the room to be overcrowded with furniture," said Anita.

"I tried to choose your favorite pieces," said Lon, hording the credit. Carrie had participated in the selection of furniture to bring.

"How did you know?"
Lon shrugged.
"I know you helped, Carrie."
Carrie smiled at her, and Anita broke into a broad smile. Lon beamed. He pecked her on the cheek, and she involuntarily drew away.

"Let's go see the rest," he said, ignoring the rebuff. The hallway led to a kitchen on one side and a dining room across from it with an arched entry. Anita peeked into the rooms approving the size and layout and proceeded to a bedroom nearly as large as the living room with a bathroom. Two windows looked out over the city, and Anita saw that she was high on a hill. A tall pine tree near her window met her gaze, and she opened the window to the smell of pine.

"It smells like Christmas," she said. For the first time, she thought she'd make it. "I'm going to get myself back together."

"You're not just saying that?" asked Lon. Anita glanced at Carrie, who retreated to the living room.

"It'll be okay as soon as I can take the world on an equal footing again. It'll happen because I'm going to make it happen."

"I know you can if you want to. I didn't know if you still love me or if all your feelings were wiped out."

"I don't know my own feelings. If you can put up with me until I regain my security, we'll see."

"Well, you know me. I'm not the monkish type. I need affection."

"I don't know how long it'll take. I'm sure the beginning is when I re-establish myself. The social worker told me I had a bad attitude, and the doctor said the speed of recovery would depend on my attitude."

"I know you better than anyone. You don't trust yourself because you believe that your decisions brought you to the circumstances that led to the break-in and attack. You have to see that your decisions bring you to where you want to be. Then your self-confidence will return."

"No, unless it was the decisions about what cases I chose, and I'd do that the same way again. It's more like being adrift in a storm. You don't know what direction to take. How do I know it wasn't something in my relationship with you?"

"Do you think it could've been?" Lon looked shocked. "Do you think if I changed something in myself?"

"I always thought you were more dependent on me than I like to be depended upon; emotionally, I mean."

Lon laughed and Anita laughed with him.

"Here," she said, turning her cheek toward him. "Kiss me quick before I change my mind." He pecked her on the cheek.

"I just need time," she said.

"We'll live it out and see what happens. Neither of us really knows."

"No. You always imagine what you'd do in a given situation, but you never know until you live it. Let's get back to Carrie." Anita returned to the living room, but Carrie was gone. She'd wanted to test her conversational ability with her oldest and dearest friend. Carrie would understand when she failed, and Carrie's confidence in her would help restore her faith in herself.

Anita looked out the window and saw Carrie step into a cab. "Do you want me to go, too?" asked Lon.
"Yes."
"Call me."
"All right."
After Lon left, Anita took two pain pills, went to her bedroom, set her cane beside the bed, and lay down to rest. She fell asleep, and when she woke up, it was dark. Getting up, she then flicked the light on, walked through the apartment with her cane on the way to the kitchen, and paused in the hallway. It occurred to her that she'd only seen one of the bedrooms. She looked down the long hall at the closed door to the other one, terrified. "There's nothing to be afraid of," she told herself. Walking slowly to the closed door, each step seemed to approach doom. Stopping at the bathroom, she then flicked on the light and looked in, a reprieve. The sight of her familiar bathmat and towels and wicker wastebasket and shelves comforted her. Pausing at the closed door, she asked herself, "What are you waiting for?"

She turned the knob and pushed the door open. It shredded the silence with a groaning creak. The room was half the size of her bedroom with some of the furnishings from the study in her house. She saw her desk, and recalled that it was the last thing she'd seen before she'd lost consciousness, but it had been dripping with her blood. The single narrow casement overlooked a slanted, gray shingle roof of the apartment building next door. Dim outlines of other buildings beyond it, like monolithic silhouettes on a freakish moonscape, conjured surrealistic city visions. The dark shadow of a leafless tree on one wall reached its branches toward her, and her throat and chest constricted. A premonition of death swept over her like wind. The room was much colder than the rest of the house, and another shadow looked like a noose swinging heavily from the tree outside weighted with a body. The rope disappeared, or was it merely a snake or branch fallen or dropped to the ground? She went to the window and looked out but saw only the tree.

Nearly overpowered with sudden vertigo, she staggered back to the door and over the threshold, shivering. Returning to the kitchen and looking down the hallway at the door that caused near panic five minutes previously, she started laughing hysterically. Listening to her moronic cackle, she changed it into a command.

"Shut up!" she said, loudly. The serenity of the warm kitchen in a flood of light was comforting. "I will not be defeated," she murmured.

Anita sat on the end of her couch, which used to be her favorite place to relax after a tough day at work, and read the newspaper Carrie had left on the coffee table. She found it enormously interesting and amusing. She'd never had time to read it when she was practicing law. On those occasions when something had been reported that pertained to her or one of her cases, she'd read only the pertinent article. Now she read the funnies and worked the crossword puzzle.

When she was finished with the newspaper, Anita went to the kitchen and looked into the pantry and refrigerator. Lon or Carrie, bless their hearts, had filled the refrigerator with a roast stuffed turkey and all the trimmings for a traditional Thanksgiving dinner. There was even her favorite mincemeat pie. The pantry was, also, well stocked.

She fixed herself a plate and nuked it before adding cranberry sauce. After eating, she cleaned up the kitchen and put a jazz CD into the player. Again she walked through the apartment, looking for something to do. At the hospital, getting out of bed and walking down the corridors was as much as she could manage.

Recalling seeing her bookcase full of books in the study, she hobbled back to it and looked over the selections. Though she could remember reading most of the books, she couldn't remember what they were about. She opened one, a novel by a popular author, and started reading the first page. The whole story came flooding back to memory. She returned that book to the shelf and selected another. The same thing happened. On her third try, she found one she couldn't recall reading, a novel, and returned to the living room with it.

She read until she felt dopey, laid the book aside, and took a walk outdoors to start checking out the neighborhood. Strolling to the corner and back home, she was surprised at how tired she was. After soaking her back in a hot tub until the water turned tepid, she put on her pajamas, robe and slippers, brewed a cup of chamomile tea, and took two pain pills to ward off the pain in her back.

Taking the tea to the bedroom, she then set it on the nightstand, and went to bed. Her old sheets and blankets were comfortably familiar, those of the successful lawyer she'd once been. She stretched out on the mattress, like an out-of-focus image seen through a camera lens. When the image of the person she was before the assault converged exactly with who she was now, her direction would be clearer.

She fell into a deep, dreamless sleep but woke several hours later terrified trying to scream, but it caught in her throat. The room was so dark she couldn't tell where she was. Arranging the pillows, so she could lean on them in a sitting position, she drew the blankets tightly around her. Her breathing sounded like thunder. Squinting into the darkness, it was impenetrable. She nestled into the pillows. This was her bed, her blankets, what was strange?

Her sensibility came to her, like an old friend a long time absent, and the years of training and career as a lawyer had laid the foundation for her ability to overcome unfounded terror with thought. She'd used it in the defense of others, and she'd use it in her own. Recalling entering this room for the first time with Lon, she visualized the night table beside the bed with the lamp and the cup of tea on it. She reached out and touched the lamp and turned it on dim, dispelling the terror. Snuggling into the blankets, she thought the conquest of each fear would have to be achieved.

*Who had attacked her and why? Was it someone she knew, someone with a grudge because of her work, or chance circumstance?* Recalling the people on whose behalf she'd filed suit, and their untimely deaths or disappearances, she shuddered. Now she knew their fear.

In the old days when she couldn't sleep, she got up and studied a brief. She pulled the covers over her head and stretched full length, letting her thoughts drift into a state of semi-consciousness which was infinitely consoling She had an intense desire to study, to prepare for a case and shut the idea away with the promise of going to her office in the morning.

After finally dozing off, she woke early, and it was still dark. She made breakfast and ate leisurely. Dropping the teacup as she went to put it in the sink, she then had to remind herself to hold onto things tightly. She swept up the glass, resolving to do better next time without condemning herself for the error.

Dressing, she then decided to enter her hospital receipts into her accounting program. It took a gargantuan effort to remember where she'd put her bag containing the envelope of receipts. She looked first in one closet and then another before pawing through drawers.

"Stop!" she said out loud. "Stop and remember." She sat down and thought back to standing outside the door with Carrie on one side of her and Lon on the other. They came in together, and Carrie had hung all their coats in the closet. She had to put her purse down to take off her coat. Yes! She'd dropped it on the closet floor and left it there because her back hurt when she bent over, and she didn't want to ask for help. She retrieved it, and gathered the receipts.

She couldn't recall how to operate her computer to enter the hospital invoices and receipts, and had to get the book and follow the directions step by step. Concentration was time consuming and demanding of intellectual energy. Thought and memory had to be lured out of some deep retreat as though they were afraid of another beating.

Encouraged by the ability to regain her lost memory and concentration, though it was a slow and painstaking process, her determination to prevail outweighed every obstacle. Each gain was a great triumph, and every time her thoughts tried to turn back to what she'd lost, she reminded herself to keep her progress going in the direction she wanted.

Establishing the first routine of her rehabilitated life, Anita walked with her cane to a shop a half-mile away she'd seen on her way home from the hospital and bought a newspaper. Pleased that she could manage the brief outing, she went home and read the news.

"Now comes the big test," she said to herself. "Lon said the car keys were in the apartment. Did he say where?"

During a lengthy search for the keys in drawers, closets, pockets, and nooks, she recalled looking out the hospital windows at the traffic, wondering if she could still drive. She found the keys on a peg on the bulletin board in the kitchen. Fixing the location firmly in mind, she resolved to put them back in the same place, so she'd never have to spend another minute of her life searching for them. Time was too valuable, and the return of her mental faculties depended on carrying out every necessity from the idea to the act.

Leaving her apartment deliberately neglecting to take the cane, she then locked the door and tried it even though she heard the click. She went down to the parking lot and located her car. Getting into the driver's seat gave her a lift. Starting the car and driving out of the parking lot was no problem, but she didn't know where she was, which way to go. The first time she'd been in this part of town was on her way home from the hospital.

The sun barely over the horizon gave her direction. She'd never had occasion to notice the position of the sun before. *I can use these new observations, or I can dribble what resources I have away on mourning my losses, but I can't do both,* she thought. She stopped at a supermarket for a street map, but to her consternation couldn't read the small print. Before the attack, she'd had twenty-twenty vision. Her next stop was a pharmacy, where she purchased a pair of reading glasses. Putting them on in the car to read the map, the names of the streets then became clear.

She followed the map to familiar territory, but even the turf she used to know was now disconnected islands. Taking a wrong turn, she then lost her bearings, pulled to the side of the street, located her position on the map, and went around the block, returning to the main street.

*I never thought driving to work would be like climbing Mount McKinley,* she thought, pulling into her parking garage. Getting out of the car in the garage brought the sensation of having done it many times before, and she instantly recalled the layout of the building.

In the old, well-known, congenial lobby, she had a moment of intense longing for her old lifestyle. Even the nick in the molding by the elevator seemed almost dear.

"Well, good morning, Anita. It's a pleasure to see you back, looking so good!" said Ron, the security guard, his good nature beaming out of dark eyes, sparkling beneath the visor of his hat.

"Good morning," said Anita, coldly. The natural cheer in her voice that had answered Ron in the before days was gone.

*Could he be one of them? No, he was too old, too fat, too innocent. His pleasure in people oozed from his pores. Were her assailants young, and slender, or was the idea based on prejudice from her practice?*

"Welcome back." He smiled at her, and Anita pasted on a smile. His face fell, and she was sorry she couldn't manage a real smile.

On the elevator to her office, she suddenly broke into tears. Two women got off, and she got off, too. To her dismay, she wasn't on the right floor. She'd regressed to the hospital days of getting off every time the elevator stopped.

"Don't panic," she said to herself. Blowing her nose and wiping tears away, she was possessed by uncontrollable grief. The others who got off the elevator laughed, and she thought they were laughing at her. Anita waited for the elevator again and rode up to her floor.

She had a long search through her bag for her keys at the office door. Tearful, with a runny nose, she fought the temptation to return immediately to the shelter of the car. Her back ached fiercely. "Stop and think. Stop! Stop!" she silently screamed at herself.

Leaning against the door, she put her hands in her coat pocket, and to her relief, the keys were there. She had the same terror of going into the office as she had of opening the door to the study in her apartment and paused in limbo.

Aubrey, the lawyer in the suite next to hers, came down the hall toward her. *Could he be one of them?* She reviewed what she knew of him. First, she'd always liked him very much and valued his opinion. She'd discussed many cases with him, and he'd occasionally showed her an approach she hadn't thought of. He was slender, middle-aged, and had never been hostile. She'd been told that he was the one who scared off the gang and saved her life by calling 911.

"Anita," he said, pleasure at her return oozing from every pore. "How are you? It's so good to see you back. Carrie said you were out of the hospital."

Anita hoped the confusion crashing through her brain wasn't visible to Aubrey. "I'm fine. How are you?" Her words were slow and hesitant.

"Same as always. Come on over. Let's have a cup of coffee just like old times, or would you rather go out?"

"I'm going to my office. Why don't you come over in an hour? I'd like to talk to you, but I have to go in alone first and have a look around. I've been afraid of my own shadow since I got out, and I have to do it this way."

Aubrey looked at his watch. "I understand," he said. "I can make it in an hour, but I'll only have ten or fifteen minutes before I have to be in court."

"Thanks, Aubrey, it's a date."

"I'll see you then," he said cheerfully and walked back to his office.

"Mourning, as though my best friend died one minute, and talking with an old friend like the lawyer I used to be the next," she said to herself, entering the quiet sanctity of her office. After walking through the lobby, library, conference room, and the offices, she went into her private sanctuary and eased herself into the chair behind her desk, wishing she'd taken Lapere's advice and brought the cane. The grief she'd experienced on the elevator was not real. She had to relearn self-confidence like everything else in order to not pick up other people's emotional overload. Beneath the confusion and doubt was the person, Anita.

Lon's words, *you believe the decisions you made led to the attack, and now you don't trust yourself,* she now knew were wrong. She trusted herself, alone, and that's what would pull her through. Before visiting her office, she wasn't sure she'd ever practice law again. Sitting at her desk, she had no doubt she'd return to practice.

"My life's a mirage," she said, addressing the portrait of Abraham Lincoln, staring down from the wall. Behind all the seeming certainties of life, there were few truths. Lincoln seemed to wink at her, and she had to laugh. She was startled out of a reverie by the phone ringing, and she answered it.

"Good morning," said Lon Dedaman.

"How did you know I was here?" she asked, irritated.

"I didn't. I called to see if Carrie's there and if there's anything I should be doing, you know...to help. You should be home recuperating."

"I'll take my office keys back."

"Anita, I've had this set of keys since you opened your office. Don't you trust me? Or is it yourself you hate, and you're trying to pin your misery on me?"

"Things are different. I'm different. Stop taking care of me. You're interfering with my ability to take care of myself."

"Alright, I'll return your keys."
"Thanks."
"You never used to say thanks. Every time you say it...oh well, never mind."

"No, I appreciate it. I hadn't realized. If you didn't tell me, I might've gone the rest of my life saying thank you every time someone speaks to me."

"I'm surprised to find you at your office. You sound like it was plenty easy, everyday routine."

Anita was suddenly exuberant that she sounded normal to someone who knew her as well as Lon, but she didn't say anything, recalling the difficulties of finding the building and the setbacks she'd encountered.

"Can you get back all right?" he asked.
"I got here, didn't I?" she retorted, belligerently.
"I wish you'd get over being so touchy."
"Bye. See you later."
"Goodbye."

She hung up, opened all her drawers and looked in, the familiarity of them bringing intense pleasure. Walking all through the suite again, she paused in the library, and looked over her collection of law books. In the lobby, she imagined it full of clients and a few of their faces came back to her. An hour slipped away in what seemed like ten minutes in her recollections and getting back in touch with her office. She stopped at Carrie's desk, and was studying the cluttered top when Aubrey walked in slick and smiling with two cups of steaming coffee.

"Still black?"
"Still black. Thathaththt...."
"You've made a remarkable recovery, Anita," he broke in. "I knew you wouldn't die."

"I get so frustrated, Aubrey, but my concentration's coming back slowly, much more slowly than I'd like." She took the coffee. "Let's go to my office." He followed her to her office, and they sat down.

"You need to come back to work. Law needs you. Greenbrier couldn't live without you."

"Now I'm sure I'll be back. At the apartment, I doubt. There's a confusion of thought that needs repair."

"They wouldn't let me in to see you for two weeks after the attack. You were critical. You didn't recognize me. What an irony that you should be subject to such brutality - you, who defended every string of bones who came your way."

"Do you have any idea where responsibility lies? I know I have enemies." She lowered her voice. "No one else would touch the cases I took."

Aubrey turned on the intercom music loudly to cover their conversation. "Does music bother you?" he asked.

"No, not in this case, not for the short time we've got. In fact, it's more like an old friend." She smiled at him.

"Of course, the attack is constantly on my mind, but there's no person or group I can pinpoint who would try to kill you like that. There are certainly similarities involving terrorism directed at other high-powered women."

"I don't know if I still believe in law and justice. Do you?"

"We're fighting hell itself for it," he answered. They chatted for fifteen minutes, and Anita enjoyed the conversation tremendously. He told her about the case he was going to trial for in such a way that she could follow it easily. He noticed that the clock in her office showed the wrong time. "I've got to get to court. I'll see you later." He got up to go.

"Good luck, Aubrey. Could you set the clock? I can't climb up on a chair to reach it yet."

"No problem," he said. He set the clock by his watch before dashing for court.

Anita struggled not to succumb to an almost irrepressible desire to sleep. Urges she'd never been subject to before plagued her. She got a stick of gum out of her bag and chewed it. Rubbing her aching back, she heard someone come in and felt a moment of panic. She opened her top drawer, grabbed the letter opener as though it were a knife, and stood up. Carrie came in, and feeling foolish, Anita put the letter opener back, laughing. "I'm glad it's you," she said. "You left before I had a chance to talk to you yesterday."

"I'm glad to see you here, Anita." Carrie smiled warmly.

"Thanks for keeping the practice alive, Carrie. Sitting at my desk, I realize a huge difference in myself before and now."

"I hope you're coming back to work."

"Yes. I need to." She looked down at the tablet on her desk with *urgent* underscored. "Who was this urgent?" She recalled writing the word and underlining it.

"Mario Dominguez."

"What did he want?"

"He was desperate. He said his wife, who worked for Senator Bold, ran away to avoid being raped on the estate. They're illegal aliens."

"Aubrey just left. We were...."

"What was Aubrey Milton doing here? Trying to finagle a date or just a favor?" asked Lon, striding into her office. His foot was so silent on the carpet in the lobby that neither of the women had heard him enter.

"You didn't have to come, Lon. You're crowding me," said Anita, her eyes narrowing.

"When I heard you on the phone, you sounded just like the lawyer you used to be. I had to come and see you in your old digs. You can't imagine my anxiety, Anita."

Unable to think of a response, Anita ignored Lon. "So this urgent wants us to locate his wife?" Anita asked Carrie.

"Yes."

"Could it have any connection to the assault? Could you tell if he was for real?"

"There was no question about it. He's a man at the end of his rope."

"Did we get anything on his wife?"

"No."

Anita sat back, thinking. "I have to consider that the assault could have been an ordinary crime that had nothing to do with any case, but it seems unlikely," she said. "Much crime comes from fear. It can be a reaction of an animal to fright. Whoever attacked me may have been afraid of something I was doing."

"Why?" asked Carrie.

"I keep coming back to the cases I take that no one else will touch."

"You're wrong, Anita," said Lon. "Crime comes from greed and lust for power."

"Their roots are in fear," insisted Anita. "Maybe the fear of exposure in the case of high level crime. I've filed countless complaints and restraining orders against Greenbrier University and the Greenbrier establishment on behalf of clients, and all of them, with one exception, have died, moved, changed identity, or withdrawn before their cases got to court. And look what happened to me."

"When I think of crime, I think of hoodlums, muggers, thugs, like your assailants, Anita, not high level criminals that participate in massive corporate scams and rip offs, or politically motivated crimes. They have a different character."

"You're prejudices are showing," said Anita. "Education and money don't give a person a corner on ethical behavior or conscience. Open your eyes and have a look at all the corporate and government scandals parading before them."

"But why; what could be the motive?" Bewilderment and concern crossed Dedaman's face.

"It's got to be the result of one of Anita's cases," said Carrie. "I don't buy the idea that it was coincidence. Somebody is afraid of something Anita is doing because if the case in question gets to court, it will expose their crimes."

Dedaman stood up, his fists at his sides, his face too red, his voice too loud. "You're always looking in the wrong place," he said. "There are two kinds of crimes. One is carried out by vicious animals. That's the kind that attacked Anita. The other is on an intellectual battleground. That's the kind that rips off millions or even billions, but it's money at stake. They don't mix."

"I say they do," said Carrie, staring at Lon, her jaw fixed, her eyes blazing.

"She's just expressing an opinion contrary to yours. Why do you get so mad when she disagrees with you?" asked Anita.

"It's in his genes," said Carrie, dryly, "from the days of Neanderthal. When someone disagrees with you, grab the club. A network out of this city is still trying to wield that club."

"Men, who are afraid of women, are worried about losing self-control and physically attacking, and an adult out of control is in deep water," said Anita, glancing at her boyfriend.

"Well, that's pretty funny today," said Lon, laughing.

"I wouldn't be laughing if I were you," said Carrie. "But they're afraid of more than losing self-control. They're afraid of losing power."

"Wait a minute, Carrie," said Dedaman. "We're getting off the track. Our law is based on justice, and it usually works. My bet is that it will work in Anita's case."

"Where's the justice in it in Anita's case?" demanded Carrie.

"The law we have works, and we're going to prove it, Carrie," insisted Anita. "We're all equal under the law, and equal justice is going to prevail. We've got the best law in human history. I still believe in it, and I'm going to prove it. What has my practice been about?"

"I wish I had your confidence in the law. I don't know where you get it after your practice of the last twenty years, not to mention your recent experience," said Carrie.

"The law works when the top echelon live by it," said Anita. "When the top of the heap turns to crime, the rest of the population follows. To discover the cause of the worse problems in any society, look at the character of those in leadership positions. You certainly wouldn't count the faculty at Greenbrier University or our high powered institutions in the poor, suffering classes, but that's where most of the people who come to me seek relief from.

"There's a type of man who'll lash out at another with his fists at a breaking point. Another type won't strike at anyone his size for fear of getting beat. This is the person who'll take out all his fears on someone who can't possibly defend against him or join a gang to give himself a preposterously unequal advantage." Anita shifted in her chair, trying to ease her back.

"Professionals with personal problems use the same technique with more subtlety in the rip off, the overcharge, the scam, the hurt under the mask of the profession. These are worse than the guy who starts a fight with an equal partner because they hide under the jargon and veneer of their professions to conceal their crimes. Often they speak in language anyone outside their narrow circle can't even understand."

"Well, a man has to have a way to get even, when a woman in the business world and the arena outside the home defeats him," said Dedaman, sitting, crossing his legs and folding his hands over his knee.

"There's the law," insisted Anita. "That's the only way we recognize. It's all laid out straight as can be if you're a man or a woman defeated by a woman or a man, inside the home or out."

"The law has broken down," said Carrie. "That's why people form secret groups that demand conformity and exclude everyone else. They're seeking protection within a self-imposed law. That's the key, the law has broken down."

"Did you bring my other set of keys, by the way?" Anita asked Lon.

"I forgot them."

"Don't forget again. You're worse off than me. At least, I remember to ask." Frowning, Dedaman started to reply and thought better of it.

The ache in Anita's back was getting worse, and she moved around in her chair trying to ease it but couldn't. "I have to go home," she said. "I appreciate you both coming, but I've got to take it slow at first." Enjoying the first return to her office, and the best conversations she'd had since the attack, she wished she'd brought her pain pills and cane so she could continue.

"I'll drive you home in your car if you like," offered Lon.

"No, I'll drive myself." Anita stood up.

"Bye, Anita," said Carrie. "Come on Lon, let's go."

"Bye Carrie. Bye Lon. Don't forget my keys next time." Anita walked her friends to the door. To give them time to get on the elevator, Anita used the restroom before leaving the suite. She was determined to make the trip home without help. After locking her office, she anxiously went to the elevator and waited for it. But when she got on, the uncertainties of the trip up were absent.

"It's going to take only time," she said to herself.

In the lobby, Ron looked up to see who was getting off the elevator, and when he saw Anita, his affable expression clouded to doubt. "Good afternoon," he said, solemnly.

Anita smiled back, with a glimmer of her old good nature. "Good afternoon, Ron. It's good to be back."

Ron's smile broke through in his eyes and transformed his whole face. He nodded. "It's going to be okay, after all," he said.

Anita went to the garage and got in her car. Retracing her way home, she lost her way after six blocks and had to painfully pull over and look at the map, but she made it the rest of the way without having to stop.

Arriving at her building, she parked, locked the car, and limped inside, her back on fire. On the elevator, she was overwhelmed with weariness. Going into her apartment, she then took two pain pills which made her drowsy. A steaming bath helped relieve the tension in her back. Getting out of the tub and wrapping in her robe, she then went into the kitchen and made a sandwich with a slice of ham and cheddar cheese on a crescent roll. She nuked it to melt the cheese and took it to her bedroom. Leaving the sandwich on the night stand, she then got the heating pad, plugged it in and leaned against it, eating the sandwich. She let her mind drift back to the night of the attack. *Did they have masks?* She couldn't remember. Snatches of the conversation with Carrie and Lon came back to her.

*Was it a conspiracy? Was the attempted murder a camouflage for something so evil that no normal person could even think it? Did Greenbrier keep coming up because they'd been discussing it earlier, or was the highest echelon of education still involved in criminal attacks on ordinary individuals? If so, why?*

As she started to doze off, the phone ring indicated someone at the door, and Anita went to the front window. The pain was gone from her back, but she was still drowsy. Carrie stood on the porch, and Anita was happy for the chance to talk to her without Dedaman. She buzzed to let her in, unlocked the door, turned the stereo on loud and sat on the couch with a pillow supporting her back, putting her feet up on the coffee table. When she heard the tap on the door, she called, "Carrie?"

"Yeah, it's me."

"C'mon in."

Carrie entered, locking the door behind her. "I wish you wouldn't leave the door unlocked," said Carrie, frowning. "I'll never quit worrying about that."

"I saw you on the porch. I just now unlocked it."

"Well, that's a relief. If you don't want company, don't hesitate to tell me. I'm having a hard time talking to you without Dedaman, and I thought I'd try one more time today."

"I was thinking exactly the same thing. I'm glad you came," replied Anita. Carrie sat beside her so they could talk quietly with the music for cover. Though neither of them thought Anita's new home was bugged, it was a habit they'd developed and used without thinking.

"On a business note, your client urgent, Mario Dominguez, is a man on the edge," said Carrie hoping to help keep Anita's interest in cases alive and thriving.

"The appointment I missed; an illegal alien with a missing wife. They work on Senator Bold's estate."

"None other," said Carrie.

"Let me have everything we've got on it."

"We have only two brief visits. Mario Dominguez is looking for his wife who disappeared from Senator Bold's estate where they both worked. Mario still works there. Our staff hasn't been able to locate his wife, Marcella. She may be using an alias which he thinks might be Sedar or Sedar Salvadore."

CHAPTER TWENTY THREE

Kate arrived at work early on Monday morning, called Maggie Hurly, the former governor's wife, and made an appointment for an interview later in the day. She then went to the morgue and scanned the newspapers published the previous year, reading those with Sue's byline pertaining to Greg Hurly. Ferrell changing her story in the computer showed her the necessity of studying the hard copy instead of electronic copies.

"What are you doing?" came Ferrell's voice from behind her.

She whirled around.

Ferrell's arms were crossed over his chest, his head tilted back with his chin pointed at her, gazing through half-closed lids. He looked like he was drunk.

"You scared the life out of me!" she snapped. "What do you mean, sneaking up on me? It's perfectly obvious what I'm doing." Slamming the volume, she returned it to the shelf, and closed her notebook.

"Leave it alone," he said, his voice alarmingly soft. "You have no idea what you're doing."

"Then why don't you tell me?" Her anger was acute, and despite Ferrell's weird actions, she couldn't fear him. He was ludicrous.

Ferrell chuckled, a dull, automatic humorless sound. "You're making trouble that can get you nowhere you'd want to go. I'm trying to help you."

"Like you helped Sue?" she demanded. Her self-control returned with an acid edge.

"I tried to help Sue. I'm the boss around here. I'll tell you what you can work on."

"This is a newspaper, not a politburo. We all find stories on our own, and they're the most interesting. Don't threaten me. I'm not afraid of you."

He gave her a long, penetrating look that made her extremely uncomfortable, but she avoided stooping to a staring contest.

"He only acts weird when we're alone," she said to herself, knowing Sue had gotten the same treatment. Kate brushed past Ferrell and stalked out in a cloak of dignity. Composing herself, she then left the office, got into her car, and met a contact for lunch. After eating, she drove to Maggie Hurly's house.

There was a place to park in the driveway, so she drove up and parked. Going to the front door and ringing the doorbell, she was then met by a servant.

"Your name please?" asked the woman.

"Kate Dolore," said Kate.

"Come this way, please." Kate followed the woman through the house and to the patio garden in back. Maggie was standing beside a patio table, and the servant left them alone.

"Hello Kate. This is my last conversation with the press," said Maggie, frowning severely, her eyes drooping at the corners. Maggie was middle-aged and dressed casually in slacks, a stylish blouse, and small gold earrings, bracelets, and four various lengths and widths of gold chains around her neck. Her brown hair was short and wavy, and she wore low-heeled shoes and no makeup.

An interior designer with an excellent reputation, she'd rarely appeared with Greg, spending most of her time on business. Maggie never intentionally campaigned, but many of her clients, hers and Greg's friends, and the general public had subtly been drawn to Greg's cause by their respect for Maggie, who had all the charm of a flesh and blood individual with none of the glitz required of politicians.

"I'm awfully sorry about Greg, Maggie," said Kate.

"I don't want to see any more about Gregory in the papers, Kate. There's been enough publicity already. I only agreed to this interview to tell you in person. I have nothing more to say to the press. Gregory never was an alcoholic. I wanted him to quash that image, but he said it was harmless. Your paper made a fool of itself not of my husband."

"Maggie, you know I never promoted the idea of Greg as an alcoholic. I never saw him drunk, and neither did Sue. That's what I want to talk to you about. The coroner said he was full of alcohol. Can we have a personal conversation, as friends, off the record?"

Maggie laughed without mirth, and Kate detected a note of scorn in it.

"There's nothing sacred to you people."

"I'm asking you to consider only what you know of me as an individual."

Maggie sighed, deeply. "I've always thought you were fair, Kate. I can't answer for the coroner's report. Sit down, please." Maggie sat on the patio, and Kate sat beside her.

"My best friend's dead, and I've a hunch that she knew something more about Governor Hurly's death; and that's why she's dead," said Kate.

"The reporter who died in the plane crash?"

"Yes. Sue Front. My suspicions are too complex and unorganized to explain. I'm only prowling around the edges of something. Who might've gained by Greg's death?"

"I don't know. He never confided his political business to me. We tried to keep the unpleasant details of his work from hampering our personal lives. And we were successful at it for forty-two years. Greg was going to retire after this term."

"I didn't know that."

"Of course, we didn't want the press to get wind of it. Nobody knew but us."

"What were Greg's plans for retirement? He was too involved to relax at the lake with a fishing pole for the rest of his life."

"He hadn't decided. There was a reason he wanted out of the business, not a superceding interest."

"You're probably the only one who knows why he wanted out."

"I didn't know. I only knew it was the first thing he came across he couldn't handle. There're things you're better off not knowing, dangerous things. You could let it be. Why don't you stick to tea parties, basketball games, and charity bazaars?"

"Sue was my best friend."

"Nothing you can do will bring her back."

"I want to know why she had to die, because the circumstances are so strange that my entire foundation is shaken."

"If you come upon some knowledge that caused the death of the governor and your best friend, what makes you think you'd escape a similar fate?"

"That's what I'm trying to avoid."

"I'm twice your age, Kate. Some things you must accept. I lost my husband. My foundations are shaken to the roots, too. I know there's foul play involved. There's nothing I can do about it."

"I have to find out what happened. That's my job."

"I'm on the other end of what you do," said Maggie. "You people create the world's mindset. Obviously, the same people own the various media, and you back each other's causes. You create a violent society by focusing the attention of everybody who reads on sex, violence, and the scam as a way of making a living. It's that mindset that killed my husband." Maggie looked straight at Kate, her chin held high. Her face was a mask of solemn purpose. She clasped her hands in front of her, her movements slow and precise as though thought out in advance.

"That's what people read," said Kate, admiring Maggie's quiet dignity.

"The media has changed so radically, I can't follow it," said Maggie. "News people have lost personal accountability. The world is starving for the good in human nature, for good to just be okay and not ridiculous."

"Truth is what sells papers...."

Laughter rolled out of Maggie's mouth and eyes. Kate stared at her, unsmiling, until she recovered her sobriety.

"The press has the function of letting the people in on what the government's doing. Sue died in the cause of freedom as much as anyone in any battle," said Kate.

"I'm sorry about your friend, Kate." Maggie stood, crossed her arms and walked across the patio and back. "Though not as sorry as I am about my husband. Every now and then the newspapers get caught in some fiction. We laughed about how the press attacked Greg, and all our friends laughed with us." Maggie spoke through a deep frown and deadly serious eyes. "But now he's dead, assassinated with a cover-up that'll never see light, and what were you saying about truth or something?"

"I believe you, Maggie. I'm on your side." She could feel Maggie's grief, and sympathized.

"Well, I'm alive, still, and I have to go on from here."

"Where're you going?"

"First, I'm going to a retreat where I can be incommunicado. After that, I'm going to bury myself in work."

"One more thing," said Kate. "Do you know what Ferrell had to do with Gregory, besides ordinary press relations?"

Maggie gave her a long look, deciding whether to answer the question. She started walking slowly, deliberately back and forth and stopped in front of Kate. Kate stood up.

"Ferrell and Gregory played golf together for twenty-five years. They had some kind of difference of opinion, I suppose. Gregory changed the number to his private line to cut Ferrell off, and their personal relations were nonexistent after that."

"When was that?"
"A long time ago."
"Six months?"
"No, I'm sure it's been longer than that. He wasn't on our list last Christmas, but of course, that wasn't so long ago."

"How about the Christmas before that?"

"Yes, I'm sure he was at some of the holiday parties. Yes, I remember Carole in her yellow gown at a benefit for the Children's Hospital."

"Did you know Sue?"

"I'd met her, of course, when she was lively and enthusiastic before she dulled out."

"About the time Governor Hurly changed his private line?"

Maggie thought a minute. "That could've been the beginning."

What might Sue have discovered to change like that?"

"I can't imagine. It could be the same thing that killed my husband."

"Thanks, Maggie. Bye. If you think of anything the Governor might've said, any indication...."

"Be careful, Kate," Maggie interrupted her. "I have to say goodbye now." She walked Kate to the front door.

"Thanks for talking to me," said Kate. She returned to the newsroom to work on another story, still thinking about Maggie's bitterness toward the press.

When she went home that evening, Maggie still on her mind, she found Burt, sitting in the recliner, one leg propped up on the hassock in a cast.

"What happened to you?" she asked in amazement.

"I broke my leg. The stair rail at work gave way, and I fell and landed on the iron rail."

"My God!" exclaimed Kate.

"I was in the rental car in New York when I made a joke about breaking my leg. The car could've been bugged. When the rail gave way, the thought flashed through my mind that it was sabotaged."

"How bad is it?"

"Plenty bad. It's a clean break. I'm grounded for at least six weeks, and I'm more determined than ever to go back to New York. My doubts were wiped out with the fall. I walk up and down those stairs every day, and the rail's never been loose. I can't grieve much over a broken leg, when I'm damned lucky to be alive."

"It could've happened to someone else at work."

"No, it couldn't. The rail collapsed at the time I always check the area before going on break. I'm the only one in that place at that time."

"Then maybe it's not me they're after," said Kate, in confusion. "You're the one with the enemy!"

"Me and Sue?" he asked, reminding her that Sue had been murdered. "No, it's definitely to get at you. It's just more subtle and stupid than your imagination is accustomed to dealing with. That's how terrorists operate. They attack indirectly, and try to obfuscate the whys and wherefores."

Kate flopped down in a chair, the wind going out of her. "Burt, I hate to be as patronizing as the ridiculous squab I have to deal with at work, but suppose we have to run like hell?"

"I'll stump along as best I can. If I'd had a cast on my leg Saturday, it wouldn't have slowed me down a whole lot. If the car we rented was bugged, so is our house and phone, and the phones we use at work. I've been sitting here all afternoon with nothing to do but think."

"We're in way beyond my capacity to deal with it," said Kate. She leaned over and kissed Burt, a worried frown tugging at the corners of her mouth. "You could've been killed."

"Why don't they just shoot us and get it over with?"

"They want something more than that or they're afraid of being found out, afraid of our deaths and Sue's unraveling to the cause."

"What can we do?"

Kate, Burt, and Sherman encountered a bleak, gray rainy day at the airport in Greenbrier Sunday morning. Kate rented a van to make Burt as comfortable as possible on the long drive. He sat in the back seat with his bum leg propped in inflatable pillows, like a fish on ice. They came better prepared this time with sleeping bags, pillows, and a change of clothes, planning to stay overnight, and Sherman and Kate loaded the gear into the van. Kate stopped for supplies in Apple Valley .

"I'll pick up extra flashlight batteries at the hardware store," said Sherman. "Anything you need, Burt?" he asked.

"No, I'm good."

"Kate? Need anything from the hardware store?"

"No, I'll take care of food after I drop you off, so you won't get too wet." Kate stopped for Sherman to get out and parked near the grocery store. She ran in, and Burt waited in the van with a best-selling thriller, a new form of relaxation since his incapacitation.

Sherman came strolling back with the batteries, under a large umbrella, pushing his glasses up, and got in the front seat.

"All set?" asked Burt, looking up from his book.

"Yeah, here comes Kate now. I better help with the groceries." He got out and sheltered Kate with the umbrella while she opened the back and put the groceries in. Sherman took a diet cola off the cold six-pack for himself and a regular cola for Burt. Kate had root beer.

"I'll drive if you want," offered Sherman.
"No, not unless you have some burning desire to. I like to drive and hate to ride."
"Okay, go ahead."
The drive seemed twice as long in the rain. No one had anything to say, and the silence irritated Kate. All her attempts to spark a conversation met gloomy one-phrase answers from Sherman, adrift in his own thought, and Burt was lost in his book. Giving up, she tired of listening to the rain pound the windshield, her eyes straining to peer through the deluge, her thought a dog chasing its tail, and flicked on the radio.

As they began the climb up the last steep ridge, Sherman started snoring. Looking up from his book, Burt smiled at Kate in the rear-view mirror and gave a thumbs up.

The rain was letting up when she found the trail leading to the house, and the ruts were now filled with water. Weary from the drive, she parked in the parking lot, climbed out, and stretched. Sherman woke up and got out with the umbrella.

"Need some help?" Kate asked Burt, who was struggling with his crutches.

"No, I've got it."

Sherman opened the umbrella over Kate and held it for her to get the food out of the trunk, while Burt extracted himself from the back seat.

"We'll soon see if anyone's been here," said Kate. She ran ahead, and to her relief, the front door was still unlocked. Going first to the kitchen, she was disappointed to find the note and card she'd left untouched. The men were close behind her.

"Looks like not a soul has darkened the door here," said Sherman, putting the perishable food and drinks in the refrigerator.

"Yeah, that's right," said Kate. "Unfortunately the place remains abandoned except for us."

They removed their wraps and left them on the coat tree in the foyer.

"I didn't have time to make any observations last visit," said Burt. "I'm going to have a better look this time. Stumping through the hallway on his crutches, he studied the floors, went back to the cedar room, and returned to the front of the house.

Kate vaguely searched for clues to the identity of the owners or meditators throughout the house starting upstairs and working her way down to the main floor, but the drawers and nooks yielded only generic material. Their trespasser status haunted her, yet the intrigue fortified her. She found Burt looking over the bookshelf in the living room.

"Did you find anything?" she asked him.

"No, I was looking for footprints in the dust, but there's not enough to make tracks. Mainly, I wanted to ascertain that nobody beside us has been here."

"What were you expecting?"

"Anything out of the ordinary."

Sherman went out to get dry wood from under the cedar room, stacked it neatly by the fireplace and went back for more. He built a blazing fire in the living room that took the chill out, and opened the windows a few inches at the top to let the stale air out. The roof overhang prevented the rain from coming inside.

Unpacking groceries and supplies in the kitchen, Kate then made sandwiches while Burt stretched out on the couch in front of the fireplace with his mystery.

"Your fire's casting a spell, Sherm," said Burt. "I'm comfortable and secure."

"Yeah, it has a strangely peaceful effect on me, too." Sherman's naturally slow relaxed speech had the effect of making Burt drowsy.

Kate brought in the sandwiches and soft drinks. The smell of the food conspired with the ping of the rain and warmth of the fire to enhance her cheer, as she took a chair near enough to the fire to feel the heat without toasting.

"This house has many moods," said Sherman, reaching for a ham sandwich. "I can't reconcile the way we ran out last time with the comfort of this moment."

"Yeah, I feel slightly high, euphoric even," agreed Burt, looking longingly at the drinks just out of reach. Getting one would be a major production. "But it makes me plenty uncomfortable."

"I'm pretty mellow myself," said Kate. She got up and handed Burt a drink.

"Thanks, Kate."

"Ham, chicken salad, or roast beef?" she asked.

"I'll take the roast beef."

Kate took Burt a sandwich and fixed herself a plate before returning to her chair of inertia, thinking the food might rid her of the lazy unfamiliar serenity.

"How can I be this spaced out stone sober? I feel like a chicken waiting my turn at the house of slaughter," she said.

"It's a different mindset," said Burt. "It's damned awful to be in such a state I didn't induce."

"Maybe we shouldn't fight it," said Kate.

"I don't want to end up like Sue," said Burt. "Sherman, what kind of meditating were they doing?"

"There are kinds?" asked Sherman.

"Yeah, did they make any noises; hums or chants or songs?" asked Burt.

"No. They sat like statues."

Sherman, whose sleep cycle had radically changed since Sue's death, when he started working overtime until he couldn't stay awake, nodded off with a smile on his face after eating. Burt read his novel, and Kate reviewed her notes.

At four o'clock, Sherman woke. Stretching, he said, "I'm going to set up the fire in the back room." Going outdoors for the wood, he then brought in an armful of tinder and kindling and went back for larger logs. He started the fire and soon had a good blaze going, after which he carried in two chairs for Burt, one to prop his bad leg on.

"The meditation room is ready," he announced, pushing his glasses up and retreating to the back room for the evening.

Kate took her notes, and went to the cedar room, also.

Burt pulled himself up on his crutches and stuffed his novel into his back pocket. His leg, uncomfortably stiff, had begun to itch. Stopping in the kitchen, he got a butter knife to poke down between the cast and his skin, but he couldn't quite reach the itch. He put on his jacket and went outdoors, stumped around the porch taking in the cold early evening mountain air not yet ready to spend more time sitting. Ordinarily active, he was accustomed to spending one full hour every day at tennis or swimming or jogging, and he was on a baseball team. Resigning himself to sitting for the rest of the evening, he retreated to the house, removed his jacket and joined Sherman and Kate in the back room. He sat in one chair, propped his bad leg on the other, closed his eyes, and tried to focus on Sue's lively vivacious days, but the ghost of her real self before she died kept usurping precedence.

The fire was now casting weird shadows over the ceiling and walls, and Kate and Sherman had the glazed over look they all acquired in the meditation room.

Sherman sat on the floor facing the fire with his legs crossed, and closed his eyes. It was easy for him to remember the Sue he'd married because even at her worst, he constantly invoked the earlier memories trying to regain their reality.

Kate leaned against the wall resting her arms on her bent knees, her notes abandoned beside her on the floor. She watched the fire until her eyes drifted closed. The unholy quiet seemed to dip into eternity, and she snuck a peek at her watch. Ten minutes had gone by. She closed her eyes again, and opened one a crack to see if Burt and Sherman still had their eyes closed. They did.

"Think about Sue," she heard. Her eyes popped open, but the men still had their eyes closed.

"Who said that?" she asked. Burt and Sherman opened their eyes and stared at her, waiting for an explanation that didn't come.

"Said what?" asked Burt, finally.

"Think about Sue."

"Nobody," said Sherman.

"I heard somebody say that."

"You must have just thought it. Nobody said anything," said Sherman.

"They didn't hear it," said Kate to herself.

The sun went down, and the room cooled as the fire dwindled; Kate shivered. Unwilling to be the chicken to break the silence the second time, she kept her eyes closed, but her thought drifted to everything but Sue, and she kept dragging it back.

"I'm turning to ice," complained Burt. His broken leg throbbed. He opened his eyes. The fire had faded to embers, and the temperature had dropped drastically.

Relieved at the absence of the wailing that had sent them dashing from the place in a panic on their last visit, Kate stood up, stretching and yawning. It was seven thirty.

"I'm going to barbecue the chicken," said Burt, hungry.

"Nonsense," said Kate. "By the time you peg leg it into the living room and stretch out, I'll have the chicken on the hibachi. Who do you think you are? Superman?"

Laughing lamely, Burt went to the living room and settled comfortably on the couch with his mystery, taking advantage of the rare opportunity to be lazy while everyone else worked. Relaxation had settled into his bones in the meditation room, and drained him of energy.

Kate took the hibachi out to the front porch and started the charcoal briquettes. She went back to the kitchen and got out the chicken. Carving it into four sections, she then seasoned the pieces, put them on a plate and carried them out to the hibachi. Leaving them on the grill, she returned to the kitchen to cut up vegetables for the salad.

Sherman brought in more firewood, refurbished the fires in the cedar room and the living room and got the sleeping bags from the car. He laid them out around the fire pit, and then went to the kitchen. "What do you want me to do?" he asked Kate.

"You could go out and turn the chicken, and give it a squirt or two of barbecue sauce," Kate replied, tossing the salad.

Sherman took a long handled fork and went out and turned the sizzling bird, squirted a little barbecue sauce on each piece, and returned to the kitchen.

"What did you think about Sue in the cedar room?" asked Kate.

"Funny thing." Sherman pushed up his glasses. "I started out thinking about the early days, but I drifted into a dream. I'm sure I was thinking about Sue, but I can't remember what I was thinking. Did anything occur to you that could be of use?"

"All my thoughts are so vague here, Sherman, to tell you the truth, I feel like I'm on another planet lost in space. This place is too weird to be real. That cedar room, for instance. I just can't picture the Sue I worked with vegging out here, although in the last days, I suppose, anything could've been possible. But that was not the Sue I know."

"I know what you mean. It wasn't the Sue I knew either. Still, I have a feeling that we're on the right track."

"How so?"

"Something's bound to turn up here. I can feel it, yet I can't explain it, anticipation is the closest I can come. They hashed over their thoughts and feelings at length.

"That chicken must be done. I'll go get it," said Sherman. He took a plate out to the porch and piled the grilled chicken on it. "Time to eat, Burt," he said, on his way into the dining room. Burt put his book aside, taking a whiff of the roast bird.

Sherman put the chicken on the table, which Kate had set with plastic plates, forks and napkins. Burt hobbled in, leaned his crutches against the chair next to him and sat in one chair propping his bum leg on the rung of the other as Kate brought in the salad and dressing and a basket of rolls. She went back to the kitchen and returned with three beers and a tub of potato salad from the grocery. They all filled their plates and talked as they ate.

"I can't meditate on Sue anymore," Burt said. "Every time I try, I think about the plane explosion and the last time I saw her. It's too hard to conjure up the earlier memories, and why should we? I'm going to take my book and a beer and laze in front of the fire in the cedar room while you guys do whatever meditations you think necessary. That's how I think of something important, by letting it cook in the underground unseen."

"I think about her night and day," said Sherman, pushing up his sagging glasses. "I think about her at work, and a little while ago, when I was bringing in the wood, I was thinking about Sue.

When I met her, she was lively and vivacious, but I lost her a long time ago. I thought for so long that I'd keep working on it until I got her back that it seems like I'm still working on getting her back. Something happened to her in this house. Why did she keep coming here? Why do we? The same thing that happened to her is happening to us. I'm not coming back. I'll leave my phone number, and if someone knows she's dead, knows her husband wants to find out why she died, and still doesn't call, coming back here won't do any good."

"We have too few leads, and our lives may be just as short-lived as Sue's if we don't hound down every trace of smoke," objected Kate. The men kept silent.

Sherman finished eating, washed his plate, and went to feed the fire in the cedar room. Burt stuffed his paperback into his back pocket, cleaned up after himself, grabbed a beer, and stumped after Sherman. He arranged the pillows on the floor under his sleeping bag to support his bad leg. He had no intention of getting up again before morning.

Cleaning up in the kitchen, Kate tried to put the pieces together to make a clear picture, but they were scattered and wouldn't congeal. She felt so peacefully serene and unfocused that she thought she should be frightened, but she couldn't work up a normal reaction. When she finished in the kitchen, she joined the men in the cedar room.

Sherman lay on his back, watching the shadows dance across the ceiling, his hands behind his head. Kate rarely saw him without his glasses and relaxed. Always pensive, he now looked fiercely intense.

Lost in his mystery, his beer gone, Burt was on the edge of sleep.

Kate added three hefty logs to the fire from Sherman's stack before crawling into her sleeping bag. "Thinking about Sue, something that happened with Ferrell crops up," she said. "Hurly hadn't died yet. Sue and Ferrell were arguing about a state statute concerning the power of the governor to order investigations outside the state in matters that concerned the state. Ferrell said he couldn't, and Sue said he could. Sue was angry and upset. Ferrell showed her a copy of his state statute. Sue stalked out of the newsroom, saying she was going to get a copy of the real statute. Sue didn't come back that day, and the next morning she let Ferrell's remarks slide off, and he was full of them."

"I know the time you're talking about," said Sherman, perking up, leaning on his elbow. "She came home early in a rage. She'd been at the State Law Library, and as usual she wouldn't talk about it."

Tuning in at the prospect of a lead, Burt put his book aside. "Suppose someone has a kind of technology we have no knowledge of?" he asked.

Kate and Sherman looked at him, waiting for him to continue.

"We don't have access to information about everything that's going on," he said. "We've got such advanced technology, who knows what's out there that's secret except to its discoverers?"

"I don't understand the secrecy angle," said Sherman. "We actually live in a very open society. Kate and Sue are the kind of people that nose out everything. Try to hide something, anything, and I guarantee Kate will ferret it out. Sue was like that too."

"That's why she's dead," said Burt.

"That's what we've always believed," said Kate. "But the international rise of terrorism has an effect on the way everyone does business. There's some underlying circumstance so close to the surface, you can almost feel it about to pop out. Sue lived in an open society, but it wasn't open for her. She was persecuted. Whatever happened to the Cloudhawk wasn't something that happens in a free country to a citizen, is it? Yet, if you buttonholed any passing person on the street, and told her your little group was singled out by a power greater than the police for murder and persecution, you'd be taken for an idiot or at the very least a mental case."

Nobody added anything to fuel the conversation, and the silence that had been threatening since morning descended like snow on a mountaintop at midnight. The fire and her surrealistic state creating a secure and agreeable feeling; Kate fell into a deep, dreamless sleep. Burt was soon snoring softly, and Sherman dozed off.

An hour before dawn, Sherman got up. The fire was almost out, and he put a stack of sticks and two logs on the embers. Going out to the van, he got in the driver's seat and started it up. It was no longer raining. Backing out to the road, he began driving slowly down the mountain.

## CHAPTER TWENTY FOUR

Kate woke in the morning looking at Burt looking at her. It was still dark outside, and the dying embers cast a weird reddish amber glow. Her watch had stopped.

"What time is it?" she asked.

"My watch stopped."

"So did mine. Where did Sherman go?"

"He must be in the kitchen cooking up some breakfast or squirreling around outside." Stretching his good leg, Burt pulled himself painfully off the floor, leaning on his crutches.

"No, he took the van." Kate got up, stretching.

"What?" Burt's alarm broke through his cool facade. "When?"

"I don't know. He got up and got in the van and drove away," she said, turning on the light.

"Why didn't you ask him where he was going?"

"I was asleep," said Kate, vaguely.

"Really, Kate! Make sense."

"I was dreaming, and in my sleep, I heard him get up and heard the van start and back up."

"How do you know that if you were asleep?"

"I don't know."

"You're talking absurdities, Kate!" said Burt.

"He got in the van and drove off, but I wasn't awake enough to ask him where he was going. Maybe he was sleep-driving." She laughed.

"We're stranded here! How could Sherman take off like that as though he didn't have to tear out of here himself in mortal terror last time?"

"How would I know? We've got food. He's bound to come back for us. Where could he go in the middle of nowhere? Did you notice how he falls asleep at odd times since Sue died? He's sleeping somewhere or lost." Kate started rolling up sleeping bags, and throwing their gear on a pile near the door to be carried out to the van. She felt the need to move vigorously.

"It's impossible to walk out of here, and we've never seen another car on the road to this place." Burt stumped around the room on his crutches, boiling.

"Nothing's impossible. Somebody may want us to think that, but there has to be a way out. I could hike back to get help if it came to that, but it won't. You know as well as I do that Sherman didn't abandon us here."

"How do you know that he wasn't lured off somewhere so we would be stranded?" asked Burt, stopping in front of her. She stood, facing him.

"Maybe he was, but what can I do about it now? I have faith that no matter what happens we'll find the solution to Sue's death. Maybe that's why we're here. And though I don't know where Sherman went, I'd almost bet my life that he's around here somewhere. After all, we're the good guys. We haven't committed any crime, and there's right and justice in the world. It applies to me personally."

"That may be, but that doesn't mean it's here. What good did it do Sue, personally?" he asked, sarcastically.

"Maybe she didn't believe in it, personally." Kate returned to packing the sleeping bag.

"Maybe she believed in it until she was convinced otherwise by a greater force than her belief."

"That doesn't lessen my belief. I don't think of myself as nothing but in relation to Sue. I am, and that's another matter. In your job, you only look at relatives, but there's much more to life than science and engineering." Finished with packing, Kate flung the pillows on the pile near the door and headed for the kitchen with Burt.

"Science and engineering go where I go," stated Burt.

"I go where it can't."

"We may have walked straight into a trap all neatly laid out, and we still haven't caught on to why."

Kate paced the kitchen, and stopped suddenly as she thought of something new. "Senator Bold is creating a retirement job for Ferrell at government expense, but what Ferrell's paying, I can't figure out. It must connect to Sue and Hurly."

"Maybe Bold got the payoff in advance in good press. Let's face it. Bold's got your little rag in his back pocket. I've never seen a criticism of him in it, and anybody who criticizes him gets lambasted."

"Keep your mindset on Sue and Hurly. They were both murdered, and there's got to be a connection."

"If there's some official con involving Bold and Ferrell, it wouldn't be the first in the world. But the most worrisome things are the plane wreck, Sue's personality change and death, Sherman driving off in the car, and my broken leg." Burt swiped at his leg. "The way I fell, it felt like I was pushed; and an electric charge went through that piece of iron. It was rock solid, Kate! Also, how could you know Sherman was leaving and not be capable of stopping or questioning him? You couldn't have been sleeping. The definition of sleep calls for unconsciousness."

"Definitions are haphazard. Language is a trick. The same words define each other with slight variations. Sleep means slumber, and slumber means sleep. The degree of awareness or unconsciousness may be as different as the sleepers, just as in wakefulness. I believed I was sleeping. I was most certainly not awake, like I am now, talking with you. We're dealing with something incredible, partly because the way we use language makes it so. What's the purpose of the news media, in your opinion, Burt?"

"To report the news."

"Yes, but before the collapse of the U.S.S.R., the job of Pravda was to report the news, too. What's the difference in that and what we do?"

"They didn't report the news. They published official dogma, illustrated with testimonials, to try to validate communism, like soap commercials. It was government controlled propaganda, not free press."

"Well, suppose Ferrell got onto some secret technology and teamed up with Senator Bold for financial benefits to both of them. What would become of your free press then?"

"What are you insinuating?"

"The job of the media is to report the news. Once it's out, people make what they will of it. Some official is caught in a crime. The media reports it, and the judiciary takes over. The criminal is impeached, or stands trial, depending on the law and the crime. Suppose that while she was investigating Governor Hurly's death, Sue discovered a high level crime that involved Ferrell and Bold? Suppose she learned that the governor found out about it and was murdered before he could start an investigation?" As she spoke, her idea gained credibility in her imagination, and she started pacing.

"Kate, if your suspicions are true, we're in extremely great danger if there is any chance of us unearthing it. Those people have money and power and ways of getting what they want that we can't even imagine."

"Not necessarily, it could be a city-wide or state-wide racket that Senator Bold is somehow facilitating. There's new political corruption exposed every day. If it involves tampering with the system on a national basis, it can't stay hidden forever. It'll come out."

"I don't want any of us to end up like Sue."

"What do you suggest?" asked Kate, her hands on her hips, "short of disappearing off the earth, in which case we end up exactly like Sue?"

"It could all be smoke and mirrors. Once one crazy thing happens, it's easier to be drawn into still more fantastic nonsense until one is led hopelessly off course. Eventually, you'd lose your mental balance."

"Everyone can't be driven crazy. Sue wasn't. That's when murder comes in. She was driven apart from us to induce a stressful state, but she didn't capitulate. When I'm alone with Ferrell, he acts like a lunatic. He doesn't act like that in the presence of any of the other staff. I'm sure he did that to Sue."

"As long as I can talk honestly to you and you to me, we have that communality of relationship, and that's what Sue lost. Maybe Sherman was ordered in a dream to drive off. Maybe someone's deliberately trying to isolate each of us in the same way Sue was," speculated Burt.

"We have our abilities to remain communicative with each other, whatever the threat. I'd rather die as the person I am than be driven to whatever horror cut Sue off from Sherman and us. Can you imagine what it'd be like to live with some awful threat with no one to discuss it with?" asked Kate.

"We tried to stick with Sue. Nobody tried harder than Sherman," said Burt. "I respected her privacy. Your concern turned into badgering, Kate. She was in way over her head, and she needed escape."

"She always said the same thing. It would be impossible to understand."

"Everything that is is possible to understand, but I don't know where we go from here."

"I'm going to explore the basement," said Kate.

"Looking for hidden doors to the catacombs?" Burt stumped after her to the basement door.

"That noise had to come from somewhere."

"I'll make breakfast. Leave the door open, and holler if you need help. I'll kick the spook with my cast."

Kate laughed, and went downstairs. The light was dim, and she carefully stepped over a broken stair. The room got colder as she descended; and by the time she reached the bottom, she was shivering. The mud floor was extremely slippery, and the walls were lined with fieldstones. Feeling a cold draft on her shins, she bent over to see where it was coming from and discovered a dark, gaping tunnel, which she couldn't see the end of. Though she wanted to know what was at the end of it, nothing could compel her to crawl through that muddy hole to further explore. She picked up a piece of broken off fieldstone and threw it into the hole but didn't hear it land.

A shadow whisked by, just beyond peripheral view, and she turned in time to see a large rat scurry across a rafter. She caught her breath in a noisy gasp.

"What?" yelled Burt, from the doorway.

"Just a rat," she shouted back.

"The animal kind, I hope."

Kate laughed.

"Anything interesting?" called Burt.

"The floor's slippery. It's mud. There are crawlways all over the place. Freezing cold comes from them, and you can't see to the end of them."

"Why don't you crawl...."

"Why don't you?"

"I've got a broken leg. What's the matter? Your voice is trembling!"

"This place is an icebox. They don't need a refrigerator in the kitchen. They've got a natural one down here." Kate returned upstairs, taking each step carefully. There was no railing, and the mud from her shoes made the steps slippery. She was covered with goose bumps when she got back to the kitchen, her lips blue. Burt rubbed her arms and hugged her until she warmed up.

"Hmm, nice," she said, putting her arms around him.

"You feel like you just got back from the North Pole." He held her close, rubbing her back, until she warmed up.

"I know. There's something down there."

"What?"

"I don't know. You can't see it. You can only feel it."

"What does it feel like?"

"Cold." Kate began cleaning the mud off her shoes.

Burt laughed. "I've heard it's always cold around ghosts."

"And meditating people. Their body temperatures drop. It's been proven. I read an article about it."

"Anything down there besides cold?"

"Whatever we felt when we heard the howling and ran out, only not as intense. It comes from underground tunnels. They seem to go down. I can't tell you how good that coffee smells."

"It's ready. Help yourself."

Kate and Burt ate cold cereal with fruit and milk, lingering over a second cup of coffee.

"There's nothing to do around here," complained Burt. "I've got to reserve the last chapter of my novel for the way home if Sherman ever comes back and we get home."

"When I was working on a story about a couple who sailed around the world, I asked what they do when there's no wind. They said, wait. That's all we can do. I can walk down the road a few miles. I sure don't relish sitting around here," said Kate, washing the cups. "Having nothing to do was great yesterday after knocking myself out at work all week, but how long can a person do nothing?"

"I've had my fill. I'll walk with you a little way. I need to move around, too."

"Let's go then." She hung up the dish towel, they put on their jackets, and Kate took her flashlight from the table. Burt grabbed the other one. They went out on the porch, and Kate switched on her light. The morning was chilly and the cold air smelled of mountains and wildness. A few day streaks had cracked the dark, but stars were still plainly visible. The cloudless sky was absent of birds and living things. *Silence*, thought Kate, *must be the point where heaven and hell meet.* Kate and Burt followed the ruts to the road, Kate taking it easy so Burt could keep up.

"Here are the tire marks where Sherm backed onto the road," said Burt, playing his light over the marks. "See, he went opposite of the way we came. He didn't know where he was going."

"I see," said Kate. "I wouldn't have noticed that, but he might've known where he was going. He said when he was here with Sue he went for a hike and discovered another road. Maybe that's where he went." She continued to walk slowly, shining her light in front of them, with Burt hobbling beside her with his light. "Maybe we'll meet him on the road."

"Hmm," said Burt, preoccupied with his thoughts. The tracks soon faded into the gravel.

"Burt, suppose Ferrell engineered Sue's death, and now he's on my case, but suppose someone with much greater power, Senator Bold, for instance, is on his case forcing his hand?" speculated Kate.

"Could be." Again they stopped talking, each sinking into their own thoughts. Continuing on, listening to the crunch of their feet on gravel and the steady whomp, whomp, whomp of his crutches hitting earth, Burt broke the silence. "The farther we get from the house, the better I feel. Did you notice there are birds here?" Daylight crept in slow, and the night faded into early morning twilight.

"Yeah, look there!" Kate pointed to a pair of magpies in a mountain laurel. Their rasping call set off a cacophony of birdsong.

Walking for several miles rejuvenated Kate, and she shrugged off the moroseness that had built up over the night. "Look! There's a groundhog," she said, pointing. They stopped to watch the fat creature waddle into the brush. Hearing crashing through the thicket, Kate turned to see a deer running away.

"We're so close to that place, yet everything's different here," said Burt. "There's life, all of a sudden."

"Yes, walking away from that house is like meeting an old friend after a hostile encounter with a stranger. The sun's barely risen. It can't be past about six o'clock," estimated Kate.

"Aha! Look at this!" said Burt. "An old gravel road comes into this one." He and Kate stopped and looked for tire tracks, but none were visible. "Sherman either kept straight down this road or he turned off onto the gravel trail."

"Or disappeared into thin air," quipped Kate.

"Which way do you want to go?" asked Burt, laughing. "Use your female intuition that gets you into so much trouble."

"Straight ahead; I think if he turned here, we'd see his tracks after all that rain, wouldn't we? That van's pretty heavy."

"Not necessarily," said Burt, thumping with his cane in the gravel. "This is pretty solid."

"This looks like the approach to civilization, and that gravel road is nothing but a hunting trail. It winds deeper into the woods," said Kate.

Burt wanted to stick to the paved road because it was easier with his handicap, so he didn't argue, though he thought Sherman would have turned onto the gravel. That was almost surely the road he'd been on before, and he may have been inspired with a hunch to check it out. They walked on for an hour. Stopping to rest, Burt sat on a fallen log, his bad leg stretched out in front of him.

Kate sat beside him, making small talk. Dawdling she was in no hurry to return to the misery of silence in the weird house. After sufficient rest, she got up, and Burt struggled to his feet.

"I can't think of a thing I hate more than going back to that house after lounging around in the sun," he said.

"I know, but there's one thing I hate worse, and that's going back to the office in the same condition I left it," said Kate.

## CHAPTER TWENTY FIVE

Marcella's leg ached and was badly swollen. She'd lost track of time. Limping, she clung to the kitchen knife she'd used to fend off the dogs. The mine could open out somewhere other then where she stumbled into it, or she could be so hopelessly lost in the underground maze that death could open its jaws and snatch her.

"Oh God," she prayed. "How am I going to get out of here?" Alone in the mine with her death, she was unwilling to go easy. Making her way through the tunnels, always in the direction from which she sensed a wisp of air, she avoided those that smelled dead and rancid. She'd no way to measure time or distance, but her instinct was heightened. When she slept, she couldn't tell if it had been for five minutes, five hours, or fifteen hours. Groggy and lethargic all the time, she imagined Mario and Rita searching for her.

"If I die down here, I'll never be found. Mario and Rita won't know what happened to me," she said. As hunger overtook her, she often forgot Mario and Rita. She thought of the food she prepared in Senator Bold's kitchen and the snake she ate on the desert. She recalled the tortillas and beans she'd lived on through the days of picking and working the fields in the hot California sun and the meals Sedar and Riva gave her at the Painter Labor Camp. The squirrels and rabbits and birds she'd eaten and the turkey she'd killed on the desert when Mario was sick tortured her, and Mary Griswold's gourmet delights teased her memory mercilessly.

Her mother used to make tacos that smelled heavenly. She smelled them now in the mine. Headaches and stomach cramps came and went, and hot dogs and hamburgers, cakes and casseroles, apples, oranges, mangos, papayas, bananas, avocados, and loaves of bread marched through her head.

When she was awake and when she was asleep, Marcella thought of food. Eventually, she couldn't tell if she was awake or asleep because the visions of food didn't distinguish between her waking and sleeping states. She longed for food with the kind of yearning she'd willed Mario to recover on the desert.

Something slithered at her foot, and stabbing frantically at it in the dark, she prayed that a rat or snake had found its way into the mine. She'd eat it raw, but when she came to her senses, she was stabbing the gravel on the floor of the mine.

"My God, my God, the night is long," she murmured. "Stay with me God and make me strong." After an eternity in hell, not knowing if she was going in a circle or maze without end, she leaned against the wall of the tomb and her legs gave out. She slid to the floor.

Sitting on the cold, damp stone unable to rise, a wail came from her that grew louder and longer and deeper. She gave it free reign, a scream of despair and pain that reached a crescendo and wouldn't quit; and she imagined riding that sound out of her prison. The terrible primal scream seemed to rise from all the persecuted souls who had found their way into some black hell to join her soulful cry; and she felt it touch the outside world. It stopped then, and Marcella fell asleep.

When she came to, she was invigorated. She stood up and felt a bare whisper of stale air which gave her direction and strength to keep moving. Stopping to rest often, her body moved like a machine. Hiking the sun-scorched desert with Mario and Rita, working the orchards and kitchens of the rich, every thought, decision, and action of her life had brought her here, and she prayed for her past to see her through.

She passed out again, woke on the cold, rock floor, and as always first felt the knife in her hand. Opening her eyes, she was back on the desert, but it was different. No human being had ever lived on this strange desert of white sand mountains and deep blue sky with clouds that were glistering white. She heard a lullaby, and hummed softly with it, and out of the mountains, riders galloped toward her on white horses. Though they came closer and closer, they could never arrive; something stood between them and her, and running toward them with open arms, she crashed into a black rock wall, and she was back in the mine. She fell on impact and lay there, recalling the riders and the music. She began to hum again, but when she opened her eyes, there was only the mine, the silence, the black stagnant air. Her lungs faltered, and she gasped for breath.

"You don't have to struggle any longer," she told her lungs. "I give you leave. Quit if you dare, if you like. I won't hold it against you." The sound of her voice was more valuable than gold. She loved the sound of the human voice, weak and raspy and scratchy though hers was, like she used to love Mario and Rita when she was alive.

"Am I alive?" she asked. And her voice answered, "Yes, you are alive."

Forcing herself to her feet, she walked until she couldn't continue; and as her walk time shortened, her sleep time lengthening, her resolve wavered. The desire to live loosened its grip at regular intervals, and she contemplated death more often. After three weeks in the mine, she often spoke aloud to herself, to hear the sweet, sweet sound of a human voice one more time. *"The cease of sorrow?"* she asked herself, *"or the beginning of it? It depends on what I've done by a judgment I can't know, yet I know the way I went is right. I'm not afraid to go from this earth; it's the love of life with Mario and Rita in it I'm not ready to leave behind."* With her voice often came visions, some bombarding, some soft as a summer dream. For a brief while, she walked a mountain trail in a jungle surrounded by innocuous wild animals who thought she was one of them. Curiously, she watched a lion watching her, as she made her way along the trail. A small herd of elephants stood by; and a black bear lumbering through the weeds with three cubs tumbling over one another cuffing each other paused on their journey. She saw squirrels and rabbits and a family of large gray wolves lying on a rock in the sun watched her trudge by.

Constantly on the verge of sleep she tripped over something on the trail and fell. Touching the obstacle, she felt a human skull and working her fingers down from the head she felt the clavicle, the ribs, the pelvic structure and the femur all the way down to the metatarsus. "That's me," she said. "Or someone else a long time down here." She sat, her feet crossed at the ankles, her legs bent, beside the bones, her sole companion. "You are my bones, aren't you?" she asked.

"Yes," replied the skull.

"We're all alone on this trail," said Marcella. "Mario and Rita were on it with me, but now we're all alone, just you and me. I've heard it called the eternal sleep, but it's not. That's only what the living call it. I have bones yet, and a voice. Bones and a voice and reason, and thought, how many parts there are to a person, how many invisible but to the sense?" As her strength gave out, her visions grew stronger. Now instead of animals and landscapes, they were populated with people. A likable young man appeared; tall and lean with a firm jaw like Mario's and a rugged face, but he was not likable enough to be Mario.

"Are you dead?" she asked.
"I don't have to answer that," he replied.
"I'd like to know. Do you mind? I'm lost, and I only want to know if I'm soon to return, or if I've left the land of the living for good. It's a great, great stress in my brain not to know."

He disappeared.

"Come back!" she called. "Come back! You don't have to answer. Tell me something, anything." But he didn't come back. Yearning for the way out of the mine, in life or death no longer mattered; she'd give anything not to wake again in the mine.

"I don't want to get up again," she said. "I don't want to walk another step," her hollow voice echoed. Yet, she did. Moving slowly, she bumped into the rock walls until she picked up the trail through hell.

Marcella heard someone screaming far off in the distance. It came closer and closer, and when it got to her, piercing her brain, she realized it came from her mouth. And then she smelled air! Unmistakably, it brushed her cheek, like the flutter of a feather. Running toward it, she stumbled over a rock and fell out of the hole. Rolling over on her back, she saw the moon and the stars, and her spirit soared. Reaching toward the moon, she grasped it and held it in her hand, drew her hand back, and left it hanging in its place in the sky.

"I'm alive!" she said aloud. "I'm alive!" Marcella stood up in the dark, and she didn't feel weak anymore. She felt strong. In a burst of energy, she started running. Crashing through the woods, she limped in a panic, like a wild animal that's been shot. She raced toward an automobile's hum by moonlight. Suppose they let the dogs out?

She ran swiftly, leaving the limp behind, listening for the baying howls, for the vibration of the earth by their paws, for their panting breath behind and on all sides, for the low, throaty growls and snarls.

Her feet hurt fiercely, but she forced them on. They felt like stones on the ends of her legs, and her legs drew energy up through them from the earth. *Suppose they caught up? Suppose they came for her tonight and suppose...stop it! Stop it!* Running through a creek, to obliterate her trail should the dogs pick it up, she then stopped to kneel and touch the earth on the other side. She kissed the soaked ground, got up, and continued running. Did it feel her feet running over it? To be always there without a thought...if it weren't for thought would life be much easier, would she care so much? Would she mind being held against her will? Would there be anything in the world of equal value to the freedom of running, running, running on her own steam where each step landed at the direction of her will?

She blinked incessantly, the shadowy trees and shrubs flying past in flashes with each shutter movement of her eyelids in the moonlight on the overgrown trail, her eyes straining hungrily after their forced fast, lustily snatching everything available at once.

This night air, unlike what she breathed yesterday, was free air, sweeter than love, greater than truth; and tonight, if it was the only night left of her life was a free night, therefore, it was the one night in all eternity that counted. She was free at this moment that crowded out the last three weeks in a single instantaneous burst of life.

Free and alive, could it be? Maybe only half of these majestic oak towers of the night showed. Maybe more than half of them lived underground, free to sink their roots deeper, to curl into the earth and find moisture, meandering their way around impediments, entwining rocks along the way, finding the underground rivers to drink from, while above ground their branches grew and matured, turning their leaves to the sun to  breathe and wave in the wind and harbor animals and shade the ground.

Her mind's eye returned involuntarily again and again to the underground tombs, but each time she wrenched it back to reality - freedom.

A muffled shriek twisted out of her mouth, a small storm, suppressing a rising image. The noise startled her. What was this free noise made, not by force but by God and nature? She begged from no one on this free night, the right to sail this noise out upon the wind; it merely happened. *What might this weed grow into? Sshh, don't spoil it with a wall.* Her free mind reached and grasped, trying to comprehend her release from the prison of the mine after the interminable confinement, and the conviction that she was dead. Nothing could fail her on this beautiful night when the air was free, and the earth oozed its life into her feet, flying through the forest, the prisoners of her direction. How willingly they cooperated, their welfare dependent upon her freedom; they flew for her, even in their distress.

The companionship of the trees, the shadows and shrubbery and the moon and the stars and the calls of night birds crowded out solitude. This desperate flight belonged to this night and these creatures. The moon showed and hid in the clouds by turns, sending out light bright as twilight. Muted rays fell directly on the path, racing away under her feet. The variously tinged clouds, some dark and gray, some eerily luminous, where the moon shimmered them glistering white, followed rapidly behind nearer slower ones.

A light rain began to fall, and she felt the drops on her skin; but that didn't impede her race through the night. Marcella lost awareness of running and of thought in the exquisite rare pleasure of freedom until the first streaks of gray before sunrise appeared in the eastern sky. A gravel road suddenly in front of her stopped her forward motion.

Shivering, she waited in the trees by the road. Glancing anxiously at the lightening sky, she waited what seemed a long, long time. At last, a lone set of headlights approached. Marcella stepped out of the woods into the path of the oncoming lights and stood facing them, waiting.

She watched the lights slow, as they caught her in their glare, piercing, hurting her unsquinting eyes that seemed to have will of their own. The car stopped, the tires crunching on the gravel. Still, she didn't move.

Sherman tried not to stop. What was he doing here half asleep on this lonesome road? This must be a dream; he'd wake at any moment. There was a hallucination ahead. Since Sue died, he'd stayed at the office working long after the others had gone home. He was accustomed to hallucinations on his way home from the office from lack of sleep and not eating properly. The vision remained three feet in front of the car. It was an Iroquois proudly totem-like in the middle of the lane, unyielding.

He shook his head to make it disappear, but it didn't go. Making up his mind to step on the accelerator to drive through it, something held him back. He stopped instead and got out of the van. A headdress blew around the head of the motionless, life-sized apparition. Walking straight toward the figment, he expected it to vanish, but as he approached, a stench that he imagined to be like the smell of death reached his nostrils, a peculiar feeling came over him, and he realized that he was much more tired than he'd known. He'd overloaded his circuits with work, and he needed rest, nothing more. Surely he wasn't mad.

Light rain diffused into thick mist rising around the figure as the light reflected in his headlights cast dim shadows. Then he saw her clearly; a woman, a living woman! The headdress was her wild hair blowing around her head. Her enormous dark eyes caught a glint from the rising sun and reflected his face back to him. He was stunned. There was something in the eyes and face that he'd never seen in the face of a human being; it horrified him. She was a living skeleton wrapped in skin with no flesh between, and a pair of eyes.

The deep wells of her eyes contained a mystery he couldn't fathom. They'd seen something he never would. She turned her eyes straight on him, but he avoided them. He looked instead at her other features; a small straight nose, firm chin, and hollow cheeks covered with beads of mist dripping off her shiny black face.

"Come," said Sherman, going to the van and opening the front door. "Get in." She came to the van and got in. He slammed the door, went around to the driver's seat, and got in.

Taking off her soaking shoes and socks, Marcella rubbed one swollen foot and let the heater blow on the other, but the pain didn't subside in either. She rubbed the other foot, and then marched them up and down on the floor.

"Got aspirin?" she asked, aching for relief.

"No," he said. "Are you hungry?" She nodded. Following the road to the foot of the mountain, he kept sneaking glances at her.

"What are you doing out here?" he asked. She didn't answer, and realizing she wasn't going to speak, he remained silent until he came to a general store and country house with a gas pump in front. At the sound of his tires stopping on the gravel, a light went on inside, and then the porch light came on.

"We're on the other side of the mountain," he said.

Making no reply, she stared straight ahead, her unnaturally bright agate eyes deep in her face, framed by a wild, tangled mass of black hair.

As he got out of the van, Sherman caught a glimpse of her feet in the pink glare of the incandescent floodlight. They were thin as her face, and long, splashed with mud and grime and blood with tiny pieces of the forest clinging to them.

He hurried in to get groceries and aspirin and dashed through the small shop yanking items off the shelf as the old store keeper watched curiously. Sherman put his groceries on the counter.

"Ain't seen you here'n these parts," said the man in denim overalls hastily pulled over long johns. "Dun woke me up."

"Sorry," said Sherman. The elderly fellow moved slowly checking out the groceries, and Sherman wished him to hurry. At last, he was ready to go. "Thanks," Sherman said.

"Any time," said the man. "Any time a'tall. Thanks fer stoppin' in."

"I'll get gas, too," said Sherman.

"Okay. I'll turn the pump on."

Sherman hurried to the van, and handed the groceries to the woman. After pumping the gas, he returned to the store to pay for it and got in the car. She was eating.

As he drove up the mountain, she ate ravenously, making noises like a starving animal and drank milk from the carton in huge gulps, not wasting a drop.

Sneaking glances at her, from time to time, Sherman had an urge to reach out and touch her to make sure she was real. There was a strange disturbing thing about her. The way she was devouring the food testified to her solidity, but her ethereal quality wasn't vanquished.

"Were you running away from someone?" he asked.

Staring at the food, she continued eating without answering.

"From something?"

He thought he detected a slight nod.

"What happened?"

She continued to ignore his questions; and after her eating binge, she fell asleep, breathing deeply, leaning against the door with a half-eaten piece of bread, cheese, and salami in her hand.

Sherman drove in dazed silence, tension rising until it became so tangible it could almost assume a form he could wrestle with and thereby dispel. When he stopped at the house, she woke with a start and clutched the dashboard.

Sherman got out.

She slipped her feet into her filthy shoes. Marcella carried her socks and followed him into the kitchen with the bag of food, shivering.

There was a note on the table from Kate. God almighty! He'd forgotten that Kate and Burt existed and had no memory of leaving the house that morning! *Sherm; Please don't leave with the van again. We went for a walk and will be back soon. Kate.*

Rubbing his jaw, absent-mindedly, he wondered where they were, but his attention quickly returned to the strange woman.

"Would you like coffee or tea? Something hot?" he asked,

"Yes, it would be nice," though she spoke very softly and slowly, as though searching out the words that fit; to Marcella, her voice sounded strange and loud and far away. She made another sandwich and ate it, made another and another. She drank a glass full of water which slid down her throat like it was poured. "Where's the bathroom," she asked urgently, standing. Sherman pointed, and she dashed to it.

After making her tea and setting it on the table in front of her when she returned, Sherman poured some hot water into a basin. Lacing it with hydrogen peroxide from his medical kit, he then soaped a washcloth and washed her feet as gently as possible. Blue veins showed through the translucent skin, contrasting sharply with the bloody gashes on the outside. Three toenails that remained were black and loose. They fell off in the water which quickly turned filthy. He emptied the basin and prepared more. Her feet swelled as he washed them, and he was surprised to see that she was white.

"Do you want to talk?" he asked. She shook her head no.

"Are you tired?" She nodded.

Sherman hoped the tea and comfort of warmth would loosen her tongue, but she sipped it slowly, silently, staring into the cup in a daze.

He opened the couch into a bed and put his sleeping bag on it for her. "I'm Sherman," he said, taking her dirty hand. He held the unresisting hand as long as it so remained; thin with muscles and veins visible under the skin. Sherman wanted to wash the dirt off, to study that hand more closely. Four of the nimble, sylph-like fingers were crooked. Fingernails on both thumbs and index fingers were missing and the rest of her fingernails, like her toenails had been, were black and loose. His fingers were drawn to the center of the inside of her hand, and when he touched it, electrical charges came from it. As her hand quickly closed and withdrew, he distinctly saw sparks fly from her fingertips. A sharp jolt electrified him.

"There's a shower in the bathroom," he said, "but the water's probably cold. I brought an extra set of clothes, though they'll be too large. You're welcome to them."

"Thanks," she said. He found his spare jeans, shorts, tee shirt, flannel shirt, and socks in his backpack and handed them to her.

"Alive," she whispered. "I'm alive!" The thought recurred slow as morning light this time, as she remembered the mine, remembered thinking she was dead, remembered never wanting to get up, trying not to get up and the sudden revelation of her death.

Sherman showed her the bathroom, and she took a shower. The water on her skin felt like the very essence of life, washing the outer grime away, but not the inner. That needed time and cicatrix.

Sherman restored the dying embers to a blazing fire, scrubbed her shoes, and set them on the hearth to dry. He attacked the socks vigorously with soap and water, rinsed them, and repeated the process until black water quit running out of them, wrung them, and laid them on the hearth beside the shoes. She returned in his clothes that were large enough for two of her, and lay down on the floor in front of the hearth. The instant she touched the floor, she fell into a deep sleep, and Sherman found a blanket in a linen closet and covered her with it.

Confused and exhausted, he took off his shoes, lay down on the couch in his sleeping bag meant for her, hoping to ponder the strange events; but unable to fight sleep, he drifted away, unsure if Marcella was really there or if he'd been sleeping and dreamed the whole sequence of events.

A noise he couldn't identify jolted him awake, violating his dream of Sue dancing alone for him. Looking to see if the stranger was there, or if he'd imagined the preposterous early morning, she was sleeping on the floor. Breathing a sigh of relief, he was nevertheless gripped with apprehension. Struggling with the intensity of two simultaneous yet incongruous emotions that he couldn't reconcile, he tried to shrug it off.

Wrinkled from dehydration, she appeared to be old. Her actions, speech, and mannerisms of the early morning told him that she was an adult but didn't indicate her age. He thought of her with extreme respect, nearly veneration. She was so still that he wondered if he should rouse her or feel her pulse to make sure she wasn't dead. As she was lying on her side, her hipbone poked up under the blanket. She should've slept on the couch where she'd have been more comfortable.

Walking in his socks to the kitchen, he then put the remains of the food in the bag, placed it in the refrigerator, and snuck back to the living room like an intruder. He wanted to talk to the woman to relieve his unbearable anxiety about what had transpired, yet he couldn't bring himself to wake her. Hungry, Sherman fixed two sandwiches, ate in the kitchen, and went out to the front porch. He stretched, paced the porch, and walked down to the lane. Not seeing a sign of Kate or Burt, he then ambled aimlessly around the grounds before returning to the house and falling asleep on the couch.

"Look!" yelled Kate, returning to the house with Burt. "Sherman's here! There's the van."

"Sherm!" yelled Burt, stumping to the house. "Sherm!" Kate sprinted past him up the front steps. Dashing into the house, she stopped so suddenly at the door to the living room that Burt crashed into her, and they clattered to the floor. Kate got up and approached the blanket on the hearth. The woman beneath it and the arm sticking out was motionless as stone.

Sherman slept peacefully on the couch in his sleeping bag, his cherubic rosy cheeks and curls poking out the opening.

"My God," said Kate, in amazement, her hands on her hips. "What has Sherman been up to?"

Before Burt had time to venture an opinion, she disappeared into the kitchen. Wanting to wake Sherman, Burt thought better of it. He heard Kate knocking around in the kitchen, went in, and leaning his crutches against the table, he then sat down clumsily.

Kate opened the refrigerator to get the food she'd brought and saw the bag of groceries Sherman had bought. She put her bag out on the table and made coffee, trying to put together a plausible explanation.

"Obviously Sherman drove somewhere to pick up that woman. She's emaciated," said Kate. "And he found someplace to shop. There's a bag of groceries in the refrigerator."

Before Burt could reply, Sherman appeared in the doorway, grinning sheepishly.

"What happened?" Kate pounced.

Sherman took off his glasses and cleaned them.

"Who's that carved bone of a woman?" asked Burt.

"I don't know," said Sherman.

"Where did you go, Sherman?" asked Kate. "What has happened to her? She looks very old and wrinkled up."

"I think she's dehydrated not old," said Sherman. "She was starving."

"Well, where did you find her, Man?" asked Burt, impatiently.

"Standing in the middle of the road."

"How could you get back without passing us? Were you on the gravel road about two miles down the mountain?" asked Burt.

"Yes. It winds all the way down the mountain."

"Well, tell us exactly what happened," said Kate.

"I don't know exactly what happened. I don't remember leaving the lodge." Sherman poured himself a cup of coffee and sat down. "I went to sleep in the cedar room with you two. The next thing I remember is driving on a narrow, one-lane road, similar to the one to this house, when I saw this woman! I'm as mystified as you. There's nothing there where she was, no place she might've come from but the woods. She looks like she's just back from...."

Sherman's sentence was interrupted by a horrendous scream, and the hair-raising tension it produced froze them like a film in stop action before they all went flying for the front door. Marcella woke, leaped to her feet, grabbed her shoes and socks off the hearth, and charged for the door on pure instinct, and all four of them jammed the doorway, trying to get through at the same time. They spilled out onto the porch, but Kate started running back into the house as Marcella thrust her feet into her socks and shoes on the porch. Burt tried to stop Kate, but she brushed him off.

"You're going the wrong way!" he shouted, turning to go after her. "Come back! Come back!"

"I've got to get my purse and briefcase!" Dashing back into the house, as though it were a burning building with a live person stranded inside, Kate snatched her purse from the table and briefcase from the foyer and raced back to the van.

As Burt had jokingly suspected earlier, his crutches didn't slow him down as he made his way to the van in one-footed leaps instead of skimpy hops. Burt and Marcella were waiting in the back, and Sherman was in the passenger seat when Kate leaped into the van. She took off in reverse, her head out the window, the tires squealing, throwing rocks and grit aside.

She backed onto the road to return the way they'd come, and tore up the mountain toward the ridge until the sharp curve ahead loomed up too soon.

Slowing, fighting for control of the wheel and losing it momentarily, she felt the vehicle swerve dangerously near the edge, and one wheel left the road. Turning the steering wheel sharply, she hit the brakes again gently, ever so gently, and felt the road beneath her. *How sweet life is in the shadow of death* she thought. Picturing the van sailing out over the precipice into space, she headed for a tree grown up from a deeper ravine. It stopped the slowly moving van with a jolt, and she felt the whiplash in the back of her neck. Unable to think, Kate was caught in the moment, her heart pounding, sweat standing out on her forehead.

Everyone scrambled out and stood looking over the edge. The front wheels were half on the road, half hung in space between the road and the tree like a surrealistic painting.

Kate's mouth was dry, and she couldn't swallow. Though she could no longer hear the frenzied scream that had catapulted them out of the lodge, she still felt the vibrations in her ear reverberating through her brain and down her spine. She felt like her guts were being forced out and that she'd surely explode from the pressure.

She could see Canada and the St. Lawrence Seaway. Looking down, the peak of a lower mountain pierced a low hung cloud. She turned to Burt, and they hugged each other as Sherman and Marcella stood gaping over the edge.

"We can't go back," said Sherman, solemnly shaken, yet his voice as steady as the tree that saved their lives. "Should I drive?"

"No," said Kate, disengaging herself from Burt's embrace. "I wish I could say yes, but I can't. I'd never drive again. I better just do it right now." Getting into the driver's seat, she carefully backed the vehicle onto the road, got out, and surveyed the damage. There was only a dent in the bumper.

"It looks like it'll run," she said.
"It'll have to," said Burt.
Marcella started laughing, and realized that it had been longer than she could remember since she'd laughed. It was contagious, and soon they were all laughing the laugh that is relief without humor. They all piled back into the van, and Kate started driving.

"I've seen you somewhere, but I can't place you," said Kate to Marcella, as she drove slowly down the mountain.

"You were at Mary Griswold's party taking pictures of Senator Bold when I was taking coats. Gordon had to throw you out. I was at the Painter Labor Camp when you came there. You took a picture of me and one of my bathroom."

"I recall both situations," said Kate, and upon identification she recognized the woman through her bony, drawn and shriveled state. She waited for Marcella to continue. Marcella related the story of their journey to New York, the work on Senator Bold's estate, the terror by television, and her escape into the coalmine.

"What a story!" said Kate. "I'm beginning to get a clearer picture, and my intimations about Senator Bold were right on target."

Marcella looked out the window nervously. "I'm hungry," she said. "I'm so hungry."

"We'll stop at the first place to eat. Marcella, I want you to tell your story to the authorities. My best friend was killed, and our lives are threatened, also."

"For telling about the farm workers?"

"I don't know why yet. That could have something to do with it. To get out of the bulls eye, I must find the answers."

"Bad, bad things happen here," said Marcella.

"Marcella, by our law, I don't have to reveal who told me about a crime by an official in public office. Because the press is responsible for finding out about crimes by officials, our sources are protected. How many people does Bold employ at the New York estate?" asked Kate.

"Two in Mario's shop, four house boys, six in the kitchen, four servers, three chauffeurs each shift, except the mechanics and gardeners, and they work the schedule, Mario the same as my shift."

"How many shifts?" asked Kate.
"Three."

"That's over fifty people in the house and garage," said Kate. "Are they all Hispanic?"

"All like Mario and me," said Marcella. "All recruited from California. Many people come there, but not servants."

"We have quite a story here, Marcella. The first thing we need to do is call the Attorney General's office," said Kate. "Bold is committing serious crimes. You have much evidence to give. Some arrangements will be made. Did you overhear anything while you worked at the Griswold place about organized movement of illegal aliens?"

"Yes. Senator Bold told Ms. Griswold she had to stop importing aliens. She told Gordon that too many illegals were escaping, and he had to keep track of everybody. I asked Belle where they went, and she said they got other jobs. At Ms. Griswold's, I was kept close to her."

"We'll go straight to the authorities," said Kate.

"But we came without papers," protested Marcella, extremely distressed.

"Are you going to spend your whole life running and hiding, exposed to situations where you have no recourse to law?"

"That seems like a hard life to you. It's the easiest life we've ever known."

"Only because you don't have the ease of life when everything is legal, and you can do whatever you want," said Kate. "You're living like a criminal, and you've committed no crime."

"We don't know. We try to stay out of trouble. I'm afraid for Mario and Rita and me, too. What if they send us back? We spent our whole lives coming here for that? It's a crime to come here like we did."

"You'll be surprised that justice comes out. You won't be deported. You can demand citizenship in exchange for your testimony, and you must talk to a lawyer before you talk to anybody else."

"How much does it cost?"

"Don't worry about that. I'll find you a lawyer who'll take the fee out of someone else's pocket."

## CHAPTER TWENTY SIX

Mario and Rita went to church on Sunday, as usual, but this time Mario's heart missed a beat when Marco walked in as the chimes sounded. Today was the day for good news! Marco came and sat next to him.

"Good morning, Mario," said Marco. "I didn't know you go to church."

"I like it; this is Rita's and my church. We started coming here after Marcella left. It gives me hope."

The congregation started singing *Rock of Ages*, and Marco whispered in Mario's ear. "Tomorrow Senator Bold will be home in the mansion. Tomorrow's Bold Done Day. Here's for Rita." He slipped Mario a note.

"I'm ready," said Mario, passing the paper to Rita. Turning first to see that there was no one behind her, she opened it in the hymnal, and Mario read over her shoulder.

"Tomorrow leave at the same time you do to go to school with your schoolbooks in your backpack. Catch the bus on your corner in front of the gas station instead of walking to school. Take #89 bus to Hillman Avenue and 48th St. Walk straight down to 4815 on 48th and ring the bell. Carmen is expecting you. Wait there until someone picks you up."

Quickly folding the paper, Rita slid it into her pocket.

"Buy Rita's birthday cake from Odetta's Bakery on your way home from church today," whispered Marco, as the congregation sang the last verse.

"Want to come over after work, Marco? It's a special day, Rita's birthday," said Mario, softly, before bowing his head to pray with the congregation.

"Maybe next Sunday. I've got too much work at home. This is my only day off. If I knew ahead of time...."

"Next Sunday would be good, but it won't be a birthday party."

A woman two pews forward turned to stare down the hum of conversation disturbing her concentration. They stayed until the service was over and Mario said, "See you at work, Marco."

"Bye Mario."

Mario and Rita left church and stopped at the bakery, which was only a little more crowded than usual, on their way home.

"I want to pick up a birthday cake for Rita Dominguez," Mario told the clerk.

"Let's see," she said, looking in the display case. "Here it is." She got out the cake with Happy Birthday Rita written on it, boxed it, and sold it to Mario. They walked home, Mario carrying the cake.

"Let's have cake and tea," said Rita, when they got home, unable to wait another minute.

"Sure," said Mario, turning on the cassette player to Frank Sinatra's rendition of *My Way*. "Make the tea, I'll set the table." He cut the cake, and the knife hit something hard on the first slice in the very middle. He extracted a small cylinder, and warning Rita with a wink not to mention it, he pocketed it.

"Want to go for a walk after we eat?"

"Yes!" said Rita, her heart skipping a beat. Eating her cake and drinking the tea so fast that she scalded her lip, she wished to hurry Mario who ate exceptionally slowly, practicing his self control. Exasperated, she thought he was deliberately making her wait because she was in a hurry. By the time he was finished with his tea and cake, Rita had her dishes washed.

When they were out on the sidewalk, Rita said, "Let's walk by the lake where we can sit in the park, and no one will notice."

"Sure, I was thinking it would be a good day for a walk in the park." They'd hiked at the lake on Sunday afternoons after church since Marcella disappeared when they didn't have to go to jobs.

This Sunday their pace was faster, and Rita won an internal battle to conceal her excitement. Reaching the park, they headed for a wooded area off the trail. Rita sat on a log; where she occasionally parked herself to feel the earth beneath her feet and look at trees and foliage, birds, squirrels, and chipmunks, and enjoy a respite from asphalt and concrete and automobile exhaust.

Mario got the cylinder out of his pocket and sat holding it, staring at it.

"Open it, Dad!" exclaimed Rita. "What are you waiting for?"

"Suppose it's all some kind of mistake, and they're not in here?"

"Open it!"

Mario brushed the crumbs off the cylinder and unscrewed it. Then he turned his pocket inside out, shaking out crumbs. Rita giggled. Finally, he righted his pockets and opened the cylinder. Three documents, tightly folded and rolled together, sprung out. Mario opened them one by one, Rita beside him, studying them as they unfurled. He was Mario House, thirty two-years old, born in Corinth, New York. Marcella's scroll came next; her birth name was Marcella Alliance born in Washington, D.C., thirty-two years old.

"This is me," said Rita, snatching her birth certificate out of Mario's hand, gleefully. "Rita House born in New York City. Naturally they'd pick me for New York. I'll probably die there, too. That's where I'm going to learn to be a doctor."

"Marcella and I will have to get married all over again," said Mario. He rolled up his and Marcella's documents, put them back in the cylinder, and returned the cylinder to his pocket. "I know you want to keep yours," he said to Rita.

"Yeah." She read it carefully, memorizing it.

"Marco says if they ever get lost, we write to the city of our birth to vital statistics. They'll send us a duplicate. They keep the original on file."

"That's valuable information," said Rita. "How did they get them?"

"Marco doesn't know. He's not on that committee."

"Somebody risked her neck for us, somebody who doesn't even know us."

"Sure," said Mario. "But he knows what we've been through. It's somebody who's been where we are now."

"What should I take, Dad?"

"Nothing but your books. You must look exactly like you're going to school on a regular school day."

"I'm ready then." Taking one last look at the note with her instructions, Rita asked, "Do you want this address?"

"It's engraved on my brain."

Rita tore up the message and threw it in a garbage can as they started walking back to the house.

"How do you feel?" asked Mario.

"If it wasn't for not knowing about Mom, I'd say excited, like when we started across the desert. You know, Dad? Scared, but happy at the adventure to pile up ahead, not knowing what's coming down the road, but looking for better than what we had. I'm scared about Mom, though. If something really terrible happened to her, and she goes to our house and we're not there, she won't know what to think."

"She won't go there. She knows the house is watched, and she'll know we're looking for her. We'll find a way to hook up. Someday you'll grow up and get married and have a family of your own, but Marcella and me, we'll be still together."

"Dad, suppose...."

"No!" interrupted Mario sternly. "Don't say that!"

"I know," said Rita, letting out a long sigh. "But no matter what Mom thinks, I'm better off talking about my worries. It lets them out. If I don't, they pile up, and there's no place for them to go. How do you know that's not just as bad as thinking what you don't want to happen? How do you know that's not the thing that caused Mom to run away at work? My friend says no one ever got away before. These are the things we don't know, because nobody studies them - what causes the causes?"

"I don't understand you, Rita. I've got too many other things on my mind. Listen carefully now, and put all that out of your head."

"Okay."

"I have to sneak out for about an hour tonight. I'm going to say goodnight, and if anyone from Bold's is tuned into our little bungalow tonight, I want them to think I'm sleeping."

"What for?" A lifetime of tension showed in Rita's expression, particularly her eyes, and though her youthful unlined face was beautiful to Mario, her eyes looked like they were a million years old.

"I can't say."

"You can trust me, Dad."

"If one part of our project was to fail, if one of us was to get caught, a substitution could be made and the rest could go on, if not this time another time. What you don't know, you can't be made to reveal if something goes wrong."

"Is it dangerous?"

"Not if I'm careful."

"Then nothing will go wrong. I can feel it beyond my body and bones and thought. I know it."

"That's what Marcella was talking about," said Mario. "And past that point where you know is a crack called will. In that brief fraction of a second, you have a choice, and your decision and faith in it makes your success or failure. I know it from the other side, because Marcella used it when I got bit by the snake. Otherwise we'd all be dead right now. But we're still alive, and it's not for nothing."

"I see," said Rita.

Mario and Rita returned to the house. Restless, Mario needed something to do with his hands. He fried some meat and made tacos for himself and Rita.

"I'll do the dishes, Dad," said Rita, after they ate.

"No, it's good for me. I miss your Mom bad. It makes me jittery. I need to do something." When he was finished with the dishes, Mario walked to the corner to get the newspaper. Then he went to the hardware store and bought a sharp, compact pair of cable cutters.

Walking home, he felt like he'd go crazy without Marcella. He saw sexual images in flowers and trees and clouds, and the pressure in his brain and body was like a continuously blazing flame. When he saw women, who even vaguely resembled Marcella, he thought of sex, and burned with shame. When the tension was unbearable, he recalled Marco and his firm denial in determination, of the escape plan that unquestionably had to work by a necessity he could neither understand, deny, nor change; and his thoughts always ended in a prayer for strength, for reunion, and for the means to get them.

His faith that he would be reunited with Marcella grew with each defeat of the monster threatening to devour him. As the time of Marcella's absence lengthened, his dreams and then his thoughts took on tones of violence. He imagined striking down men in the street, imagined enemies that weren't there, felt his father and his mother killed daily, not merely as a recollection, but he relived the experiences in all their gory horror and emotional churnings. He wanted to run down the street screaming, but when the moment of break or keep on came, he'd remember Marco. Knowing that Marco had lived through a similar experience showed him that he could, too. It would have to end some day, and when it did, would he be able to enjoy his life again or would he be behind bars or sick or dead or back in El Salvador bereft of his wife and daughter hopelessly deformed in spirit? He couldn't leave the big decisions to chance.

Putting the cable cutters in his black duffel bag in his closet, he then took the newspaper to the living room. Sitting back in his recliner, he glanced over the headlines without reading the articles, mentally rehearsing the plan.

Rita leaned over him and whispered, "Are you nervous and scared?"

He nodded yes and turned on the cassette.

"You don't have to go to your job?" he whispered. Rita shook her head no. "I'm not on the schedule today. How about you?"

"Marco said they got two new men to come in today, both illegal aliens. I'm through. He canned me." Mario grinned at her.

"Canned?" asked Rita, puzzled.
"Fired."

Watching Rita open her books on the dining room table, he thought if their plan failed, it wouldn't be on her account. He tried to concentrate on an article but soon gave up and got out the Scrabble board.

"How about a game?" he interrupted Rita at her chemistry book.

"Sure. I need a break. I'm stuck, and the answer won't come until I quit thinking about it."

Mario struggled to concentrate on the game while words flowed effortlessly from Rita's hand to the board.

"*I know* I'm going to win," she said, emphasizing know. "That's why." So much of Rita's life had been forced into the charade that she felt comfortable in the drama, yet seething below the make-believe was the deadly seriousness of their purpose. All of their lives and freedom depended on all of them getting it right. Though Mario understood the hidden meaning in her message, worry interfered with his game. They played three, and Rita won them all.

"That's enough," said Mario. "This isn't my lucky day for Scrabble. I'm going to read the book I got from the library."

"I don't have time for another one anyway," said Rita, returning to her chemistry problem.

Mario tried to read, but he kept rehashing his part in the plan. Every time he let his thoughts drift, they turned to Marcella. He lost track of the story line and read the same page over and over. Giving up, he got ready for bed, careful to do everything at the same time as usual. He heard Rita go to her room at two a.m.

Turning out his bedroom lights, Mario then got out his black trousers and a dark plaid flannel shirt and put them on over the tee shirt and boxer shorts he always wore to bed. He put on a black jacket, his black knit cap and black gloves, and got the disassembled spade in a case that looked like a briefcase out of the closet. He slunk out the back door with the case, and went to the phone booth on the corner. The street was dark with little traffic, and the wind blew freezing cold. He called a cab, and it arrived in a few minutes.

"Take me to the corner of Elizabeth Street and the highway," he said, getting into the cab and welcoming the warmth.

"Sure," said the driver. He drove Mario to the location and dropped him off, and Mario walked around the corner and down the highway along the fence around Senator Bold's estate. The telephone cable was buried two hundred yards from the entrance, around the bend. A dab of white paint on the black iron fence told Mario he had the right location.

Working in the shadows, he opened the briefcase, assembled the spade, and started digging. His spade hit ground that was hard, but not rocky. Digging steadily warmed him up, his breath visible in the cold. A foot deep the earth was softer, and the dirt flew surprisingly fast until his spade hit the cable. He worked the dirt loose all around and beneath it with the spade. After clearing a space around the cable, he filled it in with leaves. He removed a screen cut in a circle two feet in diameter from the spade case and laid it over the hole. Dirt, pebbles, and leaves were plentiful for cover, and Mario adjusted the surrounding earth so he couldn't tell by looking where the hole was. He folded the spade into the case, walked to a phone booth a half-mile away, and called a cab from a different company than the one he used before. It arrived in ten minutes. Giving the driver an address a block from his house, he was taken there. After paying the cab, he walked home to try to get a few hours sleep.

Mario repeatedly imagined finishing his job before drifting into a restless doze. He awoke ten minutes later and couldn't go back to sleep. The time crept by so slowly that he had to get up to make sure the clock was still plugged in. At last, six o'clock rolled around, and getting out of bed, he then stretched. Making coffee first like he did every morning, he then took a shower while it dripped. He made flapjacks and sausage for breakfast.

When Rita came into the kitchen and sat down to eat, she had a lump in her throat.

Mario flipped a pancake high, twirling the plate and passing it behind his back before catching the pancake on it to make her laugh. The next one he flipped too high, and stuck to the ceiling, making her laugh harder.

"Come down from there, you!" he yelled at the pancake, shaking his pancake turner at it. It plopped down, and he held the plate beneath it just in time to keep it from splattering all over the stove. Rita shook with laughter.

When breakfast was ready, Rita had trouble forcing three pancakes and sausage links down; but determined to maintain her exact routines until she got to the bus stop, she managed to eat a proper breakfast. She got up and poured herself a cup of coffee, adding milk and sugar.

"The first time you had coffee was when your friend brought it over," said Mario.

"That seems like a different lifetime." Rita snatched a glance at her watch, wishing the time would go faster. "It's a good thing we moved from there. I like my school all right."

"It's a good school. Want more pancakes?"
"No, I had enough. I'm going to a movie Friday night."
"I'm glad to see you going out in the evening a little in New York. It's good for you."
"Yeah, I know. I was studying all the time." Rita got up, and put her books in her backpack "Bye Dad," She hugged Mario, and he hugged her extra hard.

"Good luck," he whispered in her ear.

"You too," she whispered back. "We'll make it." Taking her backpack, she walked to the bus stop. Several older children with books waited for the bus, and Rita stood a few feet behind them. The #89 bus was the first one, and she got on, took a seat, and waited for her stop with her heart in her throat.

The bus turned onto 50th Street, and Rita worried, but two blocks later, it turned again and jogged onto 48th. Getting off at Hillman, she walked straight down 48th to 4815 and rang the bell, patting her pocket with the birth certificate in it. "A piece of cake," she said to herself, and Carmen opened the door.

"I'm Rita," she said.

Smiling, Carmen then put her finger to her lips for silence.

Taking her cue from the other children already there, Rita got a book out of her backpack and put the backpack on the floor. She joined seven other kids seated around a rectangular table, and Carmen sat down at one end. The table and chairs were the only furniture in the house. Noticing the others fidgeting and sighing often, Rita prayed silently, "God, let us all know what to do from here." She'd gotten no instructions except to wait and assumed all their orders were the same.

Two of the children were older teenagers, but Rita felt all their eyes upon her and knew they'd silently selected her as an example. When a small boy got up and started to wander around the house, Carmen got milk and cookies out of a paper bag and put them on the table. She opened the milk carton, and put out paper cups and napkins. Taking the little boy by the hand, she brought him back to the table, and poured some milk for him. He ate cookies and drank milk. Two of the smaller children ate cookies and drank milk, but the others, watching Rita concentrate on reading, as though their world wasn't coming unglued outside, continued reading.

A girl about ten-years-old started to ask a question, and Carmen put her finger to her lips. Falling silent, the youngster watched Carmen get out an electric pot, and warm a cup of milk, adding a teaspoon of honey and a dash of vanilla to it. Carmen gave it to the girl, and drowsy after drinking it, she fell asleep on the floor. Soon two others were sleeping on the floor.

At noon Carmen put sandwiches from a paper bag on the table, three quarts of mineral water, a bag of corn chips, and salsa. Rita ate a pastrami sandwich slowly, deliberately, aware of every person's every move. After lunch another child fell asleep.

Rita did some knee bends, sit ups, jumping jacks, and five hundred toe touches. It seemed like the morning had taken a lifetime to pass, and as she worked out, she recalled the seemingly endless trek through the Valley of the Wind. She'd had the feeling that she was on Liberty's back for life, and desperately clinging to Liberty when the branch tried to scrape her off, she knew it was the brush of death she'd escaped, and it gave her heart. The desert on the other side showed her the finality of the crossing by the feel of civilization. Though the desert had looked exactly the same, it was different. People had been on this side, and even Liberty had known it and gone into a dance of fear and frenzy. This day was another crossing, and though it seemed interminably longer because Mario and Marcella were absent, and she couldn't know what was going on with them, in the sense of it, it was alike. She was crossing a border, and regardless of the outcome, her life would never be the same.

The children who were still awake followed her example exercising; and afterwards Rita could focus her attention easier. Closing her eyes, she said a silent prayer, "Our Father, in the name of Jesus, let our people go free; let the plan work, let us find Mom."

As soon as Rita left for school, Mario got his duffel bag with cable cutters in it and the folding spade in its case out of the closet. He dressed warmly against the freezing weather. Even so, his ears and face were cold, as he walked to the corner, and got in the waiting navy blue sedan with an MC 809 license plate. The driver took Mario to the fence around Bold's estate, two hundred yards from the gate, and stopped just long enough for Mario to get out. Mario walked swiftly to the hole outside the iron fence where the main telephone cable was buried. He carefully removed the screen over the hole without disturbing the camouflage and scooped out the leaves. Lying on his stomach, and reaching into the hole, he cut the cable to the telephone system. Then he scooped the leaves back into the hole, and replaced the screen.

Marco waited in the woods across from the guard station, with a duffel bag slung over his shoulder, for Delita to show up. She came, tottering with a wine bottle in a brown sack in one hand, a disheveled blonde wig with the hair in her face, her face heavily made up, and a long coat and high heels. She went to the guard house singing loudly, and when she'd attracted the guard's attention, Marco snuck across the street in the shadows a hundred yards away and crept back to the gate. Ordinarily quiet, Delita now acted loud and brash.

"I need a bathroom bad," she yelled at the guard, slurring her words, waving the bottle in a brown paper sack. "Where's one?" She stumbled to the other side of the entrance, so the guard had to turn away from Marco's hiding place to answer. She took a long swig of water from the bottle.

"Not here. This is private property. Move along, or I'll have to call the police."

"When does the bus come by here?" She shifted her weight restlessly from one foot to the other, as Marco dived quickly through the entrance and crouched behind a bush. Catching the swift movement of a shadow in his peripheral vision, the guard turned back, but everything looked all right.

"The bus comes every half hour," replied the guard, turning back to Delita who leaned against the bus stop. It'll be along in twenty minutes."

"Thanks," she said.

Marco ran to the mechanic's shop, sticking to the darkest shadows, and used his key to get in, leaving the light off. Unzipping his gym bag, he removed the head of a dummy and screwed it to the torso. Then he snapped in the limbs, dressed it in his work clothes, and put the red baseball cap he always wore on its head. He stood the dummy in front of the car he'd been working on, leaned it over the engine, and left. He stole to the knoll, where he could see the kitchen entrance to the estate, and waited there.

The shuttle for the night shift made its last stop at the kitchen because there was no night shift for gardeners and mechanics. As the kitchen workers boarded, Mareno, Marco's wife, pulled one of three syringes filled with anesthesia from her apron pocket. She jabbed the security guard, who always sat in the front seat behind the driver, with her needle, and before he could warn the driver or protest, she shot the driver in the arm. Mareno braked the shuttle and doused the shuttle lights as they were both dragged off their seats, gagged and bound. The raucous recorded music flooding the shuttle shut out the sounds.

Mareno turned the shuttle lights back on, Marco's signal that the shuttle was liberated. He smiled and started running to the mansion at a comfortable sprint, a movie on a DVD slung over his shoulder. With wings on his feet, he was careful to stay to the darkest shadows.

Dousing the shuttle headlights, Mareno then drove in the dark to the gardener's shed. The driver and guard were quickly unloaded. The workers stripped the guard of his weapon, and the men were left to sleep off the sedative inside the gardener's shed. Mareno then drove to the mechanic's shop. She parked behind the building, and the workers silently scattered to their appointed rounds.

Mario sat in a tree from which he could see the rear of the mechanic's garage. A gathering procession of servants in a line along the fence, furtively slinking to the main gate, passed beneath him. A similar line stealthily snaked along the fence from the other direction. When Mario saw the headlights of the shuttle go out, he sounded a bob-o-link's three note call, and leaped to the ground, bringing up the rear of the line on his side of the entrance.

The two lines of workers met at the guard station, and the first two men in one line separated themselves from the rest by a distance of about ten yards. They started a scuffle to draw the guard's attention.

"Stay away from my wife, I'm telling you for the last time," yelled one of them shoving the other.

"I couldn't care less about your wife. Why would I? My girlfriend's beautiful, and your wife's a pig." The first man hit the other one as the guard turned to watch. Four men on the guard's rear slunk swiftly to the guard's station.

"Move on," he yelled at the men fighting. "You're on private property. Move on."

The four from the crew behind him yanked the guard out of the station, grabbed his pistol out of his holster, and knocked him out, as Delita darted into the crowd of servants. Dragging the guard behind the structure, they then stripped him. Parmado, selected for nearness in size to the guard's, quickly put on the guard's uniform and hat; unclipped the key ring from his belt and clipped it to his, and the workers dressed the guard in Parmado's uniform. The workers on the outside darted into the estate like a striking snake.

Parmado entered the guard station with his gym bag, which contained a navy blue sweat suit and navy pea coat and knit cap to change into later. The flashlight was off. Pulling the visor of his hat low over his brow, he then picked up the phone and listened. It was dead. Parmado smiled.

Hearing the workers inside manually slide the heavy gate closed, Parmado listened for the automatic lock to click into place. He held the only key, taken from the guard. Each worker silently set about his or her business.

Mareno drove up behind the guard house with the lights still out. Leaving his spade case behind the guard shack, Mario and three others hauled the guard into the shuttle, and Mareno injected him with a sedative that would keep him out for twenty-four hours. She stopped at the nearest tool shed, and he was unloaded and stuffed in.

Mareno then dropped Mario off at his shop. He walked in and flicked on the light. After setting his gym bag down beside the electric panel blocked from the view of the TV eye by Bold's Lincoln, he went over to the dummy, leaning over the automobile engine.

"Tough problem, isn't it?" he muttered, his thumbs in his belt loops.

"Yeah, but nothing we can't handle," he answered himself in Marco's voice.

Mario worked on a piston for fifteen minutes, with one eye on the TV screen, occasionally talking to the dummy. The screen suddenly went blank, telling Mario that Marco had separated the main house from its power supply.

Taking the cable cutters out of his gym bag, he then removed the panel covering the wires, flicked the circuit breaker to cut the electricity, and cut the power cable to the garage. Mario took the spare key to the limo parked behind Bold's mansion from the pegboard and slid it into his pocket.

He drove to the mansion in a black limousine with the lights off. His part had been so well rehearsed mentally, that his concentration was total and nothing could interfere with it. He thought only about what he was doing.

Parking in the back beside the other limo, he then left the keys in the ignition. He opened the door to the other limo and inserted the key in the ignition. Closing the limo door silently, he then entered the mansion through the basement door a night houseboy had left unlocked. He sneaked upstairs into the darkened house. At the top of the stairs, Mario made a noise like the barn owls that were often heard around the house.

Waking with a terrific headache, it was so dark Morgan Bold couldn't see a thing. Something was wrong, and he tried to orient himself. "Damned owl sounds like it's right in the house," he said. Burying his face in the bosom of the warm, sleeping Margie Parks, he had a feeling someone else was in the room. He sensed danger and reached for the phone. But when he picked up the receiver, the phone was dead. Before he could get his cellular out of the drawer, he was pinned by heavy hands on each ankle and wrist, and gagged, as his struggling girlfriend was carried from the bed, a hand clapped over her mouth.

Hearing muffled scuffling, Mario went into the room it came from to see if he could help. His eyes were adjusted to the dark as well as possible. The housemen were tying the struggling Morgan to his bed naked, a gag in his mouth.

Mario went to the next room, in the event help was needed there, and saw Bold's girlfriend meeting a similar fate in another room at the hands of the night kitchen crew.

Seeing the gardeners had easily taken care of Bold's two overnight guests, who were stripped, gagged, and tied to beds in other rooms, Mario snuck out the way he came to join the rear flank of the broadcast station contingent.

The estate retained the silence of night, as all the workers converged on Bold's broadcast station. They streamed in the basement door which the cleaning woman had left unlocked. Two lines of men crept soundlessly up the basement stairs in stocking feet, leaving an aisle in the middle of the stairway as Mario waited below with a crowd of rebels.

"Baby's home!" called Elena, loudly, from the basement. "Baby's home, Baby's home." The door to the basement opened, and before the person could ask, *who's there,* two men on the top stair grabbed him. One held a chloroformed bandana over his mouth until he quit struggling and passed him downstairs for processing. Marco threw the circuit breakers to the power in the broadcast station, and the rebels stormed the nerve center of Bold's empire.

Each of the six broadcast station operators still in the station were surrounded, bound, and gagged. Marco took the keys to the building from the broadcast crew leader.

The broadcast staffers were carried downstairs and out the basement door where Mareno waited with the van. Mario and the appointed crew loaded them like so many feed sacks. Mareno drove Mario and the securing crew to the mansion with the prisoners, where they were removed, carried to the kitchen, given sedatives, and tied to permanent fixtures.

Marco was the last one left in the broadcast station. Before leaving he restored power, opened the channel to the communication satellites, pressed the override button to alert all stations that the news from this source was of critical interest, and set Parmado's DVD made from a reel of spliced together segments on the machine. He pressed the play button, and set the machine to continuously replay the DVD.

Making sure the front and side doors were locked before leaving through the basement, he locked the basement door, tossed the keys into a stand of ivy covering a hillside, and raced for the mansion, hoping not to miss the shuttle.

When he got to the mansion, the workers were crammed into the shuttle and two limousines. Marco darted up and leaped into the doorway of the shuttle just as it was pulling away. He lost his balance, but Mario, who'd been watching for him, grabbed his arm, and tipping the balance in his favor, held him fast. The door wouldn't close, as the overloaded vehicle lumbered to the mechanic's garage, so Marco's situation remained precarious.

The two limo drivers, also, drove to the mechanic's station overloaded. Leaving the shuttle and limos parked in the garage adjoining the shop, the workers ran to the gate still speechless, the only sound the beat of their shoes and boots on grass at the approach of dawn.

Parmado unlocked the gate, and helped the workers slide it open. He counted people as they poured through the gate and scattered on the free side. Mario, Marco, and Mareno were the last ones out.

"All right?" Parmado asked.

Marco nodded. Parmado quickly slipped out of the guard's uniform and put on his sweat suit and pea coat. Leaving the guard's uniform and hat on the floor of the entrance booth, he grabbed his gym bag. He, Mareno and Mario helped Marco roll the gate closed. Parmado locked the gate, threw the key over the fence into a bed of shrubbery, and fled.

"Good luck," whispered Mario, huskily, to Marco and Mareno.

"Thanks," said Marco. "Goodbye."

"Goodbye," said Mario.

## CHAPTER TWENTY SEVEN

Lyman Mills, Jr. rose before dawn, as usual. After taking a shower and downing an eight-ounce glass of skim milk, he took his morning jog. Returning to his house at sunrise, he then flicked on his computer connected to Senator Bold's estate. He got static and blurred dots and dashes instead of an image.

"What the hell?" he muttered. He tried to call the senator on his private home line, but the senator's phone was dead. Apprehensively, he tried the public line to the estate with the same result. Dressing quickly, and speeding to the senator's mansion, he turned on the car radio and got static. As he rapidly punched buttons for different stations, a shrill whistle punctuated the electronic noise, the only sound he could tune in.

Lyman pulled up to the gate at the estate, blasting his horn. He didn't see the guard, and rolled down his window. "Open the goddamn gate!" he yelled. But the guard station was empty, and no one appeared. Trying his car phone, he still made no connection. Seeing the gate locked, Mills sped away, frowning.

The electro-magnetic equipment that had been rigged to disable broadcast satellite circuits to let the workers video through was fully activated. Broadcasts were interrupted over radio and television networks as signals returning to communication satellites caused havoc in the upper spheres. Strange things happened.

Everywhere people turned on their television sets, they tuned into a broadcast that started with Morgan Bold playing checkers with Lyman Mills. The telephone wires across the world buzzed with friends and families calling to tell one another to turn on the television until no one could get a line. Emails were jammed. In the cities, unable to get through, people went from apartment to apartment, and condo to condo; in the suburbs from house to house in hastily donned bathrobes and slippers, alerting neighbors to turn on the TV. They tuned into a conversation between Morgan Bold and Lyman Mills.

"We'll buy derelict property like Painter's labor camp and let the taxpayer pay the repair bills. I'll put over the idea of the suffering poor in my column," said Lyman.

"If some radical upstart challenges that, my chances in the next election wouldn't be worth much," replied Senator Bold.

"It's not like the old days when every rabble rouser who came down the pike had a voice. I have a lot of clout in my business."

After the conversation played out, Elena appeared without her cigar, dressed neatly, her hair carefully in place. Her mouth wasn't crooked, and she was dressed to de-emphasize her weight. "I come to the United States to escape the war in Nicaragua when I'm twelve-years-old. They tell me crop pickers are needed in California, and if I go, I get the job. You have to pay, and I use money my mother give me. Her and my dad work hard all their life to save to give one of us a chance. Lucky me because I'm the smartest. I work in labor camps five years, but I don't save no money. I always owe, no matter how hard I work. Then I go to Mary Griswold's and make sixty dollars a week doing housework. I save that.

"Then Ms. Clement tells me I make $300 a week working on Senator Bold's estate in New York. She get me a plane ticket and they find me a apartment in one of their tenements, but they only pay me $150. I can't afford no other place. The rent is $300 a month. When all my expense is paid, there's no money left. It's never enough."

Elena pulled back her hair to reveal a jagged scar from her eyebrow to her ear. "I chop vegetables and meat in the kitchen. My boss, I hate bad. A fat pig named Carlos, always trying to pinch me, always laughing in my ear, blowing his stinking breath in my ear. When Carlos and Bold's housemen try to take me to Bold's bedroom, I fight like hell. They try to kill me, but I like to die first anyway. I fight hard." Elena's voice continued as the film of the fight aired. Surrounded by men trying to drag her away, she was shown lashing out with the meat cleaver, forcing them all to back off.

"I run into Carlos' fat belly with the meat cleaver, and he die. Everybody hate Carlos. When Bold's police come, we say Carlos die in the fight, who knows how? I near die. When I can work again, I'm boss.

"I don't go to Bold's upstairs then. They don't want me no more. Good for me, but I still work in the kitchen. Only now, I make myself ugly. I don't wash. I scratch. I make a nasty face, she made one, and keep it like that. At home, I relax until I see my home's on TV, too.

"They put on closed circuit TV every detail of my life - in the shower- on the pot. When I work in the kitchen, I see myself naked on TV beaten and mutilated in disgusting, horrible ways while men and women dressed rich and fine watch; they laugh and make jokes. I want to scream and run away and hide and die. I see movies like that of other workers I know. At work they broadcast films all day of people beating and killing, stabbing and shooting and bashing, all us."

Elena's face disappeared and her words were heard over a thirty second splice of the kitchen worker's torment. "I hear screaming and crying so loud we can't talk. We walk like zombies because it goes on all day at work. We're not even allowed to go out for a break. At home, the screaming and butchering and porno is still in my head, even when I sleep.

"There's a nightmare that's America for a captive, because we're slaves. There's no way out for us, until we make this way out." The television system by which the workers were monitored was shown. Senator Bold's videos of the workers played while Marco told his story.

"Senator Bold is running a slave trade," announced Marco. "I came from Guatemala to get away from the wars. I came when I was fourteen with twenty-three other war orphans. They say I could work fields in California, but I never get paid. Here, I get $150 a week, but it's not enough. Everything costs too much.

"Hundreds come the way I come through the California migrant worker pipeline. We live only to show Bold's operation to stop him, so we can be free, and we and our children will never have to live like this again."

Kate pulled into a roadside restaurant open for early morning breakfasters. She, Burt, Sherman, and Marcella went into the cafe, which was about half full. The waitress came over immediately, and waited while they all ordered breakfast. The television mounted on a wall suddenly came on interrupting all conversation, blaring a broadcast with a shot of Mario in Senator Bold's shop working on his solar engine. "There's Mario," said Marcella, standing up.

"Sit down, plesase," said Kate, tugging on her shirt tail. She sat down.

"What's going on?" asked Burt, watching in amazement.

"It's from Bolds," said Marcella. "He makes his own TV - anything he wants. That's Mario. It must be in the shop at Bold's."

"But what's going on at the studio?" asked Burt.

The large screen had caught everybody's attention in the restaurant. Kate appeared in a sudden burst momentarily in the cockpit of the Cloudhawk.

"Did I see what I think I saw?" asked Burt.

"It went by so quick, it's hard to tell, but I thought it was me at the controls on our fatal flight," said Kate.

"That's what it was," said Sherman.

The waitress brought their breakfast, and everyone ate with eyes affixed to the screen. Senator Bold flashed on the screen again, playing checkers with Lyman Mills, a glass of skim milk in Mill's hand.

"Here's our proof," the senator said. "We can make anyone do whatever we want. We made Ferrell Sinker sell out the newspaper and keep secret the murders of a governor and a reporter who tried to tell about it. Here's Sinker addressing the International Press Convention ten years ago."

Bold pressed a button on a remote controller and a younger leaner Sinker appeared on the screen. "The American newspaper is unique," announced Sinker. "Unlike other American publishing enterprises, its function is to report true events, yet it must survive as a business. Our great latitude is protected by the most cherished of our laws, because democracy rests on the shoulders of the press. We expose corruption.

"No one can be arrested without cause or dragged off to secret interrogations as so often happens in dictatorships. We would discover and report it. We believe passionately in the sanctity of our persons, the right to security of our homes, to freely speak our opinions, and to make our lives the way we want them to be. Everyone who believes in God is free to worship without interference by the state, and those who don't believe in God are free not to.

"Each individual is guaranteed freedom with due process of law because what happens to one of us can happen to any of us. Tyranny can only operate with a media manipulated by those seeking to control others by removing their rights to life, liberty and the pursuit of happiness which we hold to be inalienable. The free world is dependent on the free flow of accurate and true information."

The speech was interrupted by shots of political figures, pornography, and flashes from ordinary movies. Kate caught her breath when Sue appeared with five other meditators around the fire pit in the lodge.

"That house and everybody that entered it was used for whatever we were used for," said Burt.

An indistinct film in black and white appeared next.

"Is that Sue?" asked Kate, squinting at the television.

"It certainly is!" said Sherman. "It's from before I met her. She's never worn her hair that way, since I've known her, and it looks dark. I've only known her with light hair." Sue appeared young, absolutely certain of herself, and more exuberant than Kate had ever known her to be. Deadly serious, Sue sat behind a desk, studying her notes, and Morgan Bold walked in.

"Thanks for coming," said Sue, standing to shake his hand. "Please have a seat, Governor Bold." They both sat down.

"What's this all about?" he asked.

"I've discovered a program from Greenbrier University known as The Beast," said Sue. You and the chancellor of Greenbrier, Dr. Anceri, initiated The Beast with the help of faculty members from Greenbrier and other prestigious universities around the world."

Senator Bold laughed nervously. "My dear young woman, my interest has been the public good since I was a student at Greenbrier. There are scientific programs and developments that you'd have no way in heaven or earth to understand, but a Beast?" He laughed again. "Give it up."

"There are serious charges of secret records, profiles of private ordinary citizens, who disagree with this inner circle, being tracked like animals, harassed and tormented with bets taken on how they'll behave," continued Sue. "Tracking devices are actually implanted in their bodies without their knowledge during ordinary medical procedures."

Sue suddenly jumped to her feet, clutching her throat, as Bold pointed at her with a small instrument that looked like a pen. She danced crazily before falling to the floor as Bold laughed softly, and the scene faded.

"Sue was a reporter in Greenbrier before being transferred to the West Coast," said Sherman.

The next feature starred former California Governor Gregory Hurly. Greg Hurly and his top aide, Morrie Phillips, sat in the front seat of a car at a railroad track. A large unmarked eighteen-wheeler pulled up behind them.

"I'm going to ask the U.S. Congress for a federal investigation into the management of California megafarms owned by millionaires and oil companies in connection with weapon buying, selling, and financing arms supplied to Central America, and illegal immigration, and their connections to each other," said Hurly.

"I'm sure it'll expose the big money and big names behind this mess."

"I agreed with you when we had friends in the media," said Phillips. "But they got to Ferrell. They've got enough money to buy anyone off, and I don't see how we can resist. They can drive a person mad with their Wizard of Oz technology."

"There are evils that must be resisted, even at death's door," said Hurly.

"I don't think we should've come this way," said Phillips, looking around uncomfortably.

"The phone call said Maggie was extremely ill," said Hurly. "I don't know a quicker way to the hospital."

"I mean you should've explained your sudden departure from the meeting."

"And have to fight my way through the media to see my wife? They said she's seriously ill...say, what's that?" Hurly looked in the rear view mirror. With the train hurtling toward the intersection, the truck behind them began bulldozing Hurly's car onto the tracks.

"Stop that! Hey...." yelled Hurly, trying to open the car door. Phillips tried to open the door on his side, but the doors wouldn't open.

The engineer saw the car on the tracks and braked too late. It collided with Hurly's car square on the rails. Hurly's car was demolished, the train derailed, the cars overturned, and Hurly, Phillips, and the train driver were killed. The driver of the rig leaped out, a syringe in his hand, and bending over Hurly's body, his back was to the camera. He jumped back in the truck, turned around in the field, and drove away.

The film continued with Morgan Bold, Lyman Mills, Jr. and Lon Dedaman, who headed the Administration of Stocks and Securities, sitting in Senator Bold's temple of the gods facing large screen computer monitors.

A crash of thunder boomed from one of the screens, and viewers watched Kate, Burt, Sherman, and Sue inside the Cloudhawk as it was hit by a stormy black cloud, which rolled out of the sky from the north, and stopped over the plane, engulfing it. The remote controlled storm, finding its target, brought laughter from the three men.

"That's not bad. To think our Technology Research Department can do that is quite amazing," crowed Senator Bold.

"It's incredible," said Mills, "a tribute to the genius of mankind."

"Be quiet," said Dedaman. "We'll miss the sound."

A view from inside the Cloudhawk of Kate opening the door of the airplane manually, and the four friends tumbling out brought the men's applause.

Watching in the restaurant, Kate's head throbbed with pain. Sick and dizzy, she felt like she was back in the plane. She ran outside and puked, followed by Burt and Sherman as Marcella remained affixed to the screen with the rest of the restaurant patrons. Running back into the cafe, nearly as turbulent as they'd been in the plane when it went down, they were in time to see Lon Dedaman featured.

"We can turn a saint into the epitome of evil," bragged Dedaman as the unrelenting show continued. "Take the incorruptible Anita Sales, the thorn in the side of an otherwise perfect New World Order, for instance. I was able to infiltrate her system." He laughed with thorough enjoyment, and Morgan Bold laughed with him.

"What a joke, Dedaman. Get real," said Mills, taking a long drink from his glass of skim milk. She's slippery as an eel. Still, I recommend the dream machine on the neighbors, all else failing."

"I've got the keys, so I'll plant the bugs," said Dedaman. "This is my show, and I'll never enjoy one more."

"There's a neighbor a few blocks away, who does nothing but watch television. He's my key player. He's got a lot of hopped up buddies seeking this kind of adventure to make enough money to keep supplied." He pressed a button to pull up the picture of the subject's apartment on the monitor, and pressed another button on a remote control computer device.

"I'm going to take a shower," Dedaman said into a speaker small enough to be concealed under his thumbnail. Dedaman deactivated the device long enough to say, "He thinks he's talking to himself. He's actually hearing those exact words and believes he's thinking them." He re-activated the device. They watched the man with long blonde hair shower and start to put on the clothes he'd just removed.

"I'm going to put on clean clothes," said Dedaman. The target wrapped himself in a towel, and got clean clothes out of his closet.

"I'm tired of watching television. I'm going to turn it off. A bottle of wine would be all right about now." Turning off the TV, the target then looked in his wallet, put it in his back pocket and left the building. He walked a few blocks to a liquor store.

"I think I'll go to a different store this time just for the hell of it," said Dedaman, into the electronic speaker. He looked like he was picking his teeth or biting his nail.

The man turned suddenly and walked in the opposite direction.

"This here looks like a good way. I don't go this way much, maybe there's a store down here. Now I'm getting uptown a little, houses instead of apartments," noted Dedaman. The man looked at the large, old houses, some of which had been converted into apartments, lining both sides of the street with a few scattered small apartment buildings. Anita was walking down the steps of her house.

"Look at that chick. I bet she thinks she's too high class to speak to me. I know that kind of chick. They think they're hot shit."

"Hello, Honey," said the man to Anita. She ignored him.

"Goddamn mother-fuckin bitch," muttered Dedaman. The man stared after Anita, scowling.

"I'll turn left at this corner," said Dedaman. The man walked to the corner and turned left.

"I think I saw a liquor store about six blocks down here," said Dedaman. They watched in silence, as the man proceeded to the liquor store and went in.

Dedaman turned off the monitor and addressed Bold and Mills.

"If she can't be set up to voluntarily overextend herself, the ways and means at our disposal are as wide as the world and the mind of man."

"I don't know," said Mills. "I've been tracking her for years. She's got friends in low places. You don't understand how they think. You've never been poor. I don't even know how they think."

"Nonsense. People are animals, and she can be controlled as any other animal. He referred to a computer program developed by Greenbrier University named Beast. "Beast contrives the circumstances and she'll react. There's not a person alive who can escape when we drop our net," said Dedaman.

"That's always been the case," agreed Mills, taking a sip of milk.

The next scene Kate, Burt, Sherman, and Marcella watched, as though it were the morning news instead of a spliced together film made by migrant workers, was the view from the precipice behind the lodge they'd just left. The camera's eye ran down as far as eye could see from the underside of the precipice and zoomed into a telephoto shot. The last scene was of a pile of human bones and skulls picked clean by vultures and other predators poking out of shreds of human's shoes and clothing. Some of the remnants had been dragged yards from the pile, and panning up the mountain, the film stopped at the underside of the jutting precipice where Kate had rested on her first visit to the country lodge.

Kate left the table and went to a public phone in the cafe. She got the number of the tax assessor's office from information, and dialed it.

"I'd like to speak to the tax assessor or any assistant who knows how to find information in the computer system," she said, getting out her notes of mileage and route numbers.

"What can I help you with?"

She described the lodge and it's location as precisely as she could pinpoint it. "Who owns this property?" she asked.

"Let me punch it up on my computer," she said. "I can find it by the route number." Kate waited for the clerk to find the information.

"I'm sorry it took so long. I had to trace it through a tangled route. The lodge is on Senator Bold's property, but the building is owned by Greenbrier University. They built it in 1960."

"Thanks," said Kate. "You've been very helpful." She hung up, and her next call was to the U.S. Attorney General's Office.

"I must speak to a deputy attorney general," she said. "It's an emergency."

"Very well. One moment, please."

Kate waited a moment, and a deputy came on the line. "Can I help you?" he asked.

"Yes. Have you seen an unscheduled television broadcast concerning Senator Bold?"

"Of course, I'm watching it now."

"I'm Kate Dolore, the pilot of the plane that went down on the segment shown a few minutes ago. I have information pertinent to the broadcasts. Also, a fugitive from Senator Bold's staff, who has been stranded in a coal mine on his property, is with me."

"Where are you?"

"We're on the road. We'll meet you at Senator Bold's estate in less than an hour," said Kate. "Where is it?"

She was given an address, thanked the deputy, and hung up.

Returning to the table, she then handed the address to Burt. "As soon as we get in the van, would you get the map out of my briefcase and locate this place? You can navigate. We've got an appointment with a deputy for the U.S. Attorney General at Senator Bold's estate," she said. "We better be going." Burt left two twenties on the table, and they all hurried out to the van, and got in.

"I don't understand why we were watched and hounded like that," said Marcella, on the way to Senator Bold's estate. "We were completely at their mercy anyway. What could they gain by watching us in the privacy of our rooms at home and putting it on television?"

"It was to intimidate and degrade you into complete submission," said Kate. "People in ordinary situations have options, and the ability to make choices to their advantage. Senator Bold had so much money and power he set himself up like a king and removed the rights of his staff in order to maintain complete control."

"It didn't work," said Marcella.

"In the history of the world, it has never worked," said Kate. "And human beings being human beings, it never will work." She stepped on the gas but stayed within five miles of the speed limit because she didn't want to be stopped for speeding so close to home. She pulled up at the gate to the senator's estate almost an hour later. A throng of media people, television cameras, and bystanders were held at bay by a contingent of armed forces.

Kate, Burt, Sherman, and Marcella elbowed their way through the throng and were met by an officer at the gate.

"I'm Kate Dolore," said Kate, getting out her press identification. "I have an appointment here with a deputy from the U.S. Attorney General's office. The people with me are all involved to the same degree I am."

"Yeah, I bet," said the officer. She went into the guard station and got out a cell phone. Kate couldn't hear what she was saying, but she soon came back out.

"An agent will be here in a few minutes. Just wait here," she said, and returned to her station.

FBI agents arrived at Senator Bold's estate with a contingent of specially trained forces. They made everybody stand back, and first shot the lock off the gate. Kate, Burt, Sherman, and Marcella stood watching. Kate thought the agents looked like the Marines in street clothes landing on a foreign battleground. They came from helicopters and cars, and one man was obviously in charge.

He sent one crew to cover the grounds. "There are dogs in the forest," said Marcella. "They're starving and vicious." She pulled up the trouser leg of Sherman's jeans and showed him her leg.

"You've been in there?" he asked.

"I escaped in the mine," said Marcella.

Kate stepped forward. "I'm Kate Dolore," she said. "We were told to meet someone from the U.S. Attorney General's office here."

Lyman Mills tried the radio once more, and the static and noise were gone. As the broadcast unrolled, his foot fell heavier on the gas pedal.

*"Reliable sources say the Attorney General's office is bringing charges against Morgan Bold for using his office to cover up a world wide slavery empire and private war trade. Federal agents have been dispatched to his estate to arrest him."*

Mills drank his milk down, and put the glass in the holder, listening to the broadcast. *"Our sources say Senator Bold owns all the buildings his servants lived in. He installed his staff in media positions and in companies he owned and corporations he controlled. He stirred up emotions with inflammatory rhetoric in the U.S. and abroad, setting special interest groups with a history of peace at war with each other. Investing fortunes in military technology, he could use it to pinpoint the hair on a target's head from satellites with sophisticated imaging. He could zap a recalcitrant resister of the Greenbrier regime with a computerized laser shot to the brain or the hand or the foot or the heart or the liver, knocking out or damaging the function."*

Hearing a siren behind him, Mills looked in his rear view mirror and saw red and blue flashing lights. "Did I run a red light?" he asked himself, looking at the speedometer. The needle was in the red. Slowing down, he pulled over and poured another glass of skim milk from his iced thermos with shaking hands, as the officer approached his car. He noticed another policeman in the car talking on his phone.

"Let me see your driver's license," said the woman, her hand on her unsnapped holster.

"I didn't realize how fast I was going," he muttered, fumbling for his billfold and then handing her his license.

"Wait here a moment," she said, and took his driver's license back to the squad car. After ascertaining his identity, she returned to his car and said, "You're under arrest."

Wiping the sweat off his forehead, Lyman feigned a laugh. "No. There's some mistake." He started to open his car door, but she kicked it closed.

"Put your hands on your head," she said. She wasn't laughing.

He put his hands on his head, protesting. "I'm Lyman Mills. Do you know who I am?"

"Get out of the car, Mr. Mills, and keep your hands on your head." She opened the car door wide and drew her weapon. A very large and statuesque woman, her blonde curls and blue-eyes and sharply beautiful face, that might have graced the pages of a bawdy magazine in a different age, froze him into submission.

Mill's expression changed as though he'd dropped a mask. He stared straight ahead out the front windshield, his mind in a whirl.

"Get out slowly right now, Mr. Mills, and keep your hands on your head," she repeated.

He obeyed.

"You're under arrest, Mr. Mills. You have the right to remain silent...."

"I know my rights," he snapped.

She continued reading him his rights as though he hadn't spoken. A second squad car pulled up, and a pair of officers got out and walked over.

"He's going easy," said the policewoman. She holstered her gun and frisked him. Opening the back door of her vehicle with a screen between the front and back seats, she motioned him in.

"Why am I being arrested?" he asked. "What are the charges?"

"I only make the arrest. You'll want to hear it with the accuracy the prosecutor will give you in the presence of your lawyer."

Mills was taken to the federal holding station and incarcerated in an interrogation room in a different wing from Senator Bold. He called his lawyer and didn't have to wait long for him to show up. "The initial charges are complicity in treason, murder, conspiracy, libel, rape, and fraud," the prosecutor's deputy told him.

Before Mills had a chance to fully digest the events since being stopped, he was in the cell of an ordinary criminal. The heavy barred door clanged shut behind him, and he sat on the wood bench with his head in his hands, pondering.

## CHAPTER TWENTY EIGHT

Mario rented a hotel room before going to the house to pick up Rita. He knocked at the door and was met by Carmen who let him in. Rita and four other children were sitting at the table. Studying, her back to the door, Rita turned when the door opened, got up quickly, and packed her books into her backpack. She hugged Carmen goodbye and left with Mario without a word.

"How did it work, Dad? Where do we go from here?" she asked as they walked down the sidewalk.

"It was beautiful, Rita. I wish you could've been there to see. Everybody did right. I've got a hotel for us for tonight. We'll eat there and talk about tomorrow." A police car drove by, and Mario and Rita went on their way unconcerned, the security of their birth certificates in their pockets.

When Mario and Rita entered the hotel, a television was on in the lobby. Mario stopped, staring at the screen. Rita grabbed his arm, gaping in amazement. Marcella was on TV! Mario looked from the screen to Rita and back at the screen.

Marcella's face was shriveled and wrinkled, her hair wild and brittle; black bags under both eyes. She looked like she was sixty years old, and clothes hung on her bones as if on a hanger.

"That's Marcella, but she's got trouble," said Mario.
"Sshh, Dad. Let's hear what they say."
A group of men in dark suits hustled Marcella into a black car at the gate of Senator Bold's estate, as armed forces held back newspaper reporters, television cameramen, and throngs of other people trying to surrounded her.

*"This kitchen maid, Marcella, on Senator Bold's estate says she was attacked on the senator's orders at work,"* announced a news woman. *"She escaped savage dogs by hiding in an abandoned mine for three weeks where she came close to death. Marcella has promised to divulge everything she knows about Senator Bold's operation in return for citizenship for herself and her family. The*

*U.S. Attorney General's office is bringing criminal charges against Senator Morgan Bold...."*

Mario went to a phone in the lobby and dialed 911.

"Emergency response."

"I have to talk to my wife. She's on television getting into a limousine on Senator Bold's estate; my wife, Marcella Dominguez. It's an emergency....." Mario was interrupted.

"Oh, okay, one moment, please." There was a long wait. He paced the room with the phone as far as the cord would reach. Rita paced with him. "She's in custody. She's safe now," came the voice.

"This is her husband. I have to speak to her. She had to run away...."

"One moment." He was transferred to a different line; and waited interminably. At last, he heard Marcella's unmistakable hello.

"Marcella!" Mario was overcome with emotion at hearing her voice. He bent over with the phone so Rita could listen, too.

"Mama!" she said. "Are you all right? Are you all right?"

"I thought you were free," Mario said. "I didn't know where to look. I knew not to think...you know."

"I know, Mario, Rita. It's going to be fine now. I can't wait to see you! I'm in the car with the federal police, but it's fine. We're out of danger."

"I saw you on television, Marcella!" said Mario. "It said that you're going to testify in exchange for citizenship for you and your family. You don't look all right. You look awful. They say you were in a mine."

"Yes, Mario. It's true. The workers at Bold's helped me get away, and I got lost in a mine. But now we're free. We'll take classes and be legal citizens. No more running. No more hiding."

"Can you leave there?"

"Not yet. Can Mario and Rita come to where we're going?" he heard her ask.

"You and Rita come to The Federal Building at 1500 Eisenhower Boulevard and tell them who you are. I have to make a sworn statement first. It's called deposition. Then I can leave. It'll take a few days, maybe a week."

"Can we stay with you?"

"Can Mario and Rita stay with me?" Mario heard her ask and waited for the answer.

"Yes. They'll want your testimony, too. I have to go now Mario. Come to that address. Bye. I love you."

"Bye, Marcella. I love you! I love you!" He kissed the receiver laughing and hung up.

"Let's go, Rita!" he said. "We're going to see Marcella! We can stay together! We're going to be legal - legitimate!" He swooped her into a bear hug and twirled her around, as people in the lobby stopped to stare, some of them laughing.

"I'm ready," said Rita. "I knew it would be all right! I knew it would be!"

They hurried out, and Mario hailed a cab. He and Rita climbed into the backseat. "We want to go to The Federal Building," said Mario.

"Sure enough," said the driver. The cab entered the stream of traffic, and when they arrived at their destination, the cab stopped. Mario paid the driver. He and Rita got out. It looked like an office building on the outside, and they hurried in. A uniformed security guard stood behind a counter, and Mario approached him.

"I'm Mario Dominguez, and this is my daughter, Rita," Mario said. "We're here to see Marcella Dominguez." The guard glanced at an appointment book in front of him and summoned a matron whom Mario and Rita followed through a long hallway, up an elevator to the sixth floor and into a private suite.

When Mario and Rita went in, the matron stayed in the hallway, and a federal agent stepped out into the hallway, also.

"Mario! Rita!" called Marcella, running across the room, throwing herself into Mario's arms. She kissed him, and included Rita in her embrace, laughing and crying at the same time in an outburst of joy and relief.

When Mario embraced Marcella, she felt like a bag of bones. She was small and frail, but he was overcome with happiness.

"We made it!" said Marcella. "Mario! Rita! We made it to the free world!" Her heart didn't feel big enough to contain the emotion she felt, and some of it ran into Mario and Rita.

"Freedom is the only thing in the world people will die before they'll live without," said Mario. "Sometimes I was afraid it would never happen, but we're through running. I'm going to find a job as a mechanic in New York, and New York needs mechanics. I'll work hard and save enough money until I can open my own shop. Then I can build my solar engine. You'll go to medical school, Rita. And you, Marcella, can we get it back together? I'll do anything."

Marcella turned to him and kissed him with the old underlying passion that he knew would come out full later when they were alone.

"I'm the happiest man alive," said Mario.

"We have to take citizenship classes to learn everything we need to know. When I'm a citizen, I'll be able to do anything myself that anyone here can. I'm going to write a book about what happened to us. It's something nobody else in the world can do," said Marcella. "But I'll never have a television in my house. If you can live with that, we'll be okay."

"Marcella! My memories of television are as bad as yours, and, anyway, there's too much to do," said Mario.

They heard a light tap on the door. Marcella opened it. The U.S. Attorney walked in with Kate, Burt, Sherman, and Anita Sales.

"I hate to interrupt a family reunion," Harlins said. She was a tall imposing woman with ice for eyes. "Our office will need every detail you can recall from your work in the labor camps and with Mary Griswold and Senator Morgan Bold," she said to Marcella. "Apparently Mary Griswold imported Latin American illegal immigrants for her own labor pool, but Senator Bold siphoned off the best of her trained staff for himself without her knowledge.

"We have proof that Senator Bold initiated and exacerbated wars in Central America for personal profit his investments in weapons brought.

Senator Bold bought off Ferrell Sinker and Lyman Mills involving the media in his web of blackmail and murder. It'll be a long time unraveling, and when something this big breaks, it's always because someone fought and won their private battle for freedom."

"There was a farm worker killed in labor camp 14 in California," said Mario. "I read it in the paper. His name was Jose Encer. Did they ever find who killed him?"

"I know the case you're questioning," volunteered Kate. "Jose Encer died from a heart attack caused by working in the grape fields too long."

"That was the only cause of death?" asked Mario.

"Yes," said Kate. "He had bruises from being kicked in the face and slugged on the jaw that set off the attack, but he was knocking at the door. I talked to the medical examiner. The cause of death on the death certificate is heart attack and stroke."

"But I read in the paper...."

"The article was wrong," said Kate.

All Mario's practice at showing nothing surged to his aid, and he gave a deep sigh. "See?" Mario said, putting one arm around Marcella and the other around Rita. "It's all going to be all right. We can stop running."

"As soon as the process of deposition is over, and your citizenship classes are arranged, you'll be free to leave," said Ms. Harlins.

"I've got to get a mechanic job," said Mario. "I started building a solar engine, and Greenbrier University stole the design. I read about it in the paper. It's in Bold's garage, not done. I have to rebuild it and design the car it goes into."

"This is a civilized country. We have laws," said Harlins. "Nobody can steal your property."

"When Ms. Harlins is finished with you, we'll talk about a lawsuit against Greenbrier University. There is no question you'll see American justice in full bloom, Mr. Dominguez," said Anita, stepping forward. "I'm your lawyer."

"Anita Sales?" asked Mario, smiling in relief.
"Yes."
"You're all right. I read what happened in the paper." He shook her hand.
"It's been a long trip for me, too, Mr. Dominguez," she said.
"Please call me Mario."
"Very well, Mario. Greenbrier University will have to answer for their crimes against you. Damages will cover the costs of your own shop, a house and car, Rita's education, and pain and suffering. You and your family will be safe."

"How could a big, rich, famous university want to steal from a beat dog not worth their spit?" asked Mario.

"Senator Bold was associated with Greenbrier University, and most of his wealth came from crime," said Anita. "The University was controlled by a few thugs, but no one's so rich and famous that they're above the law."

"We started investigating everyone connected to Greenbrier University's network long before the death of the chancellor," said Ms. Harlins, drawing the attention of everyone in the room. "Senator Bold's investments in the companies that produced the weapons of war, his international real estate holdings, and the intersecting point his power rested upon, his entrenchment on the U.S. Senate Foreign Arms Regulation Committee, which was secret even from other committees, gave him an almost impenetrable power base."

The lawyer directed her next remarks to Kate, Burt, and Sherman.

"Beneath the cliff behind the lodge of your recent visit, human remains have been found with odd shoes, clothing, and other evidence of resisters. The lodge was built using the latest electronic technology to terrorize, breakdown personalities of Senator Bold's enemies who might expose him, confuse, humiliate, and ultimately frighten to death or drive mad. These are Greenbrier University tactics. They were trying to establish a New World Order to be run by computers.

"The wealthiest individuals in the world had a secret set of investment portfolios connected to a central computer called The Beast. They moved billions of dollars around in the funds which were based on every aspect of life and human behavior. Essentially they gambled on what a target person such as Sue Front would do in a given situation.

"Investment in the known stock markets of the world were tied to money tracked and moved by the Beast by communications satellites at random and arbitrarily without regard to reason, ethics, conscience, or any of the higher functions of the human being.

"A person came to the attention of the Beast by threatening it with exposure or rousing the general public to a danger that would ultimately threaten it. Sue Front was tracked by computers worldwide, hounded continuously, and eventually murdered.

"Projecting a small storm and pinpointing its location, targeting a particular passenger was child's play to the electronic wizards who programmed the Beast."

"Why Sue?" asked Kate. "Why did she come back here?"

"She was exiled from New England when she discovered the Beast. After Hurly died, she knew the trail led back here."

"How was meditating involved?" asked Kate.

"It was a tactic to lure Bold and his fellow conspirators' opponents to their deaths. Sue infiltrated the lodge, seeking the connection to Governor Hurly's murder. She knew more about

Senator Bold and Greenbrier University than anyone, and she was passing information to us.

"When Sue reached the end of her line, she came to us. We offered her a secret identity in another country. She refused it. Too bad she couldn't have lived a few more weeks to see the results of her work.

"By supplying wrong information, changing literature and even the wording in state statutes, not by legislation but by printing new pages and replacing them in books and records, those who used the Beast could surround any person or situation with such a cloud of confusion that the truth could never be determined.

"Users of the Beast kept video and taped records of everything that transpired to entrap each other as their projects got out of hand. From the Hispanic slave trade to the repair of private property at public expense, to the Beast and control of segments of the media by a handful of criminals in high places, is a trail of blood of Governor Hurly, his aide, a railroad engineer, news people, a lawyer, and migrant workers who resisted.

"Psychiatric hospitals are full of men and women who fought off death but couldn't maintain equilibrium against their onslaught.

"Greenbrier University's Beast could electronically track every change in the body and mind from brain waves, to thought, to dreams, to glandular functions, to the speed of nerve impulses, to enzyme and chemical reactions of its victims for use at Greenbrier's Biomedical Research School.

"In the face of overwhelming evidence and the turning tide, those who were forced to participate have already started coming forth."

"How did they create those horrendous screams and pressure at the lodge?" asked Kate.

"Greenbrier University scientists were masters of terror. The recordings you heard were of the screams of victims dying, the cold and pressure from the catacombs a trick of physics. There's no way to measure how many people died of accidents, heart attacks and other diseases as a result of this new frontier technology."

"Have all Morgan Bold's people been arrested?" asked Kate.

"More are being identified every day. Lon Dedaman was the last to be picked up. The street gang that attacked Anita was influenced by remote control. All of its members have been arrested and booked on assault and attempted murder. The Beast has been dismantled."

"That's what the public was told after Greenbrier's science center burnt down and the death of Web Anceri, the head of Greenbrier University," said Kate.

"That's when it was dismantled. We've been using the information gained from the Beast for investigations of resulting crimes ever since."

"Ferrell Sinker chose the side of entrenched power to back," said Kate. "It was the wrong choice. The price of the retirement he longed for was the silence of a renegade staff - Sue, me, and Harry would've been next. Why did Sue have to die? If you had all that information, why couldn't you have arrested them before?"

"We were gathering more evidence, incriminating more people up to the time the broadcasts exposed the whole scheme," replied Ms. Harlins.

"Then the rest of the migrant workers on Morgan Bold's estate should be given immunity from prosecution and the option of citizenship, too," said Anita.

"We're making public announcements that those who escaped and so desire will have fair compensation, immunity from prosecution, citizenship upon fulfilling its requirements, and job training or whatever they need to establish themselves as U.S. citizens if they come forward and their status is verified," said Ms. Harlins, handing Kate her card. "Call me anytime," she said.

"Thanks," said Kate. "This is a valuable resource. It was a pleasure meeting you." She slipped the card into her bag, beaming.

"Marco, Mareno, Parmado, Elena, they will never come forward," said Mario. "There is nothing anyone can say that will make any of them that worked at Bold's believe what anyone says on television. They'll never even watch it, and they won't believe the newspapers either. We've seen things in the newspapers...." He stopped short of saying he'd seen himself accused of murder in the newspaper.

"I have a question, Ms. Harlins," said Burt.

"Please, ask."

"Why did they break my leg? I joked in the car in Greenbrier that I might break my leg rather than go back to that lodge, and later that week, my workplace was sabotaged, and I broke my leg."

"It's a typical Greenbrier University terror tactic. They make anything you say in speculation happen. After enough episodes of that nature accumulate, an individual becomes so intimidated, he is afraid to think or speak at all."

"Can you stop by my office so we can exchange cards before you take off?" Anita asked Kate.

"Sure," said Kate. "Goodbye, Marcella, Mario, Rita."

"Goodbye, Kate. Thanks," said Marcella.

"Bye," said Mario. "Maybe we'll meet again sometime."

"Could be," said Kate. "If you ever come back to California, call me."

"See you," said Rita. "Someday, when I'm a doctor, and I'm visiting California on a vacation, I'll call you. I want to go back there and walk on those streets again on the free side. I want to *experience* the difference." She looked at Marcella, and Marcella hugged her, laughing.

Anita, Kate, Burt, and Sherman left the Federal Building and Anita drove them to her office. She waved at Ron as she entered, led the way to her office, opened the door with confidence, and took them to the conference room where they all sat down.

"Here's my card," said Kate to Anita. "If I can be of any help, give me a call. I probably know more at this point than anyone in New York."

"Thanks for coming over," said Anita, handing Kate her card. "This is the case to restore my memory, my practice, and my emotional balance. The recovering mind needs a project to sink the teeth into. I'm sure you'll hear from me as we settle with Greenbrier University and Morgan Bold and his colleagues are prosecuted, and Mario, Marcella, and Rita go through the process of naturalization."

Carrie hurried in with a stack of folders. "Oh, I didn't realize you were busy," she said, backing toward the door.

Sherman stood up. "Don't...don't...don't just go yet," he said. Carrie's eye caught his in an embarrassingly intimate glimpse, and she looked away, as Aubrey appeared at the door.

"Oh, sorry, I didn't know you were busy. The door was open."

"Come in, Aubrey," said Anita.

"I'm on my way out," said Aubrey. "I just stopped to see if you could have dinner with me tonight, Anita."

"Yes. Call back about seven?"
"Right. Carrie?"
"Uh...." Carrie looked at Sherman.
"You remind me of someone," he said. "You work too hard and too long, and you put everything into it." He took a step toward her.

"Can you join us for dinner?" asked Carrie.
"Yes. I can take more time. Kate, Burt, I'll give you a call when I get back."

"Kate and Burt?" asked Aubrey.
"I hate to miss this," said Kate, but I've got more to do back home than I can think about right now. I'm going to use your other office to call my home office, okay?"

"Help yourself," said Anita.
"I'll be going back with Kate," said Burt, scratching at the cast on his leg.

Kate used a private office to call Harry Rosenburg. "Things are winding up here, Harry. I'll be back tomorrow," said Kate.

"I've got your desk, Kate," said Harry, his characteristic enthusiasm evident in his voice. "Ferrell was arrested this morning. I'm going to make a few changes. I heard you're moving into Ferrell's nook, and we're going to hire a new Ag editor.

Kate laughed. "You and Sue and I thought we were the radicals of the staff, but it looks like Ferrell was the true radical. He tried to change the function of the press, and we turned out to be the traditionalists."

"Life is full of ironies," said Harry. "It'll never be the same without Sue."

"No," said Kate, leaning against the desk, her pencil stuck through her hair over her ear. "The battle was tough and our losses were severe. The State is worse off for Governor Hurly's death, too. A few rich crooks tried to steal the government in broad daylight. It's damned scary what can happen when a few individuals under cover of government get their hooks into the press and starts mucking around with democracy. The line over the edge is so fine you can't see it. The hell of it is this reminds me of Watergate. They've got so much money and power they take Jesus for their savior in a posh, classy prison, and start amassing their second fortunes writing books about their crimes and hitting the lecture circuits.

"I've a line to the Attorney General, though, and I met the best lawyer in New York, maybe in the country. Our paper, at least, will never canonize a criminal whether it be a politician, business person, theologian, or sports or entertainment idol."

"Or even a lowly newspaper editor," said Harry.

www.ingramcontent.com/pod-product-compliance
Lightning Source LLC
Chambersburg PA
CBHW070625290526
45790CB00001B/1